Explorer
New York

Mick Sinclair

AA Publishing

Front cover (a): *Statue of Liberty*
Front cover (b): *Times Square*
Front cover (c): *skyline at night*
Page 4: *yellow cabs*
Page 5 (a): *relaxing outside the Metropolitan Museum of Art*
Pages 6–7 (a): *evening lights of Manhattan*
Page 8 (a): *Manhattan skyline*
Page 9 (a): *hot dog stand*
Page 9 (b): *New York City open fire hydrant*
Page 29 (b): *Bethesda Fountain, Central Park*
Page 261 (b): *Plaza Hotel*
Spine: *New York is famous for its characters*
Back cover: *Brooklyn Bridge*

Written by Mick Sinclair, with additional material by Mitchell Davis and Jane Miller
Revision verified by Mick Sinclair, Jane Miller, Tom Steele, Emmanuelle Morgen and Kate Sekules
Original photography by Richard Elliott
Revised fifth edition 2002
Reprinted 2000
Revised fourth edition 2000
First published 1994

Edited, designed, produced and distributed by AA Publishing
Maps © Automobile Association Developments Ltd 1994, 1996, 1998, 2000, 2002

The contents of this publication are believed correct at the time of printing. Nevertheless, the publishers cannot be held responsible for any errors or omissions or for changes in the details given in this guide or for the consequences of any reliance on the information provided by the same. Assessments of attractions, hotels, restaurants and so forth are for the most part generally based upon the author's own personal experience and, therefore, descriptions given in this guide necessarily contain an element of subjective opinion which may not reflect the publishers' opinion or dictate a reader's own experiences on another occasion. We have tried to ensure accuracy in this guide, but things do change and we would be grateful if readers would advise us of any inaccuracies they may encounter.

A CIP catalogue record for this book is available from the British Library.

ISBN 0 7495 3353 6

Published by AA Publishing (a trading name of Automobile Association Developments Limited, whose registered office is Millstream, Maidenhead Road, Windsor, Berkshire, SL4 5GD. Registered number 1878835).
Printed and bound in Italy by Printer Trento srl

Titles in the Explorer series...
Australia • Boston & New England • Britain • Brittany California • Canada • Caribbean • China • Costa Rica • Crete Cuba • Cyprus • Egypt • Florence & Tuscany • Florida • France Germany • Greek Islands • Hawaii • India • Ireland • Israel Italy • Japan • London • Mallorca • Mexico • New Zealand Paris • Portugal • Provence • Rome • San Francisco • Scotland South Africa • Spain • Tenerife • Thailand • Tunisia • Turkey Turkish Coast • Venice • Vietnam

AA World Travel Guides publish over 300 guidebooks to a full range of cities, countries and regions across the world. Find out more about AA Publishing and the wide range of services the AA provides by visiting our Web site at www.theAA.com

How to use this book

ORGANISATION

New York Is, New York Was

Discusses aspects of life and culture in contemporary New York and explores significant periods in its history.

A–Z

Breaks down the city into regional chapters, and covers places to visit, including walks and drives. Within this section fall the Focus On articles, which consider a variety of subjects in greater detail.

Travel Facts

Contains the strictly practical information vital for a successful trip.

Hotels and Restaurants

Lists recommended establishments throughout New York, giving a brief summary of their attractions.

KEY TO ADMISSION CHARGES

Standard admission charges are categorised in this book as following:

Inexpensive under $7
Moderate $7–$13
Expensive   over $13

ABOUT THE RATINGS

Most places described in this book have been given a separate rating. These are as follows:

▶▶▶   Do not miss

▶▶   Highly recommended

▶   Worth seeing

MAPS

To make each particular location easier to find, every main entry in this book has a map reference to the right of its name. This comprises a number, followed by a letter, followed by another number, such as 48B3. The first number (48) refers to the page on which the map can be found, the letter (B) and the second number (3) pinpoint the square in which the main entry is located. The maps on the inside front cover and inside back cover are referred to as IFC and IBC respectively.

Contents

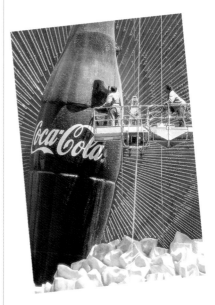

Sign-cleaning on the corner of Seventh Avenue and Broadway

Statue of Liberty

New York fire engine

Lower Manhattan – post-September 11 – seen from Brooklyn Heights

Foreword

The events of 11 September, 2001, reminded everyone that New York is a symbol as well as a city. Rising high above the Financial District, the twin towers of the World Trade Center embodied the entrepreneurial spirit that drove the city and the nation from their founding. They marked New York's place at the heart of a global economy and underlined the city's role as a flag-carrier of American values.

Like the Statue of Liberty, the Empire State Building, and carriages in Central Park, the WTC towers were as familiar to first-time visitors as they were to life-long New Yorkers. Since the attack that levelled the structures, everyday sights such as yellow cabs, also made into New York icons by TV and film, may never again reflect quite the same sense of carefree innocence. And for many years to come, the city may not be associated with something that it created or achieved but with something inflicted upon it.

Yet, after the obligatory peek at Ground Zero, as the WTC site has come to be known, visitors have turned their attention back to the architecture, the museums stocked with many centuries-worth of treasures, and the galleries that have attracted visitors for decades. The department stores that carry consumerism into a higher dimension and restaurants that define good food still captivate as well. The city's monuments and landmarks continue to beguile inquisitive travellers. How many know the Statue of Liberty was originally intended for the Suez Canal? Who can name the hard-headed 19th-century financier who asked an astrologer for decision-making assistance? And how did profits from the Lower East Side's notorious slums help give New York one of the world's greatest reference libraries?

While September 11 resonated globally, New Yorkers experienced the day's events as an attack on their own community. The immense loss of life, the trauma, and the complete disruption of daily life, tested the city mightily. Yet despite a change of mood and an awareness that things will never be quite as they were, New Yorkers themselves quickly got back to business. This determination to recover and to thrive is the best evidence of all of the strength of character that forged the city and made it great.

AA Travel Publishing

New York Is

Incredible museums, fantastic architecture, luxurious hotels and every kind of restaurant – New York has them all. But it is only by stepping out among the sights, smells and sounds that fill its streets that you will begin to feel the true pulse of the city.

NON-STOP STREETS A New York street can be a lonely place but seldom is it an empty one. Around 5 AM, the first batches of briefcase-carrying commuters emerge from the city's subway stations, just in time to see the nightclubbers heading for home. A few hours later, young people make their way to school; soon after, the first lunch-seeking office workers begin filing onto the sidewalks. By early afternoon, some commuters are already making for the stations and by dusk Midtown Manhattan is buzzing with pre-theatre diners. In Greenwich Village and the East Village, bars and clubs prepare for another long, busy night.

Despite the zero tolerance policy in New York, graffiti is still visible on some city streets

❏ The 12,000 yellow taxis that cruise New York's streets are much more than merely a quick (traffic permitting) way of travelling from A to B. Enshrined in city mythology, taxis have inspired a TV series (*Taxi*, which made a star of Danny DeVito), been represented as small yellow rectangles in a major painting – Mondrian's *Broadway Boogie-Woogie* (displayed at New York's Museum of Modern Art) – and, like taxis the world over, are infamously hard to find when it rains. Why are they yellow? Because John Hertz, who founded the Yellow Cab Company in 1907, read a survey carried out by the University of Chicago which concluded that yellow was the colour most people found easiest to spot. ❏

OFF THE STREET One contributory factor to the round-the-clock hubbub on New York's streets is the size and price of the apartments that rise above them. Most Manhattan apartments are small and, except for a few rent-controlled properties, extremely expensive. Rather than stay indoors cooking in a tiny kitchen, New Yorkers will welcome any opportunity to eat, drink and socialise outside their apartments.

STREET DEALS Free enterprise rules the New York streets. An abundance of foodstands can be found all around the city and appetites can be satisfied – often surprisingly well – without ever venturing inside a restaurant. Bookworms can shop at makeshift outdoor tables, which offer for sale all kinds of reading material ranging from brand-new discounted hardbacks to used paperbacks. Many New York apartments have been furnished by various purchases from street markets, where the merchandise ranges from eccentric junk to valuable pieces of matching furniture.

Even if it rains, there is no need to duck inside for shelter. As the first drops start to fall, street-corner traders appear, as if from nowhere, bearing armfuls of inexpensive umbrellas.

STREET TRAFFIC Listen to cyclists and lorry drivers locked in verbal combat at traffic lights, after jostling for prime position the length of the last block. Careful eavesdropping may even provide you with useful ammunition if *you* ever find it necessary to exchange insults with a New Yorker.

Watch out for rollerbladers who tempt death by weaving through Fifth Avenue's frantic rush-hour traffic – sometimes they will even grab hold of passing vehicles for a free tug.

IMPROVING STREETS After decades of cost-cutting in city services had left some city streets potholed and socially unsafe, New York's Times Square and the area around Grand Central Terminal underwent dramatic changes during the 1990s.

Designated as BIDs, or Business Improvement Districts, under a nationwide scheme funded by a tax on local businesses, both neighbourhoods now employ unarmed security forces to heighten safety and provide visitor-friendly services such as information desks and street maps. Both New York BIDs offer free walking tours of the area to highlight their success.

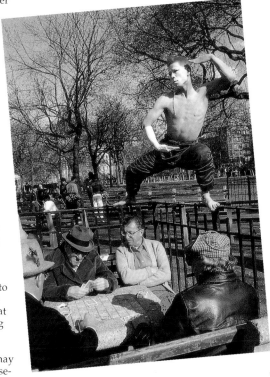

Tompkins Square Park. Street culture comes in many guises

❏ Everyone knows New York is nicknamed the Big Apple but nobody is sure of the origins of the term. Musicians, gangsters and horse-racing devotees have all been cited as its source, but the phrase's recent popularity stems from a tourism campaign launched in 1971. ❏

SAFER STREETS Through the 1990s, levels of crime in New York fell sharply. Between 1993 and 1999 there was a 55 per cent drop in reported crime. Murders fell from 1,952 to 667. Subway offences declined by 64.3 per cent in five years. However, as in most of the world's big cities, it is wise to be cautious and New York is no different. If you have particular concerns, or for further guidance, refer to page 249.

11

For anyone, anywhere, with aspirations and dreams, New York is the place to be. Whether you want to sing and dance your way to fame, make a mint on Wall Street, or start a new life in a new land, New York is – as it has always been – the beacon of opportunity.

HIGH FINANCE For those who can stand the stresses and strains, the heady world of New York high finance offers rewards unimagined and a level of power that few outside international politics ever experience.

Even without the World Trade Center twin towers, the glass-and-steel high-rises of the Manhattan skyline make it clear that this is a linchpin of the US economy, a city that provides over 3 million jobs, 80 per cent of them in the private sector.

However, there is no doubt the WTC attacks of September 2001 had a terrible impact on Lower Manhattan's

❑ While it had long dominated the US financial markets, New York also became the heart of the global economy that emerged during the 1980s and 1990s. As such, Financial District high-flyers found themselves acquiring significant performance bonuses as well as, in world terms, some of the sector's best salaries. Soaring stock prices through the bull market of the mid-1990s saw, in one year, an *average* bonus payout of $54,000 per employee. Such sudden increases in disposable income have a knock-on affect across the city as demand for goods and services rises, and property prices escalate. A downturn in the world markets can reverse the trend just as sharply. ❑

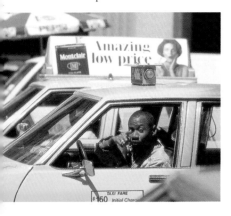

Cab driving: a steady living

office space – eqivalent to the whole of Atlanta – and their loss necessitated temporary relocation for many major players. It remains to be seen how many will return.

role as the centre of the financial world. While it still stands that many industrial giants with workers across the globe are driven by decisions made in their Manhattan boardrooms, it is also the case that many such companies moved their headquarters away from the decimated centre of the financial district. The twin towers alone housed some 50,000 workers in 88 hectares of

TAXI DRIVERS Shortly after the internal combustion engine replaced the horse on the New York streets, driving a taxi became the staple first job of arriving immigrants. Less than 11 per cent of applications for cab-driving jobs are from native-born New Yorkers. Many of these newly arrived taxi-drivers may have a university degree or years of experience in some profession in their native land, but cannot find work. Being a cabbie in New York at least means steady wages and a chance to provide their children with an education.

UNCONVENTIONAL LIFESTYLES
Many come to New York simply for the opportunity to live as they want to. Multicoloured hair and bizarre attire seldom raise eyebrows on Manhattan's seen-it-all-before streets. Avid night clubbers can go out and enjoy themselves all night

New Yorkers have learned to take the eccentric in their stride

every night, stay in bed all day and never feel that New York life is passing them by in this city that never sleeps.

New York also promises a supportive infrastructure for gays and lesbians, many of whom come to escape discrimination elsewhere.

PUBLISHING The New York-based *Wall Street Journal* and *The New York*

> ❏ An estimated 770,000 college graduates move to New York annually. ❏

Times lead the country for quality reporting and carry journalism's most prestigious jobs – coveted by ambitious news-gatherers across the country. Some New York-based magazines enjoy worldwide esteem. The *New Yorker*, *Vanity Fair* and *Vogue* have had little trouble in luring overseas talent and in the past have raised eyebrows by appointing British editors. Most of the country's major publishers are based in New York, which attracts writers – both American and émigré – to the city and gives agents and editors the chance to work with some of the world's most celebrated literary names.

THE STAGE Those intent upon a career in the performing arts ignore New York at their peril. A major early boost is to be one of the thousand students accepted every year into the city's highly rated Juilliard School of Music and Performing Arts.

For thespians, New York's place is clearly at the heart of US theatre, whether it is Broadway blockbusters or the dozens of Off-Off-Broadway productions. New York also offers acting opportunities away from live audiences: the majority of TV soap operas and commercials are cast in Manhattan, although most TV and film work is centred in Los Angeles.

New York's ballet, orchestras and opera companies, are among the world's most highly rated.

Everybody knows, or thinks they know, New York long before they actually arrive there, having seen the city depicted – be it lovingly or with loathing – in innumerable films. Here is a highly selective list of the most revealing, famous, or simply the most enjoyable, films set in New York. (Woody Allen's New York films are detailed on page 188.)

14

Breakfast at Tiffany's (1961). On screen New York has never appeared more romantic than in this adaptation of the Truman Capote novella; Audrey Hepburn stars as the free-spirited Holly Golightly who – dressed in a chic black evening gown – drinks coffee shortly after dawn as she admires the jewels in the shop window of Fifth Avenue's Tiffany and Company.

The Crowd (1928). Two years after Fritz Lang's futuristic *Metropolis*, inspired by the Manhattan skyline, came King Vidor's expressionistic study of the ordinary man's struggle in the seething city: memorable New York scenes abound.

Do The Right Thing (1989). In what might be Spike Lee's best film, the director uses the setting of a New York ethnically mixed community – such as the Korean grocer and Italian pizzeria owner who operate in a predominantly African-American neighbourhood – in a witty and provocative exploration of complex racial issues.

❏ Thomas Edison may have electrified the city but a combination of factors – royalties due on Edison-patented cinematic equipment, the demands of actors' unions and inclement weather – encouraged fledgling filmmakers to leave New York (where movies were a natural off-shoot of Broadway theatres) in the early 1900s for the sunshine of southern California. ❏

I Shot Andy Warhol (1996). A fact-based evocation of Warhol's Factory and the insularity of the 1960s New York art world as seen through the eyes of Valerie Solanas, played in marvelously intense style by Lili Taylor, whose rising anger culminates in her shooting of Andy Warhol.

King Kong (1933). The conflict between man and nature reaches its climax as the giant ape swats planes while flirting with Fay Wray beside the Empire State Building.

The Lost Weekend (1945).The bar in which Billy Wilder's alcoholic week-end began still exists – P J Clarke's, Third Avenue at 55th Street.

Mean Streets (1973). Martin Scorsese had a bigger hit in 1976 with *Taxi Driver*, but this film contrasts the New York of hippies and flower-power with the macho traditions of young Italian-Americans on the make.

On the Town (1949). One of the first MGM musicals shot on location, this fast-paced film follows three sailors (Gene Kelly, Frank Sinatra and Jules Munshin) on a 24-hour pass as they dash around the city, stopping at Rockefeller Center, the Statue of Liberty, the Bronx Zoo, the Brooklyn Bridge and other key sights.

Portrait of Jennie (1948). A lovely and appropriately haunting film in which a troubled artist is enchanted by a young girl in Central Park only to discover later on that she is a ghost.

The city's best-known screen moment: King Kong and Fay Wray in 1933

Q – The Winged Serpent (1982). Witty, low-budget piece in which a giant bird flies out of Aztec mythology to terrorise New Yorkers. It lays an egg inside the Chrysler Building, only to be discovered by a hoodlum who tries to cash in on his amazing find.

Saturday Night Fever (1977). A product of 1970s disco mania that gives a taste of the culture of young Italian-Americans in Brooklyn's Bensonhurst neighbourhood. It launched John Travolta's career.

Serpico (1973). In real life, Frank Serpico was an honest cop whose efforts to stamp out corruption in the New York police force met with intimidation and violence. Serpico's stand eventually led to a massive clean-up campaign – and to Al Pacino playing him in this highly charged thriller, which has great location shots.

Seven Year Itch (1955). Probably Marilyn Monroe's finest screen moment: her skirt is lifted by air rising from the subway grate at the junction of 52nd Street and Lexington Avenue.

Sweet Smell of Success (1957). A brilliant Tony Curtis plays the sleazy press agent currying favour with the Broadway gossip columnist, Burt Lancaster.

The Thomas Crown Affair (1999). An ingenious theft from the Metropolitan Museum is the cue for a cat and mouse game between an art-loving playboy and a wily non-conformist detective.

❏ An unknown 18-year-old actress called Lauren Bacall was crowned Miss Greenwich Village in 1942. ❏

Saturday Night Fever *in Brooklyn*

From Broadway shows to live bands in Bowery basements, New York resonates with music and has frequently attracted the composers, lyricists, musicians and those simply seeking stardom, who have reshaped popular music and created some of the world's most memorable songs.

16

TIN PAN ALLEY The sound of pianos resembling the rattling of tin pans earned a section of 28th Street the nickname Tin Pan Alley from the 1890s. George Gershwin began his career as a Tin Pan Alley composer with the song "Swanee" (1918). The pianos belonged to music publishing companies, many of which later moved to the Brill Building (1619 Broadway; see page 17).

RHAPSODIES IN BLUE Migration of African-Americans to New York underpinned the city's emergence as a jazz centre during the 1920s when emerging talents took jazz far beyond its roots. Among the innovators were Duke Ellington, pianist, composer and band leader in Harlem's Cotton Club; and jazz-influenced classical composers such as Gershwin, whose *Rhapsody in Blue* became synonymous with New York. The city also provided a launch pad in the 1940s for bebop, a new improvisational style with the glorious Charlie Parker, Thelonious Monk and Dizzy Gillespie among its practitioners.

LULLABIES ON BROADWAY In the early 1900s, Broadway's vaudeville shows beckoned aspiring songwriters. After working in Chinatown as a "singing waiter", Irving Berlin found success with the Ziegfeld Follies and composed classics such as *White Christmas, There's No Business Like Show Business* and *Everybody's Doin' It.* George M Cohan's *Give My Regards to Broadway* and *I'm a Yankee Doodle Dandy* both originated in Broadway shows. Howard Arlen penned reviews for Harlem's Cotton Club, including the song *Stormy Weather,* before heading for Hollywood and *Somewhere Over The Rainbow.*

❏ Penned at the Brill Building were: *The Locomotion, One Fine Day, Da Wah Diddy, Baby I Love You, Hound Dog, You've Lost That Loving Feeling, Da Doo Ron Ron* and *Oh Carol.* ❏

Irving Berlin at his piano

FOLK AND ROCK Through the late 1950s and early 1960s, Greenwich Village coffee houses and folk clubs provided the breeding ground for a new batch of young folk singers, often dealing with topical issues and inspired by luminaries such as Woody Guthrie and Pete Seeger. Those who emerged to wide success included Judy Collins and Bob Dylan.

Dylan's switch from folk to rock music pre-empted the psychedelic era. The streetwise cynicism characteristic of New York was at odds with the sensibilities of psychedelia, however, but provided a perfect setting for the Velvet Underground. Using violas alongside guitars, cymbal-less drumming and songs about the seedier side of urban life, the Velvet Underground (and their main singer and songwriter Lou Reed) became one of the city's most enduring influences on rock music, despite lack of commercial success during their short life.

BRILL The Brill Building was home to song-writers Carole King, Jerry Goffin, Neil Sedaka, Neil Diamond, Barry Mann and Cynthia Weill, who created some of the famous hits of the 1950s and 1960s (see panel).

NEW WAVE A Bowery basement club, CBGBs, became a venue for nascent bands of the New Wave movement from the mid-1970s,

Mr Tambourine Man, Bob Dylan

17

Musically diverse but sharing an attitude, Blondie, The Ramones and Talking Heads all regularly appeared here, as did other seminal figures such as Patti Smith and Richard Hell. Blondie evolved into the biggest-selling band in the world, reforming in the 1990s to still more success.

RAP AND HIP-HOP Also in the mid-1970s, DJs in the predominantly African-American-populated South Bronx began forging the turntable style known as "scratching", often adding beats from their own drum machine and sometimes joined by an MC providing an improvised vocal "rap" over the music.

Scratching, rap and the associated break dancing and graffiti art (collectively known as hip-hop) evolved into a worldwide phenomenon during the 1980s, with first hits from the Sugarhill Gang and Grandmaster Flash and the Furious Five and then by the Beastie Boys and Run DMC. By the late 1990s, rap-related music had a global audience, and, in the US was outselling the commercially dominant country music.

Run DMC in concert

Few areas of New York stay the same for long. Not only do entire districts undergo staggering transformations – socially, architecturally and commercially – within a few years, but sometimes a whole new neighbourhood can suddenly arise where previously there was nothing but a hole in the ground.

TIMES SQUARE AND 42ND STREET

A major programme of regeneration and development got underway, under the banner of the Times Square Business Improvement District, in the mid-1980s in and around Times Square, previously a rundown area dominated by porn theatres and pickpockets. The now transformed area – patrolled by its own security force and kept clean with frequent garbage collection – succeeds in its intention of being a safe and welcoming part of the city to shoppers, tourists and legitimate businesses alike.

New construction work over recent years has seen high-rise hotels, shopping complexes and office buildings appear and a number of the area's historic theatres have also received much-needed renovations.

Nonetheless, the new-look square has drawn a mixed response from New Yorkers. While most are happy to see crime levels reduced and relish a much-improved subway station, many fear Times Square's "Disneyfication", its character buried beneath theme restaurants and major retail franchises.

BATTERY PARK CITY Yet another testament to New York's powers of metamorphosis is Battery Park City, a $4-billion project combining commercial, residential and recreational areas on a 37-hectare land-fill site situated on the western edge of the Financial District.

Conceived in the 1970s, Battery Park City gave a new lease of life to an abandoned stretch of Hudson River waterfront, while finding a use for the thousands of tons of earth and rock excavated during the building of the World Trade Center.

Battery Park City has evolved through the labours of several prestigious architects working within a single master plan: to re-create the atmosphere of an elegant, traditional Manhattan neighbourhood.

The redeveloped Times Square

The Esplanade in Battery Park City

The residential buildings hold luxury apartments, while the commercial structures include Cesar Pelli's World Financial Center. This was completed in 1986 and noted for its palm-decorated Winter Garden atrium, which was severely damaged in the World Trade Center attacks. Escaping almost undamaged, however, was the 1.6km-long Esplanade, with Victorian-style lamp-posts and wooden benches, which restored public access to this section of the Hudson River for the first time in several decades.

CHELSEA Approximately bordered by 14th and 29th streets and Sixth Avenue and the Hudson River, the Chelsea neighbourhood began collecting the residential overspill from the increasingly upmarket Greenwich Village through the 1980s. By the early 1990s, the neighbourhood – a prominent shopping area during the 1890s and now a mixture of town houses and apartment buildings, industry and commerce – was an increasingly important nightlife and restaurant area, with a strong gay contingent among its residents and business owners.

A growing number of galleries that have appeared in the area have made Chelsea a serious rival to the longer-established SoHo art scene and have encouraged more and more shops and restaurants to open up. Many now consider Chelsea to have replaced SoHo as the city's art centre.

On Chelsea's western edge, beside the Hudson River, four early-1900s cruise-ship docks have been redeveloped into Chelsea Piers, a beehive of sports activities, dining and shopping.

Many early landmarks remain, not least the Chelsea Hotel (see page 85) and those of the Chelsea Historical District, which has examples of the diverse residental styles of 19th-century New York.

RE-ENERGISED Elsewhere, previously stagnant areas such as NoLiTa (abbreviated from North of Little Italy) and the Flatiron District have been re-energised, most noticeably with an influx of stylish shops and restaurants.

❏ The continuing eastwards migration of New York's unknown and lesser-known artists from Greenwich Village, through SoHo and the East Village neighbourhoods, now finds them located across the East River, creating loft studios in the former factories of Brooklyn's Williamsburg. Here they form a striking contrast to the area's orthodox Jewish community. ❏

Thanks to a unique combination of wealthy collectors and a wartime influx of modern European artists, New York has amassed some of the world's finest pieces of art – displaying them in several world-class museums – and evolved into a showcase for new artistic ideas and directions.

FIRST COLLECTIONS Founded in 1804, the **New-York Historical Society** (see page 165) became the city's first repository for art, acquiring a singular collection of Early American works, including many commissioned by Robert Lehman, a New Yorker who opened part of his town house as a gallery and brought American artists such as Thomas Cole to public attention.

The paintings collection of New York's **Metropolitan Museum of Art** (pages 142–148) began with a modest purchase of 174 Dutch and Flemish canvases in 1870 and grew – aided by bequests and donations – into a world-class stock, including many major pieces by Van Gogh, Turner, El Greco and Vermeer.

BUSINESSMEN BECOME COLLECTORS Having amassed wealth through their control of the industralisation of the United States, and with newly built Fifth Avenue mansions in need of decoration,

New York's 19th-century millionaires began raiding the art collections of Europe. One such was Henry Clay Frick, who acquired the phenomenal hoard now known as the **Frick Collection** (see page 110).

PATRONS Many affluent New Yorkers commissioned artists to paint their portraits, but one who did a great deal more to encourage the creativity of American artists was Gertrude Vanderbilt Whitney.

Displaying and promoting emergent artists such as Edward Hopper and John Sloan, Whitney also established an influential Parisian-style salon during the early 1900s. Her legacy, the **Whitney Museum of American Art** (page 191), continues to champion the country's unknown artists regardless of fashion and has many of the finest, long-established American artists of the 20th century represented among its permanent stock.

The Metropolitan Museum of Art

Art for Sale – a private SoHo gallery

❏ New York is said to be home to 90,000 artists and to hold over 1,000 art galleries. ❏

As Gertrude Whitney was busy furthering appreciation of American art, wealthy industrialist Solomon R Guggenheim was discovering the art and artists of modern Europe. Guggenheim's purchases of early Cubist and abstract canvases were displayed on the walls of his suite at the Plaza Hotel and later became the basis of the **Guggenheim Museum** (pages 122–124). Frank Lloyd Wright designed the building, which is as remarkable as the innovative works of art it holds and worth a visit just to see the edifice.

AN INTERNATIONAL ART CENTRE

As war loomed in Europe, New York found itself acquiring not only European art but European artists as well. By the 1940s, many of modern art's major names resided in the city, as an attempt to escape the fighting. They were to have a colossal impact on the New York art scene.

New York surpassed Paris (then under Nazi occupation) as the centre for international art dealing and the city's pre-eminence was confirmed by the emergence of abstract expressionism (see pages 128–129). Meanwhile, the **Museum of Modern Art** (see pages 158–160), founded in 1929, was evolving into the world's most prestigious and most popular modern art museum.

NEW YORK NOW New York spawned pop art, op (or optical) art, which is designed to persuade the viewer that static images are in fact moving, and minimalist art during the 1960s, and by the late 1970s the shabby warehouses of SoHo (see page 175) had been transformed into pristine galleries showcasing new trends and new talents.

In the economically buoyant 1980s, New York art became big business. The artists in vogue then – Julian Schnabel, David Salle and Eric Fischl – could expect poverty to be a thing of the past.

Today, artist-run galleries can be found in the East Village, Chelsea and on the Lower East Side. While still energetically showcasing emerging New York artists, the larger galleries also reflect interest in the relatively under-acknowledged art of Latin America, Africa and Asia.

❏ Around the city you will find a veritable outdoor art museum. There are many public sculptures, but among the best are: Barbara Hepworth's 1964 *Single Form* by the pool of the UN Secretariat Building; Louise Nevelson's 1972 *Night Presence IV* on Park Avenue at 92nd Street; and Henry Moore's 1965 *Reclining Figure* at the reflecting pool in the Lincoln Center. ❏

Not only is New York the centre of US publishing, it has also provided more material for 20th-century writers than perhaps any other city. Literary landmarks are plentiful and several New York neighbourhoods have carved out special places for themselves in the annals of literary achievement.

A PUBLISHING CAPITAL Geography made New York the publishing capital of the US in the 1850s. Before the US recognised international copyright laws in 1891, any book could be copied, printed and sold, earning its publisher fat profits as no royalties were due.

To maximise earnings, publishers vied with one another to be first with the latest foreign manuscripts. As New York became the nation's major seaport, the city's publishers could get their hands on new books and produce pirate versions of them faster than rivals elsewhere.

THE CITY OBSERVED New York has long provided rich pickings for observant writers. From a bar-stool vantage point in the early 1900s, O Henry (the pen name of William Sydney Porter) produced short stories drawing on the seamy side of city life. In a similar vein a few decades later, the

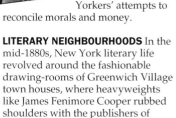

Damon Runyon

characters on the fringes of Broadway theatreland were described by Damon Runyon. Truman Capote's *Breakfast at Tiffany's* was fine-tuned to 1950s New York high life, while J D Salinger's *Catcher in the Rye* followed its young narrator through a New York night and became a benchmark of adolescent angst.

The strains and stresses of 1980s New York underpinned Tom Wolfe's comic novel, *Bonfire of the Vanities* and the same decade saw the emergence of writers such as Tama Janowitz and Jay McInerney. Their cocaine-fuelled tales were followed by more introspective, if similarly drug-centred work, such as Elizabeth Wurtzel's *Prozac Nation* and Linda Jablonky's *The Story of Junk*. The 1990s ended with Kurt Andersen's *Turn of the Century*, satirising New Yorkers' attempts to reconcile morals and money.

LITERARY NEIGHBOURHOODS In the mid-1880s, New York literary life revolved around the fashionable drawing-rooms of Greenwich Village town houses, where heavyweights like James Fenimore Cooper rubbed shoulders with the publishers of literary journals. Such times were described in Edith Wharton's *The Age*

❏ Born in Manhattan in 1783, Washington Irving might well be considered New York's first home-grown writer. His satirical *A History of New York* was written under the memorable pseudonym of Diedrich Knickerbocker. ❏

Washington Square and (below right) Henry James

❑ Rejected writers in New York have included some notable names. Born in Lower Manhattan in 1819, Herman Melville was a customs officer on the East River after his *Moby Dick* received scathing reviews. Only after his death was it acclaimed as a masterpiece. Edgar Allan Poe's poems and short stories were admired in Europe, but in New York he scraped a living from journalism before dying in a state presumed to be drunkenness. Walt Whitman penned eulogies to Manhattan and the Brooklyn Bridge in the 1840s, but every publisher in the city turned down *Leaves of Grass*, eventually acknowledged as one of the great works of American poetry. ❑

of Innocence and by Henry James in *Washington Square.*

As Greenwich Village rents fell, it drew a host of talented but impoverished writers – as diverse as Willa Cather, John Reed, Theodore Drieser, John Dos Passos, Robert Frost, Eugene O'Neill and Thomas Wolfe – who left the area filled with literary landmarks (see pages 112–118). The East Village and the Lower East Side began attracting impecunious scribes in the 1950s, when Beat writers like William Burroughs and Allen Ginsberg moved in alongside émigrés such as W H Auden. Another arrival was Norman Mailer, who formerly lived in Brooklyn Heights (and lives there now). Mass African-American migration into Harlem helped stimulate the Harlem Renaissance of the 1920s, bringing black writers such as Langston Hughes and Zora Neale Hurston to public notice. In the 1950s, Harlem-born James Baldwin created a stir with *Go Tell It on the Mountain* as did Ralph Ellison with *The Invisible Man.* More recently, Chester Himes used Harlem as the setting for a series of thrillers.

A history of New York's Jewish population can be found in *World of Our Fathers*, by Irving Howe; *Call It Sleep*, by Henry Roth; *The Promise*, by Chaim Potok; *The Assistant*, by Bernard Malamud and *Enemies, a Love Story*, by Isaac Bashevis Singer.

The Manhattan skyline is the stuff of dreams. The city's colonial structures may have almost vanished, but New York's existing buildings are a thrilling mixture, encompassing styles from the country's formative years to the contemporary adventures in postmodernism.

THE FEDERAL STYLE From 1760 to 1830, the Federal style became the first genuine American building style, though it drew heavily on British Georgian and treated public buildings to columns and domes reminiscent of ancient Rome: **City Hall** (see page 89) is a prime example.

Federal-style applied to residential architecture was distinguished by semi-detached houses of brick and wood, with fanlights above the entrances and dormer windows. **Gracie Mansion** (see page 111) is one example. A grander specimen is the former James Watson residence, now the **Shrine of Elizabeth Ann Seton** (see page 66).

❑ The zoning law of 1916, which outlawed new buildings rising sheer from their plot to rob the streets of light, shaped the look of the Manhattan skyscraper. The law led to the widespread use of cutbacks (also called step-backs), a tapering effect that has been interpreted by architects in various ways and perhaps most memorably demonstrated by the well-known profile of the Empire State Building. ❑

REVIVALS As New York enjoyed an economic surge during the 19th century, the Greek revival style – bringing floral-patterned ironwork and porticoes to the façades of the new rows of townhouses, such as those facing **Washington Square Park** – was the first of a spate of revivals, which included Italianate, Renaissance and Gothic.

BROWNSTONES A cheap form of sandstone quarried in New Jersey, brownstone was used to build swiftly and at low cost during the mid-1800s and brownstone town houses became the main residences of the middle classes. Brownstones enjoyed a surge of popularity from the 1950s and those that remain are highly prized, both as residences and offices.

LUXURY APARTMENT HOUSES By the turn of the century, property prices in Midtown Manhattan had risen beyond the pockets of the middle classes, who began colonising the new luxury apartments on the Upper West Side. Sumptuously appointed and with anything up to 10 rooms, the apartments also boasted futuristic extras such as built-in refrigerators and pneumatic mail-delivery systems. The **Dakota** (see page 96) was the first such building; several others remain near by.

EARLY SKYSCRAPERS The **Flatiron Building** (see page 106) was the city's first "world's-tallest" structure and was also the first to be supported by a steel frame – a technique that showed the way for creating even taller buildings. A 1920s building boom gave Manhattan the **Chrysler** and **Empire State buildings**, both of which not only reached record heights but bore the hallmarks of art deco (see pages 162–163).

THE INTERNATIONAL STYLE The towers of steel and glass above Manhattan resulted from the arrival in New York of Europe's most creative architects, who fled Nazism and brought with them the antitraditional ideas of the International Style.

The **Museum of Modern Art**, its original façade designed by Goodwin and Stone in 1939, gave New York a taste of the International Style. Among later examples was Mies van der Rohe's 1958 **Seagram Building** (Park Avenue between 52nd and 53rd streets), which gave New York its first plaza.

THE 1980S BOOM With the 1980s construction boom, Manhattan gained its first modern buildings not bearing the International-Style stamp. Philip Johnson's **AT&T Building** (Madison Avenue between 55th and 56th streets) became known

❏ The beaux-arts style arrived in New York in 1890 and is exemplified by Carrère and Hastings' **New York Public Library** (see page 168), Cass Gilbert's **US Custom House** (see page 190) and works by the firm of McKim, Mead, & White, such as **Washington Memorial Arch** (see page 116). ❏

as the Chippendale skyscraper and the **World Financial Center** filled its atrium with palm trees.

THE 1990S AND BEYOND The regeneration of neighbourhoods was a key theme of the 1990s. The new millennium saw the completed **Rose Center for Earth and Space** (see page 64), the beginning of an enlarged Museum of Modern Art and a new Guggenheim Museum.

The Chrysler Building and its futuristic neighbours

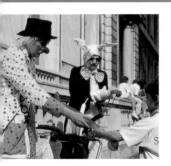

There is usually some kind of festival taking place in New York, whether a traffic-stopping parade along Fifth Avenue or a low-key neighbourhood get-together. These are just a few highlights from an exceptionally busy festivals and events calendar. For precise dates and details, check the local newspapers or contact the New York Convention and Visitors' Bureau (tel: 484-1222 or 800/NYC-VISIT).

JANUARY
Chinese New Year Celebrated by giant dragon and lion dances through the streets of Chinatown. Festive banquets are offered by the neighbourhood's restaurants. (The exact date of this depends of the lunar cycle; however, it usually takes place in February.)

❑ With a 150-year history, the St Patrick's Day Parade (along Fifth Avenue between 44th and 86th streets) is by far the biggest of New York's parades.

Green proliferates in many of the city's bars, which often mark the day with a variety of special events, as do other institutions through the city.

Tens of thousands take part in the parade itself and many more join in other St Patrick's Day-related activities. ❑

Winter Antiques Fair At Seventh Regiment Armory, Park Avenue at East 66th Street. Upmarket antiques and their dealers; browsers are also welcome (see page 226).

FEBRUARY
Black History Month Lectures and exhibitions on African-American themes are held throughout the city.
Empire State Building Run-Up Indoor joggers dash from the landmark building's lobby to its 86th floor by way of 1,575 stairs; the winner usually climbs all the steps in approximately 12 minutes.

MARCH
Greek Independence Day Parade On Fifth Avenue between 59th and 79th streets. Honours the regaining of Greek independence in 1821: a sea of blue and white as school bands

Chinese New Year celebrations: the Lion Dance

26

and Greek-Americans dressed in their national costume march jovially along the route.

Parade of Circus Animals
Creatures from the Ringling Bros. and Barnum & Bailey Circus trek from a railway siding at Twelfth Avenue and 34th Street to Madison Square Garden.

St Patrick's Day Parade (see previous page).

Check the daily papers for parade routes and arrive early for the best view

❑ The Puerto Rican Day Parade, along Fifth Avenue between 44th and 86th streets on the first Sunday in June, brings New York's huge Puerto Rican population onto the streets to celebrate their nation's Independence Day. Red, white and blue Puerto Rican flags are everywhere, traditional foods are sold from stalls, and live bands playing on floats provide a nonstop soundtrack of salsa music to wildly appreciative audiences. ❑

APRIL
Easter Day Parade Participants stroll on Fifth Avenue near St Patrick's Cathedral wearing extravagant Easter bonnets. On the Saturday before Easter a children's egg-rolling contest takes place on Central Park's Great Lawn. Check out Macy's ground floor the week before the holiday – it's wall-to-wall flowers.

Japanese Cherry Blossom Festival Highlights bloomtime in Central Park's Conservatory Garden and at the Brooklyn Botanic Garden.

MAY
Martin Luther King Memorial Day Parade Along Fifth Avenue from 44th to 86th streets. Marchers celebrate the life and achievements of the civil rights leader and highlight other African-American issues.

Ninth Avenue International Food Festival A two-day feast of the city's ethnic cuisines, on Ninth Avenue between 37th and 57th streets.

Ukrainian Festival In the East Village along 7th Street on the weekend closest to May 17: traditional foods, crafts and folk dancing.

Washington Square Outdoor Arts Show A gathering of local artists showing and selling their wares over three successive weekends.

JUNE
American Crafts Festival Lincoln Center. Over two successive weekends, exhibitors from all over the country show their skills.

Welcome to Brooklyn Festival Stalls and events along Eastern Parkway provide a focal-point while happenings throughout the borough mark local history and culture.

Feast of St Anthony of Padua Little Italy. More restrained than the neighbourhood's Feast of St Gennaro (see September), with food stalls along Sullivan Street, the feast culminates with an image of the saint carried through the streets after dark.

Puerto Rican Day Parade See box.

Lesbian and Gay Pride Day Parade Along Fifth Avenue to Washington Square Park and around Greenwich Village. New York's gay and lesbian community stands together for this assertion of strength through unity.

27

Museum Mile Celebration The museums ranged along Fifth Avenue hold special events and stay open later than usual.

The Metropolitan Opera A number of free performances in city parks, including Central Park; continues all through the summer.

Shakespeare in the Park Staged for free at Central Park's Delacorte Theater throughout the summer.

SummerStage Varied events at Central Park's Naumburg Bandshell during July and August.

JULY

Feast of O-Bon Japanese music and dance in the Upper West Side's Riverside Park, timed to mark the full moon.

Independence Day celebrations Including Macy's firework display, the site of which varies.

The horrors of Halloween

Mostly Mozart Festival At Lincoln Center's Avery Fisher Hall (see page 235); continues into August.

AUGUST

Harlem Week A two-week celebration of Harlem's history and culture.

New York Philharmonic Open-air concerts in city parks.

SEPTEMBER

New York Is Book Country Fifth Avenue between 48th and 59th streets. Major – as well as numerous minor – publishers are represented at stalls along the avenue and many well-known authors give readings and signings.

New York Film Festival At Lincoln Center (see page 234).

Feast of St Gennaro Lasts ten days along Little Italy's Mulberry Street. Makeshift kitchens serve sausages and hunks of pizza; final night sees a shrine to the saint carried through the streets and showered with dollar bills. (See also page 135.)

Washington Square Outdoor Art Show Stands with locals' artworks and ethnic food sold from stalls.

OCTOBER

Columbus Day Parade Fifth Avenue between 44th and 72nd streets. As awareness of indigenous American cultures grows throughout the US, this parade to commemorate Christopher Columbus' "discovery" of the New World has become increasingly controversial. Many Native American and Hispanic groups – and others – actively oppose the event.

Halloween Parade Outrageous drag queens and others in freakish costumes parade up Sixth Avenue in Greenwich Village to Washington Square Park.

NOVEMBER

New York Marathon Run from Verrazano-Narrows Bridge to Central Park's Tavern on the Green through all five boroughs.

Macy's Thanksgiving Day Parade Along Central Park West and Broadway starring the famous helium-filled balloons. The area around the American Museum of Natural History is mobbed the night before when the balloons are inflated.

DECEMBER

Rockefeller Center The lighting of the Rockefeller Center Christmas Tree in early December begins NYC's festive season, when many shops mount magical window displays.

❑   Thousands of New Yorkers gather in Times Square to see in the New Year. As midnight approaches, an illuminated ball (disguised as a big apple) slides down Times Tower. ❑

During the 16th century, the eastern seaboard of North America was steadily explored by European seafarers, not with the expectation of locating the site of the future major metropolis but in the hope of finding the North West Passage – a shortcut to the spice islands of the Pacific. Many years were to elapse between the European discovery of the land that now holds New York and its eventual settlement.

EARLY EXPLORERS The first European sighting of what became New York was made in 1524 by Giovanni da Verrazano, a Florentine merchant employed by the French. Verrazano described the land he found as having "commodiousness and beauty" and its native inhabitants uttering "loud cries of wonderment" as they spotted the vessels of the Europeans.

It was not until 1609 that a more thorough navigation of the area was made, this time by Henry Hudson, an Englishman working for the Dutch East India Company. Hudson's voyage was made along the river that now bears his name as far north as present-day Albany.

New Amsterdam (New York), 1673

❏ Before European settlement, the New York area was inhabited by several Native American groups, most being of the Algonquin tribe. The Native Americans, who lived by farming, hunting and fishing, did not share the European concept of land ownership but they did share the European enthusiasm for trading, which helped keep early relations fairly cordial.

A sustained series of Dutch-led attacks eventually forced the natives away from the settled areas. European diseases, to which Native Americans lacked immunity, also took their toll. ❏

Like Verrazano, Hudson failed to find the fabled North West Passage, but he did note that the Native Americans were rich in beaver, mink and otter pelts and were also eager to trade them.

THE FIRST NEW YORKERS Attracted by the prospect of commerce with the Native Americans, the Dutch West India Company was founded in Amsterdam and launched several North American settlements. In 1625, one such settlement – named

The arrival of Henry Hudson in 1609 at the mouth of what is now the Hudson River

New Amsterdam – was founded in what is now Lower Manhattan. It was made up of Dutch and French-speaking Walloon families and their African slaves. In 1626, the leader of the Dutch colony, Peter Minuit, bought Manhattan (a native term possibly meaning "Island of Hills") from a local tribe for a box of tools and trinkets worth the equivalent of $24.

Though established as a colonial trading base, Dutch New Amsterdam – soon to become British New York – quickly acquired a character of its own, partly through the ethnic and religious diversity of its inhabitants and partly through the fact that many of them came to share a desire to rid themselves of their Old World links for good.

NEW AMSTERDAM – SUCCESS AND FAILURE Much to the delight of the Dutch West India Company, New Amsterdam soon began to flourish as a trading centre. New settlers arrived, taking advantage of the company's generous land grants. Some came to escape religious persecution, seeking the freedom of worship that the company had promised.

New Amsterdam was far from being the tranquil replica of a Dutch town that the company might have hoped for, however. Violence and lawlessness were rife, unmarried couples cohabited, pigs ran wild in the streets, and – with a tavern for every 12 adults – many of the population spent their spare time drinking to excess.

A NEW GOVERNOR In 1647, the corrupt governor was dismissed and the job of bringing order to bear on the wayward colony was given to a noted disciplinarian, Peter Stuyvesant. Under his iron rule, and with a new city charter providing for elected officials, New Amsterdam doubled in population and in size, gaining its first hospital, prison, school and post office and its first real commercial institutions.

The colony also gained a protective northern wall, which would later prove ineffectual at halting British advances but did give rise to the thoroughfare named Wall Street.

Peter Stuyvesant

THE BRITISH ARRIVE Stuyvesant's unpopularity, coupled with excessive tax demands by the Dutch West India Company, caused the population of New Amsterdam to offer no resistance when four British warships blockaded the harbour in 1664. Under British rule, the colony was renamed New York, after James, Duke of York, brother of King Charles II.

Set between the major British bases to the south and north, and at the mouth of the strategically important Hudson River, it is not surprising that New York became a prominent seaport. Nonetheless, the British proved no more able to stamp their authority on the everyday life of the colony than had the Dutch, and New York remained as socially robust as ever.

By 1700 New York had acquired a population numbering 20,000, composed of a mix of nationalities and a variety of religions.

THE AMERICAN REVOLUTION After the 1763 Treaty of Paris confirmed their dominance over the 13 American colonies, the British imposed a series of punitive taxes on the settlements. Previous anticolonial uprisings had been quashed by the British, but with the world entering a postcolonial age and the theories of republicanism being universally discussed, the idea of independence became increasingly attractive to the economically thriving colonies.

❏ When the Declaration of Independence was publicly read at New York's Bowling Green in July 1776, the excited crowd overturned the Green's equestrian statue of King George III. Legend has it that the lead statue was melted down and turned into bullets, subsequently used against the British. ❏

Following the Declaration of Independence in 1776, General George Washington led the war against the British. Many British troops were billeted in New York, where they commandeered food supplies, terrorised locals and imprisoned captured rebel prisoners on board ships in which hunger and disease were rife.

New York was to remain the last toehold of British rule in the New World. Although the 1783 Treaty of Paris formally ended the War of Independence, it was not until Washington's march from Harlem down to the Bowery in November of that same year that the last remnants of the British troops were finally withdrawn from the area.

The last act of defiance carried out by the British was to grease the flagpole to hinder the raising of the Stars and Stripes.

As the country's major seaport, New York was the gateway to the New World. Through the 19th century it received the largest migration in human history: a mass movement of people which not only transformed the city but shaped the future of the entire nation.

New York's population had been markedly cosmopolitan from the earliest days of settlement, and a steady influx of immigrants continued after the Revolution.

Some new arrivals were attracted by the prospect of shaping the first democratic mixed-nationality society, others were radical intellectual rebels driven into exile by governments who feared them and a few were simply adventurers or fortune-seekers.

In the mid-19th century, however, came the great waves of mass immigration into New York that were to change the city completely.

MASS MIGRATIONS There were three major factors all of which contributed to the mass waves of European migration into New York during the first half of the 19th century: the social upheaval which had been caused by the Napoleonic wars, the potato famines in Ireland and Germany, and the industrial revolution, which spread across Europe and robbed many skilled craftsmen and smallholding farmers of their livelihoods.

Arriving in the New World: an engraving of 1892

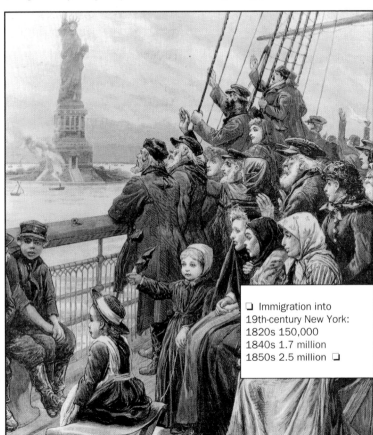

❏ Immigration into 19th-century New York:
1820s 150,000
1840s 1.7 million
1850s 2.5 million ❏

On the receiving end of a mass movement of people on a scale never before known, New York's overstretched Castle Garden (now called Castle Clinton) immigrant processing centre was replaced in 1890 by the federally funded Ellis Island complex. The new receiving centre, which was a pristine, state-of-the-art affair, was a far cry from the slums that awaited most new arrivals once they set foot in New York as American citizens.

While not all of the new arrivals stayed in New York, many did; and they placed a massive burden on the city's resources. The 1860s saw the creation of tenements in an effort to fit more people into small areas – five- or six-storey buildings where an entire family would sometimes occupy a single windowless room. These tenements earned the nickname "lung blocks" due to the high incidence of tuberculosis among their inhabitants. Inadequate drainage and sewage systems made diseases such as yellow fever and cholera a constant threat.

In a city of immigrants, a mix of guile, initiative and extremely hard work in appalling conditions usually bore rewards and the major ethnic groups became assimilated and began climbing the city's social ladder comparatively swiftly (particularly as child immigrants reached adulthood fully conversant with the ways of the New World).

The northwards spread of Manhattan's grid-style streets was matched by a steady northwards flow of wealth. As the city's rich occupied the newest, most northerly homes, their previous dwellings were occupied by prospering ethnic groups while the poor – the latest

immigrants – were housed in the south, usually in the tenements of the Lower East Side.

ANTI-IMMIGRATION LAWS
Established and powerful groups campaigned for tighter immigration controls. They feared loss of jobs, the spread of disease and the decline of Anglo-Saxon supremacy (after the Revolution, 60 per cent of Americans had been of English origin). In 1882, the Chinese Exclusion Act banned further Chinese immigration into the US. The Act reflected an anti-Chinese feeling that also led to lurid stories about New York's Chinatown.

The US entered the 20th century as the world's richest industrial power and the calls for protecting its economic position and well-being grew much stronger.

The outbreak of World War I encouraged the isolationist stance that paved the way for the immigration curbs of the 1920s (although the granting of US citizenship to Puerto Ricans in 1917 was an exception). Mass immigration as seen in earlier decades came to an end.

35

❏ Immigration into New York is not a thing of the past. Easing of immigration restrictions in the 1960s caused a dramatic expansion of Chinatown (where many inhabitants are now actually Vietnamese or Cambodian). Indians, Koreans, West Indians, Filipinos, Latinos, Middle Eastern nationals and Eastern Europeans from the former Iron Curtain countries are among the 90,000 people who still settle in New York every year. ❏

Seldom has the entrepreneur (or the rogue) had such opportunities to make a name and a fortune for himself as in 19th-century New York. The city, rapidly evolving from an outpost to a great metropolis, was alive with speculation, sharp dealing and money-making. From those heady times, a handful of names are still remembered – fondly or otherwise.

JOHN JACOB ASTOR (1763–1848)

A fur-trade millionaire, John Jacob Astor switched his attentions to property in 1834, buying New York land while currying favour with city politicians and ingratiating himself into New York high society. Profits from slum housing helped Astor become the country's richest man by the time he died in 1848. In a rare act of generosity, however, Astor bequeathed $400,000 for the creation of the US's first public library, now the Public Theater in the East Village.

ANDREW CARNEGIE (1835–1919)

Andrew Carnegie started in industry as a cotton-factory worker and rose to become a magnate with interests spanning iron, coal, steel, ships and railways. Believing in the motto "a man who dies rich, dies disgraced", Carnegie financed numerous trusts, some 2,000 libraries and gave $2 million for the building of Carnegie Hall – yet still had $23 million when he died in 1919. The Carnegie mansion on Fifth Avenue is now the home of the Cooper-Hewitt National Design Museum.

From mill-worker to multimillionaire: Andrew Carnegie

❑ When Caroline Schermerhorn married into the Astor family in 1853, she became the fabled "Mrs. Astor", a New York high-society legend whose annual balls were regarded as the city's definitive social barometer. The 400 people invited (the number of people in New York who, it was thought, would fit into her ballroom) could consider themselves "in"; those not invited – which included anyone who worked for a living or who had made their millions in railways – were definitely "out". ❑

HENRY CLAY FRICK (1849–1919)

A partner of Andrew Carnegie in the Carnegie Steel Company, Henry Clay Frick was credited with few redeeming qualities. He instigated the blackest event in the history of US labour relations: hiring a mob to bring a steel-mill strike to a violent and murderous end. Some of Frick's fortunes went into acquiring the great stash of European art that now forms the Frick Collection, housed in his Fifth Avenue mansion (see page 110).

JAY GOULD (1836–1892)

Robber baron, dealer and socialite, Jay Gould made his first fortune at 21. He would bet on the outcome of Civil War battles, having learned the result by tapping telegraph lines. In 1869 he manipulated the price of gold, made himself a hefty profit of $11 million on the gold market and brought about the calamitous "Black Friday" financial crash.

JOHN PIERPONT MORGAN

(1837–1913) Much of the European money invested in the US during the 19th century was channelled through banker and financier John Pierpont Morgan. Able to wield influence on every new project that needed money, Morgan gained considerable wealth and importance. He had a finger in every entrepreneurial pie and oversaw the creation of the US Steel Corporation, which became the world's first billion-dollar business in 1901.

Morgan spent $25 million buying gold to help save New York – and the nation – from bankruptcy in 1907. He is the founder of the library that carries his name: the Pierpont Morgan Library (see page 169).

CORNELIUS VANDERBILT

(1794–1877) Beginning with a ferry service between Staten Island and Manhattan in the early 1800s, Cornelius Vanderbilt built a steamship empire that dominated transportation across New York Bay and plied routes as far afield as Latin America and – at the height of the Gold Rush – to California. In 1864, Vanderbilt diversified, placing some of his $20 million into railways. Tracks were laid that linked the steel-producing factories of Pittsburgh and the dairy farms of rural New York state to the city's docks, where his cargo ships awaited loading: Vanderbilt had once again cornered the market.

When he died in 1877, Vanderbilt was worth $105 million.

❑ J P Morgan fully deserved his reputation as a hard-headed businessman, but he regularly consulted society astrologist Evangeline Adams before making decisions. Evidence of the banker's interest in astrology is easy to find at the Pierpont Morgan Library, where symbols of the zodiac are incorporated into the lavish decoration. ❑

An early wheeler-dealer: investment banker John Pierpont Morgan

Unusually for a major city, the pattern of New York's expansion is easy to trace. The city's growth was a simple case of the long, narrow island of Manhattan being smothered with urban development, starting at one end and working systematically towards the other.

The European settlement of the island of Manhattan began at its southern tip, the easiest place for ships to berth. Here the first businesses and homes became established. As the settlement grew, therefore, it could only expand northwards. In the process, it acquired the haphazard street pattern which remains largely intact in today's Financial District.

38

THE GRID PLAN In 1811, the Board of Commissioners ratified a rectangular, grid-style street plan formulated by a surveyor, John Randel. Ignoring all existing streets except for Broadway – a track that followed an ancient Native American route – the design called for numbered streets (intended for residence) running east–west and numbered avenues (intended for commerce) running north–south.

The new Brooklyn Bridge must have seemed a miracle in its day

The grid plan provided a blueprint for Manhattan's development. In 1820, with a population of 123,000, New York was already the US's largest city, despite barely extending beyond Canal Street. North of Canal Street, a few villages had taken root in what are now Chelsea and Greenwich Village, and the areas that now comprise the Upper East Side and the Upper West Side were a mixture of farms, wasteland and squatters' camps.

When the Erie Canal opened in 1825, it linked New York to the Great Lakes and the agriculturally productive Midwest and left the city unchallenged as the major American seaport – the gateway to lucrative international trade. This, coupled with the waves of mass immigration which began in the 1840s, set the scene for New York's rapid expansion throughout the 19th century.

Harlem was speedily developed by 19th-century speculators

MONEY MOVES NORTH Property developers wasted little time in moving northwards through Manhattan, flattening hilly land and erecting new buildings. In the mid-1800s, the first of the city's handsome brownstones appeared, which provided comfortable accommodation for New York's expanding moneyed classes on the city's northerly fringes.

In the Lower East Side, meanwhile, the first tenement houses were erected, sheltering penniless immigrants and swiftly maturing into desperate slums.

As its poor toiled in sweatshops, New York generated incredible wealth for its already well-heeled élite. By the 1860s, several hundred millionaires were calling Manhattan home. Many of them occupied the luxury apartment houses recently erected along Fifth Avenue, facing the newly created Central Park – and the Upper East Side became the lasting domain of the rich.

A METROPOLIS IS BORN Steadily, the city gained an infrastructure worthy of the metropolis it was becoming. In 1868, the first "El" (or Elevated) train went into service. Two years later the first subway line was drilled. Work on the Brooklyn Bridge – the engineering miracle of its day – began in 1870 and was completed in 1883. Thomas Edison's company began the electrification of the city, opening its first generating station in 1882.

In 1898, the creation of Greater New York linked the five boroughs – Manhattan, Brooklyn, the Bronx, Queens and Staten Island – under a single municipal government. New York City's population was now 3.8 million, making it the second largest city in the world.

❏ When work began on New York's City Hall in 1803, the building stood on what was then the city's northern edge. Marble was used for the building's front and sides, but the north-facing rear was made from cheap red sandstone in the expectation that nobody would ever see it. Such was the rate of New York's expansion, however, that by the time of its completion in 1812, City Hall was already ringed by new buildings. ❏

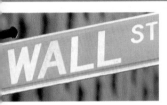

The USA's early years were coloured by frequent financial uncertainties, but none of the early banking troubles quite prepared the city for "Black Tuesday", the Wall Street crash of 1929, which dragged the country – and the world – into the Depression.

New York lasted only a year as the capital of the US, but the financial institutions on and around Wall Street – most notably the Stock Exchange, which began as a trading place for the $80 million-worth of bonds created to pay Revolutionary War debts – remained at the heart of the nation's monetary system.

As unscrupulous investors played on the insecurities and inexperience inherent in the new nation's financial systems, crashes were numerous. The panic of 1837 wiped $60 billion off the value of shares and left 50,000 people without jobs; 20 years later, another crash put 40,000 out of work. A further stock-market tumble occurred in 1873 and in 1907 New York's banks had to be saved from insolvency by the wealthy financier J P Morgan.

THE ROARING TWENTIES As the federal government came to replace independent financiers and the US emerged from World War I as a rich and powerful nation, financial uncertainties seemed to be very much a thing of the past.

The economy boomed and rumours of fortunes being made overnight caused the stock market to trade faster than ever before, its ticker-tape machines struggling to keep up with the developments.

Even economically irrelevant events, such as Charles Lindbergh's successful first solo flight across the Atlantic in 1927, were enough to quicken dealing. Trading levels regularly broke new records during 1928.

THE CRASH OF 1929 Although the warning signals had been observed – industrial production was declining and the economy was beginning to stagnate – few people paid any heed

until the third week of October 1929 when everyone began selling at once. Millions of shares were traded at a loss, causing 11 dealers to kill themselves and the date 29 October, 1929, to go down in history as "Black Tuesday" – the day the Depression began.

> ❏ "Sooner or later a crash is coming, and it may be terrific" – financial expert Roger W Babson, speaking in September 1929. ❏

By 1932, the Depression's bleakest year, more than a third of New York's 29,000 manufacturing firms had closed down, leaving a quarter of the city's work force idle. Many people, unable to afford rent, lived in the shanty towns that appeared in Central Park (dubbed "Hoovervilles" after the incumbent president, Herbert Hoover) and lined up for free food provided by soup kitchens.

Many of the city's most enduring skyscrapers had appeared through the buoyant 1920s, but now the building boom ground to a halt. The Empire State Building, opened in 1931, had to pay for its upkeep on the proceeds of tourist visits rather than office rents.

LA GUARDIA LEADS RECOVERY
For New Yorkers, the woes of the Depression were made worse by the incompetence of their mayor, Jimmy Walker, better known for his song-writing skills than for his political abilities. Not the first – nor the last – city mayor to be embroiled in a corruption scandal, Walker departed from office in 1932 and fled to Europe. His replacement was Fiorello

La Guardia, a young, credible politician who pledged to end corruption and lead the city out of the Depression.

While La Guardia engineered the social policies which did lift New York from the Depression, it was Robert Moses who oversaw city planning and development from the 1930s to the 1960s and gave New York a new look. Old neighbourhoods were razed to make way for the expressways, tunnels and bridges of the modern city, as well as for specific projects that included the creation of the Lincoln Center and Battery Park City.

Staged in Queens, the 1939 World's Fair was intended to symbolise New York's emergence from the Depression, but it was the country's entry into World War II in 1941 that really restored the city's finances, as tens of thousands of soldiers and streams of tanks, trucks and planes passed through New York on their way to Europe.

❏ In 1940, the capital budget of New York City was $1. ❏

Below: the drama of the Wall Street crash, as illustrated by an Italian magazine of the day

Police being paid off by criminals and the mayor using public funds for private gain are enduring images of New York – and with good reason. Corruption was part of New York life from the city's earliest days and has proved hard to shake off, even in recent times.

THE TWEED RING A former volunteer fireman and street-gang member, William Marcy "Boss" Tweed got himself elected in 1851, age 21, as assistant alder-man to a council body popularly nicknamed "The 40 Thieves".

Tweed quickly rose to the top of the thuggish faction of New York's Democratic Party (called Tammany after a Native American chief) by promising (and delivering) jobs and money to people – often freshly arrived immigrants – in return for votes.

The administration was soon under the thumb of the "Tweed Ring", a coterie of corrupt officials who, during their brief reign, are estimated to have helped themselves to $300 million of public money.

As commissioner of public works, Tweed extracted fat commissions from construction companies as a reward for giving them lucrative contracts and extorted large sums from businesses in return for providing essential services. A share of the ill-gotten gains was earmarked for bribes to the police and others, to dissuade them from speaking up.

Tweed's most spectacular swindle involved the construction of the New York County Courthouse (now known informally as the Tweed Courthouse). Having started in 1862 with a budget of $250,000, the courthouse eventually cost New York taxpayers $14 million, of which the Tweed Ring creamed off around $12 million.

THE "BRAINS"

The secret of success: one 1871 cartoonist's view

❏ Since most of the people who voted for him were illiterate, Tweed claimed to have little interest in what newspapers wrote. He considered the satirical cartoons published in *Harper's Weekly* – which he called "them damn pictures" – to be more damaging to his career than reports on his dirty dealings documented in words. ❏

Eventually, an angry City Hall clerk (said to have been offered a $500,000 bribe to keep quiet) passed incriminating documents to *The New York Times*. Whilst in gaol, Tweed was allowed out each day for lunch and escaped to Chile before being recaptured. He died in 1878 in a gaol which his corrupt regime had commissioned.

Mayor William O'Dwyer at his desk in City Hall (below)

MAYORS Quaker Fernando Wood was viewed as the man who would end corruption at City Hall in 1844, despite previous accusations of fraud and the fact that he was elected mayor with more votes than there were voters. In fact, Wood sold the job of city commissioner for $50,000 and provided guarantees of naturalisation to immigrants in return for their electoral favours.

A symbol of the booming 1920s, songwriter and playboy Jimmy Walker was elected mayor in 1925. Walker dressed in white suits, frequented nightclubs and never arrived for work until the afternoon. After raising his own salary from $25,000 to $40,000, Walker skipped town in 1932 as the news broke that he had taken $1 million in payoffs for city contracts.

After the term of the admired mayor Fiorello La Guardia, it was dirty business as usual at City Hall. The subsequent incumbent, William O'Dwyer, made a swift exit to Mexico in 1951 as his links with organised crime were about to be exposed.

THE POLICE In a city corrupt from head to toe, it was little surprise that 19th-century New York police similarly veered off the straight and narrow. Patrolmen routinely acted as

paid lookouts for illegal gambling dens and brothels, while higher ranks improved their salaries with bribes and the proceeds of bank robberies. Crimes were liable to "disappear" in return for payments and many robberies were investigated only if a reward was offered.

Actual arrests were usually intended to improve the appearance of the city for its affluent classes, removing any "lewd women", beggars or homeless people from well-to-do areas.

Within the force, payments secured a popular beat and would bring promotion. According to a newspaper report of 1892, a fee of $300 was required to become a patrolman, while $14,000 was the asking price for a precinct captain's job.

It may be a bastion of big business, high finance, the media and the arts, but New York's lofty position in the hierarchy of world cities is largely due to the simple matter of possessing an outstanding natural harbour. This stroke of geographical good fortune made possible its rise from an obscure colonial trading post to the world's greatest port.

EARLY DAYS New York's discovery by Europeans stemmed from the search for the North West Passage, a short-cut to the spice islands of the Pacific. Early explorers did not find the short-cut, but they did record that New York Bay provided a safe, sheltered anchorage in an area that enjoyed a comparatively mild climate and was relatively free of fog. With the Hudson River, the bay also provided access to a navigable route inland.

Even so, New York was but one of several moderately busy ports on the continent's east coast and was fortunate when the British – then ruling over the American colonies – chose it in preference to Boston as the main recipient of their exports.

THE ERIE CANAL The trigger of New York's phenomenal rise as a seaport – and its subsequent emergence as a major world city – was the building of the Erie Canal. The Hudson River provided a transportation route between the city and the upstate

44

❏ New York's waterside streets were traditionally among the dirtiest, most dangerous and crime-ridden in the city. The glamour accorded to Fifth Avenue partially derived from its geographical position: plumb in the centre of Manhattan and as far from the rivers as it was possible to be. ❏

farms (and the important towns of New England), but the Erie Canal – begun in 1817 and completed in 1825 at a cost of $7 million – connected the Hudson to Lake Erie and thereby opened a swift, direct line of communication between New York and, via the Great Lakes, the newly settled farmlands of the Midwest.

Using the canal, the 804km journey between Buffalo (on Lake Erie) and the city could be completed in

Manhattan and several of its numerous busy piers in the 1860s

The 20th-century port: South Street Seaport today (above) and (right) the Queen Mary *at 51st Street Pier*

ten days. With the American heartland opened up, ships from almost every nation converged on New York bearing products destined for the interior.

THE PORT EXPANDS By the turn of the 20th century, the southern end of Manhattan was lined by 35km of docks, with 270 piers extending along the East River and the Hudson River.

The advent of the railways did more to improve New York's transportation links. Many freight lines ran directly to the docks, while Grand Central Station (now Grand Central Terminal) became the country's foremost rail passenger station.

By the 1930s, "the freighter, the river boat, the ferry and the soot-faced tug" plied the city's rivers – making the Hudson River itself barely viewable below 23rd Street. These craft were among the 3,500 vessels that berthed in New York each month.

OCEAN-GOING LUXURY Cargo may have been the bread and butter of the city's docks, but its place among the world's great ports was symbolised by the graceful ocean liners of the 1910s to the 1950s. Greeted by low-flying planes and water jets, the *Queen Mary* arrived in New York for

the first time in 1936 as one of several vessels regularly ferrying the rich and famous between Europe and the US, where New York welcomed them in a blaze of publicity.

GRADUAL DECLINE Changing patterns in international trade caused New York's port to lose its commercial importance. Also the rising popularity of air travel reduced the demand for ocean-going liners and the great passenger ships made their last farewells to New York, although the *QE2* (as well as modern cruise ships) is still a regular visitor. Nonetheless, the city's port is the third busiest in the US (after New Orleans and Houston) and annually handles around 118 million tonnes of freight. Meanwhile, the fall in passenger routes failed to deter the construction of a new passenger ship terminal on the Hudson River in 1974.

Nobody waking up on 11 September 2001, an ordinary Tuesday, was remotely prepared for what was about to happen: New York and Washington DC were under terrorist attack and the world stood still to watch the tragedy unfold.

Just before 9 AM, TV and radio programmes were interrupted: a plane had flown into the north tower of the World Trade Center, ripping a great burning gash in its top floors. Then, exactly 15 minutes later, as New Yorkers stared in disbelief, the top of the south tower exploded in flames. It took several minutes before footage was found and replayed on television: it was another jet, apparently a commercial flight. Suddenly it was clear this was no freak accident. New York had been attacked.

A MORNING OF UNSPEAKABLE HORROR Two Boeing 767-200s left Boston's Logan airport at 8 AM, both loaded with fuel for their flights to Los Angeles. At 8:48 AM, American Airlines Flight 11 crashed into the north tower, slicing into floors 96 to 103; and at 9:03 AM, while the whole world watched, United Airlines Flight 175 decimated floors 87 to 93 of the south tower. At 9:59 AM New York stared in horror as the south tower crumpled, taking a mere 12 seconds to sink, its steel trusses and exterior columns having softened and buckled like spaghetti in a furnace thought to have reached 1,100°C. A lethal tidal wave of smoke, dust and debris thundered up the narrow streets of the Financial District, shrouding it in blackness. As office workers continued to evacuate the north tower, they passed hundreds of firefighters grimly mounting the narrow stairways. When, at 10:28 AM, that tower too collapsed, it consumed 343 members of the New York City Fire Department.

New York did not suffer alone. Reports came in of other hijackings: one plane was flown into the Pentagon in Washington DC, another crashed in Pennsylvania after passengers apparently tried to regain control. All on the flights died, with more loss of life on the ground.

A TERRIBLE TOLL New York mobilized instantly. The Manhattan hospitals' emergency rooms prepared for a huge influx of the wounded; in all five boroughs, hopeful blood donors started queuing up for hours; doctors rushed to what had become known as Ground Zero to help with triage. But the hordes of injured never materialized. Spouses, children, relations and friends of the twin towers' 50,000 occupants roamed from hospital to hospital desperately scouring lists for their loved ones' names. Some had had their hopes raised by mobile phone calls after the towers' collapse. Soon, photocopied notices appeared all over Manhattan – the vital statistics, WTC office location, and a smiling snapshot of the missing person. Around the hastily set up Lexington Avenue Amory disaster centre, twenty blocks were papered with these heartbreaking posters. At Union Square, New Yorkers congregated in an impromtu vigil, gazing at the missing posters, praying, unrolling half a mile of paper to write messages of hope. Across the East River, the Brooklyn Heights Promenade, with its famous panoramic view of the Lower Manhattan skyline, was packed with people staring in silent disbelief at the gigantic plume of dense, acrid smoke

❏ "U.S. ATTACKED. Hijacked Jets Destroy Twin Towers"— 13 September *New York Times* headline. 14 September "Stunned Rescuers Comb Attack Sites, But Thousands Are Presumed Dead." ❏

billowing from the place where the towers had stood since 1973, obscuring their absence. Everywhere flowers were stuck in railings and candles burned. But the temporary morgue in the Brooks Brothers store at Ground Zero remained ominously empty.

It was more than two weeks before Mayor Giuliani could bring himself to announce that the gruesome round-the-clock labor of clearing twisted steel, flattened fire engines, masonry, and human remains from the 6.5-hectare disaster site was no longer a search-and-rescue operation. DNA testing was used to verify identity whenever a shard of bone was picked out from the rubble, but a huge number of the missing seemed to have vaporised. The city offered the bereaved an urn filled with dust from the site in lieu of a body where no trace was found.

❏ "I don't know what the gates of hell look like, but it's got to be like this. I'm a combat veteran, Vietnam, and I never saw anything like this." A WTC firm's security director, quoted in the *New York Times*. ❏

HOPE FOR THE FUTURE By Christmas 2001 the towers' site was as clean as a car park after three months of excavation. The world, and especially New York, still marvels at the heroism displayed that day – and as casualty lists are revised down to below 3,000 – at the miracle that so many thousands had escaped.

Smoke drifts over the city from the damaged twin towers after the impact

47

New York City

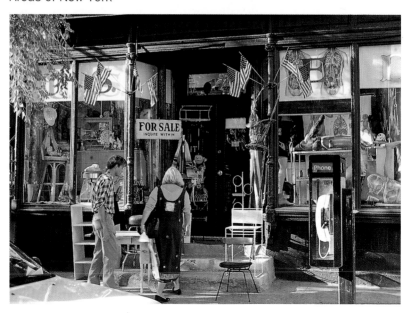

Browsing in Greenwich Village makes good entertainment: shops here range from the mildly quirky to the completely outlandish

Not for nothing did they name New York twice. What most people think of as being New York is really Manhattan, a long, narrow island squeezed between two rivers. Manhattan is the kernel of New York life, home to much of the city's affluence and élan. Most New Yorkers live in the so-called Outer Boroughs which form the remainder of New York City: Brooklyn, the Bronx, Queens and Staten Island.

MANHATTAN As far as the rest of the world is concerned, the island of Manhattan – just over 19km long and for the most part 4km wide – is everything that defines New York, with its towering skyscrapers, teeming streets, ceaseless noise and giant neon advertisements that turn night into day. However, it quickly becomes apparent to visitors travelling beyond Midtown that only a fraction of Manhattan actually fits this image. The island divides into an almost countless number of separate areas and each has its own distinctive history, looks, atmosphere and residents.

Lower Manhattan At Manhattan's southern extremity, the modern high-rise towers of the **Financial District** rise above the oldest part of New York. It was here that the first Dutch settlement took root and, while few markers of the colonial days remain, the entrepreneurial spirit with which the colony was founded remains very much alive – from the floor of the New York Stock Exchange to the street-side foodstands dispensing all kinds of ethnic food to power-dressed brokers.

Pressed hard against the Financial District's northern edge, the short busy streets of **Chinatown** make up one of New York's longest-established ethnic areas. Lately, Chinatown's banks, bakeries and dim sum houses have spread across the traditional boundaries into **Little Italy** – a tiny area where freshly made cappuccino and creamy pastries can still be consumed at pavement tables.

To the west, the ethnic atmosphere gives way to artiness in compact **SoHo** and **TriBeCa**, trendy locations that, not long ago, were derelict industrial areas – prime examples of the neighbourhood transformations that are a New York speciality, as is the thriving **Chelsea** further north.

By contrast, the elbow of land jutting towards the East River is consumed by the **Lower East Side**, a long-time first base of newly arrived immigrants and now the home of cut-rate stores and street markets where the work-hard-and-prosper ethos that built the city remains strongly in evidence despite a substantial number of newer shops and bars.

Greenwich Village is packed with restaurants, cafés, bars and clubs. This area also has some fine houses, intriguing narrow streets, and even today, a knack for attracting the writers and artists who, historically, have shaped American culture.

Across Broadway – which runs the length of Manhattan – the **East Village** provided a less costly alternative for those dispossessed by Greenwich Village's rising rents and gentrification during the 1980s. With offbeat shops and cafés, the area still has a modestly radical atmosphere, although the writers and artists who once colonised it are being replaced by trendy professionals.

**H G WELLS ON
NEW YORK**
"To Europe, she was America, to America she was the gateway of the earth. But to tell the story of New York would be to write a social history of the world".

Choose from a few skyscraper viewing galleries to contemplate the almost unbelievable panorama of Manhattan and beyond

51

THE WPA GUIDE TO NEW YORK CITY (1939)

The guide, which was commissioned during the Depression to create jobs for writers, gave this description of the scene around the Hudson River docks: "A surging mass of back-firing, horn-blowing, gear-grinding trucks and taxis".

OGDEN NASH ON THE BRONX

"The Bronx? No thonx", wrote Ogden Nash in 1931, his four words summing up many a New Yorker's attitude to this particular Outer Borough. Nash later offered an apologetic update: "The Bronx? God Bless Them". Unfortunately for the Bronx, few remember the latter verse as well as the former, which is usually the one to be quoted.

LEON TROTSKY ON NEW YORK

"New York impressed me tremendously because, more than any other city in the world, it is the fullest expression of our modern age".

Little Italy – one of several ethnic areas that make up New York's complex cosmopolitan patchwork

To the east of Fifth Avenue are **Murray Hill** and **Gramercy**. There is an air of elegence here and the various squares and parks, including **Gramercy Park**, offer a respite from city life. The **Flatiron District** is just across Fifth Avenue and another of New York's regions, similar to Chelsea, that has seen a revival in its fortunes, becoming a chic place to eat and shop.

Midtown Manhattan Unlike Lower Manhattan, where the streets tend to have names and to be short and crooked, Midtown Manhattan is all numbered streets and avenues that fortunately make the visitor's life a simple one. These broad, busy thoroughfares, with their dizzying pace of life, hold many of the city's highlights.

Midtown's northern border is defined by the southern perimeter of **Central Park**, an imposing and precisely rectangular chunk of greenery which re-creates a piece of the country in the heart of the city. At this, Central Park succeeds admirably.

Upper Manhattan To the east of Central Park, gaining much of its long-lasting prestige from the mansions and apartment houses erected to face the bucolic expanse, the **Upper East Side** is far and away Manhattan's wealthiest neighbourhood, a fact borne out by its exclusive clothes shops, gourmet restaurants and sizeable gathering of upmarket art galleries.

Three of the city's major art museums are located here: they are the Metropolitan Museum of Art, the Guggenheim Museum and the Whitney Museum of American Art. To enjoy art in a luxurious setting, it is hard to beat the Frick Collection, still housed in Henry Clay Frick's 19th-century mansion.

Across Central Park, the **Upper West Side** offers the Lincoln Center, the Cathedral of St John the Divine and the American Museum of Natural History as its major attractions. The neighbourhood's tall apartment houses – among them the Dakota, which has been home to celebrities ranging from Judy Garland to Leonard Bernstein and John Lennon – were the height of luxury living at the turn of the century and are still coveted addresses in what has grown into a vibrant bastion of the upper middle class.

Stretching across the northern reaches of Upper Manhattan, **Harlem** has played a key role in the history and culture of black America from the turn of the century. The economic and social infrastructure that had traditionally held back African-Americans also contributed to Harlem spending many years in decline.

Similar problems derived from institutionalised racism have been experienced in **East Harlem**, above the Upper East Side, a major base for the city's enormous Hispanic population. Like Harlem, however, local initiatives as well as the passing of time have helped reduce long-held assumptions that the area is off-limits and has nothing to interest those from outside the resident community.

THE OUTER BOROUGHS Locals would no doubt disagree but, unless your time is limitless, the Outer Boroughs probably merit only day-trip excursions from Manhattan.

Brooklyn, with the exceptional Brooklyn Museum, the enjoyable Brooklyn Heights neighbourhood and Prospect Park, has most in its favour. On the coast, Brooklyn also has Coney Island. Its glory days are gone, but the amusement area and boardwalk remain a curious piece of Americana. The latter leads to the New York Aquarium and to the lively Russian community of Brighton Beach.

Staten Island is also worth a visit, partly for the fun of the ferry ride to reach it, but also to enjoy the pastoral pace and the scattering of low-key museums.

In the **Bronx**, the Bronx Zoo (also called the Wildlife Conservation Park) is an excellent stop for children. The New York Botanical Garden is just next door. A more sombre relic is the cottage in which author Edgar Allan Poe resided for two troubled years.

The predominantly residential surburbia of **Queens**, named in honour of the wife of England's King Charles II, includes thriving ethnic communities and the American Museum of the Moving Image.

The Wollman Memorial Rink in Central Park

53

LE CORBUSIER ON NEW YORK
"A hundred times I have thought New York is a catastrophe and fifty times: it is a beautiful catastrophe".

New York may appear to be a complicated city to navigate, and due to its past reputation, may even daunt some travellers. However, by following some simple advice and guidelines, visitors can be confident of enjoying all that the city has to offer without feeling too much like a stranger in a strange land.

MANHATTAN ADDRESS CALCULATOR

To find the cross street of any avenue address:
1. DROP the last figure of the building number (944 Third Ave becomes 94).
2. DIVIDE the remainder by 2 (94 divided by 2=47). If a number is not evenly divisible, this indicates it is between two streets (46.5 is between 46th and 47th streets).
3. ADD or SUBTRACT the number on the following chart (47+10=57 or 57th Street).

Avenue	Number
1st	+4
2nd	+3
3rd	+10
6th	-12
7th	+12
8th	+9
9th	+13
10th	+13
A,B,C,D	+3
Amsterdam	+59
Columbus	+60
Lexington	+22
Madison	+27
Park	+34
Park South	+8
West End	+59
Fifth Avenue	
to 200	+13
to 400	+16
to 600	+18
to 775	+20
to 1286	-18
Broadway	
755–846	-29
to 953	-25
above 953	-31
Central Park West	all +6

The subway is a great way to travel

Addresses Walking is the best way to explore Manhattan, but before you start, take time to orientate yourself and to learn a few basic rules about how New York's grid system works. First, work out which way is north, which way is south, and so on. North of Houston (pronounced *how*-ston) Street, where the streets and avenues are numbered this is relatively easy: streets run east to west, avenues run north to south. Broadway is like an avenue, in that it runs north to south, but cuts diagonally through the length of the island. Fifth Avenue is the dividing line between East and West in Manhattan. On each side, street addresses start at 1 and climb higher the further you go towards either river. New Yorkers usually give addresses in terms of intersections: 3rd Avenue at 50th Street, for example, or 29th Street between Park and Lexington. Below Houston Street, the West Village is a tangled web of tiny streets. Without a map, there is no foolproof method to manoeuvre your way around, although its labyrinthine quality is part of the area's charm.

The subway Using the subway is the cheapest and fastest way to get around during the day. There is over 1,000km of track in the subway system, which is open 24 hours a day and can be travelled on at any one time for $1.50. For more information on tickets see page 257. Study the Metropolitan Transit Authority (MTA) map, which is free from the ticket booths and posted in the stations and on the trains. Before you go through the turnstile, check that you are taking the train going in the right direction and whether you need an express or local train. Signs above the tracks will indicate this, as will the train number: 1, 6 and 9 are always local, while 2, 3, 4 and 5 are always express.

Many New Yorkers feel the subway in Manhattan is safe around the clock, although waiting for the infrequent trains at night can be very frustrating, particularly if construction work affects services (check signs in the stations). However, if at night you are travelling alone or going to the outer boroughs, consider taking a taxi.

Take a bus instead of the subway if you're not in any special hurry. You will see a lot more of the city and, because buses are air-conditioned, will be more comfortable in summer (if the bus isn't crowded). Buses are particularly useful to go across town above 59th Street, where there is no east-west subway service. Be aware that on weekdays at rush hour (8–9:30 and 4:30–6) all buses and trains are packed. During these times be careful on subway platforms and safeguard your purse or wallet. Whenever you are on the street, especially in Midtown where business people are rushing about, stay with the flow and be careful not to stop suddenly or stand for too long in the middle of the pavement: it is considered discourteous.

After dark No matter how safe New York may seem during the day, you should always be more careful at night. If you are in a group, a dark or deserted street may not feel threatening. However, if you are out walking alone or in a couple, remember to use your common sense and stick to busy and lighted streets. Several areas that you might visit with comparative nonchalance in daylight hours are considered to be potentially unsafe after dark. These areas include Alphabet City beyond Avenue C (avenues A and B are fine), Central Park, Riverside Park, Harlem, and parts of the Lower East Side, just north of Canal Street.

To help orientate yourself within the city, remember to use the bridges

CROSSING THE WATERS
New York's bridges are useful landmarks for navigating around the city. Among them are the Queensborough Bridge (or 59th Street Bridge), which crosses into Queens and is to the northeast of Manhattan island, level with the bottom of Central Park; the Triborough Bridge, which is further north, past the top of Central Park and close to East 125th Street; the Manhattan Bridge, which stretches from the Lower East Side to Brooklyn; and the Brooklyn Bridge, to the southeast of the island in the Financial District.

WALKING TOURS

A number of organisations run walking tours of various Manhattan neighbourhoods (see Travel Facts, page 260). Historical walks led by Columbia University historians are run by Big Onion (tel: 439-1090) and walks through the Lower East Side are organised by the Lower East Side Tenement Museum (see page 138).

Itineraries

You could spend your entire life in New York and never feel you had seen the whole city. Nonetheless, these itineraries will provide a balanced view of New York.

Weekend itinerary

Day one In the morning, visit the Empire State Building and continue on foot to the New York Public Library, Rockefeller Center and St Patrick's Cathedral. Have lunch in Midtown Manhattan and spend the afternoon at the Museum of Modern Art.

Day two Take an early-morning ferry to the Statue of Liberty and Ellis Island. Lunch at the World Financial Center and then spend the afternoon in Greenwich Village.

Despite losing its world-record status, the Empire State Building is still a magnet for visitors

One-week itinerary

Day one As day one of weekend itinerary.

Day two Take an early-morning ferry from Battery Park to the Statue of Liberty and Ellis Island. After returning, take the subway to Union Square for lunch and then spend the afternoon travelling through the universe at the Rose Center for Earth and Space.

Day three Spend the whole day at the Metropolitan Museum of Art. If a whole day seems too long, spend part of it shopping for clothes in Midtown and along Madison Avenue, or in the discount outlets of Lower Manhattan.

Day four In the morning, you can explore Central Park. Travel to Greenwich Village for lunch and spend the afternoon exploring Greenwich Village, SoHo, Little Italy and Chinatown.

STATUE OF LIBERTY FERRY

Due to the events of 11 September, the ferry service to the Statue of Liberty and Ellis Island is subject to change. It is advisable to call ahead for the latest information (tel: 269-5755), or check online at www. statueoflibertyferry.com. You will also need to allow plenty of time (currently about an hour) to pass through the new security system. Don't take backpacks, coolers or any packages with you.

Day five On the Upper East Side, tour the Frick Collection or the Cooper-Hewitt National Design Museum. After lunch, continue to the Guggenheim Museum or the Whitney Museum of American Art.

Day six Travel by subway to the Brooklyn Museum. Spend the day at the museum, pausing to eat a picnic lunch in the Brooklyn Botanic Garden. Alternatively, spend the day exploring Brooklyn Heights, dropping into the Brooklyn Historical Society and continuing to the New York Transit Museum.

Day seven Tour the Lower East Side and the East Village. After lunch, explore the Gramercy Park area and then conclude at the Pierpont Morgan Library.

Two-week itinerary

Day one As day one of weekend itinerary.

Day two As day two of week itinerary.

Day three As day three of week itinerary.

Day four In the morning, explore Central Park. Have lunch on the Upper West Side before visiting the American Museum of Natural History.

Day five Spend the whole day on Staten Island, visiting the Snug Harbor Cultural Center, the Richmondtown Historic Restoration and the Jacques Marchais Center of Tibetan Art.

Day six Tour the Lower East Side and Chinatown. Have lunch in Chinatown and spend the afternoon exploring Greenwich Village.

Day seven As day six of week itinerary.

Day eight On the Upper East Side, zip through either the Frick Collection or the Cooper-Hewitt National Design Museum. After a late lunch, continue to the Museum of the City of New York.

Day nine Visit the Forbes Galleries and idle away the rest of the morning in Washington Square Park. Have lunch at a café in Greenwich Village and then continue on to the East Village, or explore the Gramercy Park area and conclude your sightseeing at the Pierpont Morgan Library on 36th Street.

Day ten Explore Harlem and the museums of the Audubon complex on West 155th Street. After lunch, tour the Columbia University campus and the Cathedral of St John the Divine.

Day eleven Pay a visit to the Bronx Zoo and the New York Botanical Garden.

Day twelve Divide the day between the Whitney Museum of American Art and the Guggenheim Museum.

Day thirteen Travel by subway to Coney Island, tour the New York Aquarium and continue to Brighton Beach.

Day fourteen Spend the morning at the Cloisters, returning to Midtown for lunch and to visit the Museum of TV and Radio, or the American Craft Museum – and any landmark building you have yet to view at close quarters.

The Statue of Liberty is essential viewing, even if you're on a flying visit to the Big Apple

GUIDED TOURS OF HARLEM
Harlem is one of New York's most celebrated areas but can be intimidating for the first-time visitor. One way to see Harlem without worries is with a guided tour. Harlem Spirituals, Inc (tel: 391-0900) offers a choice of several: a Sunday or weekday tour that combines a gospel church service with a tour of historic Harlem, another that offers a soul-food lunch and a local history commentary and an evening fling based around several hours of jazz at a local venue.

The ultimate New York viewing platform is no more, but even without the magnificent panorama that was available from the World Trade Center's Tower Two, New York has views that no other city comes close to matching. The sun setting and the lights going on across Manhattan as seen from the Empire State Building is still as breathtaking as ever. Another option is to leave Manhattan itself and view it from afar. The Staten Island Ferry or the Brooklyn Heights Promenade both afford stunning vistas of the famous skyline

Empire State Building This is the star of virtually every Manhattan view except those from its own 86th-floor observation level. On a clear day, the eagle-eyed can see through the wire mesh into Massachusetts and Pennsylvania and peer down at jets swooping into New York's airports. Come after dusk to see nighttime Manhattan: the building is open until midnight at weekends.

Waterside Restaurants Fewer restaurants than you might suppose have staked a claim to the best dinner show in town: the New York skyline. One, however, is rightfully famous for its food as much as for its prime vistas of lower Manhattan: Brooklyn's River Café. Several top-rated chefs have made their reputations devising menus to compete with that view – Larry Forgione, Charlie Palmer and Rick Laakonen are just three – and ensuring the steep bill is money well spent. In Queens, the Water's Edge affords a different take on Manhattan, the Midtown east skyline. Finally, a barge on the East River called the Water Club lets you see in both directions, though, being tethered just off 34th Street, Queens is the easier shore to spot.

Rockefeller Center Look out from the 65th-floor windows of the Rainbow Room restaurant complex in the GE (formerly RCA) Building and you will see the Empire State Building rising regally to the south. Look north, and the green rectangle of Central Park cuts between the stately apartment buildings of the Upper East Side and the Upper West Side towards Harlem.

STATUE OF LIBERTY VIEWS
At the Statue of Liberty, which sits on an island between Manhattan and New Jersey, the outlook is stirring; at time of press Liberty Island was open to visitors though the statue itself was closed. This may well change – check on arrival.

Above the East River From its terminal at the junction of Second Avenue and 60th Street, the cable-car that crosses the East River to Roosevelt Island gives clear views of the island's former hospitals and lunatic asylums. The memorable views, though, are in the other direction, taking in a lengthy swath of riverside Manhattan from Midtown's United Nations complex northwards, far into the Upper East Side. A bonus is a bird's-eye view of any passing river traffic.

Fort Tryon Park Close to the northern tip of Manhattan, Fort Tryon Park offers not only the unexpected sight of a reassembled medieval European monastery (the Cloisters) but also, from the hilltop site of the fort itself, views across the Hudson River to New Jersey's Palisades Park and, on the other side of Manhattan, the Harlem River.

Brooklyn Some of the most rewarding views of Manhattan are found by leaving it. From Brooklyn Heights Promenade, the eastern edge of the Financial District – the so-called Water Street corridor, a heady mix of glass, steel, limestone and marble – walls the East River. In the foreground are the tall ships of South Street Seaport. Behind Water Street's forest of high-rises, you should be able to pick out the world's one-time highest building, the Woolworth Building, while two more, the Chrysler Building and the Empire State Building, are visible in the cluster of skyscrapers marking Midtown Manhattan.

Brooklyn Bridge Be sure not to use up all your film on the Promenade: returning to Manhattan on foot across the Brooklyn Bridge reveals the same scenes from continually shifting perspectives behind the struts of the bridge, providing endless scope for inventive photographers. The outlook is familiar from countless films and TV shows.

Staten Island Ferry Look across the harbour from Brooklyn Heights to see the green hills of Staten Island rising to the south. You might also spot the Staten Island Ferry as it plies between the island and the southern tip of the Financial District.

Riding the ferry is much more interesting than looking at it, however. Dramatic views of Manhattan's skyline can be seen from the vessel (best on the return leg, when the skyscrapers appear to grow bigger and bigger) as well as slightly less dramatic ones of Governors Island (occupied by the US Coast Guard), the Statue of Liberty and one of the world's longest suspension bridges, the Verrazano-Narrows Bridge, which forms a link from Staten Island to Brooklyn.

H G WELLS ON NEW YORK VIEWS, 1906
"Suddenly as I looked back at the skyscrapers of lower New York a queer fancy sprang into my head. They reminded me quite irresistibly of piled-up packing cases outside a warehouse. I was amazed I had not seen the resemblance before".

View over Midtown – one of the most recognisable skylines in the world

59

THE TOMPKINS SQUARE PARK RIOT

In the heart of Alphabet City, Tompkins Square Park was the scene of a heavy-handed police operation on a steamy August night in 1988, when 12 mounted police, soon joined by 400 re-inforcements, battled for four hours to clear the 6.5-hectare park of the homeless people who were occupying it.

The incident was recorded on video by a local artist and the police brutality that the playback showed triggered outrage across the city, and nightly violence at the park. Mayor Dinkins closed the park for major renovations, posting police guards to keep out anyone but dog-walkers and basketball players. Reopened, the park is now fairly peaceful during the day.

Tompkins Square Park, in Alphabet City, has seen its share of problems, but it is now a fairly safe and peaceful place in daylight

▶ Abigail Adams Smith Museum 151D3

61st Street at York Avenue (tel: 838-6878)
Open: Tue–Sun 11–4; Jun and Jul until 9 on Tue.
Admission: inexpensive
Subway: N, R, 4, 6; 59th Street

Neither Abigail Adams, daughter of John Adams, the second president of the US, nor her husband, William Stephens Smith, an aide to George Washington, ever lived here. Instead, the ashlar stone building was the carriage house of their intended 9.3-hectare country estate on the banks of the East River.

It was financial decline that caused the couple to move to alternative accommodation in 1799, however. The stables were converted first to an inn and then to a private residence before being purchased in 1924 by the Colonial Dames of America, an organisation pledged to preserving the history of the revolutionary period. The building was gradually equipped with Federal-period furnishings and objects which now fill nine of its rooms, making for an entertaining half-hour's viewing.

▶ Alphabet City IFCC3

Subway: B, D, F, N; Second Avenue

The process of gentrification that spread through Greenwich Village in the 1970s continued into the East Village. By the mid-1980s it had reached Alphabet City (so-called for having lettered rather than numbered avenues), which lies east of First Avenue between Houston and 14th streets. With its restaurants offering cuisines from Asia to Eastern Europe, the area draws mainstream New Yorkers in search of new dining experiences. Among its resident population are those wealthy enough to inhabit a classy, if usually small, renovated apartment in one of the many former tenement blocks.

Most of Alphabet City's population, however, are Puerto Ricans who have informally dubbed the area "loisaida"

(pronounced "low-ees-SIDE-ah"), a phrase reputedly first used by a local poet and playwright. The neighbourhood suffered from urban blight into the early 1980s, but the efforts of the local community and a major police initiative – and the rising interest of property developers – all contributed to regeneration. Much poverty remains though, and the area east of Avenue B can seem intimidating.

▶ American Academy and Institute of Arts & Letters IBCD2

Broadway at 155th Street (tel: 368-5900)
Open: Thu–Sun 1–4. Admission free
Subway: C, D, 1; 155th or 157th streets

Two august cultural bodies – the National Institute of Arts, founded in 1898 and the American Academy, founded in 1904 – unified in 1977 and jointly honour American achievements in art, writing and music.

Although much of its activity seems little more than mutual backslapping, the organisation also administers grants to deserving artistic causes and stages temporary seasonal exhibitions highlighting individual members. If your favourite author, painter or composer is being featured, it could be worth a visit.

▶ American Bible Society 151D1

Broadway at 61st Street (tel: 408-1500)
Open: Mon–Wed and Fri 10–6, Thu 10–7, Sat 10–5.
Admission free
Subway: A, B, C, D, 1, 2, 3, 9; 59th Street

A 1960s cast-in-place concrete structure a bagel's throw from busy Columbus Circle makes an unlikely home for the American Bible Society, founded in 1816 in order to circulate the Bible "without note or comment".

Over the years, historic bibles from near and far have been collected to form the society's extensive library and archive. The collection includes an illustrated Armenian account of the Four Gospels dated to the early 1400s and also a 16th-century bible translated by a New England preacher into Massachusetts (an Algonquin Native American dialect).

A few changing selections are displayed on the second-floor level, alongside a reconstruction of a Gutenberg printing press and a feature on the Dead Sea Scrolls.

AUDUBON TERRACE

The American Academy and Institute of Arts & Letters occupies one section of Audubon Terrace, a Renaissance Revival complex planned in 1908 and intended to provide a suitably imposing setting for several venerable national institutions – others among them including the American Numismatic Society (see page 65) and the Hispanic Society of America (see page 126).

Situated between Riverside Drive and Broadway and 155th and 156th streets, the scheme was never entirely successful: not only a poor architectural job, it also left its tenants in a humdrum residential area far removed from the ebb and flow of New York life.

The terrace was built on a part of the estate of John James Audubon, the eminent American naturalist of the early 1800s.

Changing exhibitions of pottery, textiles, furniture and other artefacts can be viewed in spacious surroundings at the American Craft Museum, which showcases the work of contemporary craftspeople

MUSEUM OF AMERICAN ILLUSTRATION
Within a few steps of the American Federation of the Arts, the Society of Illustrators (63rd Street between Lexington and Park avenues), established in 1875, holds the small but interesting Museum of American Illustration. Through lively temporary exhibitions, the museum highlights the contribution made to Americans' self-image through cartoons, advertising, book and magazine drawings and much more.

▶▶ American Craft Museum   151C2
53rd Street between Fifth and Sixth avenues (tel: 956-3535)
Open: Tue, Wed and Fri–Sun 10–6, Thu 10–8.
Admission: inexpensive
Subway: E, F; Fifth Avenue
From teapots and tapestries to baskets and brooches, the exhibits of the American Craft Museum are always stimulating. Chosen from the museum's own vast collection or using loaned pieces, the displays illustrate design trends and techniques and often feature the work of the most artistic and skilful 20th-century American craftspeople.

The museum is run by the American Craft Council, whose purchase of a brownstone house on this site in 1959 turned out to be a wise investment. A 1980s property speculator eager to erect a high-rise here agreed to give the museum a spacious chunk of the new building's first floor, enabling the displays to be mounted around a lovely three-storey atrium.

▶ American Federation of the Arts   151D2
65th Street between Park and Madison avenues (tel: 988-7700)
Call for opening times and admission fee
Subway: 6; 68th Street
The American Federation of the Arts arranges travelling exhibitions for the small museums of the US, often finding time to display tasters of some in its own galleries. It is pot luck what might be on display but a look inside also reveals the building's lavishly decorated interior, a 1960s restoration of what was originally the home, built around 1910, of a successful stockbroker.

▶▶ American Museum of Natural History   IFCF2

Central Park West and 79th Street (tel: 769-5100)
Open: Sun–Thu 10–5:45, Fri–Sat 10–8:45. Admission: moderate
Subway: 1, 9, B, C; 79th Street or 81st Street

With 36 million exhibits, this is one of the world's best-stocked museums. Whether you are gazing at a sabre-toothed tiger or an ancient Guatemalan inscription, there is a strong chance it will be among the foremost examples of its kind on show anywhere in the world.

Darwin's theory of evolution and Mendel's law of heredity were two of the natural science breakthroughs that provided the stimulus for the museum's founding in 1869. Within a decade, the collections had acquired a specially built home, a stately Romanesque structure beside Central Park.

The sheer size of the collections of the American Museum of Natural History makes it a daunting prospect even for the most enthusiastic visitor. One way to discover the best of the museum without fatiguing yourself too much is to join a free hour-long guided Highlights Tour. These depart several times daily and details can be obtained from any of the museum's information desks. Greatly improved by a $30 million restructuring, the museum's fossil collection – which was already among the best in the world – now forms part of a six-room, state-of-the-art complex revealing the intricacies of the evolutionary relationships as far back as the Jurassic period (180–120 million years ago). The climax of this section are the two Dinosaur Halls, which feature magnificent skeletons of Tyrannosaurus Rex and Apatosaurus.

CARL AKELEY

The Akeley Gallery at the American Museum of Natural History is named after Carl Akeley, a naturalist, explorer and inventor. Akeley twice narrowly escaped death by dangerous animal. In 1911, he was gored by an elephant but saved himself by swinging beneath the creature's body; on another occasion, he ran out of bullets while confronted by an angry leopard but saved himself by strangling it. Among his many technical innovations was a new taxidermy technique, which he employed on the seven elephants that stand in the gallery. Ironically, Akeley died in 1926 from complications arising from a gnat bite.

63

Massive exhibit in a massive museum – the Barosaurus at the Museum of Natural History

THE ROSE CENTER

A 42-metre steel and glass cube provides a striking (particularly so when illuminated) transparent exterior for the Rose Center for Earth and Space. Inside, a giant sphere orbited by models of the planets of our solar system holds the Hayden Planetarium and a series of walkways and galleries offering displays on astronomical subjects, from the mysteries of black holes to the birth of a star. The state-of-the-art planetarium offers 3D trips through the universe and temporary presentations for imminent astral phenomena such as eclipses. The Center's design is especially bold when viewed alongside the main museum's 19th-century architecture and the neighbouring apartment buildings. For planetarium tickets tel: 769-5200.

Native American life and the evolution of animal and bird species in North America are outlined by fairly dreary, but comprehensive, habitat dioramas.

More enjoyable, however, are the excellently arranged anthropological collections on Africa, Asia and Central and South America. This last section is particularly strong, including thousands of curious religious, ceremonial and everyday objects. Look for the Aztec musical instruments made from human bones, the 17th-century sheet-metal ornamental llamas from the Andes and shrunken heads from the Amazon rain forest – and be ready for intriguing insights into Mayan astronomy.

The museum unveiled a new permanent exhibition in 1993, the Hall of Human Biology and Evolution. It studies the workings of the human body, traces ancestors over the centuries and features a computerised archaeological dig and an electronic newspaper with information on human evolution.

Measuring 29m in length and weighing 10 tonnes, what is thought to be the world's largest museum exhibit replicates the world's largest mammal – the blue whale – above the Hall of Ocean Life and Biology of Fishes. The fibreglass whale steals the show, although the room's dioramas and fish skeletons do a commendable job in unravelling the mysteries of reproduction, feeding and self-defence far beneath the ocean's waves.

Moving on, even the mindbogglingly priced gems of Midtown Manhattan's jewellery shops pale into insignificance when compared with the contents of the museum's

The gorilla diorama at the American Museum of Natural History. Few aspects of the world's wildlife are left untouched by the museum's vast collections

Hall of Minerals and Gems, a collection valued at $80 million. A great chunk of crystal-impregnated copper and scores of darkened display cases filled with sparkling, spellbinding stones are just part of a cleverly planned exhibition focusing on the natural forces that create the world's most prized pieces of rock. Some of the stones are the size of a pinhead, others are as big as your fist; the 21,000-carat Brazilian Princess Topaz weighs a quarter of a tonne and is the world's largest uncut gem.

Entered directly from the museum, the **Nature Max Cinema** has screenings on natural history themes using the giant-screen IMAX system. If you have ever wanted to inspect a lion's teeth at close quarters, this is the safest way to do it. Adjacent is the museum in the **Rose Center for Earth and Space** (see panel).

► American Numismatic Society   *IBCD2*

Broadway at 156th Street (tel: 234-3130)
Open: Tue–Sat 9–4:30, Sun 1–4. Admission free
Subway: C, D, 1; 155th or 157th streets

A vast hoard of coins and medals that is unsurpassed anywhere in the world, the collections of the American Numismatic Society are primarily intended to aid the research of devoted coin collectors and academics. There are, however, two engaging first-floor exhibitions. The first is a spirited documentation – using maps, photographs and remarkable specimens of very ancient money – of the origins of, and the spread of, coins throughout the world.

After viewing the coins, you may not have sufficient energy left to do justice to the extensive display of medals housed in the second exhibition. Upstairs, there is a public information desk where you can find out whether the unusual coin you have just found in your change is likely to improve your lifestyle dramatically.

►► Asia Society   *151D3*

Park Avenue at 70th Street (tel: 517-ASIA)
Open: Tue–Wed and Fri–Sat 11–6, Thu 11–8, Sun 12–5.
Admission: inexpensive
Subway: 6; 68th Street

Founded in 1956 with a pledge to improve understanding between Asia and America, the Asia Society hosts conferences, concerts, workshops and film shows, and mounts stunning temporary exhibitions of Asian art drawn from the world's foremost collections. Displays from the society's own collections include Chinese ceramics from the 11th century BC, some very fine pre-Angkor Cambodian sculpture and wonderful Japanese Edo-period prints, all donated by John D Rockefeller III. The decorative lion above the entrance is based on an 18th-century bronze of a Nepalese guardian lion.

ST JAMES CHURCH
The Sunday services at St James Episcopal Church (861–863 Madison Avenue), a short walk from the Asia Society, draw many of New York's most wealthy believers from their Upper East Side homes. Drop in during the week to admire the church's impressive stained glass and reredos.

65

The bright interior of St James Church on Madison Avenue – one of several notable places of worship on the Upper East Side

ST ELIZABETH ANN SETON

The well-preserved Federal-style building at 7 State Street (tel: 269-6865) – its columns said to be cut from ship's masts – was erected in 1783 for the prominent Watson family but has found longer-lasting fame as the Shrine of Elizabeth Ann Seton. She founded the Sisters of Charity, the first order of nuns in the US, in 1812 and in 1975 she became the first native-born American woman to be canonised by the Roman Catholic Church. This was her home from 1801 to 1803. Usually *open* Mon to Fri 6:30–5, on weekends and holidays. *Admission free*; ring bell for attention.

66

Above and right: Battery Park, the gateway to the Statue of Liberty, combines history and small-time commerce

▶ Battery Park

104B1

Subway: 4; Bowling Green

A welcome open space on the edge of the Financial District, Battery Park provides nine hectares of greenery with outstanding harbour views. Historical texts are pinned to its lampposts, leaving you with no excuse for not discovering something of early New York simply by strolling the tree-lined pathways.

The park took its name from the row of cannons that the British stored during the 17th century along State Street, which now borders the park but which then marked the Manhattan shoreline.

If you are taking the ferry to the Statue of Liberty and Ellis Island, you will enter Battery Park's most interesting structure to reach the ticket booth, which is situated on the one-time parade ground of **Castle Clinton** (tel: 344-7220; *Open* daily 9–5. *Admission free*). This circular fortification, finished in 1811, was built to repulse British attack.

Though there is little evidence of the fact today, Castle Clinton – which originally stood some 90m offshore and was linked to land by a causeway – has enjoyed a prominent place in New York life. As its defensive importance declined, the fort was planted with floral gardens and became the scene of well-attended concerts (some presented by 19th-century showman P T Barnum) and exhibitions; subsequently, it predated Ellis Island as a landing and processing point for immigrants, almost 8 million of whom came ashore here between 1855 and 1889. The castle also served a 46-year stint as aquarium for the city.

Elsewhere in Battery Park is the pint-sized Peter Minuit Plaza named after the Dutchman who bought Manhattan from its Native American inhabitants for the equivalent of $24 paid in the form of tools and trinkets. Occupying a granite building topped by a distinctive six-tiered roof in nearby Battery Park City (see page 18), the **Museum of Jewish Heritage** (18 First Place; tel: 509-6130; *Open* Sun–Wed 9–5, Thu 9–8, Fri 9–3. *Admission: moderate*) traces Jewish life through persecution in Europe to the creation of Israel and the growth of Jewish communities in the US.

With its manic streets and towering sky-scrapers, it is easy to forget that Manhattan is an island. One of the best ways to get a grasp of its size and shape is from the water that surrounds it, on a guided boat trip.

Most boat-tour operators seem to be offering much the same thing—a sightseeing trip along the Hudson and East rivers that includes a stop at the Statue of Liberty and a view of any New York landmarks visible from the water. There are variations, however, so consider all the options to find the trip that suits you best.

In-depth sightseeing The most comprehensive of the sight-seeing cruises is run by **Circle Line** (tel: 630-8888). This comprises a three-hour narrated circumnavigation of Manhattan Island, passing beneath seven major bridges on the way. The same company operates a two-hour cruise after dark (Manhattan at night is not a sight to be easily forgotten) and several other options including a speedboat ride and a Latin DJ dance cruise.

Other options A touch more decadent are the eating and sightseeing trips of **Spirit Cruises** (tel: 727-7735). The company offers a two-hour Tropical Lunch Buffet cruise daily except Sunday, voyaging around Manhattan's southern tip and passing some of the city's major sights. On Sundays, the champagne-fueled Jubilee Lunch Cruise follows a similar route. Dinner and dance cruises (the food from a substantial buffet and the music from a live band), depart nightly and offer memorable views of Manhattan by moonlight.

The catamaran used by **Express Navigation Tour** (tel: 262-8743) has the swiftest tours, zipping from the Statue of Liberty to the United Nations in 75 minutes. By contrast, **Seaport Music Cruises** (tel: 630-8888) operated by Circle Line (see above) offers cruises around the city's waterways accompanied by live jazz and blues and a DJ playing NY-themed oldies.

EAT AS YOU GO
Visitors love to sightsee but New Yorkers love to eat and they are the people most in evidence on the lunch, brunch, and dinner cruises offered by World Yacht (tel: 630-8100). These are not calorie-counting affairs: lunch and brunch are lavish buffets and dinner is a four-course treat followed by dancing.

Even on a short stay, sightseeing by boat can make a pleasant change from hot sidewalks and traffic jams

BROADWAY'S FIRST BEND

Broadway's angular scythe through Manhattan's otherwise largely grid-style street plan gave rise to squares such as Union, Madison and Times. Its first bend – after travelling for 5 ruler-straight kilometres north from Bowling Green – was due to the refusal of a Dutch landowner, Jacob Brevoort, to allow it to cross his property, a site now occupied by Greenwich Village's Grace Church.

Broadway's nerve centre: the theatre district near Times Square

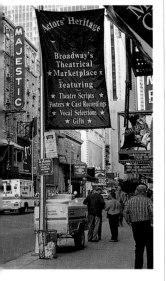

TIMES SQUARE TOURS

Call into the Times Square Visitors Center, inside the Harris Theatre, 1560 Broadway, for the story of Times Square, told with posters and assorted memorabilia. Each Friday at noon, the centre is the starting point of a free two-hour walking tour of the neighbourhood, pointing out places of interest.

►► Broadway

The story of Broadway is the story of New York. This is the city's oldest and longest thoroughfare – in one guise or another, Broadway not only runs north–south through Manhattan but continues for 225km to Albany. It has witnessed every good, bad and indifferent phase in the city's growth, while its internationally famous theatre district of Times Square and adjacent streets is, for many, what New York is all about.

Originally part of a Native American trail, Broadway was known to early Dutch settlers as De Heere Straat, or Main Street. It has remained New York's major (and perhaps most famous) artery ever since.

Broadway acquired the city's first numbered housing in 1793 and was also the first New York street to see its residential properties put to commercial uses. The commerce came in contrasting forms, with seedy bars, brothels and gambling dens alongside the city's finest retail outlets. In the 1880s, a popular saying held that if you fired a shotgun in any direction at the junction of Broadway and Houston Street, you would not hit an honest man.

In the days before traffic signals and one-way streets, Broadway was bedlam. Holding the city's major businesses and being the main route north, Broadway's sidewalks were packed with pedestrians and its centre a crush of handcarts and horse-drawn wagons. Police had to physically intervene to prevent the thoroughfare becoming completely blocked. Walkers took their lives in their hands when attempting to cross Broadway. The junction with Fulton Street was so infamously hazardous that, in 1867, the authorities erected a footbridge – only for it to be torn down at the insistence of shop owners fearful of losing their side's share of captive pedestrians.

What evolved into New York's theatre district began in Broadway's southern reaches and steadily moved north, one of the first theatres opening in 1798 at the junction with present-day Park Row. Broadway's theatres quickly forged a reputation for entertaining the city's well-to-do classes with productions of artistic merit and were therefore considered a cut above their Bowery counterparts, popularly regarded as offering low-brow titillation for the consumption of the masses.

By the 1880s, the heyday of vaudeville and the age of stars such as Lillie Langtry, the Broadway theatres had pushed north to Union Square. Around this time, however, the Metropolitan Opera House opened on an unlikely site 26 blocks north and began drawing the city's élite to an area then dominated by livery stores and stables. Broadway crossed this area at Longacre Square.

Ten years passed before a theatre opened at Longacre, but by then a section of Broadway around 34th Sreet had been famously labelled "the Great White Way" on account of its giant advertising billboards lit by hundreds of electric light bulbs.

Soon, **Times Square** – as Longacre Square was renamed after the publisher of *The New York Times* got permission to build an office tower above it – was similarly illuminated. Once joined to the subway system, it quickly became the heart of the city's theatre district.

Broadway continued north but the theatre district stayed where it was. By the 1920s many of the theatres were showing films and, 50 years on, the oldest of them were demolished in a spate of office building.

As if to echo the sleaziness of an earlier Broadway, the area around Times Square degenerated into a centre for porn shops, prostitution and drug dealing – though the sheer gaudiness of the place and the many legitimate theatres showing hit plays and musicals continued to attract crowds of tourists.

With the help of several billion dollars, a different Times Square began to appear through the 1990s: numerous new commercial developments and considerable improvements in appearance and safety have utterly transformed the area (see page 18).

The night-time neon of Broadway – still as dazzling to visitors as it was the day the electricity was switched on

Above and opposite: riding above it on the Skyfari aerial tramway is a good way to view the re-created habitats found at the Bronx Zoo

BRONX ZOO PRACTICALITIES
The zoo's Browndale entrance is a short walk from the Pelham Parkway subway stop. An alternative route from Manhattan is with the Liberty Lines Express Bus (BxM11), which runs from Madison Avenue to the Bronxdale entrance (for details, tel: 718/ 652-8400).

Though busy, early on summer days is the best time to visit (*Open* Mon–Fri 10–5, Sat and Sun 10–5:30). During the winter (Nov–Mar) many of the zoo's open-air sections are closed and the animals moved indoors (opening hours are then 10–4:30). Admission is inexpensive but free on Wednesdays. For general information on the zoo, tel: 718/367-1010.

▶ The Bronx   49E4

That the Bronx has had a worse press than any other New York borough is largely because one section, the South Bronx, became an international symbol of the most extreme forms of urban decay. Since the 1970s, abandoned buildings stripped clean of their fittings and regularly targeted by arsonists have littered the area. A major injection of funds for the building of affordable housing for the predominantly low-income population and widespread community initiatives are steadily, if slowly, having an impact, but the South Bronx's image as a place depressed is a hard one to lose.

The rest of the Bronx is quite different. Off **Grand Concourse**, a stately thoroughfare laid out in 1892 and still (though no longer deserving of its title) cutting south-north through the borough, lie safe and tidy residential areas, immense parks and the **Bronx Zoo** (see below).

In the South Bronx, **Yankee Stadium** (161st Street and River Avenue, tour info tel: 718/579-4531) has been the home of the New York Yankees since its completion in 1923. A $100-million renovation programme carried out in the mid-1970s was intended to improve the area as much as the building. If you visit the stadium, continue to the **Bronx Museum of the Arts** (1040 Grand Concourse). Opened in 1971, the museum has exhibitions of local art and Bronx-related cultural topics.

If they are not fans of the Yankees, many New Yorkers visit the Bronx for just one thing: the **Bronx Zoo**▶ (officially called the **Wildlife Conservation Park**), the largest city zoo in the nation. Spanning 107 hectares, the zoo puts its emphasis on herds and flocks rather than single animals and on re-created natural habitats rather than cages. The indoor rain forest of JungleWorld, for example, finds gibbons and monkeys leering at their human visitors from across artificial rivers. You should also spot a few Indian gharials, a type of alligator whose ancestry goes back 180 million years. Rare snow leopards are the highlight of the Himalayan Highlands, while World of Darkness – where day is transformed into night – allows glimpses of aardvarks, bushbabies, and bats (including the vampire variety, which receive a daily ration of blood).

The animals of the zoo's principal open space, Wild Asia, can be viewed only on a 25-minute narrated monorail ride. The open-sided cars glide above a plain roamed by antelopes, elephants, rhinoceroses, and sika deer – a species now extinct in its native habitat.

More traditional exhibits include the ape and reptile houses, and the MouseHouse, its cages inhabited by innumerable tiny furry things. There is also a Children's Zoo, intended to provide young minds with an insight into animal behaviour and offering plenty of cute and cuddly creatures for stroking.

Beginning across Fordham Road from the zoo, the **New York Botanical Garden**▶ (tel: 718/817-8700; *Open* Tue–Sun 10–6, 10–4 in winter. *Admission: inexpensive*) is a wonderful mixture of formal gardens, rock gardens and rugged woodlands – including a 16–hectare hemlock forest. In the northwest corner, the Enid A Haupt Conservatory is filled by a glorious array of banana plants, palm trees, cacti and other vegetation and stages seasonal flower shows. After

enjoying the vegetation, stop for refreshment at the Snuff Mill Terrace Café (*Open* summer only), invitingly shaded by trees and overlooking the Bronx River.

The **Edgar Allen Poe Cottage**▶ (off Grand Concourse at East Kingsbridge Road, tel: 718/881-8900; *Open* Mon–Fri by appointment, Sat 10–4, Sun 1–5) is where the writer lived for two years during the 1840s, in the hope that the country air would improve his wife's health. In the unheated dwelling, Poe's tubercular spouse died during the first winter. Holding a few of the Poes' sparse furnishings, the cottage is an aptly bleak memorial to a man whose short life was seldom a happy one.

In the grounds of the **Bronx Community College**▶ (181st Avenue and University Avenue) is the **Hall of Fame for Great Americans**. Here the bronze busts of

THE BRUNO HAUPTMAN HOUSE
The house at 1279 East 222nd Street, east of the Bronx's Woodlawn Cemetery, looks like any other but it was here in 1934 that police arrested Bruno Hauptman on the charges of abducting and holding to ransom (and subsequently murdering) the baby of flying-ace Charles Lindbergh.

The celebrated case galvanised the media and popularised the term "kidnapping". Hauptman was found guilty and executed, but doubts over the verdict rose with the discovery that the police had kept vital pieces of evidence from the jury.

The site where the $50,000 ransom was paid is also in the Bronx: St Raymond's Cemetery, between East Tremont Avenue and Eastern Boulevard, just south of Throg's Neck.

YANKEE STADIUM'S FIRST GAME
Financed by brewery magnate and then Yankees owner Colonel Jacob Ruppert, Yankee Stadium staged its first game in front of 60,000 people in April 1923. The legendary Babe Ruth hit three home runs, a major contribution to the Yankees 4–1 win over Ruth's former team, the Boston Red Sox. That same year, Ruth helped the Yankees win their first World Series.

71

RIVERDALE

When New Yorkers talk of the Bronx, they are not usually thinking of Riverdale, part of which is the site of enviable homes and which reaches from the eastern edge of Van Cortlandt Park to the Hudson River.

One place worthy of a visit is the 1846 Fonthill Castle, a Gothic Revival structure modelled on an English folly and originally the home of actor Edwin Forrest. It now serves as the admissions office for the College of Mount St Vincent, at Riverdale Avenue and 263rd Street. Another is Wave Hill (675 West 252nd Street; tel: 718/549-3200), 11 hectares above the Hudson River holding two 19th-century mansions with gardens and greenhouses. It is the site of horticultural exhibitions and summer concerts.

The New York Botanical Garden

around 100 prominent Americans are lined up along an open-air colonnade. The neo-classical style of the Hall of Fame is noteworthy and is replicated across the campus, much of which is credited to the prominent turn-of-the-century New York architect Stanford White (of the firm McKim, Mead, & White).

Predating the college, as well as most other buildings in the Bronx, the **Van Cortlandt Mansion**▶ (off Broadway between 240th and 242nd streets, tel: 718/543-3344; *Open Tue–Fri 10–3, Sat and Sun 11–4. Admission: inexpensive*) was built in 1748 for a family that was prominent in politics and farming, their land holdings consuming what are now the wild expanses of **Van Cortlandt Park**. The mansion, built in Georgian style with Dutch adornments, also provided a part-time base for George Washington, who marched from here into Manhattan to celebrate the end of the Revolutionary War. The mansion does an excellent job of highlighting its English, Dutch and Colonial furniture, and a few other 18th-century odds and ends. From time to time there are demonstrations of brick making and open-hearth cookery.

Strange as it may sound, a more intriguing stop than the mansion is **Woodlawn Cemetery**▶ (East 223rd Street and Webster Avenue). Rather than raid the art collections of Europe or finance Manhattan skyscrapers, some ultra-rich early New Yorkers chose to spend their fortunes on extravagant mausoleums. Among those buried here are merchants Richard H Macy, J C Penney, and F W Woolworth – whose sphinx-guarded, pseudo-Egyptian palace defies belief. Smaller tombs honour writer Herman Melville and jazz giant Duke Ellington.

New York's first black immigrants were slaves who arrived with the Dutch, by whom they were treated with comparative benevolence. A change for the worse occurred during the era of British dominion, when the colony's new rulers showed no respect for people whom they regarded merely as chattels. They responded to slave uprisings with public hangings and burnings. Since then, the struggle for civil rights has been a long, uphill battle.

Early racism After the Revolutionary War, a few freed slaves attained respectable social positions, but others were illegally transported to the Deep South. All were subject to racial hostility.

By the early 1800s, New York's African-Americans encountered segregation in public places and were prevented from obtaining the necessary work skills to be employed as anything other than labourers and servants.

The rise and fall of Harlem In response, the first black churches and mutual aid societies were formed and, after years of enduring racism in the city's slums, it was amid the stylish brownstones of Harlem (originally built for wealthy whites) that New York's blacks first felt they had found a secure and self-supporting enclave.

Harlem's population doubled during the 1920s, a period when its art, music, and literature flowered into the "Harlem Renaissance". Swiftly, however, the Depression made Harlem a ghetto, and its problems, along with those of African-American communities in other boroughs, were never tackled by the authorities. The Civil Rights Movement – and the Harlem speeches of Malcolm X – brought racial issues into the public spotlight during the 1960s.

Modern times David Dinkins became New York's first black mayor in 1990, as Harlem was evolving into one of Manhattan's newest areas of tourist interest. Meanwhile, Harlem institutions such as the Schomburg Center of Research in Black Culture have earned widespread recognition.

The raising of black consciousness in the 1960s was helped by public campaigners such as Malcolm X, seen here addressing a Muslim meeting in Harlem. He was assassinated in 1965

GREEN-WOOD CEMETERY

Henry Pierrepont, the man who developed Brooklyn Heights, was not only concerned with providing homes for the living. With Green-Wood Cemetery (main entrance at Fifth Avenue and 25th Street), he created a 193–hectare landscaped plot to be enjoyed by some of the most prominent New Yorkers on their earthly demise. The cemetery drew 100,000 visitors a year in its Victorian hey-day to wander its 32km of footpaths, take in the views over New York har-bour, and contemplate the many richly decorated tombs. Richard Upjohn's remarkable Gothic Revival gate and gatehouse, at the Fort Hamilton Parkway entrance, just marks the beginning. Among the 500,000 interred are Henry Ward Beecher, William Marcy "Boss" Tweed, Peter Cooper and Samuel Morse.

Absorbed into New York City in 1898, fiercely independent Brooklyn at least has its own view of the Statue of Liberty

▶▶▶ Brooklyn 48C3

Brooklyn was once a full-fledged city in its own right, with an affluent population and revered cultural institutions. In 1898, buoyed by the opening of the Brooklyn Bridge spanning the East River, it decided (by a narrow majority) to become part of New York City.

The decision has been cursed by Brooklynites ever since. Post-independence humiliations have been many: the Depression and a huge influx of immigrants turned many of Brooklyn's stylish neighbourhoods into slums and created breeding grounds for organised crime; the naval shipyards were closed down; Brooklyn's award-winning *Daily Eagle* newspaper bit the dust after a strike. Perhaps most galling of all, the Brooklyn Dodgers moved to Los Angeles in 1955.

Despite these setbacks, Brooklyn does remain the most distinctive and enjoyable of the Outer Boroughs. The moderate tempo of its streets comes as a welcome relief after the bustle of Manhattan.

If it were still a city, Brooklyn would be the sixth most populous in the US. Within its metropolitan sprawl are four pockets of special interest. Downtown Brooklyn and the historic Brooklyn Heights lie closest to Manhattan. To the north, Fort Greene is gaining a reputation as the home of the new black artistic community. South of downtown, the elegant Eastern Parkway leads past the massive Brooklyn Museum and the Botanic Garden; further south, on the coast, is the Russian-dominated Brighton Beach and the fabled but faded Coney Island amusement park.

From the Brooklyn Bridge, any turning to the right leads into the short leafy streets of **Brooklyn Heights▶▶▶**. The 1814 invention of the steam-powered ferry made this district, set on bluffs above the East River, a residential area coveted by the bankers and speculators active in Manhattan's Financial District, just across the water.

(Continued on page 76)

Where Brooklyn meets the Atlantic Ocean you will find not only a coastline but two contrasting images of New York life: Coney Island amusement park, world-famous but now a pale shadow of its former self, and Brighton Beach, a declining seaside resort energised and transformed since the 1970s by a massive influx of Russian émigrés.

Coney Island Up until the mid-1940s, this was many New Yorkers' idea of heaven. For a nickel subway fare they could spend a day of fun beside the ocean, munching cotton candy, making themselves dizzy on the roller coasters, or lurking around the side shows. Coney Island is undoubtedly a legend, but today it is also – in every sense – history. In the amusement park area between Surf Avenue and the Boardwalk and West 8th and West 16th streets, little more than run-of-the-mill fairground rides suggest the old days, though a 1927 roller-coaster, the fearsome Cyclone, is still in business, offering a 26-metre drop at a 60-degree angle.

On summer days, Coney Island's beach still gets plenty of users, while remaining surprisingly clean, and the Boardwalk beside it is as atmospheric as ever – windswept, breezy, and with an exhilarating polyglot flavour.

New York Aquarium (tel: 718/265-FISH; *Open* daily 10–4:30 or 5. *Admission: moderate*) Five species of shark, beluga whales, dolphins and sea lions are among the inhabitants of the Coney Island Aquarium, accessed from the boardwalk. Visitors will also find the Sea Cliffs exhibition, a re-creation of a rocky coastal habitat, which is populated by walrus, seals, penguins and sea otters.

Brighton Beach Continue east along the Boardwalk to reach this revitalised area where between 10,000 and 20,000 ex-Soviet immigrants form the largest Russian community in the US, beneficiaries of the USSR's relaxing of restrictions in the years before its collapse. With caviar and ice-cold vodka advertised in Cyrillic script, and the riotous restaurants along Brighton Beach Avenue known to round off the evening with frenzied dancing and the odd drunken brawl, so-called Little Odessa (many settlers arrived from the Black Sea port) is becoming one of the most celebrated areas of New York City. Bakeries and restaurants here offer Russian culinary specialities.

CONEY ISLAND'S NAME
The most plausible of many theories as to how Coney Island acquired its name is that it derives from the Dutch *Konijn Eiland* – Rabbit Island.

MAXIM GORKY ON CONEY ISLAND, 1906
"Fabulous and beyond conceiving, ineffably beautiful, is this fiery scintillation".

From its beginnings as an ash dump, the Brooklyn Botanic Garden has developed into an inspiration and delight for its visitors

(Continued from page 74)

Brooklyn Heights subsequently became covered with brownstone dwellings – Gothic, Greek, or Romanesque in style – which largely survive intact in an area that became a National Historical Landmark in 1965.

Structure your explorations sufficiently to include Orange Street and its **Plymouth Church of the Pilgrims▶** (tel: 718/624-4743 for opening hours). It was here during the 1800s that abolitionist minister Henry Ward Beecher (see panel on page 78) delivered eloquent and impassioned sermons against slavery and made the church a platform for the leading abolitionists. He is remembered by a statue in the adjoining garden. **Brooklyn's Historical Museum▶** (128 Pierrepont Street, tel: 718/624-0890; *Open* Tue–Sat 12–5. *Admission: inexpensive*), with its exhibits of local memorabilia, is another worthwhile stop.

Below the Heights, downtown Brooklyn spills along Fulton Street, which bends around Borough Hall, an unappealing Greek Revival building erected in 1848. Of far greater interest, the **New York Transit Museum▶▶▶** (tel: 718/243-8601; *Open* Tue, Thu–Fri 10–4, Wed 10–6, Sat and Sun 12–5. *Admission: inexpensive*) occupies a former subway station at the junction of Boerum Place and Schermerhorn Street. Inside, art deco air-vent coverings and mosaic-tiled station name plates recall the care that went into the early years of what became the world's second-largest mass transit system.

Between downtown Brooklyn and the former naval dockyards, **Fort Greene▶** is another district well endowed with leafy streets and elegant brownstones, now owned by Brooklyn's more affluent blacks among others. Many became rooming houses during the Depression, causing the area to fall into neglect.

Though signs of inner-city poverty remain apparent, Fort Greene is very much on the rise. African-Americans still make up 70 per cent of the district's population, a significant number of them being successful in the arts. Artist Ernest Critchlow is a long-established local; another is film-maker Spike Lee, who resisted the lure of Hollywood and located his production company here.

STROLL: BROOKLYN HEIGHTS

An enjoyable way to walk off a good lunch is with a stroll along the Brooklyn Heights Promenade. Also called the Esplanade, this wide pathway overlooks the East River, and has views of Manhattan strong enough to draw Brooklyn office workers with picnic lunches and to push the prices of west-facing penthouse apartments along nearby Columbia Heights into the realms of the phantasmagoric.

Lee grew up in Fort Greene and his 1986 film, *She's Gotta Have It*, made use of a local landmark: **Fort Greene Park**, designed in 1860 by Olmsted and Vaux (better known for Manhattan's Central Park). The Doric column was added later in memory of the 12,000 American patriots who died on British prison ships during the Revolutionary War and lie buried beneath the park.

Fort Greene sees comparatively few tourists. It would be sensible to keep to the area south of the park, where you will find the most impressive of the brownstone buildings and also several churches (visit on Sunday morning for the best atmosphere).

There are many more brownstones to be viewed in the surrounding residential streets between Flatbush Avenue and Sixth Avenue, which is an upmarket section of the Park Slope neighbourhood. A much more spectacular sight in this area, however, is located at the centre of Grand Army Plaza: the oversized Soldiers' and Sailors' Memorial Arch, raised in 1892 to commemorate the

BORN IN BROOKLYN
Mae West (1892), George Gershwin (1899), Aaron Copland (1900), Clara Bow (1905), Phil Silvers (1912), Veronica Lake (1919), Mickey Rooney (1922), Woody Allen (1935), Mary Tyler Moore (1937), Philip Glass (1937), Elliot Gould (1938), Neil Sedaka (1939), Barbra Streisand (1943), Barry Manilow (1946).

Brooklyn

THE HASIDIC JEWS

Since the 1940s, Brooklyn's Williamsburg district (north of Downtown) has been a base of the ultrastrict Hasidic community. Men wear beards, side curls, dark frock coats and hats; the heads of married women are shaven and covered by a wig. The Hasidim adhere rigidly to kosher diets, and some eschew TV and radio. Another large Orthodox Jewish community in Brooklyn is the Lubavitchers, adherents to a Hasidic sect that originated in 18th-century Russia.

HENRY WARD BEECHER

Clergyman at the Plymouth Church of the Pilgrims for some 40 years in the latter half of the 19th century, Henry Ward Beecher spoke out against slavery and in favour of women's suffrage. Equally controversial for the time, Beecher's writings supported Darwin's theory of evolution. His later years were dogged by allegations of adultery, charges of which he was cleared only after his death in 1887.

Brooklyn Heights. Not all of the city's best skyscrapers are in Manhattan

Union forces who died during the Civil War. This can be found on Flatbush Avenue by the main entrance to Prospect Park, described below.

This Brooklyn version of an imperial Roman arch was designed by John H Duncan, who was also responsible for the similarly grandiose General Grant Memorial (see pages 110–111). The memorial's sheer size makes it much more of an architectural curiosity than a fitting shrine to the dead. The sense of pomposity is compounded by the heroic sculptures added to the memorial in 1898, though some amends are made by the finely detailed bas-reliefs that decorate the walls on the inside of the arch.

Prospect Park▶ itself is a broad and bucolic open space completed in 1874. With none of the restraints that were imposed with Central Park (such as incorporating major traffic arteries) architects Olmsted and Vaux gave their imaginations free rein here and considered Prospect Park their finest work.

The grand streets and landscaped open spaces – as well as the triumphal monuments – that Brooklyn acquired during the late 19th century were the hallmarks of a city very much on the rise. In keeping with the optimism of the times – and in an effort to create a symbol of Brooklyn's cultural superiority over Manhattan –

the **Brooklyn Museum**▶▶▶ (200 Eastern Parkway, tel: 718/638-5000; *Open* Wed–Fri 10–5, Sat–Sun 11–6, 11–11 first Sat of the month. *Admission: inexpensive*) was founded in 1897 with the intention of becoming the largest museum in the world. Such great ambitions were never fulfilled, however, and this fine museum does play second fiddle to the better-known Manhattan museums. It is probably most renowned as the resting place for the world's third largest stock of ancient Egyptian artifacts.

The museum's fifth floor has an exceptional collection of 19th-century American portraiture, including Gilbert Stuart's iconographic image of George Washington. Elsewhere, Francis Guy's airy *Winter Scene in Brooklyn* of 1817 stands out, and a quality selection from the Hudson River School culminates in Albert Bierstadt's *Storm in the Rocky Mountains, Mt Rosalie*, an intense landscape of rugged granite beneath brooding storm clouds.

The fourth floor of the museum has colonial-period ceramics, and interiors ranging from 17th-century farmhouses to 1920s art deco lounges. Note the Moorish Room: a dreamy conglomeration of patterned tiles, gold-brocaded walls, oak panels and velvet drapes which once graced John D Rockefeller's Manhattan mansion.

Other floors are filled by comprehensive Asian art collections, while the first floor holds pottery, figurines and votive objects from Africa, Oceania and Central and South America. Most striking among the latter is perhaps the Paracas Textile, a 2,000-year-old Peruvian burial cloth. The Native American collections, on the same floor, feature diverse tribes and exhibits ranging from buckskin jackets to totem poles.

After exploring the museum, head for the 21 divinely landscaped hectares of the **Brooklyn Botanic Garden**▶▶ (tel: 718/622-4433; *Open* Tue–Fri 8–4:30, Sat–Sun 10–4:30, extended hours during summer. *Admission: inexpensive*), just to the rear.

The quiet charm still to be found in parts of Brooklyn Heights contrasts with the frenetic streets of Manhattan, just across the East River

LITERARY BROOKLYN HEIGHTS
Brooklyn Heights has strong literary associations. Poet Hart Crane and novelist John Dos Passos both lived at 110 Columbia Heights during the 1920s (Crane also resided briefly at 77 Willow Street). Henry Miller spent a short time at 91 Remsen Street during the 1920s and Truman Capote wrote *Breakfast at Tiffany's* in the basement of 70 Willow Street. Norman Mailer wrote *The Naked and the Dead* while living with his parents at 102 Pierrepont Street (he now lives elsewhere in Brooklyn Heights). At the same address Arthur Miller wrote his play *All My Sons*, before moving to 155 Willow Street, where he is remembered by a plaque – though he wrote *Death of a Salesman* at 31 Grace Court.

BAD LUCK AND THE BROOKLYN BRIDGE

In its early years, the Brooklyn Bridge saw more than its share of tragedy. Its designer, John A Roebling, died following an accident before his bridge was complete. His son, Washington, took over, but became paralysed as a result of "the bends", and had to supervise the construction work from his sick bed. Twenty of the 600-strong work force died during the construction. Six days after the bridge opened, the screams of a woman who tripped on the approach caused a panic in which 12 people lost their lives, mistakenly believing the bridge was about to collapse. In 1884, however, circus-owner P T Barnum led 21 elephants across it; since then there have been few doubts as to the bridge's strength.

Brooklyn Bridge—"the crowning glory of an age memorable for great industrial achievements"

▶▶ Brooklyn Bridge   77D1

Subway: Brooklyn Bridge

Completed in 1883, the Brooklyn Bridge was the world's first steel suspension bridge, and, for 20 years, the longest. It formed the first fixed link between Brooklyn and Manhattan Island.

Enhanced immeasurably by its two Gothic 83m high stone arches (when they were finished, only the spire of Trinity Church rose higher into the New York sky), the bridge is an aesthetic as well as an engineering master-piece. Many writers, including Brooklyn-based Walt Whitman, have waxed lyrical over its beauty.

Cyclists, skaters, joggers and high winds can all be a hazard to walkers on the bridge's pedestrian path, easily the best way to appreciate the structure. From Manhattan, the views used to be of Brooklyn's busy shipyards, a scene re-created by a display beside the footpath, while another recounts the bridge's origins. In the other direction is a fabulous view of Manhattan.

▶ Carnegie Hall   151C2

57th Street at Seventh Avenue (tel: 247-7800)
Guided tours: Mon–Tue, Thu–Fri 11:30, 2 and 3.
Admission: inexpensive
Subway: D, E, N, R; Seventh Avenue or 57th Street

Financed by a $2-million gift from steel magnate Andrew Carnegie, Carnegie Hall opened to the public in 1891 and quickly gained an international reputation for its out-standing acoustics. Its horseshoe-shaped auditorium is modelled on those of Italian opera houses. Refurbishment has restored the hall, best appreciated by attending a concert – a must if you have time. Tours of the building end at the **Carnegie Hall Museum** which records the hall's origins and the long list of famous names that have graced its boards. Besides Benny Goodman's clarinet and Arturo Toscanini's baton, the museum has a 1964 bookings diary with a handwritten entry recording the first New York appearance of "The Beetles"(sic).

Gothic vaulting (left) and (below) a sculptural detail of what will, if and when it is completed, be the world's biggest cathedral

▶▶ Cathedral of St John the Divine   *IBCB2*

Amsterdam Avenue at 112th Street (tel: 316-7540)
Open daily 8–6. Admission free
Subway: 1; Cathedral Parkway (110th Street)

The cornerstone of the Cathedral of St John the Divine was laid in 1892, marking the beginning of what is now an immense Episcopalian edifice spread across 4.5 hectares – the largest church in the US, and the largest Gothic church in the world, yet still years short of completion.

The original plans were for a church of Byzantine/Romanesque design, but delays caused by engineering problems and lack of finance meant that only the choir and four stone arches were completed in the first 25 years. Changing tastes (and the death of the project's original architect) saw the structure remodelled in French Gothic form, and it was given a façade rather reminiscent of Notre-Dame in Paris.

The nave, covering a staggering 3,000sq m, was completed in a comparatively swift 10 years, but the US's entry into World War II again halted progress, as did a decision during the 1960s to divert building money to the needs of the community. Another building programme got under way in 1978, when funds were available to import a master stonemason from England to cut the Indiana limestone used in the towers and to train a small army of local apprentices.

As its towers still rise, enclosed by scaffolding, the cathedral's exterior takes on a strangely surreal appearance. Inside, the scale is breathtaking. The clash of Gothic and Romanesque/Byzantine styles is most apparent from the unfinished crossing, where the structure's anatomy is revealed and above which the red-tiled dome, installed as a "temporary" shelter during 1909, remains in place even today.

Foremost among the cathedral's decorations are two sets of religious tapestries: the Mortlake Tapestries, woven in England during 1623 from cartoons by Raphael, and the 17th-century Barberini tapestries, which were woven on papal looms.

NEW YORK PUBLIC LIBRARY: 115TH STREET BRANCH
The main branch of the New York Public Library on Fifth Avenue (see page 168) is one of the city's greatest architectural delights, and the 115th Street branch (between Seventh and Eighth avenues) is no mere pile either. Dating from 1908, the library was the work of the firm of McKim, Mead, & White, and its imposing Renaissance style was intended to match the grandeur of early Harlem.

1 Charles A Dana Discovery Center
2 El Museo del Barrio
3 Museum of the City of New York
4 International Center of Photography
5 Jewish Museum
6 Cooper-Hewitt National Design Museum
7 Guggenheim Museum
8 Cleopatra's Needle
9 Delacorte Theater
10 Belvedere Castle
11 Swedish Cottage
12 American Museum of Natural History and Hayden Planetarium
13 San Remo Apartment Building
14 Loeb Boathouse
15 Alice in Wonderland Statue
16 Hans Christian Andersen Statue
17 Frick Collection
18 Bandstand
19 Holy Trinity Lutheran Church
20 Tavern-on-the-Green
21 Heckscher Playground
22 Wollman Memorial Rink

►►► Central Park   IFCF2

From almost any high point in Manhattan, what holds the eye longest is not the Empire State Building or the World Trade Center but the great rectangle of greenery in the heart of the dense urban clutter. Central Park fills 340 hectares and runs for 50 city blocks between the Upper East and Upper West sides.

The candidates in New York's mayoral campaign of 1850 were agreed on just one issue: the need for a large public park of the kind civic leaders and journalists had been advocating since poet and newspaper editor William Cullen Bryant raised the idea in 1844. At that time, property developers were breaking all records in their northwards streak across Manhattan.

In 1856, the city paid $5.5 million for a tract of land, which was in an area well to the north of the city as then established, dotted with pig farms and squatter camps and mostly used as a rubbish dump. Two years later work began on the park, to the plans of Frederick Olmsted (a farmer-turned-engineer-turned-journalist-turned-landscape architect) and English architect Calvert Vaux.

The park's design called for a major earth-moving project as glades, copses and rock outcrops were created, and some 5 million trees planted. Bridges linked the park's internal thoroughfares and cross-park traffic was carried by sunken roads to keep the pastoral view intact.

With tree-lined driveways for the wealthy to parade in horse-drawn carriages and footpaths for the working classes (who typically at the time toiled in sweatshops and lived in filthy tenements) to experience, as Olmsted expressed it, "a specimen of God's handiwork", the park was an instant success.

Though now fully enclosed by buildings and with far more monuments than Olmsted would have liked, Central Park is still a great escape from the city streets. The Fifth Avenue and Upper West Side apartment buildings that appear above the treetops simply add to the park's country-in-the-city effect. Getting lost temporarily in Central Park is surprisingly easy. Be sure to pick up a map from one of the information kiosks before you enter.

From the south, the first place to make for is the **Dairy**. In pursuit of a romantic rural vision, the Gothic-style Dairy was built here in 1870 as a place where traditionally attired milkmaids would serve fresh milk to mothers and young children. The quaint building now holds the park's main Visitor Center, with displays and several leaflets describing park walks.

North of here, across the 65th Transverse, the 9-hectare **Sheep Meadow** did indeed hold sheep during the park's earliest years, the resident flock being led across the park's West Drive twice a day to the Sheepfold, which occupied the site of the present Tavern on the Green.

Just east of the Sheep Meadow begins the **Mall**, one of the first completed sections of the park and its only formal area. Many 19th-century New Yorkers got their first taste of European-style promenading along its tree-lined esplanade, and some also gained their first experience of donkey- and goat-cart riding, both of which were offered to visitors here.

Olmsted initially resisted attempts to have statuary in the park but eventually agreed to the memorials of writers – Shakespeare, Robert Burns and Sir Walter Raleigh among them – which are grouped around the Mall's southern end to form the **Literary Walk**. Continuing north, the Mall leads into the **Concert Ground** and the **Naumberg Bandshell**, the scene of free live music on most summer weekends.

Cross the 72nd Street Transverse and you enter **Bethesda Terrace**. At its heart is the Bethesda Fountain and the elegant *Angel of the Waters* statue. One of the few pieces commissioned especially for the park, the statue, inspired by the biblical story of the Bethesda Pool in Jerusalem, was unveiled in 1873 to commemorate the opening of the aqueduct that gave New York its first regular supply of fresh water.

There is more water directly north of Bethesda Terrace, in the form of the **Lake**. A leisurely paddle along this imposingly calm body of water is a fine way to round off a park visit. Boats can be hired from the Loeb Boathouse, on the eastern banks of the lake.

If you are determined to do something more energetic, you could always cross the lake on foot by way of the Bow Bridge – one of Central Park's seven original cast-iron bridges – to **The Ramble**. Comprising 13.4 hectares of painstakingly re-created rurality, complete with rustic

STROLL: STRAWBERRY FIELDS

From the Upper West Side, entering Central Park on 72nd Street leads into Strawberry Fields, a 1.2-hectare section maintained by an endowment from Yoko Ono, as a memorial to her late husband John Lennon.

Overlooked by the Dakota apartment building, where the Lennons lived (see page 96), Strawberry Fields is planted with 161 species of plant, representing 161 nations of the world. The authorities were not unanimous in agreeing to the tribute: conservative elements wanted a memorial to Bing Crosby.

Central Park's Bethesda Fountain

CENTRAL PARK IN STYLE
One way of seeing the park is as the city swells of the 1880s did: by horse and carriage. Buy a ticket from the stand at Grand Army Plaza (at the junction of 59th Street and Fifth Avenue) and climb aboard. Prices have risen over the last hundred years, however: expect to pay around $34 per person for a 25-minute trot.

birdhouses and beehives, The Ramble is excellent for exploration and for birdwatching. It is not advisable to ramble alone, however, as this is an isolated area.

Across the 79th Street Transverse from The Ramble, a replica Scottish castle, **Belvedere Castle** (tel: 722-0210; *Open* Tue–Sun 10–4. *Admission free*), was erected in 1869 for no reason other than fun and holds displays on park wildlife.

To the left, a path leads to the **Shakespeare Garden**, planted with trees and plants mentioned in the bard's works, passes the **Delacorte Theater** (scene of a summer Shakespeare festival), and continues to the immaculate **Great Lawn**. Free open-air concerts are given here each year during the summer by the New York Philharmonic.

Central Park has had its share of well-publicised crimes

but is generally no more dangerous than the average New York street, though there are isolated areas where lone wandering is not wise. Do not visit the park after dark except for a major event.

▶▶ Chelsea   IFCD2

West of Fifth Avenue between 14th and 34th Street
In the 1990s Chelsea evolved into one of Manhattan's most stylish neighbourhoods. Former warehouses close to the Hudson River have been converted into gallery space, and Chelsea has become a thriving quarter for new art, exhibited amid truck supply stores and courier firms.

Among the galleries is the main site (there are three others in Manhattan) of the **DIA Center for the Arts** (548 West 22nd Street, tel: 989-5566; *Open* Wed–Sun 12–6. *Admission: inexpensive*), with low-key exhibitions often featuring major names. Meanwhile, several river piers (west of 23rd Street) became the imaginatively designed recreational complex of **Chelsea Piers** offering skating, bowling, golf, river cruises and a waterside promenade.

The commercial heart of Chelsea is around the junction of 23rd Street and Eighth Avenue. The residential areas nearby are a mixture of tasteful townhouses and high-rise apartment blocks.

Top: a sedate tour or (above) the more energetic pastime of rollerblading

When the Chelsea opened in 1888 at 222 West 23rd Street, it was the first apartment building in New York to have a penthouse. Its façade featured wrought-iron balconies decorated with sunflower motifs. Converted to a hotel in 1905, the Chelsea became famous as a haunt of writers, painters and composers, who gave it an unconventional ambience.

Painter John Sloan and writers Mark Twain and O Henry (the pen name of William Sydney Porter) were among the Chelsea's early guests, but the hotel hit its artistic stride during the 1930s, after poet Edgar Lee Masters eulogised it in verse and novelist Thomas Wolfe took up residence. Impressed by the size of his suite, Wolfe dubbed his bathroom the "Throne Room" and kept 4,000 loose pages of prose strewn across his floor. Selections from these would be assembled and supplied to his publisher as finished works.

The 1950s and 1960s Its literary links were already established by the time Dylan Thomas made the Chelsea his New York base during the early 1950s. His last conscious hours, after he had claimed to have downed 18 whiskys in a Greenwich Village bar, were spent in room 205, and he died in hospital a few days later of suspected alcohol poisoning.

A decade later, the Irish writer Brendan Behan took shelter at the Chelsea and begged to be commemorated by a plaque – as he now is. Besides Behan, Beat writers William Burroughs and Gregory Corso, expatriate Russian novelist Vladimir Nabokov, and abstract expressionist painter Jackson Pollock were among the renegades who gathered at the Chelsea's bar (which is now a Spanish restaurant).

Pop and punk The hotel provided a backdrop for Andy Warhol's rambling split-screen film *Chelsea Girls* (which starred Warhol acolyte Edie Sedgwick, a Chelsea resident) and through the 1960s its guests included many pop-music icons – among them Bob Dylan, who wrote his epic song *Sad Eyed Lady of the Lowlands* in one of its rooms.

The hotel's most ignominious night came in 1978, when punk rocker Sid Vicious allegedly stabbed his girlfriend to death in their suite – Alex Cox's movie *Sid and Nancy* actually featured the hotel.

Step into the Chelsea's lobby and you will find plaques commemorating its most illustrious residents and many works donated by artist guests. The Chelsea's rooms vary greatly in style, size and price, and many of them are occupied by eccentric long-term guests.

Its decorative design may once have been ahead of its time, but the Chelsea has long been known not as an architectural landmark but as a cultural one

PRE-CHINATOWN REMNANTS

On St James Place you can find the First Shearith Israel graveyard, predecessor of the cemeteries of Greenwich Village and Chelsea. The first Jewish cemetery in the United States, the site was consecrated in 1656, when it was considered to be well outside town.

On nearby James Street, St James Church is an 1837 Greek Revival edifice. Al Smith, once an altar boy at the church, rose from this poor then-Irish neighbourhood to become New York's governor and a 1928 Democratic presidential candidate.

Frenetic but fascinating, Chinatown's streetlife never takes a break

▶▶▶ Chinatown   *IFCB3*

New York streetlife enters a new dimension on the tightly clustered, densely crowded sidewalks of Chinatown, which lies between the courthouses, Little Italy and the Lower East Side.

Stalls are laden with seafood, vegetables or fruit; herbalist shops dispense wondrous remedies; bakeries concoct sweet cakes; and rows of gaudy neon signs advertise (in both English and Chinese) the noodle stores, tea parlours and dim sum houses that bring the majority of non-Chinese New Yorkers to the area.

There has been a Chinese presence here since the 1850s, but only with the relaxing of immigration laws in 1965 did Chinatown really begin to expand. Spilling beyond its traditional boundaries, Chinatown now holds around half of New York's estimated 300,000 Chinese population and has been swelled by arrivals from Vietnam and other parts of Southeast Asia.

The handover of Hong Kong to Beijing has also been felt. Hong Kong banks have opened here, and brightly lit shopping malls stuffed with jewellery and electrical goods have spread along Canal Street.

Beyond the business and the people, there is not a lot for visitors to see in Chinatown, although a notable exception is the **Museum of Chinese in the Americas** (second floor, 70 Mulberry Street; tel: 619-4785; *Open* Tue–Sat 12–5. *Admission: inexpensive*). This one-room exhibition presents a small, absorbing documentation of Chinese settlement in the US. The many exhibits are a hotchpotch of family photos, items from Chinese-run businesses and objects of symbolic significance carried from the homeland. Part of the museum's aim is to help young Chinese-Americans understand their history, although the temporary exhibitions examine many aspects of the Chinese Diaspora.

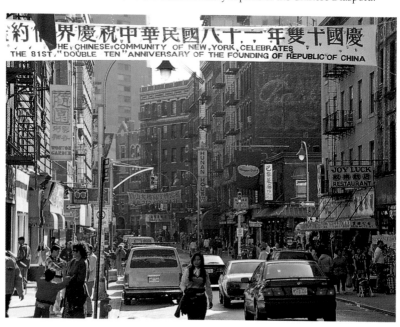

約世界慶祝中華民國八十一年雙十國慶
THE CHINESE COMMUNITY OF NEW YORK CELEBRATES
THE 81ST "DOUBLE TEN" ANNIVERSARY OF THE FOUNDING OF REPUBLIC OF CHINA

CHINATOWN

Walk

Chinatown streetlife

Effervescent streetlife is the main attraction of Chinatown, which holds few specific sights. This walk covers the main ones and captures the atmosphere of the area.

Begin at **Columbus Park**, which replaced a notorious slum and red-light area of the mid-1800s. Across Mulberry Street is the entrance to the **Museum of Chinese in the Americas**. Walk up to **Canal Street** for Chinatown's biggest and brightest shopping emporiums before reaching Mott Street.

At 64 Mott Street, the **Eastern States Buddhist Temple** is a genuine temple but also sells souvenir Buddha figures, arranged in eye-catching rows. Built in 1801, the Georgian **Church of**

the **Transfiguration**, at 25 Mott Street, predates Chinatown. Not far away, **Doyers Street** was once the

domain of opium dealers and prostitutes, and its bend was used as an ambush point during 19th- and early 20th-century Tong Wars, when rival Chinese gangs fought over who should have control of drug-trafficking, prostitution and gambling. Nowadays perfectly safe, Doyers Street is lined by numerous restaurants.

Chinese faces were few and far between in early 19th-century New York, but nowadays the Chinese community is expanding fast in both size and importance. Whether in academia or business, Chinese-Americans are frequently among the city's most spectacular achievers.

CHINESE IN THE US

Although only a few Chinese were present in New York prior to the late 1800s, they were already established in California where 25,000 had arrived in 1852. Most of them worked in the California gold mines and, subsequently, on the transcontinental railway that linked the West Coast to the rest of the country. The Chinese gained a reputation as dependable labourers, but in the economic depression that followed the Gold Rush, they found themselves prevented from opening businesses or owning land. Banding together, the Chinese settled in what became the "Chinatown" districts of many California communities, some making the cross-country trip to the less hostile atmosphere of New York.

88

The 75 Chinese immigrants estimated to be living in New York in 1870 were mostly individuals who had jumped ship and assimilated themselves as best they could into established ethnic groups. By 1890, however, New York's Chinese population had rocketed to 12,000. Many of the new arrivals came here from California, where they had provided labour for the transcontinental railway.

With their language and culture at odds with European New York, the lone Chinese males (denied the company of their relatives by an anti-immigration law of 1896) rarely strayed from Chinatown. Aided by family-based self-help organisations, they toiled in shops and laundries, sending any spare money back home.

The seamy side The popular imagination saw Chinatown as a neighbourhood of incredible exotica. Gambling, prostitution (provided by white women) and opium dens did in fact exist, but usually in upstairs rooms or basements. These activities were overseen by the Tongs – an American term for a Chinese-American secret society. Many Tongs claimed long histories to impress recruits and, at a time when the Chinese were excluded from the American legal system, provided a vehicle for settling grievances.

Acceptance and expansion The Japanese invasion of China in 1937 helped unite warring factions in the Chinese community, and the subsequent US–Sino military alliance reduced anti-Chinese feeling among New Yorkers. A bigger change came in 1965, when limitations on Chinese immigration were lifted and waves of new arrivals from Taiwan and Hong Kong came to Chinatown.

The new Chinese were eager to embrace American ways. They quickly made their presence felt in mainstream New York life. Their success and prosperity enabled them to become fully integrated into New York life, and to leave cramped Chinatown for more comfortable homes. Many left the inner city for suburbia as soon as they made the climb up the economic ladder.

Chinese take-away. Chinatown's eateries cover a vast range of styles and regional cuisines

The unmistakable Chrysler Building – New York art deco at its finest, and everyone's favourite skyscraper

THE CHEATING SPIRE
The Chrysler Building's "world's tallest" title was acquired through some slightly devious behaviour by its architect, William Van Alen. The needle-like spire that tops its 77 storeys was secretly assembled inside the tower and pushed through the roof. In this way Van Alen outwitted his former partner, H Craig Severance, whose contemporaneously completed Bank of Manhattan Building (40 Wall Street) would otherwise have earned the accolade.

POLICE RIOTS
In 1857, City Hall Park was the scene of violence between New York's two rival police forces, the discredited Municipal and the newly formed Metropolitan. Their battles continued into City Hall and ended only when National Guardsmen drew their bayonets.

In September 1992, New York's finest again disgraced themselves in the park, when a poorly planned demonstration against Mayor Dinkins culminated in officers (some of them clearly the worse for drink) stepping over the barricades and blockading the entrance to City Hall.

►► Chrysler Building   *151B3*

42nd Street at Lexington Avenue (tel: 682-3070)
Open: Mon–Fri 8:30–5:30. Admission free
Subway: 4, 6, 7; 42nd Street/Grand Central

The definitive symbol of New York art deco and briefly the world's tallest building, the 318m Chrysler Building was completed in 1930. Its tower is still among the city's most recognisable landmarks. More impressive than the exterior view, however, is the lobby, retaining its walls of red-veined African marble and a mural by Edward Trumbull depicting the glories of world transportation. The elevators, too, still have their original décor of laminated woods, and the entire 77-storey building is studded by automobile motifs.

► City Hall   *104C2*

Broadway and Park Row (tel: 788-6879)
Open: Mon–Fri 9–4. Admission free
Subway: N, R; City Hall

A cluster of municipal buildings stands near the foot of the Brooklyn Bridge. The oldest, the **City Hall**, a mixture of Federal and French Renaissance styles dating from 1811, is still in use for its original purpose. The barriers that line the front of the building are intended to prevent the frequent demonstrations in City Hall Park from blocking councillors' access to the building. Inside, a circular staircase winds beneath the eye-catching rotunda to the second floor, where the **Governor's Room** is lined by portraits of early New York notables and items of furniture mostly contemporaneous with the building. To the north stands the **Old New York County Courthouse**, intended as a shrine to justice but a building whose financing was one of the biggest swindles in New York history (see page 42). It is now used as municipal offices. Across Centre Street, the present **New York County Courthouse** has a hexagonal shape and a magnificent Corinthian portico.

City dwellers love to root for the home team, and New Yorkers – with their city represented by two professional teams in football, hockey and baseball – are no exception. Loyalties and rivalries run deep, even though the closest most people get to actual games is the TV in their living rooms: tickets, especially for football games or for playoff games in other sports, tend to be hard to get hold of and expensive.

THE NEW YORK MARATHON

What began in 1970 with 127 runners is now one of the world's largest urban marathons. Its 42km course is contested by some 22,000 runners and watched by over 2 million spectators. Usually held on the third or fourth Sunday in October, it begins on Staten Island at the Verrazano-Narrows Bridge, passing through each of the city's five boroughs to finish at Central Park's Tavern on the Green.

A great New York sporting event

Baseball The exceedingly successful New York Yankees, with a string of World Series wins echoing the glory days that saw them dominate the sport from the 1920s to the 1960s, play at Yankee Stadium in the Bronx (tel: 718/293-6000). The season runs from April to October. Ticket prices range from around $8 (on the day) for the bleachers, where you will hear the New York crowd at its most witty but also get the worst view, to around $23 as you move up into the tiered seating.

The slightly less successful New York Mets (who met and were beaten by the Yankees in the World Series "subway series" in 2000) play at Shea Stadium in Queens (tel: 718/507-8499) where ticket prices are similar to those for the Yankees.

Basketball From fall to spring, basketball fans can watch the New York Knicks (short for "Knickerbockers") playing at Madison Square Garden (tel: 465-JUMP). The Knicks had an all-win "dream" season in the early 1970s, but their record has been off and on since. Ticket costs vary upwards from $20 and are particularly difficult to get for the end-of-season play-offs. The advent of professional women's basketball quickly found New York Liberty (tel: 564-9622) among the country's top WNBA sides. Like the Knicks, they play at Madison Square Garden, with tickets priced from $8 to $55.

Hockey The incredible lack of success of the city's New York Rangers was dramatically ended by their winning of the Stanley Cup in 1994. The Rangers face off at Madison Square Garden (ticket info, tel: 307-NYRS) in a season lasting from late fall to spring. New Yorkers who want to see a local hockey team with a more regular success rate are inclined to travel to Uniondale on Long Island, where the New York Islanders play at the Nassau Coliseum (tel: 516/794-9300).

Football Both of New York's two professional football teams play outside the city's boundaries, at Giants Stadium, the Meadowlands, East Rutherford, New Jersey (tel: 201/935-8222). Despite being thrashed in the 2001 Super Bowl, the Giants have been slightly more successful than New York's AFC team, the Jets. The football season runs from August to December and tickets for the Jets start at around $25. Particularly for Giant games, however, tickets are virtually impossible to obtain without making reservations many months (if not years) in advance. Shuttle buses carry spectators from Manhattan.

Horse-racing At daily races held from May to July and from September to mid-October, thoroughbreds can be seen stampeding along the turf at Belmont Park, Elmont, Long Island (tel: 718/641-4700), and from late October to May at the Aqueduct Racetrack, Ozone Park, Queens (phone number as for Belmont Park). During August, the state's horse lovers move upstate to follow events at the Saratoga Equine Sports Center (tel: 518/584-2110) for a month-long series of meetings.

Betting on horse races If your interest in horses extends only as far as betting, aim for one of the many branches of New York City Off-track Betting, where bets can be placed and races watched on TV simulcast. Other venues for a wager are The Inside Track, Second Avenue between 53rd and 54th streets (tel: 752-1940), a sports bar in the style of an English pub with 15 TV monitors, or the Winners Circle, 515 Seventh Avenue (tel: 221-5200).

Tennis Early in September the US Open takes place at Flushing Meadows, Queens (tel: 718/760-6200). Tickets for the later stages of the Open are snapped up in advance, though it's usually possible to see international stars play at short notice – people with extra tickets sell them outside the stadium area. The springtime Tournament of Champions draws many top players to the West Side Tennis Club in Forest Hills, Queens (tel: 718/268-2300). A top women's event, the Chase Championships, takes place at Madison Square Garden (tel: 465 6741). The male stars of yesterday are on view at Central Park's Masters championship at Central Park's Wollman Ice Rink (tel: 396 1010) in June.

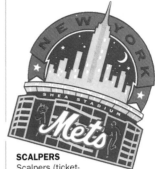

SCALPERS
Scalpers (ticket-touts) offering tickets for all major sporting events are usually found on the approach routes to the venue. Be wary of forged tickets and that prices, which can start well in excess of the ticket's face value, will drop as game time approaches.

SPORTS BARS
The city's many sports bars provide alcohol and TV screens tuned to every sports event anyone could possibly want. If a New York team is involved, you can also be sure of loud and frequent partisan comments and suggestions.

Informal basketball

THE GEORGE WASHINGTON BRIDGE

Look southwards from any high point in or around the Cloisters and you will be able to admire the elegant form of the George Washington Bridge, spanning the Hudson River from 178th Street and once described by famed modernist architect Le Corbusier as "the most beautiful bridge in the world".

Altarpieces and chapel furnishings at the Cloisters

▶▶ The Cloisters   IBCF1

Fort Tryon Park, Washington Heights (tel: 923-3700)
Open: Tue–Sun 9:30–4:45. Admission: moderate
Subway: A; 190th Street

Manhattan and medieval European monasteries may seem an unlikely partnership, but at **Fort Tryon Park**, close to Manhattan's northern tip and perched on a spectacular site above the Hudson River, parts of five 12th- to 15th-century monastic buildings from France and Spain have been brought together to form the Cloisters, a fitting home for a large portion of the Metropolitan Museum of Art's medieval collection and enclosed by beautiful gardens.

Although much of the Cloisters' architecture is new disguised as old, the genuinely historic parts – assorted columns, cloisters, chapels, apses and much more – were gathered by sculptor George Gray Bernard as he roamed the back roads of Europe during the early 1900s. Bernard grabbed all the forgotten religious art and architecture he could lay his hands on. Some of his pieces were discovered lying in pigsties and ditches near old churches, others were being used as garden ornaments. Bernard

put the rather haphazard collection on show in Manhattan and it was brought to the Met in 1925 with funds provided by John D Rockefeller, who subsequently commissioned the construction of the Cloisters to put it on permanent show. The exceedingly wealthy Rockefeller also owned the land that became Fort Tryon Park (see panel page 93) and donated to the Cloisters its most memorable exhibit – the Unicorn Tapestries (see page 93).

Each section of the Cloisters is arranged more or less chronologically, and highlights particular aspects of medieval creativity. The Romanesque Hall, for example, is entered through one of three sculptured church door-ways, demonstrating the stylistic shift from 12th-century Romanesque to 13th-century Gothic. Most impressive of the three is the latest: a High Gothic masterpiece from Burgundy which shows Christ crowning the Virgin, flanked by Clovis, first Christian ruler of France, and his son, Clothaire. The two men are so realistically sculpted they seem ready to reach forwards and shake your hand.

TWO FOR THE PRICE OF ONE

If you visit the Metropolitan Museum of Art and the Cloisters on the same day, a single ticket is valid at both. During the summer there is also a direct bus link between the two museums, which is quicker though more expensive than public transport.

Off the Romanesque Hall you will find the apse of the 12th-century Fuentidueña Chapel, which survived as its church crumbled around it: note the frescoes and the statues of St Martin and the Annunciation of the Virgin, both of which remain highly impressive despite the ravages of age.

Next door, stroll around the cloisters of the Benedictine Saint-Guilhem Monastery admiring the 12th-century carved capitals before passing through the Romanesque room for the Langon Chapel. During the 12th century, few places produced better wood sculpture than Autun, in Burgundy. Gaze long enough at the chapel's major piece – an Enthroned Virgin and Child – and its many subtleties of form and texture gradually become clear.

Beyond the Langon Chapel are several Gothic rooms and the Cuxa Cloister, its pink arches and columns built in 1188 for a Pyrenean monastery. Across the cloister are the amazing Unicorn Tapestries, probably 16th-century and of Flemish origin. Depicting the hunt for the mythical unicorn as an allegory for Christ's Incarnation, the Unicorn Tapestries are vivid in colour and rich in detail. Pick out the images of love and fertility (within the flora and fauna), which mingle with the Christian symbols and suggest that the series may have been commissioned to celebrate a wedding.

The beauty and glowing colour of the tapestries tend to outshine everything else in the Cloisters, except for the six glorious stained-glass lancet windows in the adjoining Boppard Room. Produced during the 1400s, the panels originally stood in the Carmelite Church of St Severinus in Boppard-on-Rhine in Germany. With stunning artistry and craftsmanship, the glass shows several saints occupying canopied niches around the central figure of the Virgin.

Another important exhibit is a few steps away: Robert Campin's *Annunciation* altarpiece, an early Flemish triptych pioneering the use of oils on wood panels and also breaking new ground by using a contemporary domestic setting.

A "medieval" home for medieval treasures: the Cloisters

FORT TRYON PARK
This park, in which the Cloisters stands, was the site of the Battle of Washington Heights during the Revolutionary War. The fort that stood here then was renamed Tryon by the victorious British, after the last British governor of New York. Subsequently, its 27 hectares were divided into private estates which, one by one, were later purchased by John D Rockefeller. Rockefeller gave the land to the city in 1930, and the Olmsted Brothers (descendants of Frederick Olmsted, architect of Central Park) were commissioned to landscape the lawns, terraces and picnic grounds that stand here now.

RIVERSIDE CHURCH

Just south of the Columbia University campus, the Cathedral of St John the Divine rises in its monumental and still unfinished form (see page 81). Another substantial example of religious architecture sits just to the north, between 120th and 122nd streets off Riverside Drive, in the very imposing French Gothic form of Riverside Church.

The church – now inter-denominational – has championed the under-privileged, and radical liberal views have often been aired from its pulpit. A lift runs to the tower's 20th-storey observation level for views of the Hudson River and over Upper Manhattan. Go after Sunday morning service to hear world's largest carillon, housed in the tower. *Open* Tue–Sat 11–4, Sun 12:30–4. *Admission free* (tel: 870-6700).

Alma Mater, *Daniel Chester French's statue, outside Columbia University's Low Library*

▶ Columbia University

IBCB2

114th–120th streets between Amsterdam Avenue and Broadway (tel: 854-4900 for free guided tours of the campus, which run most weekdays)
Subway: 1; 116th Street

Founded in 1754 with a charter from the British king George II (it was originally named King's College) on a site in Lower Manhattan, Columbia University was intended to raise New York's cultural profile at a time when the fast-growing city was regarded as an uncouth, money-crazed upstart by the comparatively refined communities of Boston and New Haven, where the universities of Harvard and Yale were well established.

The campus occupied various locations in Manhattan. Through its steady movement northwards, Columbia acquired ownership of the land that was later occupied by Rockefeller Center; it sold the prized plot during the mid-1980s for $400 million. The university arrived at its present location in 1897.

The specially designed campus (on the grounds of a former lunatic asylum) placed the academic buildings around a series of fountain-dotted plazas at the heart of which stands the majestic **Low Library**, based on Rome's Pantheon. This was the gift of Seth Low, a university president and briefly, starting in 1902, mayor of New York.

An elegant three-tiered stairway leads up to the library's colonnaded entrance. Inside, you will see 16 green marble columns supporting an impressive octagonal rotunda. What you will not see is students poring over weighty tomes: the library is used only for ceremonies and exhibitions. On the second floor, the Columbiana Collection charts the history of the university with a mass of drawings, documents, paintings and assorted paraphernalia.

On the library's steps you will pass Daniel Chester French's symbolic sculpture, *Alma Mater*, which was

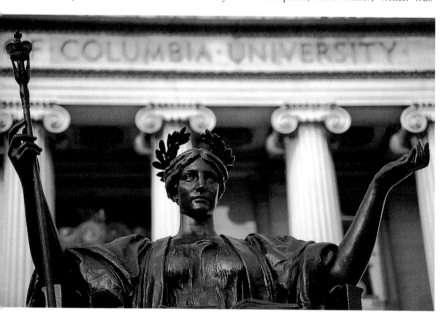

covered in gold leaf until 1962 and which formed an unlikely rallying point for the anti-Vietnam War demonstrations that spread across the campus in 1968. Just east of the library is the Italian Renaissance **St Paul's Chapel,** which has a masterly vaulted interior.

▶▶ Cooper-Hewitt National Design Museum   187C1

91st Street at Fifth Avenue (tel: 849-8400)
Open: Tue 10–9, Wed–Sat 10–5, Sun 12–5.
Admission: inexpensive
Subway: 4, 6; 86th or 96th streets

Inspired by their 1897 visit to London's Victoria and Albert Museum, the three Hewitt sisters set about creating a visual library of design that would inspire new ideas. From their motley assortment of wallpaper, keys and unusual jewellery, the Cooper-Hewitt Museum has grown into a collection of more than 250,000 items. It includes ceramics, wall coverings, textiles, decorative arts, drawings and prints, plus encyclopaedic reference and picture libraries devoted to design matters.

Selections from the eclectic stocks make up the museum's thematic shows. Whether they feature 17th-century French needlework, contemporary Italian typewriters, Middle Eastern embroidery, American hatboxes or three centuries' worth of maps (to mention a few past shows), this is where you will find some of New York's most imaginative, and sometimes most controversial, exhibitions.

The status of the museum rose greatly in 1967 when its collections, previously displayed in Lower Manhattan, were put into the care of the prestigious Smithsonian Institution and later moved to their present home, the former residence of industrialist Andrew Carnegie.

Carnegie was one of the world's richest men when he announced his intention to have built the "most modest, plainest and roomiest house in New York": the 1901 Georgian mansion, in red brick and limestone, has 64 rooms and sits amid extensive gardens – intended for Carnegie, his wife and daughter, and their 19 servants.

As you wend your way around the exhibitions, notice the vaulted ceilings, the Tiffany glass windows and the Louis XVI music room furnished with French antiques and with a set of bagpipes moulded into the decorations – a reminder of Carnegie's Scottish origins.

▶ Daily News Building   151B3

220 East 42nd Street
Open: during business hours (lobby only)
Subway: 4, 6, 7; Grand Central Terminal/42nd Street

Created by Raymond Hood, who with it established his credentials as the father of New York skyscraper architecture, the 1930 Daily News Building (now called the News Building) is a landmark, a no-frills structure of thrusting verticality. Inside the largely original lobby, a frieze recounts the rise and rise (though its immediate prospects are in question) of the New York newspaper that became a legend for its punchy headlines and salacious stories. An immense revolving globe sits at the centre of displays on meteorological themes. If the building seems familiar, you may be remembering the 1980s *Superman* films, in which it starred as the offices of the *Daily Planet*.

COLUMBIA UNIVERSITY RIOTS

By 1968, the student activism that had begun a few years earlier with the Free Speech Movement at the University of California at Berkeley had escalated into nationwide campus demonstrations protesting against US involvement in Vietnam and inept academic administrations. In April, Columbia University saw marches, sit-ins and the taking of five university officials hostage for 26 hours. The besieged university president eventually asked city police to clear the campus, in the course of which they arrested 698 students and injured 100 – and united the student body and university staff in allegations of police brutality.

95

PETER COOPER

The fortunes of inventor and philanthropist Peter Cooper, grandfather of museum founders Sarah, Amy and Eleanor Hewitt, were built on glue and iron. The Cooper foundry, in New Jersey, was where the tracks of the US's first great railways were forged. Recognising that his riches stemmed from the "cooperation of the masses", Cooper founded the first free college, the Cooper Union, which still stands in what is now the East Village (see pages 98–99).

THE DAKOTA IN FILMS AND BOOKS

Plenty of the Dakota's residents have had leading roles in films. So, too, has the building. With its turrets, towers and gables, the Dakota provided a suitably unsettling location for Roman Polanski's 1968 story of demonic possession, *Rosemary's Baby*. It also played a part in the 1970 time-travel novel, *Time and Again*, by Jack Finney.

The Dakota Apartments – home of the stars, and a screen star itself

96

▶ Dakota Apartments 151D2

1 West 72nd Street
Subway: 1, 2, 3; 72nd Street

Wealthy New York house owners of the 1880s had yet to be convinced that apartment living was the lifestyle of the future when Edward S Clark, heir to the Singer sewing machine fortunes, commissioned a luxury apartment house in what is now the Upper West Side but was then wild, open land dotted by shanty dwellings and not even linked to the city's power supplies.

So far out was the site that critics suggested it might as well be in the Dakota territories – which is how the building got its name and the ears of corn, arrowheads and the Native American head that decorate its entrance.

As the city spread northwards and Midtown Manhattan house prices rocketed, there were suddenly lots of enthusiastic takers for the Dakota's marble floors and oak- and mahogany-panelled dwellings. The building quickly became – and continues to be – a prestigious address, with a roll call of rich and famous residents that has included Leonard Bernstein, Lauren Bacall, Judy Garland and John Lennon – who was murdered while entering the building in 1980.

> *More inspired by Manhattan's celebrity-filled soirées than by its art museums, Andy Warhol might be the one world-famous artist New York can call its own.*

Born Andrew Warhola to Czech immigrant parents in Pittsburgh, Andy Warhol moved to New York in 1949 and within seven years was among the city's most sought-after commercial artists, much of his work appearing in high-society magazines.

Fame in a soup can Warhol loved the party-going life of New York but found his own fame – and artistic vocation – after a trip to a supermarket in 1962. As pop artists created collages of consumerist images, Warhol began painting soup cans, according the gravity of serious portraiture to each one.

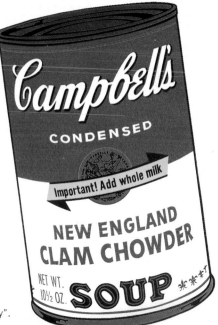

He then went on to depictions of dollar bills, electric chairs and Brillo boxes, relishing the publicity that his work aroused. A reviewer wrote that Warhol's silk-screened images of Marilyn Monroe were "as sentimental as Fords coming off the production line". In reply, Warhol declared, "I want to be a machine" and named his studio the Factory.

In the mid-1960s, Warhol's Factory became a magnet for oddball characters in New York, many of whom starred in the underground movies that the artist began making, including *Chelsea Girls*, described by one critic as "an image of the total degeneration of American society".

Getting rich The Factory's excesses ended in 1968, when Warhol narrowly survived an assassination attempt and found his financial affairs under scrutiny. Feeling he should be earning more money, the guru of pop art became a society portrait painter, charging $25,000 a time, while his revamped *Interview* magazine began providing lucrative advertising alongside its celebrity gossip.

Warhol's wealth and fame became greater than his creativity. Moving to an expensive Upper East Side house in 1975, he spent a lot of time and money on several ill-fated projects and appeared happiest during his daily shopping expeditions.

Shortly before his death in 1987, Warhol commented, "Getting rich isn't as much fun as it used to be".

ANDY WARHOL SAID
"In the future, everybody will be famous for 15 minutes".
"I don't think my art has any lasting value".
"I never wanted to be a painter. I wanted to be a tap dancer".

LITTLE UKRAINE
In an area of the East Village around Second Avenue between 4th and 14th streets is New York's Little Ukraine. Ukrainians began settling here in the late 1800s and, though their numbers have been greatly depleted, are still much in evidence among the neighbourhood's many Slavic restaurants and shops selling traditional Ukrainian crafts – such as painted Easter eggs. The tiny Ukrainian Museum, 203 Second Avenue, has changing exhibitions on past and present Ukrainian life in New York and in the homeland.

▶ The East Village   IFCC3

In the 1950s, rising rents in Greenwich Village began pushing New York's more radical artists and writers across Broadway into the East Village. Here they took cheap apartments in tenement buildings otherwise inhabited by hard-up Eastern European immigrants, many of them from the Ukraine.

The heart of New York hippiedom in the 1960s and the epicentre of its 1970s punk rock scene, the East Village was regularly at the vanguard of alternative culture. Despite increasing signs of gentrification, expect to see at least one person dressed head-to-toe in leather and sporting bright green hair. Bizarre one-of-a-kind shops, ethnic eateries, and a vibrant street scene are the things the East Village does best, although a handful of historical sights are also worthy of attention.

Astor Place carries the name of John Jacob Astor, one of early 19th-century New York's wealthiest men. Like the similarly extremely affluent Cornelius Vanderbilt, Astor owned one of the series of marble-fronted houses that became known as **Colonnade Row**. Once the grandest residences in New York, those that have managed to survive, now looking rather shabby, are on Lafayette Street (numbers 428 to 434).

Across Lafayette Street, Astor financed the city's first free public library in a brownstone building which, since the 1960s, has been the **Public Theater** (originally known as the Joseph Papp Public Theater), a venue for varied theatrical, cinematic and other arts events.

Another 19th-century remnant is the **Cooper Union Building**, just south of Astor Place. Founded in 1859 by the millionaire railway tycoon Peter Cooper to provide free education for all, the college was the first of its kind in the US and also became an airing place for a range of political views: Abraham Lincoln was one of the famous orators who spoke here.

East of Astor Place is St Mark's Place, where the unprepossessing building at number 77 was home to Anglo-American poet W H Auden from 1953. This was where, four decades earlier in the basement, Leon Trotsky had plotted the Russian Revolution.

Nearby, the church of **St Mark's-in-the-Bowery** (tel: 674-6377; *Open* for events only) arose on the estate of New York's Dutch governor, Peter Stuyvesant, in 1799. Its original body was later topped by a spire and fronted by a cast-iron portico. The church serves its congregation with Episcopal services, poetry readings and performance art. On the church's eastern side, Stuyvesant and six generations of his descendants lie buried.

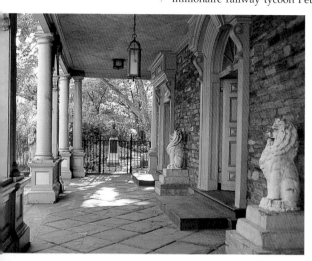

St Mark's-in-the-Bowery carries on the area's cultural tradition by staging poetry readings

Walk

The East Village shops and sights

This walk touches historical sites and also highlights the contemporary flavour of the East Village.

Begin at the 1799 church of **St Mark's-in-the-Bowery** and continue along Stuyvesant Street to the **Cooper Union Building** (1859), the US's first free college.

In Astor Place is the huge Bernard Rosenthal **Alamo** cube sculpture which spins on a point when pushed. Turn into St Mark's Place, once the centre of the punk rock movement, now a touristy collection of piercing shops, cafés and T-shirt kiosks. You can eat cheaply at **La Palapa** (77 St Mark's Place) or at **Café Mogodor** (101 St Mark's Place).

Unusual shop in the East Village

Turn on Avenue A to 7th Street and walk west to 2nd Avenue for funky vintage shops, such as **Tokio 7** (64 East 7th Street). Stop for a beer at **McSorley's** (15 East 7th Street), a local landmark since 1854.

99

THE WALL OF HONOR

Running around the edge of Ellis Island close to the ferry dock, the American Immigrant Wall of Honor records 200,000 names – just a small percentage of those who became American citizens here. Ellis Island arrivals you may have heard of include Isaac Asimov, Irving Berlin, Bela Lugosi, Golda Meir, Edward G Robinson and Rudolph Valentino.

Ellis Island: the future of many a would-be American was determined in these buildings. Museum displays now bring to life the hopes, fears and disappointments of those newly arrived immigrants

►►► Ellis Island   48C2

Telephone for latest information: 269-5755

Approximately 100 million present-day Americans have ancestors who passed through Ellis Island, a modest speck of land in the shadow of the Statue of Liberty in New York's Upper Bay. From 1892 to 1924 this was the country's busiest immigration centre.

Later serving as an army hospital and as an enemy alien detention centre, Ellis Island was closed in 1954 and suffered total neglect until a $160-million restoration project reopened its major building as the Ellis Island Immigration Museum in 1990.

Those who arrived at Ellis Island hoping to become Americans were drawn from Europe's underclasses (immigrants of means were processed elsewhere and allowed immediate entry into the US). The elation they experienced on seeing the Statue of Liberty quickly dissipated as they reached the place nicknamed the "Island of Tears" and faced the bureaucracy that stood between them and American citizenship.

These would-be Americans were screened for signs of insanity and contagious diseases and questioned about their relatives and their work skills. Any sign of sickness, or giving the wrong answers, could mean being detained and perhaps deported.

Some also got their first taste of American corruption at Ellis Island: among the many scams were bribes for immigration officers and overpriced train tickets for onward travel in the US.

From statistics projecting the country's future ethnic make-up to trunks and string bags that carried treasured possessions from overseas, the museum has many eye-opening exhibits. However, it is the taped oral histories of former arrivals that do most to suggest the hopes, the fears and the sheer sense of bewilderment that most of the would-be immigrants experienced as they stepped into this building.

►►► Empire State Building   151B2

34th Street at Fifth Avenue (tel: 736-3100)
Open daily 9:30–midnight, last lift 11:30 PM.
Admission: moderate
Subway: B, D, F, N, R; 34th Street

The Statue of Liberty may be a more potent national symbol, but New York's most enduring emblem is the Empire State Building, which rises above Midtown Manhattan with a gracious, ageless aplomb. As construction mania

EMPIRE STATE BUILDING FACTS

Height: 449m.
Weight: 331,128 tonnes.
Number of bricks:
10 million.
Budget: $60 million.
Actual cost:
$40,948,900.
Tallest visitor: King Kong, 1933.
Greatest tragedy: plane crashing into the 79th storey in 1945, killing 14.

The lobby of the Empire State Building

NEW YORK SKYRIDE

If the views from the observation levels of the Empire State Building fail to satisfy, get an aerial view of the city on the New York Skyride – a flight simulator tour of the city at dizzying speed. The Skyride is on the Empire State Building's second floor. *Open* daily 10–11 PM; tel: 1-888 SKYRIDE.

swept through New York during the booming 1920s, the Empire State Building was the winner in the financiers' race to create the world's tallest building, snatching the title in 1931 from the Chrysler Building and holding it until the first World Trade Center tower was finished in 1973.

Although the building rose to 380m (gaining an extra 70m with a TV mast in 1951), it was constructed in only two years. The zoning laws (see page 24) of the time resulted in the tiered design that tempers the impact of

At Federal Hall National Memorial, the statue of George Washington commemorates his inauguration as president, which took place in an earlier building on the site

THE ORIGINAL FEDERAL HALL
The historic significance of the present Federal Hall is eclipsed by that of its predecessor, which housed the first US government and which was where, in April 1789, George Washington was sworn in as the country's first president.

Despite its role in US history, the original building reached such a dilapidated state that it was sold for scrap in 1812.

the structure's bulk and contributes to its elegant profile.

Conceived in an economic boom, the building was completed amid the gloom of the Depression, the Wall Street crash occurring as the 0.8 hectare site – which held the original Waldorf-Astoria Hotel – was being cleared. Consequently, much of the office space remained unrented for years, and most of the building's early income was from tourists visiting for the views.

Once you have admired the art deco fittings of the lobby, descend to the concourse for a ticket and ride the express lift to the 86th-floor observation level. On a clear day you can see for 130km. The enclosed 102nd-floor level has been closed to the public due to long queues.

▶ Federal Hall National Memorial　　104B2
Wall and Nassau streets (tel: 825-6888)
Open daily 9–5, closed Sat and Sun during winter.
Admission free
Subway: 2, 3, 4, 5; Wall Street
Its finely proportioned steps and Doric columns impose themselves grandly in the heart of the Financial District, but a sense of history is disappointingly missing from the echoey interior of the 19th-century Federal Hall. Built as the first US Custom House, it later served as a bank before being declared a national memorial in 1939.

If you are exploring the Financial District, Federal Hall ought to be on your itinerary, but do not expect anything spectacular. Inside, only a short film and a rather tame collection of exhibits record events that took place on the site: a glass-encased section of balcony railing, on which Washington leaned when addressing the crowds after his inauguration and a pair of the great man's belt-buckles form the highlights.

▶ Film Center Building　　151C1
Ninth Avenue between 44th and 45th streets
Open: business hours (lobby only)
Subway: A, C, E; 42nd Street
You may not want to visit any of the film companies that have offices here, but the Film Center Building justifies a visit to view one of the city's most stunning art deco interiors: its foyer, cloakroom and entrance hall are all the work of Ely Jacques Kahn. Already an outstanding modernist architect, by the late 1920s Kahn had also built up a reputation for his distinctive interior decoration which was based on interlinked geometric forms – employed here to wonderful effect.

▶▶ Financial District　　IFCA2
The nation's monetary institutions took root in Lower Manhattan from the early 1800s, and as the city grew, so did its Financial District, quickly becoming a global centre of trade and commerce. Side by side in this compact area stand grandiose neo-classical buildings, whose form signified their status as repositories of wealth, and the high-rise glass and steel blocks that are the contemporary towers of mammon.

The exuberant 1980s saw Wall Street (just one of several thoroughfares, but internationally synonymous with the highest of high finance) yield millions and give birth to the yuppie. But the party was over by the end of the decade, when a succession of scandals put the greedy behind bars and heralded the economic uncertainties of the 1990s.

Facing Wall Street from Broadway, the striking neo-Gothic form of **Trinity Church** (tel: 602-0800) has, since the 1840s, been reminding the Financial District's power brokers of a force greater than money. Note the bronze doors and the reredos, and continue into the small church museum to look at drawings showing a Manhattan skyline dominated by church spires rather than high-rise towers. In the 17th-century graveyard (*Open* daily 8–4:30) lies Alexander Hamilton, the first US treasurer.

Predating Trinity Church by almost a century is **St Paul's Chapel** (tel: 602-0872; *Open* Mon–Sat 9–3, Sun 7–3), Manhattan's only surviving pre-revolutionary church, which faces Fulton Street from Broadway. Laid out in a graceful Georgian style with a surprisingly bright interior, the chapel was regularly visited by George Washington, and dutifully maintains the Washington Pew, where the first president sat during the service marking his inauguration in 1789.

WALL STREET'S NAME
An oaken barricade erected by Dutch governor Peter Stuyvesant in 1653 to mark the northern boundary of New Amsterdam and deter British invaders was the "wall" that gave the world-famous street its name. The wall never quite fulfilled its promise, because its planks were steadily removed to build and repair the wooden homes of settlers. In 1699 its remains were finally demolished by the then well-entrenched British.

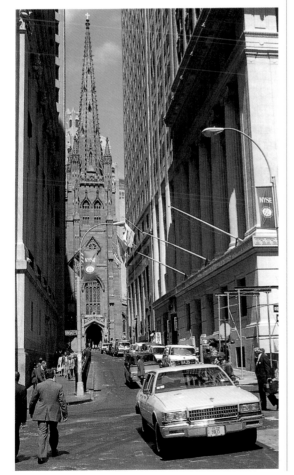

Now dwarfed by skyscrapers several times as high, Trinity Church began life as the city's tallest building, at 80m high

103

THE FEDERAL RESERVE
Many Financial District buildings house major financial corporations where every day millions of dollars are traded and transferred in paper and electronic transactions. One of the few that actually holds money – in the form of gold – is the Manhattan branch of the Federal Reserve (33 Liberty Street; tel: 720-6130), formally known as the Federal Reserve Bank of New York. Nationally, the Federal Reserve acts as banker to major banks and to the US government, regulates monetary policy and sets interest rates. The high security of the fortress-like building can be lawfully penetrated on free guided tours, but tickets must be acquired well in advance. *Open* Mon–Fri 9–5; tours at 10:30, 11:30, 1:30 and 2:30.

FINANCIAL DISTRICT

Walk

Financial District architecture

Encompassing historic churches and financial and architectural land-marks, this walk is an excellent way to explore the varied facets of the Financial District.

Begin at **Trinity Church** (page 103) and continue along Wall Street,

stopping at **Federal Hall** and detouring along Broad Street for the **Stock Exchange** (page 182).

Continue along Nassau Street for **Chase Manhattan Bank**, the first international-style structure in Lower Manhattan. Across Maiden Lane, you can gaze at over 11,000 tonnes of gold – the wealth of many nations – stored below ground at the **Federal Reserve Bank** (advance reservations essential, tel: 720-6130). Otherwise, examine the richly decorative ironwork of the enormous building's façade.

On the corner of Broadway, the much-detested 1915 **Equitable Building** rises for 40 sheer storeys; this was New York's first ever high-rise office building and the first to plunge its neighbouring buildings – and much of the street below – into relative darkness. Continue along Broadway for **St Paul's Chapel** (page 103); aim to arrive for a free lunch-time concert, and finish in the lobby of the Woolworth Building (page 192).

Tussles during the 19th century among Eastern Europe's Slavic peoples – Poles, Ukrainians and Russians – and the totalitarian suppression of more recent times helped create two of New York's most stridently nationalistic communities: the Poles and the Ukrainians, who now coexist peaceably alongside their former foes, the Russians.

Polish-Americans Struggles against colonial oppression in their own country made New York's Poles natural allies of the Americans in the revolutionary battles with the British. Not much later, New York offered refuge to those who had led an unsuccessful Polish republican uprising in 1830. The 234 immigrants who arrived were among Poland's finest minds, and were to give New York its first Polish cultural institutions.

Later Polish arrivals found factory jobs in the Greenpoint area of Brooklyn, though some opened the shops and bookshops that would become community focal points. Soviet control of post-war Poland brought exiled intellectuals, while the collapse of Communism in the 1990s led to more arrivals.

The Ukrainians Enforced military service in the tsar's army caused many Ukrainians to flee their Russian-dominated homeland during the 1800s. Arriving in New York with their families, they turned a section of what is now the East Village into the world's largest urban Ukrainian community by 1919.

Russian immigrants The bulk of Russian immigrants were Jewish refugees who had fled persecution under the tsar (see page 139). More symbolic of the effect of European political upheavals, though, were the Russian aristocrats who arrived in New York as Leon Trotsky (here since the abortive 1905 revolution) left for Moscow to help the Bolsheviks seize power. Another arrival was ground-breaking choreographer George Balanchine. These newly arrived Russians quickly became integrated into New York society – a far cry from the former Soviet Russians who later settled in Brighton Beach (see page 75).

THE PULASKI AND KOSCIUSZKO BRIDGES
Two of the bridges – the Pulaski and the Kosciuszko – linking Brooklyn and Queens bear the names of Poles who aided the American cause in the Revolutionary War. Cavalry expert Casimar Pulaski was noted for his bravery in battle (he died in an attack on the British); the engineering skills of Thaddeus Kosciuszko were crucial in preparing the anti-British fortifications at West Point and Saratoga.

105

The first taste of America for European immigrants: Ellis Island

*The Flatiron Building –
an unmistakable Fifth
Avenue landmark*

23 SKIDOO
A story goes that in the
days when well-dressed
ladies had skirts to their
ankles, high winds would
find voyeurs lingering outside the Flatiron Building
on 23rd Street hoping to
spot female legs exposed
by the breeze. The shouts
of the police when moving
the gentlemen on are
thought to be the origin of
the term "23 skidoo".

DANIEL H BURNHAM
The architect of the
Flatiron Building, Daniel H
Burnham, made his name
in Chicago in the 1880s,
where, in partnership with
John Root, he pioneered
the modern skyscraper
by making the first use of
a steel frame to support a
high-rise structure.
Burnham's design ideas
became a fundamental
element in the highly
influential "Chicago
School" of architecture.
Burnham's Chicago work
was made possible partly
because of a devastating
fire that required the
entire downtown area to
be rebuilt. He also played
an important role in the
reshaping of San
Francisco, wrecked by the
earthquake of 1906, for
which he planned a new
Civic Center.

▶ Flatiron Building   *151A2*
Broadway and Fifth Avenue at 23rd Street
Subway: N, R; 23rd Street

Architect Daniel H Burnham solved the problem of fitting
a building into the triangular plot of land where Broadway
crosses Fifth Avenue with the most logical solution: a
triangular building. It was the world's tallest (87m) on its
completion in 1902 and was one of the first to be erected
around a steel frame – the basic support of every subsequent skyscraper.

Nowadays, it is not height or building techniques that
make the Flatiron Building one of New York's most-loved
structures but its pretty French Renaissance features and
the fact that its limestone body tapers to an impossibly
slender 2m-wide corner curve on 23rd Street. In recent
years, the building has provided a convenient sobriquet
for the immediate area, now known locally as the
"Flatiron District".

▶ The Forbes Galleries

113C2

Fifth Avenue between 12th and 13th streets (tel: 206-5548)
Open: Tue, Wed, Fri, Sat 10–4. Admission free
Subway: L, N, R 4, 6; 14th Street/Union Square

Even in New York, few magazine publishers have broken the speed record for ballooning across the country or have hurtled along Fifth Avenue on a motorcycle. Malcolm S Forbes did both of those things, and more, in a career that began by accident and left him with wealth estimated, at his death in 1990, to be in excess of $700 million.

Born in 1919, two years after his father had founded *Forbes*, a ground-breaking magazine of investigative financial journalism, Forbes had turned the ailing title into a thriving concern by the time he took it over in 1964. One of the secrets of his success was a genius for garnering maximum publicity for himself and the magazine. Through the 1970s the media doted on Forbes and his colourful activities, which ranged from lavish parties to his off-beat collecting interests.

The Forbes Galleries bear the fruits of Forbes' quirky collecting passion. They occupy the first floor of the Forbes Magazine building. Among the displays are 500 model boats and submarines (some of them in bathtubs) viewed to the accompaniment of what purports to be the sound of the Battle of Jutland. Some 12,000 model soldiers are arranged in battle-ready poses, and there is an amazing room of trophies awarded for achievements such as having the best pure-bred bull of 1878 and the best 2 hectares of turnips grown with Bradburn's manure.

The Presidential Papers room holds less eccentric material, drawn from the Forbes collection of 3,000 historical documents, while another special room displays gem-encrusted Easter eggs – and scores of other priceless objets d'art – made by master jeweller–goldsmith Peter Carl Fabergé for the last two tsars of Russia.

▶▶ Fraunces Tavern

104A2

54 Pearl Street (tel: 425-1778)
Open: Mon to Fri 10–4. Admission free
Subway: 1, 4, 9; Bowling Green, South Ferry or Broad Street

This Federal-style brick building, which looks like a dolls' house beneath the glass-and-steel high-rises of the Financial District, stands on the site of the original Fraunces Tavern, a hotbed of subversion during the 18th century, when its customers included George Washington and his fellow revolutionaries.

At the successful completion of the Revolutionary War, Washington made a famously emotional farewell to his officers here after a meal in the Long Room. The revolutionary era is commemorated by the Tavern with displays of period furniture, paintings and other objects of interest.

It may seem strange today, but the tavern became the unofficial seat of several government bodies during the earliest days of nationhood and spent three years as the recognised base of the Department of Foreign Affairs, the War Department and the Treasury, before being unceremoniously sold to a Brooklyn butcher.

If you visit the tavern at lunchtime, the atmosphere is enhanced by the smell of food wafting up from the renovated restaurant.

For those with money and a well-known face (or name), New York is the ultimate playground. What follows is a very selective Manhattan list for the well-heeled person about town. For visitors who need to budget carefully, a peek inside one or two of these establishments offers a glance at the luxurious end of New York's wide spectrum of lifestyles.

Daniel (East 65th Street between Madison and Park avenues, tel: 288-0033). One of the reasons Daniel Boulud decided to relocate his gastronomic temple was that he couldn't accommodate all of the power players and food lovers clamouring for reservations. Some $15 million and 40 additional seats later, you still have to book a table four weeks in advance. The restaurant is a formal affair, an elegant combination of contemporary style and stateliness. The food is every bit as good as at the previous restaurant (now home to his more casual, more moderately priced Café Boulud). Think ethereal soups, whole-roasted fish, succulent braised meats and a seasonality and freshness of ingredients unsurpassed by any of the city's great restaurants.

Jean Georges (Trump International Hotel, 1 Central Park West at Columbus Circle, tel: 299-3900). Like superstar chef Jean-Georges Vongerichten himself, this four-star restaurant is sleek, elegant and welcoming. During the day it is flooded with sunlight, at night the glow radiates from the beautiful crowd. In keeping with the environment, the food is conceptual and artfully presented: for example seared sea scallops with raisin caper sauce. Equal emphasis is placed on service, and the tableside show is like a fine ballet. Don't miss the extravagant tea service and the homemade marshmallows in a variety of flavours, paraded around the room in glass apothecary jars and snipped ceremonially onto your plate.

GETTING AROUND LUXURY NEW YORK
When money is no object, travel between expensive shops in a chauffeur-driven stretch limousine. Equipped with VCRs, telephones and bars – and other features that make Manhattan's traffic-stopping gridlock almost seem attractive – stretch limos can be rented from around $50 per hour. Carey Limousines (tel: 599-1122) and Imperial Limousines (tel: 229-9292) are among the operators awaiting your call.

Four Seasons (East 52nd Street between Park and Lexington avenues, tel: 754-9494). The serious trade here is power-lunching corporate executives – plus a sprinkling of lawyers, politicians and publishers. On the ground floor of Mies van der Rohe's landmark Seagram Building, this Philip Johnson-designed restaurant features a large Picasso tapestry and other noted modern pieces. The lunch menu is designed to be good but simple, so it does not detract from the deals being struck across the tables. At dinner, the chef presents ably prepared contemporary American creations, some of which are finished at your table. A full dinner here is liable to cost $100 per person; lunch should be around $40.

The "21" Club (West 52nd Street between Fifth and Sixth avenues, tel: 582-7200). A row of cast-iron model jockeys stand to attention along the façade of the "21" Club, which opened on New Year's Eve 1929 and was – in those Prohibition times – just one of scores of speakeasies lining 52nd Street. The others quickly disappeared but the "21" Club endured, maturing into a favourite watering hole of the New York establishment. Despite a complete refurbishment in the 1980s, the "21" Club's dark, wood-panelled walls and deep-pile carpets offer a picture of old-style luxury New York that is rarely found today. Although appearances suggest otherwise, it is not an exclusive club, but there would be no point in showing up without a reservation. Many regulars come here to confirm their place in the New York social pecking order as much as to dine: the kitchen is experiencing a renaissance since the addition of a creative chef. You might try the famous "21 Burger", or the pre-theatre prix fixe dinner, but you probably won't have change from $30 and $50 respectively.

Le Cirque 2000 (New York Palace Hotel, 455 Madison Avenue at 50th Street, tel: 303-7788). No restaurant in New York has quite the razzle-dazzle of this celebrity shrine. Adam Tihany's futuristic circus décor for the ornate Villard mansions has been likened to a Ferrari parked in an Italian palazzo. (You either love it or you hate it.) He doesn't miss a detail of the operation. Chef Pierre Schaedelin's food can be sublime, but it isn't the point. You are there to see and be seen, or to watch the people who are.

SIGHTSEEING BY HELICOPTER

One way to beat the crowds at the Empire State Building is to view it, and the rest of Manhattan, from a helicopter. Sightseeing helicopter flights are operated day and night by Island Helicopter Sightseeing (tel: 683-4575) and Liberty Helicopter Tours (tel: 800/542-9933 or 967-6464).

109

SPECIALITY GROCERS

Manhattan's avid food lovers are willing to pay high prices for superior quality and variety at fancy food emporiums such as **Balducci's** (Sixth Avenue at 9th Street) in Greenwich Village, with exquisite produce, meat, fish and pastries, and the huge SoHo trendsetter **Dean & Deluca** (560 Broadway at Prince Street) where food is displayed like art. On the Upper West Side, there's **Zabar's** (2245 Broadway at 80th Street), which sells fine foods on the street level and kitchenware upstairs. On the Upper East Side are the **Vinegar Factory** and **Eli's**, also owned by the Zabar's clan. The **Chelsea Market** (88 Tenth Avenue) is a block-long food mall with good quality, independent shops, and the new **Garden of Eden** (East 14th Street near Fifth Avenue) rivals Balducci's in its heyday.

The luxurious Plaza Hotel: evocative of Old World elegance

110

Having made his fortune in Pittsburgh, industrialist Henry Clay Frick moved to New York, where he had this elaborate mansion built to house his superb collection of European art

MOVING PICTURES
Each summer, Henry Frick had his fantastic art collection packed into crates and transported in a special railway car so he could enjoy it while staying at his estate in Massachusetts. Asked if he was worried about losing the priceless canvases through an accident in transit, Frick allegedly replied, "No, they're insured".

▶▶ Frick Collection   151D2

70th Street at Fifth Avenue (tel: 288-0700)
Open: Tue to Sat 10–6, Sun 1–6. Admission: moderate
Subway: 6; 68th Street

Henry Clay Frick made a fortune through coke and steel, and was little loved in his day for his mean-spirited business practices. Ironically, the Frick Collection of 14th- to 19th-century European art, housed on the first floor of the French-style mansion in which Frick spent the last five years of his life (he died in 1919), is perhaps the most loved of New York's many art collections.

The absence of ropes, descriptive texts, and other museum trappings is intended to make seeing the collection akin to visiting a private house. The collection is a triumph of quality over quantity, and there is not one painting that does not deserve its wall space.

Highlights are many and naturally vary according to individual taste. Few could fail to be impressed, however, by Gainsborough's *The Mall in St James's Park*, a refined vision of privileged promenaders that stands out in a dining room lined by 18th-century English portraiture. The living hall has two particularly potent canvases: Titian's *Portrait of a Man in a Red Cap* and El Greco's *St Jerome*. But the cream of the collection is hung in the west gallery: two of Turner's studies of northern European ports resonate on facing walls, close to Rembrandt's 1658 *Portrait of a Young Artist – Self-Portrait* and his much debated (its authenticity is disputed) *Polish Rider*.

After leaving the final room, take a break in the garden court before starting through the collections once again, this time concentrating on the outstanding sculptures, tapestries and decorative arts exhibits.

▶ Garment District   IFCD1

On and around Seventh Avenue between 30th and 40th streets, the Garment District is the heart of New York's renown fashion industry, its warehouses and factories packed with the latest work of designers whose creations are displayed in showrooms. Many local shops specialise in rag trade items such as fabrics, ribbons, buttons, trimmings and lace. The sharp contrast between fashion's glitzy public face and the reality of low-paid workers who stitch and sow has long stained the area, although the divisions are receding as the district's warehouse-to-office conversions attract more diverse professions. Designers such as Ralph Lauren and Calvin Klein are among those honoured with bronze and granite plaques embedded in Seventh Avenue, locally titled "Fashion Avenue".

▶ General Grant Memorial   IBCB2

Riverside Drive at 122nd Street (tel: 666-1640)
Open: daily 9–5. Admission free
Subway: 1; 116th Street

The largest mausoleum in the US, its grey granite form rising 46m beside the Hudson and its entrance fronted by six Doric columns, the General Grant Memorial (commonly known as Grant's Tomb) holds the remains – in 9-tonne marble sarcophagi – of Ulysses S Grant and his wife Julia. As commander-in-chief of the Union forces in the Civil War, Grant achieved enormous fame: an estimated million people lined the route of his funeral procession in 1885.

Inside, a chilled atmosphere prevails, and your footsteps echo as you walk around reading the brief accounts of Grant's distinguished military service and his much less successful eight-year tenure as 18th US President. Outside, the mosaic-decorated benches result from a community arts project.

▶ Gracie Mansion   187C2

East End Avenue at 88th Street (tel: 570-4751)
Guided tours: Apr–Oct, Wed 10, 11, 1, 2. Admission: donation
Subway: 4, 6; 86th Street
The official residence of the mayor of New York since 1942, Gracie Mansion was built in 1799 as a country retreat for shipping magnate Archibald Gracie. After his business collapsed, Gracie sold the mansion, and it spent an ignominious period as a refreshment stand before being purchased by the city. Renovations have made the mansion a finer example of Federal architecture (the first architectural style considered distinctly American) than it ever was in its infancy. The house can be fully appreciated only on guided tours.

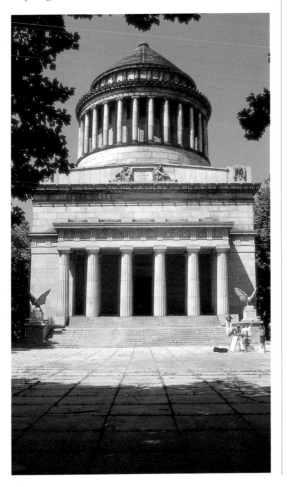

GRANT'S MILITARY CAREER
Following an unremarkable graduation (21st in a class of 39) from West Point Academy, Ulysses S Grant distinguished himself in service, but resigned from the army in 1854 while stationed in California. Grant failed as a farmer (his subsequent occupation), and was working as a clerk in his father's store in Illinois at the outbreak of the Civil War. His military experience led to his appointment as brigadier of the Illinois Volunteers. A series of battle successes followed, showing a strategic brilliance that culminated in Grant's capture of the Confederate stronghold of Vicksburg after a 47-day siege in 1863. The following year, Grant was made commander of all Union armies. As president, Grant faced the postwar Reconstruction period and difficulties that would have tested the skills of the most experienced politician – his battle planning skills proved no match for the chicanery of Washington DC.

HENDERSON PLACE
In a cul-de-sac on the north side of 86th Street, close to Gracie Mansion, stands the lovely row of 24 Queen Anne-style houses that constitute the Henderson Place Historic District. The houses were commissioned during the 1880s by fur-hat manufacturer John C Henderson to provide homes for "persons of moderate means".

The grandiose mausoleum of Civil War general Ulysses S Grant was inspired by Napoleon's tomb in Paris

Greenwich Village second hand shops may not offer such good bargains as less fashionable areas of the city, but they are hard to beat for sheer variety

GRACE CHURCH
One of the few things in Greenwich Village likely to bring to mind the European Middle Ages is the 1846 Grace Church, on Broadway between 10th and 11th streets. The church's finely proportioned Gothic Revival design – among the earliest examples of the style in the US – helped its architect, James Renwick, win the commission for the larger, grander St Patrick's Cathedral in Midtown Manhattan. Set on Broadway's first curve, the church's spire could originally be seen from as far south as what is now Battery Park.

►►► Greenwich Village IFCC2

No place in New York has a greater cultural aura than Greenwich Village. For almost 100 years this has been a breeding ground and rallying point for the nation's most inventive and imaginative minds.

From its earliest days, Greenwich Village has kept its distance from mainstream New York life. Its first homes were built to enable the wealthy to escape the outbreaks of disease that were common in the 1790s, pushing back the boundaries of the city that, until then, had been contained within present-day Lower Manhattan.

By the late 1800s, the rich were moving north again, and their Greenwich Village town houses were being converted into shops, factories and boarding houses for immigrants. By the turn of the 20th century, Greenwich Village's diverse ethnic mix had fostered an atmosphere of tolerance that, coupled with low rents, attracted the unconventional elements that gave birth to the country's first, and its most celebrated, enclave of non-conformity.

Over three decades, writers and artists from Walt Whitman to Edward Hopper were to turn American culture upside down from their Greenwich Village bases. During the 1950s, the earliest Beat writers began taking Greenwich Village still further away from the materialist values of middle America, but rents were soon on the rise as new transit links made Greenwich Village the target of moneyed professionals in search of a well-placed neighbourhood full of character.

Living in Greenwich Village today certainly requires financial security, but the lawyers and investment bankers who have flocked here have certainly not dampened the community spirit or Greenwich Village's rebellious streak. A Bohemian mood still percolates through its innumerable Italian cafés and restaurants, even though today most Greenwich Village visitors are on shopping or nightlife expeditions rather than seeking creativity's cutting edge.

(Continued on page 116)

GREENWICH VILLAGE

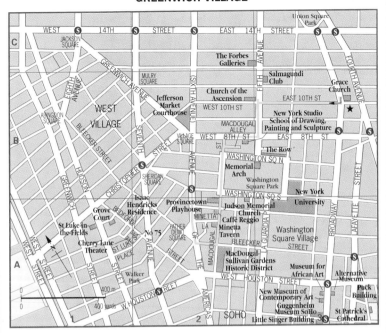

Walk

interior has been seen in films such as *Godfather II* and *Serpico*.

On Sixth Avenue, Village Square is dominated by the gables, turrets and towers of the 1877 **Jefferson Market Courthouse**, now a library. Across Sixth Avenue is **Balducci's**, a long-established purveyor of groceries and very fine foods.

The heart of Greenwich Village

From Grace Church in the east, this walk goes through the heart of Greenwich Village, ending at the foot of Christopher Street.

Leaving Grace Church, walk along 10th Street to the 1840 **Church of the Ascension**, by English architect Richard Upjohn, also known for Trinity Church in the Financial District.

Eighth Street holds many shops and the New York Studio School of Drawing, Painting and Sculpture, first home of the Whitney Museum. This was founded in 1931 by Gertrude Vanderbilt Whitney; her own studio was a converted stable at 17½ MacDougal Alley (a private street).

In business since 1785, **Caffé Reggio** is the oldest of many cafés lining MacDougal Street; its dark

Washington Square Park

Like delis and subway stations, bars are among the stock images of New York life. From rough-and-ready Bohemian hangouts to elegant hotel cocktail lounges, New York bars come in all sizes and forms. Don't miss this quintessential experience. (For guidance on bar-going etiquette, see pages 224–225.)

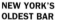

WINE BARS

In New York nowadays any restaurant that wants to be taken seriously offers several decent wines by the glass. But a proliferation of wine bars offering hundreds of wines has upped the ante. Wines are sold either as single servings or in tasting "flights" (wines grouped by region, style, vintage or other characteristics). Check out Divine Bar (244 East 51st Street and 55 Liberty Street), Le Bateau Ivre (230 East 51st Street), and Enoteca i Trulli (122 East 27th Street).

NEW YORK'S OLDEST BAR

In business since 1854, McSorley's Old Ale House (15 East 7th Street) is justified in its claim to be New York's oldest surviving bar. For years a men-only establishment patronised by career drinkers from the Bowery's Skid Row, McSorley's began admitting women in 1970 and now attracts a young, mainly student crowd.

Writers, artists and bars Greenwich Village is littered with bars where major names of art and literature have gathered to eat, drink, and (not infrequently) be carried home very much the worse for wear.

On his New York stays, Welsh poet Dylan Thomas held court at the **White Horse Tavern** (567 Hudson Street). One night in 1953, a drunken Thomas spluttered, "I've had my 18th whisky, and I think that's the record". Within a few days he was dead. The literary associations might seem all but buried beneath the throng of customers, but cuttings on the wall remind drinkers at **Pete's Tavern** (129 East 18th Street) that this was once a lair of O Henry, the pen name of William Sydney Porter, short-story writer and a trenchant New York observer in the early 1900s. To sample the East Village's Bohemian ambience, slip into something black and then into **d b a** (41 First Avenue), a popular local hangout with minimalist décor and a good variety of beers and single malts.

No longer in its original location, the **Cedar Tavern** (82 University Place) was a meeting place for the painters of what became the New York School of Abstract Expressionism. As Jackson Pollock and others loudly lamented the state of art, Beat writers such as the late Allen Ginsberg and William Burroughs eavesdropped from neighbouring tables.

Bars for beer-drinkers Beer connoisseurs will welcome the 200 imported varieties sold at the **Peculier Pub** (145 Bleecker Street). The wooden bench tables here often overflow with New York University students. Detailed menu descriptions will help you choose from the 50 or so beers served at **The Blind Tiger** (518 Hudson Street). There's no such help at **The Ginger Man** (11 East 36th Street), but the selection of beers and single malt scotches is even larger. **Heartland Brewery** (135 Union Square West) offers microbrewed beer. What would you expect from a bar called Brewsky's (41 East Seventh Street)? Yes, beer, but this wood-floored, no-frills East Villager serves a whopping 700 varieties, so you are bound to find something to your taste.

Bars with a view In Midtown Manhattan, try the 39th-floor **Top of the Sixes** (666 Fifth Avenue), or the now refurbished **Top of the Tower** at the Beekham Tower Hotel (3 Mitchell Place, off 49th Street) for a splendid view across the East River. The **Pen Top Bar** at the Peninsula Hotel (700 Fifth Avenue) offers its drinks from a roof-top terrace.

Bars for the beautiful people Rande Gerber's newest watering hole, **Underbar** (201 Park Avenue South), located in the subterranean environs of the W Union Square hotel, has caused quite a sensation with its sleek, black-clad waitresses and mesh-curtained booths. The minimalist Philippe Starck designed **Hudson Bar** (256 West 58th Street) in the Hudson Hotel, which is a white-on-white fantasy of minimal design. Though actually a restaurant, **The Park** (118 Tenth Avenue) attracts a discerning crowd for nightly quaffs and nibbles; opened by the man behind B-Bar so expect a who's who crowd. **Astor Lounge** (316 Bowery) has the feel of an underground brasserie with tin ceilings, worn mirrors and clouds of cigarette smoke. **Lotus** (409 West 14th Street) is *the* in place, if you can get past the bouncers.

Hotel bars Many are favoured by locals for their elegant surroundings and the fact that you do not have to shout over loud music to hold a conversation. The **King Cole Bar** at the St Regis Hotel (2 East 55th Street) serves drinks in front of an impressive Maxfield Parrish mural. For a private tryst, try **Fifty Seven Fifty Seven** at the Four Seasons Hotel (57 East 57th Street), which draws publishing and media bigwigs. The scene at the lobby bar of the **Mercer Bar** (99 Prince Street) in SoHo is white hot, and the **Grand Bar** at the SoHo Grand Hotel (310 West Broadway) attracts the fashionable every night.

MARIE'S CRISIS CAFÉ
Few places symbolise changing New York better than Marie's Crisis Café (59 Grove Street). Nowadays, do not be surprised to find this lively bar packed by gay men singing hit songs from famous Broadway shows. Two centuries ago it was a home of Thomas Paine, whose publication, *Crisis*, helped fuel the American Revolution.

The photos and flags that adorn the walls of McSorley's Old Ale House suggest a time when New York bars provided informal employment centres and enabled many new immigrants to land their first jobs in the United States

115

GREENWICH VILLAGE WRITERS

James Agee, James Baldwin, Willa Cather, James Fenimore Cooper, Hart Crane, Theodore Dreiser, e e cummings, Henry James, Ruth McKenney, Herman Melville, Edna St Vincent Millay, Eugene O'Neill, Anaïs Nin, John Dos Passos, Edgar Allan Poe, John Reed, William Styron, Mark Twain, Tennessee Williams, Edmund Wilson, Thomas Wolfe.

Washington Square Memorial Arch

INSIDE THE MEMORIAL ARCH

In 1916, maverick artist Marcel Duchamp and friends forced their way through the locked door of Washington Square Park's Memorial Arch and climbed the 110 steps to the top. Once there, they hung balloons, Chinese lanterns, and banners proclaiming Greenwich Village as the independent republic of New Bohemia. After having a picnic, Duchamp and company were forced down by militiamen.

With somewhat less of a spectacle, a man is thought to have lived in the arch for seven months during World War II. He was noticed only when he hung his washing out to dry.

(Continued from page 112)

There is no better place to begin exploring Greenwich Village than **Washington Square Park**▶▶▶ where jugglers, actors, unicyclists and chess-players put on a show for the families, visitors and the street-wise kids who promenade along the park's pathways.

On the park's northern side, the triumphal **Washington Memorial Arch**▶▶ stands at the foot of Fifth Avenue, 23m high and erected by Stanford White in 1892 on a spot where he had earlier raised a wooden marker to celebrate the centenary of Washington's inauguration.

What the white marble arch does not commemorate, however, are the 22,000 people who were buried beneath the park when it served as a mass cemetery during epidemics. There is also no reminder of the fact that during the early 1800s some of the park's trees were, in fact, used for public hangings.

Besides ending hangings and covering over the burial ground, the creation of the park in 1827 greatly increased the social cachet of the immediate area. Fashionable town houses rose around it, the only survivors being **The Row**▶▶ on the north side: note their porticoes, shuttered windows, and elongated stoops – emphasising the distinction between the owner's entrance and the servants' entrance at ground level.

To the park's south and east are a few of the buildings of New York University. With 14 separate schools scattered throughout Greenwich Village, the university is one of the city's major landowners.

(Continued on page 118)

New York City is home to one of the most vibrant gay and lesbian communities in the USA, centred around Chelsea and Greenwich Village. The contributions of its members help to make New York what it is in publishing, advertising, art and design, theatre, dance, restaurants, law, business and other fields.

The census of 1880 found five men in prison for "unspeakable crimes against nature" – a euphemism of the time for homosexual activity. By the 1930s, a small network of gay rendezvous points had spread across Manhattan; places where discretion was uppermost and which remained invisible to the heterosexual world.

In the period following World War II, when the values of family life were extolled to the hilt, gays and lesbians increasingly felt the backlash. Sexual minorities were pilloried in the press, and the police were urged to clamp down on behaviour that was feared and perceived as a menace to society.

Gay Pride In 1969, the two days of rioting that followed a police raid on Greenwich Village's Stonewall Inn became a turning point in gay history: for the first time, the community had risen up to defend itself against the authorities, and its newfound solidarity led to the founding of the Gay Pride movement.

The movement's many achievements are celebrated annually by the Gay Pride Parade along Fifth Avenue and through Greenwich Village (see page 27).

Gays have steadily become established and largely accepted throughout the city. Gay issues are now widely debated throughout mainstream media, while legal breakthroughs include the formal recognition of gay couples in 1993. In the last few years gays have also featured prominently in the rejuvenation and gentrification of the Chelsea neighbourhood.

INFORMATION
For general information and the latest on gay and lesbian events, nightclubs and more, contact the Gay and Lesbian Community Center, One Little West Twelfth Street (tel: 620-7310; www.gaycenter.org). Many other useful online resources can be found at the New York Gay–Lesbian Guide: www.woofbyte.com/newyorkcity/nyc_directories.htm.

117

Christopher Street in Greenwich Village, is home to a substantial gay and lesbian community

STROLL: GREENWICH VILLAGE

The maze of side streets off Christopher Street holds some of Greenwich Village's quietest and prettiest corners. Take time to admire the lovely row of brick and brownstone Italianate houses on St Luke's Place and venture into Bedford Street for the Isaacs-Hendricks Residence (see page 130) and the 3m-wide house at number 75½. Its dainty dimensions did not deter actor John Barrymore, poet Edna St Vincent Millay or screen star Cary Grant from living in it at various times.

Its subway station has preserved its original blue tiles and the street stalls on Bleecker Street recall its place as a home for Beat writers in the 1950s and 1960s

(Continued from page 116)

Not content with his Memorial Arch, Stanford White also erected the **Judson Memorial Church▶**, on the park's south side, in largely Romanesque style. More noteworthy than the architecture are the church's stained-glass windows, the work of Hudson River artist John LaFarge.

A block away, on MacDougal Street, the unremarkable exterior of the **Provincetown Playhouse** does nothing to suggest that the group based here forged new ground in American drama in the 1910s, helped in no small measure by the talents of Eugene O'Neill.

Just south, on the corner of Minetta Lane, the **Minetta Tavern▶** displays photos and mementos from Greenwich Village's earliest days as a centre for the arts.

Running across MacDougal Street, **Bleecker Street▶▶▶** holds the best of Greenwich Village's bars and clubs, though nothing these days matches the stirrings of the early 1960s when local folk clubs spawned talents such as Bob Dylan, Judy Collins and Arlo Guthrie.

A decade earlier, the cafés in Bleecker Street had reverberated to the performance poetry and drunken debates of embryonic Beat writers: Gregory Corso, Jack Kerouac, Allen Ginsberg and William Burroughs (see page 119).

More restaurants, bakeries and cafés line Bleecker Street as it continues westwards across Sixth Avenue into the West Village, the main artery of which, Christopher Street, cuts westwards from Village Square and the extraordinary **Jefferson Market Courthouse** (see page 113), towards the Hudson River; on Sixth Avenue is Balducci's (see page 113).

At 53 Christopher Street was the **Stonewall Inn**. It gave its name to the "Stonewall Riots", which united the local gay community in 1969 and led to the founding of Gay Pride (see page 117), which was to spawn a number of similar organisations in many parts of the world.

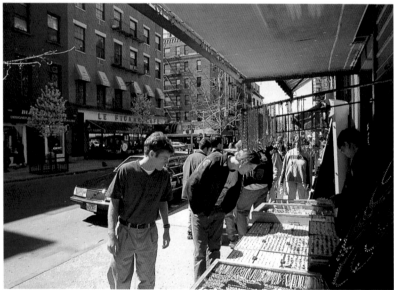

A small group of characters frequenting the bars around Columbia University and Greenwich Village in the 1940s evolved into what became the Beat Generation, the USA's first postwar subculture and one that used drugs, jazz, and Eastern religion to inspire the new forms of writing that, for a brief time in the 1950s, seemed set to tear US society to pieces.

If the Beat Generation had a starting point, it was the West End Café (on Broadway between 113th and 114th streets) in the mid-1940s. Here teenaged student Allen Ginsberg, 30-year-old William Burroughs and 22-year-old Jack Kerouac swapped ideas, later adjourning to an apartment at 421 West 118th Street to hold lively discussions to the sound of the newly emerged bebop jazz.

Beat writing Ginsberg began writing "serious" poetry, Kerouac worked on his breathless prose style, and Burroughs steadily assembled the pieces that would evolve into his novels. By the end of the 1940s, the chief hangouts were the San Remo (189 Bleecker Street) and the Cedar Tavern (then at 24 University Place).

Success and notoriety Ginsberg was living in San Francisco in 1956 when, besides working for an advertising agency and studying Buddhism, he wrote his epic poem, *Howl*, describing characters and ideas from the past few years. The poem was published to enthusiastic reviews – and an obscenity trial that greatly increased the notoriety of "the Beats", as did *On the Road*, Kerouac's novel published the next year.

When Ginsberg and Kerouac returned to New York, the *Village Voice* proclaimed "Witless Madcaps Come Home to Roost", and the events of a decade earlier quickly became, and continue to be, a source of legend.

WHY "BEAT GENERATION"?
Ginsberg and another writer, John Clellon Holmes, conceived the term "Beat Generation", partly from the "Lost Generation" of the 1920s and partly from a Times Square junkie who always described himself as "beat". When Holmes's novel *Go* was published in 1952, the New York Times reviewer seized on the handy phrase, but this did not help Ginsberg, Burroughs or Kerouac find publishers for their work.

The late Allen Ginsberg (left) listens to a speaker at a 1960s anti-Vietnam War rally near Tompkins Square Park

For every major religious edifice such as St Patrick's Cathedral or the Cathedral Church of St John the Divine, New York has dozens more that seldom receive a visit from passing travellers. Many of these are mentioned in the A–Z section of this book, but those described below are especially notable for illustrating the city's many forms of ecclesiastical architecture or for highlighting the city's endless diversity.

SAME CHURCH, DIFFERENT RELIGION

Indicative of the changing ethnic make-up of the Lower East Side, the 1895 Russian Orthodox Cathedral at 4th Street between Avenues C and D is now San Isidro y San Leandro Orthodox Catholic Church of the Hispanic Rite, which is serving the Lower East Side's now predominantly Puerto Rican population.

120

Greek Orthodox New York's earliest Greek church, **St Nicholas Greek Orthodox Church**, was tragically buried by the collapse of the World Trade Center. The Greek community's religious focal point had already moved north, however, to the icon-rich **Greek Orthodox Cathedral of the Holy Trinity** (74th Street near First Avenue; tel: 288-5876), which opened in 1931.

Episcopal Although a near neighbour of St Nicholas's, the 1849 neo-Gothic **Trinity Church** (74 Trinity Place; tel: 602-0800) did survive the attacks of September 2001. Along with its Georgian annex, St Paul's Chapel, the church serves a 300-year-old parish.

Jewish Also in what is now the Financial District, New York's first Jewish residents established the city's earliest synagogue some 300 years ago on what became William Street. A replica of the 20-seat shrine can be seen on the fifth floor of the **Wall Street Synagogue** (47 Beekman Street; tel: 227-7800). Completed in 1887, the Eldridge Street Synagogue (12 Eldridge Street, between Canal and Division streets, tel: 219-0888; *Open* Sun 11–4, Tue and Thu at 11:30 and 2:30. *Admission: inexpensive*) is also deeply rooted in New York history, being the first synagogue raised by eastern European Jews. The past is documented within its museum.

Roman Catholic In 1918, just north of the Central Synagogue, architect Bertram Goodhue produced an accomplished and imposing façade for the **Church of St Vincent Ferrer** (Lexington Avenue at 66th Street; tel: 744-2080), but he saved his best touches for the expansive interior. Note the reredos and Charles Connick's exceptional stained-glass windows.

Russian Orthodox The seat of the Russian Orthodox Church in North America is on New York's Upper East Side, where the **St Nicholas Orthodox Cathedral** (97th Street near Fifth Avenue; tel: 876-2190) was erected at the turn of the century, financed by donations collected across the tsarist Russian empire. The cathedral's splendidly ornate style – red brick patterned with blue and yellow tiles and five bulging onion domes – is based on the church architecture of 17th-century Moscow.

The statue of Shinran-Shonin outside the New York Buddhist Church

AN EMBARRASSED ARCHITECT
With Grace Church (see page 112) and St Patrick's Cathedral (page 150), church architect James Renwick made his name. Among his less acclaimed works, however, was the 1846 **Calvary Church** (Park Avenue at 21st Street; tel: 281-2192). The church still stands but without its steeples.

Muslim The design of St Nicholas is strikingly different from the drab buildings around it, as is that of the **Mosque of the Islamic Culture Center** (Third Avenue at 96th Street; tel: 722-5234), which also deviates from the usual grid-style alignment of Manhattan buildings by being pointed towards Mecca. The first permanent place of worship for New York Muslims, the $12-million mosque was largely financed by the government of Kuwait.

Buddhist On the other side of Central Park, you might easily go right past the **New York Buddhist Church** (Riverside Drive between 105th and 106th streets; tel: 678-0305) without realising the fact – were it not for the unmistakable bronze statue of Shinran-Shonin, the 13th-century founder of a Buddhist sect, that stands outside.

Abyssinian Baptist Harlem's **Abyssinian Baptist Church** (138th Street near Lenox Avenue; tel: 862-7474) was founded in 1808 by, and to serve, New York's black community and quickly acquired the largest black congregation of any church in the US. Past ministers include Harlem's first black member of congress, Adam Clayton Powell. His struggles to end racial discrimination and raise African-American living standards made him a nationally controversial, but locally revered, figure in the 1940s. The present Gothic-style church dates from 1923 and has a display recording Powell's achievements.

From the Central Synagogue (above left) to the Episcopalian St Mark's-in-the-Bowery (above): New York's places of worship mirror its diverse ethnic make-up

▶▶▶ Guggenheim Museum   187C1

Fifth Avenue between 88th and 89th streets (tel: 423-3500)
Open: Sun–Wed 9–6, Fri and Sat 9–8. Admission: moderate
Subway: 86th Street

A member of an ultrawealthy New York family whose fortunes were founded on copper and silver mines, Solomon R Guggenheim followed the usual track of an Upper East Side millionaire with more money than he knew what to do with by dabbling in art. Guggenheim's first purchases were unremarkable Old Masters, but his tastes were changed radically in 1927 when he met Baroness Hilla Rebay von Ehrenwiesen, an outspoken and energetic enthusiast of European abstract art.

Through the baroness, Guggenheim met artists such as Robert Delaunay, Fernand Léger and Albert Gleizes and quickly amassed a superb stock of their work and works by other contemporary artists, particularly Wassily Kandinsky, hanging them on the walls of the rooms he occupied with his wife at New York's Plaza Hotel. At the suggestion of the baroness, Guggenheim commissioned architect Frank Lloyd Wright to design and build a museum to be called (with an ideological correctness insisted on by the baroness) the Museum of Non-Objective Painting.

Guggenheim had been dead for 10 years by the time Wright's extraordinary achievement opened in 1959, its name changed to the Solomon R Guggenheim Museum. It proved to be the architect's only New York building, and he referred to it as his "Pantheon". By this time, Guggenheim's initial collection of abstracts had been enlarged and greatly broadened in scope by purchases and bequests, particularly the Thannhauser Collection of impressionist and post-impressionist paintings which were bequeathed by a prominent dealer and collector.

The best way to see the collection is to take the elevator to the top level and slowly work your way down the museum's remarkable spiral ramp. In this way you can study the exhibits, look over the parapet to the lobby below, and finish up where you began without ever getting lost.

Precisely what will be on show when you visit has been scheduled years in advance; the museum stages several special exhibitions each year, often focusing on the work of an individual artist. What you can be fairly certain of seeing, however, is the permanently displayed Thannhauser Collection, hung in comparatively orthodox fashion in several galleries reached off the second level of the ramp.

Highlights of the Guggenheim's permanent collections include works by Kandinsky, Modigliani, Klee, Mondrian, Braque, Chagall, Gleizes and Malevich.

Among these, Van Gogh's painting entitled *Mountains at Saint-Rémy* is outstanding, its vibrant swirls of colour painted in 1899 as the artist recovered from one of his bouts of mental illness.

Works by Cézanne include *Still Life: Flask, Glass and Jug* and *Bibémus*, a shimmering pre-abstract landscape, and the slightly mystifying *Man With Crossed Arms*, described as a "proto-Cubist" piece, whose figure has been thought to embody the spirit of quiet resignation that the artist possessed during the last years of his life.

GUGGENHEIMS AROUND THE WORLD

A 1998 exhibition, the Art of the Motorcycle, sponsored by BMW, and a subsequent fashion-magazine-sponsored retrospective of the work of clothes designer Giorgio Armani, caused the Guggenheim to upset art purists as many questioned the increased role of business in the museum's displays. Nonetheless, the exhibitions gave the museum some of its best-ever attendance figures and provided further impetus for its global expansion plans. The summer of 2001 saw the first Guggenheim exhibition in Las Vegas, as well as advanced plans for further branches in Rio de Janeiro, Vienna and St Petersburg. These follow the continuing success of the architecturally-stunning Bilbao Guggenheim. The latter's architect, Frank Gehry, is also behind the new Manhattan Guggenheim, planned for the East River at the foot of South Street.

A couple of paintings by the enigmatic artist Henri Rousseau (also known as "Le Douanier" – the Customs Man) are amusing and defiantly odd. In *The Football Players*, five handlebar-moustached and ludicrously attired figures strike up absurd poses while frolicking with a ball in a forest; similarly handlebar-moustached but more correctly attired soldiers make up the core of *The Artillery Men*.

The earliest of several canvases by Picasso, *Le Moulin de Galette*, was painted in 1900 when the artist was only 19 years of age and was inspired by his first visit to Paris. The gloomy but angular figure of 1904's *Woman Ironing* is a product of the latter stages of what is known as Picasso's Blue Period; from a year or two later, *Fernand with a Black Fortilla* marks a change of style – and perhaps the first step towards Cubism.

The most striking piece in the Thannhauser Collection is also the earliest: *The Hermitage at Pontoise*, an 1867 landscape by Camille Pissarro. The artist later became a leading impressionist (Gauguin and Cézanne were among Pissarro's students and associates) but here uses a realist style that goes hard against the grain of traditional French landscape painting – and seems to make the idyllic rural scene radiate from the canvas.

RAYMOND HOOD
Architecture buffs impressed by his subsequent Daily News Building and Rockefeller Center's RCA Building (as the GE Building used to be known) may care to cast an eye over Raymond Hood's 1928 apartment block at 3 East 84th Street, bearing many of the features – such as pressed-metal spandrels – that later appeared in a refined form on his more well-known works.

The vertiginous interior of the Guggenheim

123

It has been called a doughnut, a snail, and an insult to art, but Frank Lloyd Wright's Guggenheim Museum is one of the outstanding contributions to New York architecture – even though it often steals the show from the art that it exhibits. Wright inserted the inscription "let every man practise the art he knows" in bronze on the entrance floor – intended perhaps as a lasting riposte to the building's critics.

124

THE GUGGENHEIM ADDITIONS

In 1993, the completion of Gwathmey/Siegel's 11-storey tower, welded to the rotunda, provided much-needed extra office and exhibition space despite being widely criticised for its failure to blend with Wright's original building. Meanwhile, in addition to the long-established SoHo Guggenheim (see page 175) plans are underway for a third Guggenheim, intended to rise on piers in the East River.

More than 40 years after it opened, the Guggenheim remains a unique feature of the New York landscape

Organic architecture The originator of the "Prairie style", Wright in his best architecture blended buildings into the organic, natural forms around them. The Guggenheim's predominantly curving exterior is totally out of step with the vertical lines of the neighbouring Upper East Side apartment houses but has a great deal in common with the trees and shrubbery of Central Park, directly across Fifth Avenue.

With the Guggenheim Museum, his only major New York commission, Wright also made a radical departure from the traditional room-by-room gallery style. The exhibits here occupy partitioned spaces off a 400m-long spiral walkway that rises six storeys high, steadily growing wider as it climbs.

Controversy The architect persistently battled with the city authorities and disagreed with the museum's director over the structure's supposed failure to meet the practical needs of an art museum. All this contributed to delays, and 16 years elapsed between Wright's finished plans and the Guggenheim's opening in 1959, the year of his death. The aesthetic debate has raged ever since, though the museum is now very much part of the Upper East Side landscape.

► Harlem

IBCC2

Increasingly a part of the city's tourist circuit and long a vital and distinct component in New York's character, Harlem begins north of Central Park at 110th Street and splits into two sections.

Above the Upper West Side, West Harlem (or Harlem proper) is the longest-established home of the city's African-American population. Above the Upper East Side is East Harlem – or **El Barrio** ("the Neighbourhood") – which has become New York's largest Spanish-speaking enclave. The majority of East Harlem residents have Puerto Rican origins.

During the 1890s, eager to repeat the success they had had on the Upper West Side, property speculators covered West Harlem with brownstones and apartment blocks. The anticipated buyers never materialised, however, and Harlem's homes were rented out largely to black tenants. Rents were inflated because of housing pressure – thousands of African-Americans were arriving in New York, and the competition was great. Tens of thousands of the nation's blacks fled the Deep South for Harlem, seen at the time as a promised land. By the 1920s, the Harlem Renaissance was in full swing: a flowering of African-American culture through art and literature as jazz and blues percolated through Harlem nightclubs such as the **Cotton Club** and **Smalls' Paradise**.

On the main commercial strip, West 125th Street, stands the **Apollo Theater** (at number 253), legendary for its

FIDEL CASTRO IN HARLEM

Arriving to address the United Nations in 1960, Cuban leader Fidel Castro and his entourage spent several nights in a Midtown Manhattan hotel, reputedly running up a $10,000 bill for damage before being asked to leave. No other hotel was eager for Castro's patronage, but Harlem's Teresa Hotel (272 West 125th Street), long known as a radicals' meeting place, filled the breach. During its week-long stay, the Cuban contingent was cheered by locals and was visited by Soviet leader Khrushchev. In 1971, the Teresa was converted into an office building.

125

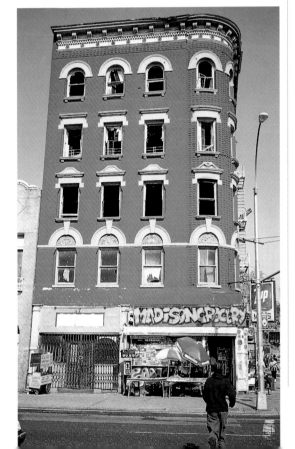

Not many people visit Harlem for its architecture, but the buildings can be just as lively as the atmosphere

MARCUS GARVEY IN HARLEM

Arriving in Harlem from Jamaica in 1914, Marcus Garvey predated the Black Panthers in the 1960s in encouraging black pride and assertiveness. Winning many followers through his brilliant powers of oration, Garvey founded the Universal Negro Improvement Foundation, published the *Negro World* newspaper and purchased two ocean liners to carry out his promised repatriation of America's blacks to Africa.

Eventually, Garvey was arrested on trumped-up charges and deported. He died in London in 1940. Garvey's doctrines became crucial elements in Rastafarianism, and in 1973 the Harlem park that straddles Fifth Avenue between 120th and 124th streets was renamed in his honour.

Unfortunately, the park, which holds a curious fire-watch tower dating from 1856, is a drug-users' hangout and is best left unvisited.

Harlem gospel choir

amateur talent nights and for showcasing every African-American jazz, blues and soul act, from Billie Holliday in the 1930s to James Brown in the 1960s. Brown's *Live at the Apollo* album was recorded here in 1962 and captures some of the venue's raw excitement. You will also find the temporary exhibitions and photographic archive of the **Studio Museum in Harlem** (144 West 125th Street; tel: 864-4500; *Open* Wed–Fri 12–6, Sat and Sun 10–6. *Admission: inexpensive*) and more soul-food restaurants than anyone could wish for.

Rare books, documents, art and artefacts pertaining to African-American history make up some of five million items housed at the **Schomburg Center for Research in Black Culture** (515 Malcolm X Boulevard; tel 491 2200). It also hosts drama, concerts and temporary exhibitions.

For the best of early Harlem architecture, explore the **St Nicholas Historic District** on 139th Street. The stylish 1890s town houses between Seventh and Eighth avenues were occupied by successful blacks from 1919 and hence earned their lasting nickname "Striver's Row".

Upbeat Sunday gospel services have become one of the major points of visitor interest in Harlem, although the tour group numbers at some churches have led to complaints that local congregations are being ignored. One of Harlem's most celebrated churches for its outstanding choir and history of community involvement, is the **Abyssinian Baptist Church** (see page 121).

Always shabbier than its westerly counterpart, **East Harlem** was first settled by working-class Italian and Irish families but, from the 1920s on, it steadily evolved into the city's major Puerto Rican neighbourhood. The **Museum of the City of New York** and **El Museo del Barrio** (see pages 156–157) stand on its fringes, but the place to make for is **La Marqueta**, found under the Park Avenue viaduct between 110th and 116th streets, where salsa music resounds among the market stalls and food stands.

► **Hispanic Society of America**   *IBCD2*

Broadway at 155th Street (tel: 926-2234)
Open: Tue–Sat 10–4:30, Sun 1–4. Admission free
Subway: 1; 157th Street

Paintings by Velázquez, El Greco and Goya are among the most prized possessions of the Hispanic Society of America, founded in 1904 by Archer M Huntington, son of magnate Collis P Huntington. However, this collection of Spanish and Portuguese art, archaeology, tilework and tomb decorations is overall less impressive than its setting: a sumptuous two-storey Spanish Renaissance interior, decorated with ruby-red terracotta.

> *As their country is a self-governing common-*
> *wealth territory of the US, Puerto Ricans are*
> *automatically US citizens. The right to settle*
> *freely led to Puerto Ricans forming the biggest*
> *Spanish-speaking community in New York.*

Early 19th-century New York drew Puerto Ricans active in the sugar and coffee trade. Others, who were inspired by the American Revolution, came here hoping to use the city as a base to plot the overthrow of their Spanish colonial masters.

The US in Puerto Rico In 1898, Puerto Rico was deeded by Spain to the United States, which established a military government on the Caribbean island and allowed American interests to rule its economy. In return, Puerto Ricans were granted United States citizenship (although not until 1917) and so were able to settle freely in the United States.

The profiteering of American companies encouraged Puerto Rican migration and, by 1930, around 45,000 Puerto Ricans had settled in New York. Many were employed in jobs formerly held by upwardly mobile Jews and Italians; others worked in their traditional trades such as cigar-making.

El Barrio Although there were a number of Puerto Rican neighbourhoods across Manhattan, the area around the low-rent apartments of East Harlem became *El Barrio*, base of Puerto Rican cultural institutions and Spanish-language cinemas and publications. Over a period of time, Fiorello La Guardia (who took office in 1933) recognised the political power of the Puerto Ricans by encouraging them to register to vote.

In the 1950s, when inexpensive flights began operating between New York and San Juan – the Puerto Rican capital – the Puerto Rican population in New York soared to 600,000, some spilling from El Barrio into the Bronx. The majority of the new arrivals had been rural-dwelling farm labourers, who subsequently found it difficult to adjust to big-city life.

Americans of Puerto Rican descent are now a major part of the city's ethnic jigsaw puzzle. While the area is celebrated among trendy New Yorkers for its spicy foods and for its salsa music, El Barrio unfortunately continues to struggle with every contemporary inner-city problem.

SAN JUAN HILL
When Yankee Stadium was completed in 1923, it was dubbed "the House that Ruth built", after baseball's most famous player. One might well call Lincoln Center "the House that Bernstein built". The great irony is that the construction of the new home of Leonard Bernstein's New York Symphony Orchestra required the utter destruction of the neighbourhood that was the setting for his most famous work, *West Side Story*. More than 1,500 families in the area then known as San Juan Hill – most of them black and/or Puerto Rican – were displaced.

127

At an exhibition in Los Angeles in 1956, the phrase "the New York School" was first coined, referring to the group of artists who, in New York a decade or so earlier, had spearheaded abstract expressionism, the country's first modern art movement, thus creating a worldwide audience for American art.

THE CEDAR TAVERN

Rare is the major art movement that was not influenced to some degree by drunken debate. Abstract expressionism was no exception. The favoured gathering place of many of the artists who became the New York School was the Cedar Tavern, then at 24 University Place. Here, discussions would rage into the night and sometimes culminate in an inebriated rearrangement of the furniture.

Fans of abstract expressionism who also like a drink may be pleased to know that the Cedar Tavern still exists (though it has moved to 82 University Place). These days, however, it is plain and rather uninteresting.

The Armory Show of 1913 (see page 149) not only brought modern European art to the US for the first time, but also made it plain that the country had no modern style to call its own. Dadaist Marcel Duchamp summed up America's contribution to world art as "her plumbing and her bridges".

Even if they viewed it only as a stop on the way to Paris, however, New York was still a magnet for young American artists. They arrived to escape humdrum rural towns, to take classes at the city's Art Students League, and to paint in spacious light-filled loft studios available for cheap rents.

European influences As Europe moved towards war, many of the continent's most innovative and influential artistic minds fled across the Atlantic. When the Nazis marched down the Champs-Elysées, New York eclipsed Paris as the nerve centre of international art.

In the late 1940s, as the conclusion of the war seemed to present a world free of the shackles of traditionalism and filled with new possibilities, a new group of abstract expressionists emerged.

Jackson Pollock A farmer's son from Wyoming, Jackson Pollock had arrived in New York in the 1920s and was later employed for a short time at the embryonic Guggenheim Museum.

In 1947, Pollock seized one of his paintings from its easel, fixed it to the floor, and started applying paint directly from the can in great sweeping arcs across the canvas. Soon after, Pollock dispensed with easels and brushes entirely, pouring paint onto the flat canvas and manipulating it with "sticks, trowels or knives".

As the final product depended entirely on the act of Pollock dripping and throwing paint (compared to a western cowboy's lasso skills), the technique gave rise to the term "action painting" (also called "gestural painting").

De Kooning, Gottlieb and Rothko Another key abstract expressionist was Willem de Kooning. While de Kooning used figures much more than Pollock – often formed by white contours on black – he was every inch the action painter, attacking his canvas with an energy that sent specks of paint flying in every direction.

A major influence on the abstract expressionists was the *Pictographs*, a series of paintings by Adolph Gottlieb, each of which was divided into compartments holding a mythological figure or symbol.

The abstract expressionists sought to transmit primal emotional states through their work – a goal that went beyond what was possible within traditional painting and which the horrors of the war had helped awaken.

Mark Rothko, an associate of Gottlieb's, became the foremost figure of what was termed the "colour field" branch of abstract expressionism. As the full terrors of the Nazi concentration camps emerged, there was a special poignancy when Rothko, the Latvian-born son of Russian Jewish émigrés, asserted that "human incommunicability" had rendered figurative painting obsolete. Rothko's work evolved into floating rectangles of colour, which, he said, provided "a spiritual basis for communion".

Barnett Newman and after Barnett Newman likened the colour field artists' work to that of "primitive" cultures, keen to reach a "metaphysical understanding". In the late 1940s, Newman produced the first of his "zip paintings", their flat field of colour split by a narrow vertical line.

Ironically, it was a misinterpretation of Newman's work that influenced later artists such as Jasper Johns. These later artists paved the way for the break away from the mentally wrought canvases of abstract expressionism to the re-casting of familiar images practiced by the 1960s pop art movement.

Perhaps in keeping with the anguished soul-searching of their work, the lives of abstract expressionism's two major figures both ended prematurely: Jackson Pollock died after driving his car into a tree in 1956 and Mark Rothko committed suicide in 1970.

ABSTRACT EXPRESSIONISM ON DISPLAY
The Museum of Modern Art (see pages 158–160) has an excellent collection of abstract expressionist works and, besides those mentioned on these pages, also features work by other highly influential members of the movement such as Robert Motherwell, Franz Kline and Arshile Gorky.

The Guggenheim Museum (pages 122–124) has a fair number of abstract expressionist canvases in its possession (sometimes on display in temporary exhibitions), and important works by Pollock, de Kooning and Rothko can be seen at the Whitney Museum (page 191).

One, a huge canvas of 1950 by Jackson Pollock, now in MoMA

PHOTOGRAPHY HOUSE

One of the most handsome neo-Georgian mansions on the Upper East Side is home to a branch of the International Center of Photography. The four-storey red-brick building was completed in 1914 by the firm of Delano & Aldrich for Willard Straight, a wealthy ex-diplomat who founded the influential *New Republic* magazine.

▶▶ International Center of Photography   187D1

1133 Sixth Avenue, at 43rd Street (tel: 860-1777)
Open: Tue 10–8, Wed–Sun 10–6. Admission: inexpensive
Subway: B, D, Q; 42nd Street

The International Center of Photography (ICP) is one of the world's few museums entirely devoted to photography. It has several galleries mounting changing exhibitions of both internationally established names and lesser-knowns.

One gallery is usually filled with selections from the Center's permanent collection, which holds prints by almost every notable photographer you can think of: Henri Cartier-Bresson, Ernst Haas, Weegee and Robert Capa to name a few.

▶ Intrepid Sea-Air-Space Museum   151C1

West end of 46th Street (tel: 245-0072)
Open: Mon–Fri 10–5, Sat–Sun 10–6. Admission: moderate
Subway: A, C, E; 42nd Street

The flight deck of the *Intrepid*, a Navy aircraft carrier, is the core of this militaristic museum. Permanently moored on the Hudson River, the *Intrepid* saw action in the Pacific during World War II and served in an antisubmarine role during the Vietnam War.

The vessel is stuffed with exhibits from its own wartime adventures – its aircraft shot down 650 enemy planes and destroyed 289 ships – and from its peacetime role of retrieving Mercury and Gemini space capsules. On its deck sits an A-12 Blackbird, the highest, fastest spy plane ever built.

Other maritime vessels on show include the *Edson* destroyer, which saw 30 years of service, and the *Growler*, a strategic missile-carrying submarine built in 1958. A tour of its innards includes the missile command centre and brings the sobering realisation that World War Three could have started at this very console. Also displayed are a variety of American, British and French fighter aircraft. An additional (inexpensive) fee brings the chance to fly a simulated mission over the Persian Gulf at the controls of an F-18 fighter.

▶ Isaacs-Hendricks Residence   113A2

77 Bedford Street, Greenwich Village
Subway: 1; Christopher Street

You could be forgiven for walking right past the Isaacs-Hendricks Residence without noticing it. Alterations in 1836 and 1928 have detracted from its Federal style, of which it is one of the earliest surviving examples, having been erected in 1799. The clapboard wall on the side that backs onto Commerce Street is the main clue to the house's architectural pedigree.

▶ Jan Hus Presbyterian Church   187B2

74th Street between First and Second avenues
Subway: 6; 77th Street

Named after the Czech martyr of the Reformation, the Jan Hus Presbyterian Church was founded in 1914 to serve Czech settlers in an area that was known as Little Bohemia into the 1930s. The church, with a bell tower modelled on the Powder Tower in Prague, is more popular for its secular activities than for its services. Musical and dramatic events are staged at the church's hall.

Only a small fraction of New York's Czech-American population now lives in Little Bohemia and, besides the church, there are only a couple of notable reminders of the Czech presence, such as the run-down Bohemian National Hall, on 73rd Street between First and Second avenues, raised in 1895.

▶ Jewish Museum   187D1

Fifth Avenue at 92nd Street (tel: 423-3200)
Open: Sun, Mon, Wed, Thu 11–5:45, Tue 11–8.
Admission: moderate. Subway: 6; 96th Street

An imitation French Gothic château might seem a strange home for the largest stock of Judaic ceremonial art and historical objects in the US, but the fine collections of New York's Jewish Museum have been housed in just such a place since 1944. It was then that the premises were bequeathed to the museum by the widow of their original owner, banker Felix M Warburg.

Some of the tremendous stash of coins, household objects and religious pieces date back to Roman times; much more is representative of Jewish life from medieval times into the present century. One exemplary feature is the re-created turn-of-the-century café in which visitors can select oral histories of Jewish lives in various European cities of the time, and of early Jewish arrivals to the United States.

The Jewish Museum also stages lively and sometimes provocative temporary exhibitions that are designed to explore the Jewish experience from new and challenging perspectives. There is also a Childrens' Activity Center which offers arts and crafts projects related to Jewish culture and traditions.

CZECHS IN NEW YORK

The first significant group of Czechs in New York arrived in 1848 to practice the free thinking denied them by the ruling Hapsburg Empire. Nicknamed the "48ers" they founded many of the institutions that were to provide assistance to the second wave of Czech immigrants who arrived in the 1870s.

The Nazi invasion, the Soviet coup, and the failure of the 1968 Prague Spring also brought fresh waves of Czech migration, most of the newcomers becoming quietly assimilated into suburban American life.

The Intrepid Sea-Air-Space Museum

Informed to the point of overload, New Yorkers enjoy TV spanning national networks and public access channels, countless radio stations and newspapers that range from venerable nationals to neighbourhood freesheets.

Television Alongside the networks with their mixture of national and local programming, the Time-Warner-owned NY1 brings a lively blend of news, weather, sport and entertainment gossip focused solely on New York. While all hotel rooms have televisions, budget-priced rooms may lack extra cable channels, and even medium-priced options tend to be skimpy on the selections available. Therefore, one perk of more costly hotels is a fuller range of viewing options, sometimes including Manhattan's public-access channels on which people – ranging from astrologers to self-styled sex therapists – pay to make a half-hour show. New York's daily newspapers carry full listings of TV programmes. A full week's listings are also included as a separate magazine with the Sunday *New York Times*.

Radio New York has many radio stations. FM frequencies offer a wide choice of stations, each with its own special-ity, from round-the-clock hip-hop, soul, funk, jazz, country, heavy rock or classical sounds. Stations on the AM wave-bands are primarily spoken word, and include phone-ins of the kind that should, at the very least, quickly acquaint visitors with the New York accent.

The cast of international comedy hit "Friends", which is set in New York

Newspapers Of New York City's daily newspapers, *The New York Times* is unmatched for in-depth coverage of international and national affairs, while its Metro sec-tion delivers the New York news that matters. The special features of the *Times* provide intriguing insights into city life, and the Friday edition is invaluable for its listings of weekend events and activities. The Sunday edition, particularly as the Christmas-shopping season begins to advance, becomes, literally, a heavyweight as its pages fill with ever more tempting advertisements. While the city once had several flourishing dailies, there has been a general falling off in newspaper readership that has left the *New York Times* as a virtual monopoly when it comes to the serious-minded reader.

While the *Times* is regarded as politically liberal, the tabloid *New York Post* is the home of conservative reaction, despite having some sharp columnists. The Page Six gossip column (which may not be on page 6) is avidly read. New Yorkers who hate the *Post*'s politics but love tabloid headlines turn instead to the *Daily News*. The *Daily News* has built its reputation on well-written racy stories which match its famously racy headlines. It can be relied upon to reveal the most heinous of crimes and the juiciest of scandals.

The weekly *Village Voice* began in the mid-1950s as an alternative paper (author Norman Mailer was one of its co-founders) and is now as much a part of the city as the Empire State Building. It explores city politics and fringe issues with relish and carries comprehensive arts and entertainment listings. However, the *Voice* faces competition from other weeklies such as the entertaining, easier-to-read and better presented *New York Press*, the smaller *Time Out New York*, with comprehensive listings and sharp, compact reviews, and the *New York Observer* with its engaging news, features and arts reviews.

Magazines Appearing in weekly editions, the *New York* magazine is a glossy celebration of the New York lifestyle and has an extensive events-listing section. The *New Yorker*, also published weekly, is noted for long, detailed articles written by literary heavyweights. The *New Yorker* is hardly light reading, although there are many who buy it solely for its thoughtful film reviews, its cartoons and its humour columns.

Free publications Many free publications are found in New York's shops, restaurants, bars and hotel lobbies, and in special bins around the city. Some specialise in particular areas, such as pet care, advancing your career, or the beliefs of the New Age; others are neighbourhood publications such as *The Villager, Resident* and *Tribeca Trib* and well worth reading for gossip and local news. *New York Blade* is a free weekly with news and features of interest to the gay community.

133

A sense of occasion is never lacking at the Metropolitan Opera House: the crystal chandeliers above the auditorium are sucked into the gold-leafed ceiling before a performance

GUIDED TOURS OF LINCOLN CENTER
Hour-long guided tours depart from the concourse level four times daily on weekdays. The anecdote-packed tours weave through the major buildings (except the Metropolitan Opera House; see below), visiting backstage areas and often catching rehearsals in progress (tel: 875-5350). Tours of the Metropolitan Opera House leave from the entrance foyer of the Met, Mon–Fri at 3:45 PM and on Sat at 10 AM (tel: 769-7020).

▶ Lincoln Center for the Performing Arts   151D1

62nd to 66th streets between Columbus and Amsterdam avenues. Subway: 1; 66th Street/Lincoln Center

Parts of the Lincoln Center for the Performing Arts may reflect the less enduring aspects of 1960s design, however, the music and drama staged there is rarely considered unimpressive.

The complex arose in the 1960s as part of a Utopian plan to give New York a single cultural rendezvous point. One element in Lincoln Center's genesis was the decision of the New York Philharmonic, faced with what seemed likely to be the imminent destruction of Carnegie Hall, to seek a home of its own. Philharmonic Hall was completed here in 1962, changing its name in 1973 to Avery Fisher Hall in honour of the man who parted with $10 million to improve its atrocious acoustics (not completely brought up to scratch until the 1980s).

The Philharmonic's search for new premises coincided with that of the Metropolitan Opera; the 10-storey **Metropolitan Opera House** (tel: 362-6000) now rises boldly above the plaza, two enormous Marc Chagall murals visible through its windows.

Home of the New York State City Opera and New York City Ballet, the **New York State Theater** (tel: 870-5570), designed by Philip Johnston, was successfully remodelled in the 1980s. Two of the better 1960s contributions are Eero Saarinen's **Vivian Beaumont Theater** (tel: 239-6200), and the neighbouring **New York Public Library for the Performing Arts** (tel: 876-1630), from the firm of Skidmore, Owings and Merrill. The library holds 50,000 tomes and has three galleries for temporary exhibitions.

On the north side of the complex is the world-famous Juilliard School, which numbers violinist Itzhak Perlman and actor William Hurt among its alumni. Beside the school, **Alice Tully Hall** (tel: 875-5050) provides a refreshingly intimate and acoustically brilliant home for the Lincoln Center Chamber Music Society – and for free concerts given by students, which usually take place on Wednesday lunchtimes.

►► Little Italy

87B2

Both Italian and not very large, Little Italy has had its boundaries steadily eroded by the expansion of Chinatown and by the drift of its original inhabitants to Italian enclaves in the Outer Boroughs. Between 1890 and 1924, however, 145,000 migrants from Sicily and southern mainland Italy settled here, in an area between Houston and Canal streets.

After years of decline the area is now showing signs of gentrification with shops and restaurants spreading from SoHo and the East Village into its northern edge, now dubbed **NoLiTa** (north Little Italy). Many of the few thousand Italians remaining in the neighbourhood are employed in the restaurants, cafés and bakeries along Grand and Mulberry streets. The food is good but far from cheap, and the cost-wise way to take in Little Italy's atmosphere is with a cappuccino at an outdoor table.

The closest the district comes to a genuine Italian landmark is **Umberto's Clam House** (129 Mulberry Street), which acquired fame for all the wrong reasons in 1972, when, in settlement of a gangland feud, "Crazy" Joe Gallo was shot while dining on a seafood supper.

The local Irish, who predated the Italians, had their spiritual needs fulfilled by what is now **"Old" St Patrick's Cathedral** (264 Mulberry Street; tel: 226-8075; Open daily 7–8:45). The city's earliest Gothic-style building, it lost its original façade in an 1866 fire and was demoted to a parish church after a new St Patrick's Cathedral was consecrated in Midtown Manhattan in 1879.

Take a look at the **Old Police Headquarters** at 240 Centre Street. This Renaissance palace, topped by a green dome, was an immeasurably imposing symbol of law and order when it arose in the midst of one of the city's most crime-ridden districts in 1909.

Walk on to the **Puck Building** at 295–307 Lafayette Street. This was completed in 1886 to house the *Puck* satirical magazine and, with its deliriously complex red brickwork, was instantly revered as a prime example of New York commercial design.

FESTIVAL OF ST GENNARO

Each September, Little Italy's Mulberry Street is lined by makeshift stalls selling homemade sausage, calzone and other Italian specialities (plus an increasing number of Chinese ones) and jumps to the sound of marching bands in a two-week celebration of the Feast of St Gennaro. The religious aspect of the festival, honouring the patron saint of Naples, is evident as a likeness of the saint is carried along the streets and showered with dollar bills. In 1995, the festival was almost cancelled following allegations that most of the estimated $10 million raised by the event went to one of New York's Italian crime families. Mayor Giuliani refused to licence stallholders until guarantees were made that the proceeds would reach charities.

135

The tenements of Little Italy. Many of them have a restaurant or a café at street level – worth a stop at any time for a cappuccino, ice-cream or a pizza

Italians first arrived in large numbers in New York during the 1880s. Through a combination of hard work, traditional values and business acumen, the Italian community had become sufficiently prosperous to take the helm of the city by the 1940s.

A refuge for Italian liberals and revolutionaries through the 19th century, New York's first Italian neighbourhood was on Bleecker Street during the 1860s. Its population was chiefly made up of sophisticated northerners. By contrast, the grinding poverty of rural southern Italy triggered the massive influx of the late 1800s, and 145,000 people were soon packed into the tenements of what became, and still is, Little Italy.

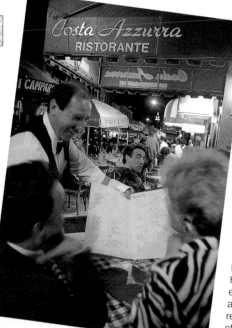

Many Italians work in the restaurant industry, providing New Yorkers and visitors alike with pasta, pizza and other universally popular specialities

Exploitation of immigrants

Speaking little or no English, these new arrivals were exploited, not least by their fellow countrymen who had been in the US long enough to learn the language yet who still knew enough about traditional Italian values to overwork and underpay the immigrants.

Little Italy's men built New York's sewers and subways and its women worked in garment industry sweatshops. Any spare money was sent home to their villages. Many Italians had escaped Little Italy for East Harlem by the 1910s, and by the 1940s had become wealthy enough to move to suburban areas in the Outer Boroughs.

Rising fortunes It was from East Harlem that Fiorello La Guardia emerged. This Protestant Italian son of a Jewish mother was destined to be remembered as the best mayor the city of New York ever had. La Guardia's rise was a symbol of the assimilation of Italian-Americans into city politics, a sphere where they replaced the Irish as the dominant ethnic group.

With descendants of the first Italian-Americans excelling in every walk of New York life, a new wave of immigrants appeared almost unnoticed during the prosperous 1980s. In contrast to the Italian arrivals of a century or more earlier, these Italians were affluent and stylish. They moved into the Upper East Side and opened the up-market boutiques and critically acclaimed Italian restaurants that won the hearts and wallets of New Yorkers who could afford to shop and eat in them.

▶ ▶ ▶ Lower East Side   *IFCB3*

Don't come to the Lower East Side expecting epoch-making architecture, fashionable faces, glamourous boutiques or expense-account restaurants. While new bars and boutiques are making in-roads, this is still downbeat New York with few pretensions. It is traditionally the first stop for newly arrived immigrants from around the world whose priority is to work hard and earn enough money to move on.

The first to arrive in the Lower East Side were the Irish, fleeing their homeland's famine in the mid-1800s. They were followed by successive waves of German and Eastern European immigrants, including the two million Jews who turned the Lower East Side into the world's largest Jewish community.

Living in windowless rooms in overcrowded tenements and often working in sweatshops for breadline wages, the immigrants nonetheless founded cultural institutions and places of worship and established the educational organisations that were to make their children's lives easier than their own.

The 1924 tightening of immigration laws slowed the European influx into the Lower East Side, although by then its more successful inhabitants had moved on and established ethnic pockets elsewhere, and it was to these districts that new arrivals headed.

With land here yet to become valuable, many Lower East Side tenements remain, as do the delis, garment and jewellery shops on which the first locals made their money. Nowadays, the owners are likely to be Indian or Korean, representing the latest waves of immigration.

Less immediately obvious to outsiders are the Lower East Side's Caribbean immigrants, including the many Puerto Ricans who dominate a broad area east of Essex Street and spill north across Houston Street into Alphabet City (see page 60).

It is the shops and their heavily discounted prices that bring most visitors to the Lower East Side. The area is at its busiest on Sundays when bargain-hunting New Yorkers descend on the narrow streets off Delancey Street

TENEMENT LIFE: THE ANNUAL MOVE
Few Lower East Siders ever stayed in a particular tenement for longer than they had to, and the offer of a free month's rent in return for a year's tenancy was usually sufficient inducement for tenement dwellers to up stakes and move every 12 months. It also became common for entire families to move back and forth across the same street, often moving in and out of the same tenements many times at yearly intervals.

137

For vast stocks of cut-price clothing, the shops and stalls of Orchard Street, at the heart of Jewish New York on the Lower East Side, are hard to beat

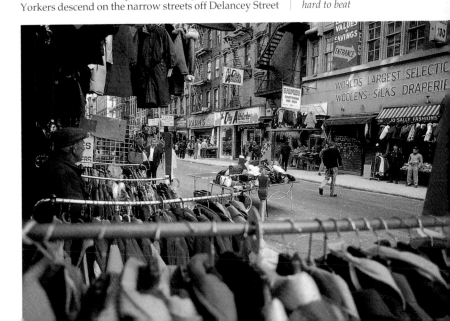

HOW THE OTHER HALF LIVED

Photographs and text by Jacob Riis, published as *How the Other Half Lives* in 1894, focused attention on the grim realities of everyday life in the Lower East Side and were instrumental in bringing about laws improving housing and working conditions. Nonetheless, for most Lower East Side residents, the only real escape was to save enough money for a move to Brooklyn, the Bronx or Queens.

WALKING TOURS

The Lower East Side Tenement Museum organises various walking tours, each concentrating on a specific facet of Lower East Side life – such as ethnic heritage, the lives of women, tenement architecture and the exploits of New York's earliest street gangs. The walks are not cheap but they are enjoyable and informative. For details and reservations, tel: 431-0233.

Typical Lower East Side tenements on Delancey Street. Buildings like these sprang up in the 19th century to house newly arrived immigrants – often in very overcrowded and unhealthy conditions

for some of the biggest clothing discounts to be found in the city. The crush is fiercest outside the garment shops lining **Orchard Street▶**. When the crowds become overwhelming, explore the marginally less busy neighbouring streets such as Allen, Grand and Essex.

The tumult of Sundays is not repeated during the week, when the streets are much quieter – and actually rather dull. An exception to this is the **Essex Street Market▶**, where Lower East Siders buy their fresh meat, vegetables and fruit.

The current ethnic mix of the area is evident in the conversations carried out here in Yiddish, Spanish and Chinese – and in the plantains and bean sprouts sitting alongside the Jewish staples. The market is closed on Sundays. If you plan a weekend visit, it is useful to bear in mind also that many shops are closed on Saturdays in observance of the Jewish Sabbath.

After shopping, taking in the atmosphere and sampling fresh-made knishes (doughy pastries filled with meat or potatoes) from one of several dozen Jewish bakeries, be sure to visit the **Lower East Side Tenement Museum▶▶▶** (97 Orchard Street; tel: 431-0233; *Open daily 11–5. Admission: inexpensive.* Guided tours are available Apr–Dec) which is situated in a six-storey tenement that was built in 1863 and housed 11,000 people over a 70-year period.

The museum provides a fascinating background to Lower East Side life and reveals countless illuminating facts about the deprivations of tenement living, at least for those tenement dwellers of an earlier age. The upper floors have been re-created to show the conditions that the house's tenants endured.

Since 1654, when 23 Sephardic Jews deported from Brazil landed in New York and resisted the Dutch governor's attempts to remove them, the Jewish community has shaped the character of New York life. The city's Jewish population has given the world everything from bagels to Irving Berlin.

Established and respected in the commercial life of colonial America, the Sephardic community – which traces its origins back to Moorish Spain – continued to flourish after the American Revolution.

In the 1830s, arrivals from Germany, the Ashkenazy – who had a different set of Jewish traditions – began looking for new opportunities in the city.

Germans and Russians Assisted by mutual aid societies, the Germans settled in the Lower East Side and were soon establishing the area's jewellery and garment industries. Such businesses employed other Ashkenazy: Russian Jews who arrived during the late 1800s, fleeing the pogroms of Tsar Alexander III. For the most part, these Russians shunned the charity offered by the German Jewish aid societies and formed their own self-help organisations. In the garment industry sweatshops, the Russians formed powerful labour unions.

The Ashkenazy immigrants also brought a rich cultural life to the Lower East Side, particularly with the Yiddish theatres in an area which became known as the "Yiddish Rialto". Although the Yiddish theatre began with vaudeville and farce, the arrival of Jacob Gordin, a leading Russian playwright, helped it develop serious drama and stage works by the likes of Norwegian playwright Henrik Ibsen and Russian playwright Maxim Gorky. Future stars such as Walter Matthau and Edward G Robinson cut their teeth before the lively Yiddish theatre audiences. At the same time, the smoke-filled Lower East Side cafés became centres of political and literary debate, as well as the venues for closely fought chess matches.

Some anti-Semitism was encountered, but New York immigrants never suffered the hostilities that had been their fate in Europe, and Jewish culture soon became deeply embedded in New York life.

Later arrivals The Lower East Side was still the first area of settlement for poor Sephardic arrivals from Turkey, Greece and Syria during the Balkan Wars of the 1910s. By the 1930s, however, Europeans fleeing the rise of Nazism were able to move directly into comfortable Jewish enclaves established in the Upper West Side and the Outer Boroughs.

In the 1970s, Soviet Jews began settling in Brooklyn's Brighton Beach. Today, the most conspicuous aspects of New York's Jewish community are seen in areas dominated by ultra-orthodox sects, such as the Satmarers and Lubavitchers.

Black hats (fur trimming denotes a rabbi) and matching long coats make men belonging to the rigidly orthodox Satmar sect instantly recognisable

Many visitors come to New York for no reason other than to shop. Once the designer outlets and the big-name department stores have been exhausted, however, the attention of the serious shopper turns to the city's flea markets and second-hand shops – where the quest for that elusive item at a giveaway price can bring hours of sheer pleasure to many.

THRIFT SHOPS

The intrepid bargain-hunter might not want to leave New York without delving into at least a few of its thrift shops. Often linked to a church and run by volunteer labour with the proceeds going to charity, thrift shops are filled with cast-off clothing, household objects, books and other items. Of particular note are the Upper East Side thrift shops that are run by prominent charities and attract donations from the moneyed neighbourhood residents. These sprawling stores sell everything from fine furniture to up-market clothing to costume jewellery. Try your luck at **Memorial Sloane-Kettering Thrift Shop** (1440 Third Avenue at 86th Street), **Housing Works** (202 East 77th Street, between Second and Third avenues), **Spence-Chapin Thrift Shop** (1473 Third Avenue between 83rd and 84th streets) and **Cancer Care Thrift Shop** (1480 Third Avenue at 84th Street). For a full list, consult the *Yellow Pages*.

Flea markets Wherever the New York sidewalk is wide enough you are likely to find an impromptu flea market. The merchandise will probably range from out-and-out junk to stolen goods (often with fake designer labels). Resist temptation and instead visit one of the city's four main official flea markets, where better fare turns up.

Every weekend between March and December, the **Annex Antiques Fair and Flea Market** (Sixth Avenue between 24th and 26th streets) features a varied stash of bric-a-brac, clothing and jewellery. The quality is highly variable, but a browse can be worthwhile. Nearby is the **Chelsea Antiques** building (110 West 25th Street), where vendors sell everything from exquisite jewels to novelty items. Next door is the **Chelsea Antiques Garage** (112 West 25th Street), a weekend emporium of fine and mediocre used goods.

Prices are higher at the Saturday **Greenwich Village Flea Market** (Greenwich Street at Charles Street), although this small market merits a visit if you are exploring the neighbourhood.

On Sunday, the **Green Flea Indoor/Outdoor Market** (Columbus Avenue between 76th and 77th streets) is a larger and somewhat more commercial affair, with clothing, jewellery, ornaments and furniture. On Saturday, the same market can be found at 67th Street, between First and York avenues.

Books Not only do they love bargains, New Yorkers also love to read. Spend a whole day browsing in the **Strand Book Store** (Broadway at 12th Street) and you will barely make an impression on its 13km of shelves; the stocks range from dog-eared paperback best-sellers to discarded review copies of pristine hardbacks – all sold for a fraction of their original price.

Much smaller but equally interesting, the intimate **Bleecker Street Books** (350 Bleecker Street) carries general-interest subjects. By contrast, a massive, unclassified clutter of paperbacks fills **Ruby's Book Sale** (119 Chambers Street), where you might also be tempted by piles of vintage magazines.

Clothing The city's more affluent elements may shop for clothes among the designer-name shops that proliferate in Midtown Manhattan, but the sartorially adventurous – and those in search of a bargain – target the array of vintage clothing shops downtown in Greenwich Village and SoHo.

Left: you will find plenty of junk (and, just possibly, a bargain or two) on sale in Canal Street

It is hard not to be overwhelmed by the sheer volume of print at the Strand Book Store, which claims to be the world's largest second-hand bookshop

The enormous stocks of **Antique Boutique** (712–714 Broadway) have plenty to keep the vintage-clothes fanatic engaged, although dedicated bargain-hunters might be better served by a search through the racks at **Stella Dallas** (218 Thompson Street) or **Cheap Jack's** (Broadway between 13th and 14th streets).

Clothes of the 1950s are the specialities – though far from the total extent – of the reasonably priced stock at **Love Saves the Day** (119 Second Avenue at East 7th Street), while **The Family Jewels** (832 Sixth Avenue at 29th Street) carries everything from 1920s evening gowns to 1960s miniskirts, along with an eclectic mix of hats, purses and shoes. **The Quilted Corner** (Fourth Avenue at Twelfth Street), stocks vintage clothes alongside curtains and fabrics. Another happy hunting-ground is **Alice Underground** (Broadway between Broome and Grand streets). Resale shops such as **Ina** (101 Thompson Street and 21 Prince Street) and **Ina Men** (262 Mott Street) sell used haute couture like Prada and Gucci at a fraction of the original price.

CDs and Records New York has a massive audience for all kinds of music, but predominant on the second-hand racks are indie rock and classical rarities. Underground rock music and hot dance cuts are found at **St Mark's Sounds** (20 St Mark's Place). **Stooz Records** (122 East 7th Street) has a stellar supply of new and used records and cds ranging from jazz to hip-hop. **Footlight Records** (113 East Twelfth Street) is the city's prime source of show music, big band records and movie soundtracks, and also has a strong jazz selection. Classical music fans should explore the used records section of **Academy Records** (12 West 18th Street) and seek out the costly rarities at **Gryphon Records** (33 West 72nd Street).

The Met's imposing neo-classical entrance

THE ORIGINAL BUILDING
Few New York façades are as overwhelming in their grandeur as that of the Metropolitan Museum of Art, even though the exuberant neo-classical features that greet visitors to the Met's Fifth Avenue entrance are but one of many additions made to the museum's original body. In 1880, in an effort to blend the planned museum into its setting on the edge of Central Park, its original architects Jacob Wrey Mould and Calvert Vaux (one of the park's co-designers) devised a High Gothic form for the main façade, which then faced the park.

As its collections grew, so too did the museum building. In 1902 it gained the Fifth Avenue entrance that remains in place today. Only a segment of Mould and Vaux's work can still be seen, inside the much more recent Robert Lehman Wing.

▶▶▶ **Metropolitan Museum of Art**   *187C1*
Fifth Avenue and 82nd Street (tel: 535-7710)
Open: Sun, Tue–Thu 9:30–5:15, Fri and Sat 9:30–9.
Admission: moderate donation. Subway: 4, 6; 86th Street
Founded in 1870, the Metropolitan Museum of Art is now among the world's most important museums. Over the years, the collection itself has been greatly swelled by donations from some of America's richest people.

The Met will exhaust you long before you exhaust it. The best way is to think of it as a dozen or so separate museums. Plan your visit bearing in mind that some galleries close in rotation. Schedules are available from the desk. If you cannot decide where to begin, aim first for the European paintings on the second floor.

The Dutch galleries include almost a whole room of Rembrandts and five of Vermeer's 40 extant paintings.

Among the Spanish contributions, focus on El Greco's *View of Toledo*, a striking depiction of the 16th-century religious centre below menacing clouds and Velázquez's *Juan de Pareja*, a portrait of his assistant, painted in the 1640s during his second trip to Italy.

Moving on, the French rooms reveal choice works that span three centuries. Among many striking pieces, George de la Tour's *The Penitent Magdalen* has a rare ability to draw the viewer into its dark corners, and Rousseau's *The Forest in Winter at Sunset* seems to resonate with the primeval forces of nature.

After the changing displays of drawing and photography you reach the 19th-century European painting and sculpture. The galleries of French impressionists and post-impressionists include contributions from Manet, Monet, Cézanne, Gauguin and Renoir, but winning the day are the canvases of Van Gogh, among them *Self-Portrait with a Straw Hat* and the stunning *Cypresses*.

(Continued on page 144)

Detailed explanatory labels are an essential aid to comprehending the Met's Egyptian collections, an otherwise overwhelming stash of 40,000 objects that stretch from pre-dynastic times to the arrival of the Romans.

You don't need to be a scholar to enjoy the collections or the lasting impression they provide of one of the world's greatest civilizations. Some of this colossal stock of treasures were donated by individuals but many come from the Met's own 40-year excavation programme. The single biggest exhibit, the Temple of Dendur (see panel), was a gift from the government of Egypt to the United States in the 1960s.

Although the walk-through Tomb of Perneb – a structure that draws attention as soon as you enter the Egyptian galleries – is a reconstruction, most of the objects on display are originals in such excellent states of preservation that they seem far younger than they really are; their imagery, and their often extravagant use of colour are surprisingly forceful.

The trappings of death The most powerful examples are the numerous brightly decorated coffins, that of the 12th-dynasty (1897–1843 BC) Khnumnakht being particularly notable for its painted eyes – intended to allow the dead to look into the land of the living.

The smaller items, too, can be striking. From the Ptolemaic period (332–30 BC) are a sculptured Anubis, the jackal-headed god of embalming who watched over the dead, and the erect and disconcertingly alert bronze likeness of a cat, used as a coffin for the animal regarded by some ancient Egyptians as sacred. Look also for the detailed 11th-century (2009–1998 BC) house and garden models from the tomb of Mekutra, used to show the layout of the deceased's property.

THE TEMPLE OF DENDUR
Destined to be submerged following the construction of the Aswan Dam, this 2,000-year-old temple was packed up and transported to the museum from its original site on the banks of the Nile. The sandstone temple, a monument to Isis and two Egyptian brothers who drowned in the Nile, was constructed around 15 BC in an effort by the Roman emperor Augustus to win the hearts of the conquered locals. It manages to be both spectacular and disappointing, overwhelmed by the modern gallery that was built to contain it and overlooked, through a vast glass wall, by the trees of Central Park and the penthouses of Fifth Avenue.

143

The Temple of Dendur stands in its own huge gallery

(Continued from page 142)

The American Wing holds an outstanding collection, defining the development of art and design in the US as European traditions were by stages mimicked, absorbed and finally submerged, as American styles developed.

Foremost among the paintings are the finely detailed landscapes of the Hudson River artists, many of which captured the continent's natural breadth and diversity as white settlers steadily forged westwards. A series of period rooms shows the progress of the decorative arts, from Queen Anne armchairs and Philadelphia Chippendale chests of drawers to the unique art nouveau glasswork of Louis Comfort Tiffany, who worked in Long Island, and a large living room that brilliantly expresses the vision of Frank Lloyd Wright's Prairie-style architecture, intended to replicate the wide open spaces of the American heartland in a domestic setting.

Compared with their American counterparts, the European period rooms seem vulgarly stuffed with finery – they include Venetian bedrooms, English interiors by Robert Adam and a Louis XIV state bedchamber. The phenomenal collection of clocks, mirrors and objets d'art lining the adjacent passageways is enough to bring tears to the eyes of any passing antique dealer.

Just steps away, a flamboyantly decorated 16th-century Spanish patio leads to the stairwell and the main entrance to the museum's cache of medieval art. Should medieval art be your abiding interest, make this your first call. Only with a clear head are the 4,000-odd exhibits – from the fall of Rome to the dawn of the Renaissance and from a tiny 3rd-century Alexandrian medallion to a three-storey-high wrought-iron choir screen from 17th-century Spain – likely to fall into a comprehensible pattern.

(Continued on page 146)

MORE MEDIEVAL ART
After a thorough rummage through the Met's main collections, true medievalists might consider forsaking the remainder of the museum for New York's second batch of medieval treasures, displayed at the Met's Cloisters wing (see pages 92–93). Admission tickets are valid at both locations on their day of issue.

One of the less well-known and more restful corners of the labyrinthine Met: the Petrie Sculpture Court

Documenting the origins and spread of Islam through the highly skilled and often beautiful art and craft works that it inspired, the Met's Islamic art collections fill 10 galleries on the second floor: they make up one of the finest such displays in the world.

After a bright introductory room describing the founding of Islam by Muhammad in 622 and the religion's steady outward spread from Mecca, the sides of the initial galleries are lined with dozens of well-stocked display cases, each holding a wonderful assortment of gold and silver pieces such as beads, pendants and plaques from the craftsmen of Egypt, Iran and Syria during the 9th, 10th and 11th centuries.

A side room is even more copiously stocked, holding the enormous collection of ceramics unearthed during the Met's own excavations in Nishapur during the 1930s and 1940s. The Iranian town was a 10th-century centre of Islamic creativity.

Calligraphy and ceramics Flanked by exquisite mosque lamps and perfume sprinklers, another gallery holds a series of leaves from the Koran, demonstrating the development of calligraphy from angular kufic scripts on parchment from 9th-century Egypt to the final refinement of cursive scripts achieved by the oblique cutting of the pen nib in 13th-century Iraq. In the same room stands a 14th-century prayer niche (Mihrab), each of its tiny ceramic tiles individually fired to maximise the glaze and heighten the floral decoration. Since it showed the direction of Mecca, the Mihrab was (and still is) the most important item in a Muslim place of worship.

Small is beautiful Many exquisite examples of 14th-century miniature painting, used in text illustration and characterised by pure and harmonious colours and a strong sense of patterning, are displayed in rotation. The influence of miniature artwork was carried over into Islamic carpet design in later years, and carpets and prayer rugs are the prize exhibits of subsequent galleries. Look especially for the lavish textiles – some decorated with gold leaf – with which Mogul emperors lined their tents. Finally, peer into the Nur ad-Din Room, a reassembled winter reception room typical of a wealthy Syrian home of the early 1700s: heavily decorated wood-panelled walls rise from a patterned marble floor and reach up to stained-glass windows and a sumptuous beamed ceiling.

A 14th-century gilded and enamelled glass mosque lamp

145

PRINTS AND PHOTOGRAPHS

As comprehensive and as engrossing as any other section of the museum, the Met's collections of prints and photography include everything from Rembrandt etchings to Russian constructivist photography. Every print-maker and shutter-clicker that you have ever heard of – and many less familiar – are represented.

(Continued from page 144)

Unlike the tightly packed rooms of the main museum, the newer Lila Acheson Wallace Wing holds spacious, light-soaked galleries and makes an excellent setting for the museum's 20th-century art.

Picasso's portrait of Gertrude Stein is a piece that stands out, though the bulk of the collection is provided by Americans – de Kooning, Lichtenstein, Pollock and O'Keeffe among them. This is not the greatest collection of modern art in New York (for that, see the Museum of Modern Art, pages 158–160), but the side room holding selections from the Berggruen collection of Paul Klee drawings is a definite plus. So, too, is the rooftop sculpture garden, reached by a lift. Its views across Central Park tend to draw your attention away from the sculpture, which is

146

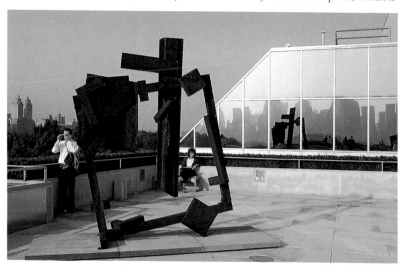

Changing exhibitions of sculpture and sweeping views over Central Park are two good reasons to visit the Met's rooftop

taken from the permanent stock in the museum and exhibited on a rotating basis.

The Michael C Rockefeller Wing, named after the collector who disappeared (presumed drowned) on a trip to Papua New Guinea in 1961, houses the art of Africa, Oceania and the Americas. Of a large, wide-ranging and constantly intriguing assemblage, items from the Asmat tribe of Irian Jaya (the region of Indonesia adjoining Papua New Guinea) are perhaps the most absorbing.

The **Greek and Roman art** collections include Cypriot, Greek and Roman sculpture, painted Greek vases, Roman portrait busts, one of the few surviving Etruscan chariots, and some remarkable wall paintings from a villa at Boscoreale, buried by the AD 79 eruption of Mt. Vesuvius. Another engaging piece is the diminutive *Seated Harp Player,* a marble Cycladic sculpture.

Since the early 1970s, the museum has developed its **Asian Art** holdings into one of the world's best. The collection of early Chinese art includes major Buddhist sculptures, ceramics and jade.

(Continued on page 148)

Bequeathed by a millionaire banker who allegedly spent his youth roaming Europe tracking down masterpieces and telegramming his father for the money to buy his discoveries, the Robert Lehman Collection provides a relaxing interlude from the museum's more popular galleries.

The Lehman Collection's more important paintings, chiefly 14th- and 15th-century Italian works, are all on display on the first floor in reassembled period rooms from the Lehman house at West 54th Street. The various other paintings vie for attention with the temporary exhibitions of drawings at the lower level, including work by Dürer and Rembrandt.

Botticelli Modest in size but immense in its importance, the highlight of the collection is perhaps Botticelli's *Annunciation*, revealing the achievements of late 15th-century Florentine art in the use of perspective. The painting sets a row of classical pillars between a resonant Virgin and the Archangel Gabriel. God's message arrives as light through a doorway, the rays cutting a diagonal path, splitting the painting's horizontal and vertical lines and linking the two figures.

Venetian painters The Bellini family is represented with a Madonna and Child by Jacopo Bellini and an early work by his more famous son, Giovanni, placed at around 1460 and depicting the Madonna and Child in intense poses before an eerily still landscape. From a few years later, another Venetian, Jacometto Veneziano, contributes two portraits: *Alvise Contarini* and *Nun of San Secondo*, intriguing works prefiguring the Venetian portrait style that came to prominence during the 1500s.

Giovanni da Paolo Among a strong complement of Sienese works, da Paolo's *Expulsion from Paradise* stands out, not least for its lively use of colour. The painting shows God soaring above an intensely vibrant constellation, pointing a finger at a barren Earth – the destination for a spindly Adam and Eve who are being shooed out of Eden by a nervous angel.

Another interesting Sienese contribution in the Lehman pavilion is the painting, *Temptation of Saint Anthony Abbot*, credited to the Osservanza Master.

FRENCH WORKS
The collection's 19th-century French paintings are less inspired despite bearing famous names: Monet's unusually airy *Landscape near Zaandam* is worth a look, as are *Promenade among the Olive Trees* (above) by Matisse, and Cézanne's *House behind the Trees on the Road to Tholonet* and *Girl Bathing*.

Jacopo Bellini's Madonna and Child

EATING AND DRINKING AT THE MET

A thorough exploration of the Met calls for great stamina, and even if you have consumed a hearty breakfast before arriving, you will be in need of further nourishment well before it is time to leave.

On the museum's first floor, near the entrance to the Michael C Rockefeller Wing, a spacious atrium holds a self-service cafeteria, with a choice of hot and cold dishes at reasonable prices, and a slightly more expensive waiter-service restaurant.

If you are only pretending to visit the museum – or its size simply becomes too much to bear – you could while away the day over a glass or two of something deliciously tempting at the atrium's bar.

Figures and figurative art: visitors and exhibits at the Metropolitan Museum of Art

(Continued from page 146)

Astor Court, a re-creation of a Ming-era scholar's garden in Soochow built by craftsmen from that city, is a centre for traditional garden architecture.

The Japanese collections span thousands of years but their strongest pieces are undoubtedly the wonderful screen paintings of the Edo period, when years of peace and stability enabled great blossoming of artistic talent: Ogata Korin's *Waves* is just one eye-catching example.

The Met has a couple of off-beat departments that – though not designed for the purpose – might well come as a godsend if you have young minds to keep occupied.

The Musical Instruments galleries house 4,000 weird, wonderful, and sometimes priceless tune-making devices. Among the displays, look for the remarkably unattractive legs of the world's oldest existing piano – dated 1720 and a product of the workshops of Bartolommeo Cristofori – and a Stradivari violin made in 1691 which has been restored to its original appearance.

Strange instruments are plentiful, such as the 19th-century Indian mayuri, a kind of bowed sitar in the shape of a peacock, and a Native American shaman rattle, its carved animal emblem intended to symbolise the transfer of magical power from the spirits to the shaman.

Though it gets comparatively scant attention from the public, the Met's Arms and Armor collection is among the best of its kind to be found. Close study of the massed rows of suits of armour, from the 15th century onwards, reveals the high level of artistic flair and craftsmanship that went into the creation of battle apparel.

In temporary exhibitions, the **Costume Institute** displays selected parts of its enormous wardrobe of 60,000 items – from every corner of the world – of clothing and accessories, spanning everything from 19th-century Parisian ballgowns and Mary Quant mini-skirts to Korean bridal gowns and African tribal wear. Items from the US include 1940s clothing and 1920s "flapper" attire.

▶▶▶ Midtown Manhattan   *IFCD2*

Midtown Manhattan is the New York of popular imagination: a place where battalions of office-workers march along packed sidewalks to the sounds of wailing police sirens and bumper-to-bumper traffic, as street vendors dispense hot dogs and pretzels in the shadows of the striking high-rise buildings.

It is here that many of New York's main attractions are found – the Empire State Building, the United Nations complex, Rockefeller Center, St Patrick's Cathedral, the Chrysler Building, the Museum of Modern Art, Grand Central Terminal, Times Square and the Broadway theatre district, as well as a number of major department stores such as Macy's and Bloomingdale's – all of which are detailed elsewhere in this book and explored by the walks on page 150.

▶▶▶ Murray Hill, Gramercy and Flatiron   *IFCD3*

Murray Hill and neighbouring Gramercy, north of 14th Street and east of Fifth Avenue, retain much of the refined ambience that made them fashionable addresses for the well-to-do of the late 1800s. Spared the relentless bustle of much of Manhattan, a wealthy mood remains despite many of the orginal brownstones being replaced by comfortable apartment buildings. Just across Fifth Avenue from Gramercy is the trendier, resurgent Flatiron District, while **Union Square▶** (see page 183) can be found on the area's southern fringe.

Just east along 14th Street, the offices of Consolidated Edison – the firm responsible for providing New York's power supply – fill a building notable at night for its illuminated façade and clock tower and by day for its **Energy Museum▶** (tel: 460-6244; *Open* Tue–Sat 9–5. *Admission free*), which records the triumph of Thomas Edison in electrifying the city. Audiovisual displays explain the vine-like entwinements of pipes and cables beneath a typical New York street.

(Continued on page 152)

Stroll through the vast skyscapers of Midtown and past the famous Macy's department store

THE ARMORY SHOW
The 69th Regiment Armory, on Lexington Avenue between 25th and 26th streets, is not the only National Guard barracks to be modelled on a medieval fortress, but it is the only one to have staged the legendary Armory Show of 1913, the first exhibition of modern European art in a country then still obsessed with traditional landscapes and portraiture. The work of Marcel Duchamp and others shocked critics and public alike and the Armory Show's effect on American art was profound. A small plaque on the Armory's façade notes the historic event.

Midtown Manhattan landmarks

Beginning at the Empire State Building and finishing at the United Nations complex, this walk passes seven decades' worth of landmark New York architecture.

After visiting the **Empire State Building** (pages 100–102), continue north along Fifth Avenue to the **New York Public Library** (page 168), its entrance set back from the street and guarded by sculptured lions. Behind

the library is the restored **Bryant Park**, landscaped in 1934. Walk east along 42nd Street to Grand Central Terminal (pages 166–167) and the **Philip Morris Headquarters**, on Park Avenue, a modern building with a gallery holding exhibits from the Whitney Museum of American Art.

Further east on 42nd Street, pass through the cast bronze doors of the 1923 **Bowery Savings Bank** (now the Home Savings Bank of America) to see the lavish Romanesque interior. Close by, note the stunning art deco bas-reliefs by Edward Trumbull on the exterior of the **Chanin Building**. Ahead are the unmistakable **Chrysler Building** (page 89) and **Daily News Building** (page 95), while turning north on First Avenue reveals the **United Nations** complex (page 184).

Midtown churches and museums

Beginning and ending at Rockefeller Center, this walk includes several Midtown churches, the **Museum of Modern Art** (pages 158–160), and the **American Craft Museum** (page 62).

Facing **Rockefeller Center** (pages 173–174) across Fifth Avenue, the twin-spired **St Patrick's Cathedral** was completed in 1878 in rich, carved Gothic form. Inside, the chapels and shrines glow with candlelight.

On East 50th Street, the art deco **Waldorf-Astoria Hotel** has accommodated royalty and every US president since its opening in 1931. Inside, admire the art deco interior and the lobby shops that cater to every whim of the well-heeled traveller. Nearby, the slim octagonal brick tower of the **General Electric Building** is another art deco landmark. Byzantine-style **St Bartholomew's Church** boasts a splendid triple-arched entrance portal and a mighty dome which adds to the interior's sense of airyness. Back on Fifth Avenue, a single corner tower gives **St Thomas' Episcopal Church** a disjointed look, but don't miss the striking reredos inside. The architect, Bertram Goodhue, also designed St Bartholomew's and had a hand in several other noted Manhattan churches.

View of St Patrick's Cathedral and the Olympic Tower

MIDTOWN MANHATTAN

Madison Square Park: the square holds several tributes to notable figures in US history

(Continued from page 149)

It was from the mid-1800s that the city's élite began to relocate from Greenwich Village into the new areas of Murray Hill and Gramercy. Particularly prominent citizens favoured elegent brownstones overlooking **Gramercy Park► ►**. Between 20th and 21st streets, the park was the centre-piece of a town plan modelled on the great, aristocratic squares of London. Still the city's only private park, local residents are given a key in return for an annual fee towards its upkeep. Amid the park's luxuriant foliage, and visible through its iron railings, are several statues including that of actor Edwin Booth in the role of Hamlet.

It was Booth, one of the leading tragic actors of his time (and brother of John Wilkes Booth, assassin of Abraham Lincoln), who founded the influential **Players Club►** at 16 Gramercy Park South. Designed by noted architect Stanford White, the building is easily spotted by the ornamental theatrical masks decorating its entrance.

The co-designer of Central Park, Calvert Vaux, added the Ruskin-influenced Gothic features to the building next door, now the **National Arts Club** but earlier occupied by Samuel Tilden, governor of New York from 1874. Tilden's stand against corruption in New York public life did not alleviate his fears of public insurrection: he had a secret passageway set under the house to hasten his escape if angry mobs barricaded the entrance and rolling steel barriers set behind the windows.

Theatrical connections continue north into **Murray Hill►**. When asked to provide a funeral for an actor in 1870, one Murray Hill church representative said "we don't accept actors but there's a little church around the corner that does". From then on, the 1849 Church of the Transfiguration, on 29th Street just off Fifth Avenue, became better known as the **Little Church Around the Corner► ►**, serving New York thespians in spiritual need.

BASEBALL'S BIRTHPLACE
Baseball was introduced to the US in 1842, but not until 1845 did a group of enthusiasts – who had been playing the game regularly at what later became Madison Square Park – band together to create a fixed set of rules and the first baseball club, the Knickerbocker Club. As baseball spread in popularity across the country, it was known at first as the "New York Game".

A picturesque garden fronts the church, and the intimate interior holds several memorials to actors.

Stylish hotels and a smattering of elegant restaurants tucked into quiet residential streets characterise the bulk of Murray Hill, where a rare surviving brownstone is the grand home and library of financier J Pierpont Morgan (see page 169).

To the west of Murray Hill at the foot of Madison Avenue, **Madison Square Park▶** is dotted with 19th-century statuary and overlooked by the unmistakeable 1909 clocktower of the Metropolitan Life Insurance Building. The park was the original site of Madison Square Garden, a venue for entertainment and sports events up until the 1920s. Its much larger namesake now looms between Seventh and Eighth avenues.

Near the park, the Flatiron Building (see page 106) gives its name to the surrounding Flatiron District. This area was dubbed "Silicon Alley" during the 1990s when it gained many of the city's internet and multi-media companies, along with some up and coming publishers and advertising companies. These, along with a batch of new restaurants and shops, have helped turn a once nondescript neighbourhood into one of Manhattan's most fashionable few blocks.

THE ALGONQUIN HOTEL
In the Oak Room of the Algonquin Hotel at 59 West 44th Street stands a round table that, from 1919, became *the* Round Table. Around it a legendary coterie of critics, playwrights and journalists engaged in sparkling wit and repartee. The exchanges were reported in Franklin P Adams' widely read column in the *New York World* magazine.

Cheek-by-jowl Midtown skyscrapers – with a view!

153

It was an Irishman, Thomas Dongan, who gave his name to the charter of 1686 that created New York's modern system of administration. As governor of a British colony, however, Dongan probably never expected that in years to come his countrymen would flock to New York to free themselves of British oppression and take a controlling grip on New York life.

THE UNWELCOME IRISH

Most of the large numbers of penniless Irish that arrived in the city during the 1800s were forced to occupy the worst areas, and some turned to petty crime in order to make a living. In so doing, they incurred the wrath of many long-established New Yorkers. Some turned against Irish immigrants as a whole. The auctioneer and one-time city mayor Philip Hone wrote of New York's Irish population: "they increase our taxes, eat our bread and encumber our streets, and not one in twenty is competent to keep himself".

Under British rule, Protestant and Catholic Irish were established in professional life in New York, but – mindful of British treatment of the Irish at home – both groups embraced the American Revolution and saw their chance to build a truly democratic, self-governing society.

Fall and rise The potato famines brought tens of thousands of Irish into New York during the 1800s. They arrived on the "Irish berths": cramped, airless sections of ships where disease was rife, and once ashore, the penniless Irish – faced with residents' growing anti-Catholic feeling – were forced to occupy crowded rooms, often in atrocious conditions.

By 1860, Irish Catholics made up a quarter of the city's population and were the backbone of the police force, fire-fighting teams and building trades. Irish organis-ational skills created powerful unions and paved the way for Irish domination of New York's entire administrative machine from the 1870s to the 1940s.

Church and tavern One symbol of the Irish Catholic ascendancy in New York was the building of St Patrick's Cathedral in 1878. But while the church was important in Irish immigrant life, so too was the tavern. A first stop for new arrivals, taverns were informal clearing-houses for jobs. Some served free lunches to Irish workmen.

Irish-Americans are still strongly represented in New York public office. New York's last outpost of authentic Irish culture is Bainbridge, in the Bronx. First settled in the 1840s by Irishmen who saw its enticing greenery while working on the Harlem Railroad, Bainbridge's bars are the genuine article, without an ornamental leprechaun or bottle of green beer in sight.

St Patrick's Day (17 March) sees the city's biggest street parade, along Fifth Avenue

▶ Museum for African Art   *113A3*

Broadway between Houston and Prince streets (tel: 966-1313)
Open: Tue–Fri 10:30–5:30, Sat and Sun 12–6. Admission:
inexpensive. Subway: N, R, 6; Prince Street or Spring Street
Arts and crafts from sub-Saharan Africa form the core of the temporary exhibitions staged in this highly respected museum, one of the US's major spaces for African art, along with the Smithsonian Institution. Far from being static displays, the shows frequently take provocative directions.

▶ Museum of American Financial History   *104B2*

Broadway at Bowling Green (tel: 908-4110)
Open: Mon–Fri 11:30–2:30. Admission free.
Subway: 4; Bowling Green
This one-room collection need not detain you long, but it is an appropriate stop when touring the Financial

Woven hangings at the Museum of American Folk Art – a showcase for the talents of craftspeople from all over the Americas

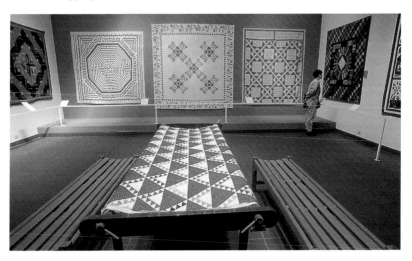

District. Inside the former Standard Oil Building, once presided over by multimillionaire John D Rockefeller, the changing exhibitions explore diverse historical avenues in the US economy.

▶▶ Museum of American Folk Art   *151D1*

45 West 53rd Street (tel: 265-1040)
Open: Tue–Thu, Sat 10–6, Fri 10–8. Admission moderate
Subway: E, F; Fifth Avenue
From toys and weather vanes to carved walking sticks and gravestone rubbings, the collections of the Museum of American Folk Art are drawn from the output of artists and craftspeople – many of them revered figures within their own communities – from all over the Americas. Be it Mexican wooden animal figures or Navajo blankets, the work on display is frequently of an exceptionally high standard and decorated with symbolic detail that only becomes apparent with close inspection.

In a city that often seems focused on honouring the art of Europe, these exhibitions of indigenous American culture are very welcome, and they are now housed in one of New York's most striking contemporary buildings.

The Museum of the City of New York, whose dignified grand entrance on Fifth Avenue is the gateway to a mixed collection charting aspects of the Big Apple through the ages

THE NEW YORK ACADEMY OF MEDICINE
A short walk from the Museum of the City of New York is the New York Academy of Medicine (2 East 103rd Street; tel: 822-7200), which occupies a 1926 building raised with Byzantine, Italian, and Romanesque features. Inside, the academy's library is open to the public. One reason to drop in might be to view the collection of 4,000 cookbooks (many of them rare), donated by a physician who believed that the key to good health was a nutritious diet. *Open* Mon–Fri 9–5.

SPECIAL EVENTS
The Museum of the City of New York organises numerous special events, including puppet shows for children and classical concerts and lectures for adults. During the spring and fall, the museum also runs four-hour guided walking tours through different sections of the city. For details on any or all of these events, tel: 534-1672.

▶ **Museum of the City of New York**   *IBCA3*
Fifth Avenue at 103rd Street (tel: 534-1672)
Open: Wed–Sat 10–5, Sun 12–5. Admission: moderate
Subway: 6; 96th Street

Chronicling the rise and rise of one of the world's most diverse and colourful cities is no easy task, and while the Museum of the City of New York has its share of interesting bits and pieces from the early years of the great metropolis, it struggles to bring them together with any cohesion. Many of the museum's exhibits seem lost in the spacious innards of this neo-Georgian building.

The devoted history buff will find plenty here to mull over, however. Chronologically, things begin on the third floor with staid dioramas of Native American life in the years leading up to European discovery. Far more intriguing are the earliest maps of the New York area and drawings and paintings from the mid-1600s, thought to be the earliest depictions of what was then the Dutch trading post of Nieuw Amsterdam.

Six undistinguished period interiors give a very general impression of the furnishings – from simple Dutch tables to ornate English colonial cabinets – that stood in New York drawing rooms from the 17th to the early 20th century. Close by, several cases hold a glittering array of New York-made silver tea caddies, tankards and cutlery that graced the kitchens of the city's most illustrious residents from the late 1700s.

A few figureheads and many model ships and boats are the principal pieces in a forgettable room intended to document the city's growth into a major seaport. Take care, though, to look at the paintings – such as Alonzo Chappel's simple but expressive *Bowery on a Rainy Day*, painted in 1849, and another that shows ice-skaters in Central Park during 1865 – that hang on nearby walls and do more to evoke the New York of their period than many of the more valuable exhibits around them.

The museum enjoys its finest moment on the third floor, where a glorious collection of toys (some dating to the mid-1700s) includes a room filled by elaborate three- and four-storey dolls' houses. The dolls, too, are as impressive as the houses and include a specimen of almost every type produced in the US from the late 18th to the mid-19th centuries. The oldest doll is a French-made import dating from 1724.

The Rockefeller Rooms on the museum's fifth floor comprise the master bedroom and dressing room from the mansion purchased in 1884 by John D Rockefeller at West 54th Street – a site which is now consumed by the garden of the Museum of Modern Art. A wealth of intricately carved woodwork with mother-of-pearl inlays inspired by English designer Charles Eastlake, the rooms were the height of fashion in Victorian New York. What is not on view here is the mansion's wonderful Moorish room, which is now to be found in the Brooklyn Museum (see page 79).

Temporary exhibitions fill the first-floor rooms, while the museum's basement is occupied by poorly arranged memorabilia from New York's earliest fire-fighters. The centrepiece is a well-maintained hose-carriage of 1865, but smaller and more revealing pieces fill the surrounding display cases. Among the helmets, lamps, model fire-appliances and press clippings detailing New York's most famous fires and the men who put them out, look for the fire-fighters' ear trumpet – a device intended to improve communication in blazing buildings. When plugged at one end, it also served as a beer-drinking vessel and a handy weapon for when the "fire laddies" (as they were known) gathered for an evening in a tavern.

EL MUSEO DEL BARRIO

A few strides across 104th Street from the Museum of the City of New York, El Museo del Barrio (tel: 831-7272; *Open* Wed–Sun 11–5. *Admission: inexpensive*) is very much a product of its East Harlem environment, evolving from a local school classroom into a museum devoted to the cultures of Latin America, particularly that of Puerto Rico. The small permanent collection of pre-Columbian objects is regularly eclipsed by temporary exhibitions that span paintings, sculpture, video and more, reflecting diverse aspects of Latin American life, past and present.

157

Times change: one of the museum's dioramas shows what New York's East River waterfront looked like in the 1850s

Queuing for a special MoMA exhibition

THE MOMA BUILDING
In 1939, MoMA acquired not only its current home but also what would, on completion, be one of the first international-style buildings in the US. Architects Philip Goodwin and Edward Durrell Stone interrupted the row of brownstones on West 53rd Street's with a façade of marble, tile and glass. The very term "international style" had been coined at a MoMA exhibition in 1932 by Philip Johnson, who was later to oversee several additions to the building, most notably the Sculpture Garden.

Van Gogh's Starry Night

▶▶▶ **Museum of Modern Art**   *151C2*

53rd Street between Fifth and Sixth avenues (tel: 708-9480)
Open: Sat–Tue, Thu 10:30–6, Fri 10:30–8:30.
Admission: moderate. Subway: E, F; Fifth Avenue

Nowhere else in the world will you find a museum so well stocked, so aptly designed to illustrate art's principal movements and trends, or showing so many of the major works of the last 160 years of artistic achievement.

Be it Picasso, Mondrian, Matisse or any number of others whose names are writ large in the history of art, the Museum of Modern Art (MoMA) not only has them but often has some of their most influential works too, including Van Gogh's *Starry Night*, Picasso's *Les Demoiselles d'Avignon* and Pollock's immense and mesmerising *One*.

Since World War II, MoMA has played a pivotal role in defining the way art is assessed, understood and displayed. As New York eclipsed Paris as the centre of the art world, MoMA was uniquely placed to play a leading role. As European artists arrived in New York (destined to have a great impact on the new generation of American artists who helped make the city the dynamic heart of contemporary creative art from the 1940s to the 1960s) so too did their art, not least Picasso's *Guernica* held by the museum on extended loan throughout the Franco dictatorship before it returned to Spain in 1981.

In the late-1990s, however, MoMA began to dramatically change its thinking and, in a major departure from its long-held adherence to a linear, chronological approach to arranging its collections (so large that only around 12 per cent could find space in the museum's airy and well-lit galleries), began undertaking a daring new approach.

The new millennium was marked by the museum with a series of temporary shows collectively titled MoMA 2000. In this, the accent was on thematic exhibitions which mixed artists from different times and cultures and work spanning painting, photography, design, video and multi-media, and room-sized installations. The series was to divide both the critics and the public alike, but seemed to show the museum's future direction, emboldened by a major expansion and renovation project.

Another MoMA strength is the ability to raid its stock – and those of other museums – to mount significant smaller exhibitions. One such, Van Gogh's Postman, displayed portraits and drawings by Van Gogh of the postman Joseph Roulin, who was a friend and major figure in the artist's life during a troubled period.

The museum's apparently radical approach might be seen as entirely in keeping with the ground-breaking early days of the museum, founded in 1929 to "help people enjoy, understand and use the visual arts of our time".

Hard to believe it may be but when MoMA staged its first exhibition, the artists featured – Cézanne, Gauguin, Seurat and Van Gogh – were not represented in any other New York museum. Even the otherwise all-emcompass-ing Metropolitan Museum of Art considered such names

THE SCULPTURE GARDEN (*Currently closed due to building work*) Directly opposite the lobby, and a great place to pass an hour on a sunny afternoon after viewing the interior exhibits, is MoMA's Abby Aldrich Rockefeller Sculpture Garden, filled with an excellent and diverse collection of sculpture. Highlights include Henry Moore's *Family Group*, Picasso's *She Goat* – and Rodin's striking *Memorial to Balzac*, a towering bronze that was rejected by its Parisian commissioning committee in the 1890s.

159

to be too avant-garde. Nonetheless, 47,000 people visited the MoMA exhibition in a single month.

A decade later, MoMA acquired its present site (a gift of the Rockefeller family, one of whom was among the museum's founders) and through the energy of its young director, Alfred H Barr Jr, and the benevolence of a host of millionaire benefactors, steadily became the world's pri-mary repository for many of modern art's most important works, gaining a prestige that few rivals can match.

Acquiring the site of the Dorset Hotel and two town-houses adjacent to the present museum in 1995, MoMA began its building expansion project, expected to be com-pleted in 2004. Architect Yoshio Taniguchi has promised "to transform the Museum of Modern Art into a bold new museum while maintaining its historical, cultural and social context". Among the benefits of the new-look museum will be a doubling of its existing gallery space.

Exhibitions will continue at MoMA's 53rd Street base until summer 2002, at which point they will move to a temporary home in Queens (to be known as MoMA QNS; map reference 48D3), where it will stay until late 2004.

Inside MoMA's 53rd Street building – New York's earliest piece of architecture in the inter-national style and a fitting home for some of the most famous paint-ings and sculptures of the 20th century. Clever design, using plenty of natural light and with space to stand back and relax, allows unhurried appreciation of the exhibits

The highlights of MoMA's collection provide a changing but unfailingly impressive gathering of seminal items that provide a thumbnail sketch of modern art's major twists and turns.

WHAT'S ON AT MOMA

Changing shows can be great news for art-loving New Yorkers but less so for visitors who may have travelled to New York only to find that their favourite artworks are in storage or away on loan. To discover the latest on the building expansion project and find out what exhibitions will be on during your stay, visit visit the museum's web site, www.moma.org, or tel: 708-9480.

160

Europeans Key European works include Van Gogh's much eulogised *Starry Night*, the intense swirls of colour indicative of his painting at Arles in the late 1880s; one of Monet's *Water Lilies* paintings, a study of the subtleties of light and shadow on water where the colours appear to undulate before your eyes; and an example of Matisse's *The Dance*, one of the series of large murals created by the French artist in the early 1930s. Picasso's *Three Women at the Spring* and Braque's *Man With A Guitar* and *Woman with a Mandolin* are formative Cubist statements, while Mondrian's *Broadway Boogie-Woogie* reveals the impact of New York, its jazz rhythms and grid-style streets, on the Dutch artist. Among MoMA's surrealist holdings are Magritte's *The False Mirror* and Dali's *The Persistence of Memory*, painted in 1931 – a landmark in itself as it denoted the first appearance of the soft watches that became Dali's most original and celebrated images.

The Americans The first American modern art movement, abstract expressionism (see pages 128–129) and the so-called New York School is well represented with works by Pollock, particularly *One*, the mightiest of his drip canvases; Rothko's shimmering blocks of colour; and pieces by the Dutch-born De Kooning. As a prime example of gesturism, look for Motherwell's *Elegy to the Spanish Republic*. Partly as a reaction to abstract expressionism came noted works such as Johns' *Flag* and *Target* series, Rausechenburg's bold collages depicting an excessively consumerist sociey, and the comic-strip blow-ups of Lichtenstein.

Allow yourself time whilst you are in the museum to appreciate the works

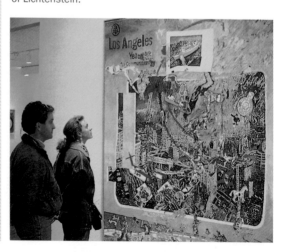

▶▶ Museum of Television and Radio   151C2

*25 West 52nd Street (tel: 621-6800 for daily events, 621-6600
for general information)*
Open: Tue–Sun 12–6, theatres open later.
Admission: inexpensive. Subway: E, F; Fifth Avenue

For serious media students and couch-potatoes alike, the
Museum of Television and Radio is the stuff that dreams
are made of. For almost anyone else, a visit will be a
highly entertaining experience – and a perfect antidote to
the more run-of-the-mill forms of sightseeing. More than
40,000 American television and radio broadcasts from the
1920s to the present are stored here, all of them available
to the public at little more than a flick of a switch. Several
thousand new programmes are added every year.

A number of small screening rooms show selections
from the museum's televisual archive (schedules are
available from the lobby, or tel: 621-6800), while the
headphones in the cosy radio listening room can be
switched to one of five separate channels, each exploring
a different area of broadcasting history – from a landmark
Metropolitan Opera broadcast to a wartime comedy

*A TV addict's dream
come true – the Museum
of Television and Radio
offers your own choice of
viewing at one of around
100 individual video
consoles*

161

show. If you have a special interest you can riffle through
the library's computerised cataloguing system and make
your own selections from the entire collection. Not only
listing television programme titles, the database also carries details of the personnel involved in each production –
a handy resource if you have forgotten who played Thing
in *The Addams Family* or want to discover the real-life
identity of your favourite *Batman* villain.

Once you have made your choice (restricted to two
hours of viewing time), leave the library for the viewing
room, where your selection will be made ready for you
almost immediately (though there may be a three-day
wait for particularly obscure items) for private watching
at one of the video consoles.

Commercials – of which the museum has 10,000 in stock
– feature among the daily screenings. Also on view are
television shows from other countries, from heavyweight
documentaries to vintage episodes of *Monty Python's
Flying Circus*.

THE MUSEUM BUILDING
You may be too eager to
renew your acquaintance-
ship with Perry Mason or
Lou Grant to notice, but the
building that houses the
Museum of Television and
Radio is a curious blend
of classical and modern
styles by architects Philip
Johnson and John Burgee.
With its 16-storey
limestone-clad tower, the
structure has been
described as the world's
first vertical museum.

The advent of art deco coincided with the skyscraper boom that gripped New York during the 1920s, and the new decorative style was seen as the natural accompaniment to the world's most adventurous architecture. Walk around the city and you will find the art deco influence everywhere, from world-famous buildings to fine details of decoration.

ZONING LAWS

In 1915, when the Financial District's Equitable Building rose straight up in the air, robbing adjacent streets and buildings of their sunlight and breezes, the city authorities responded with the US's first set of building regulations – or zoning laws. The Zoning Law of 1916 divided New York into commercial and residential plots; high-rise buildings had to recede as they rose above the street. This greatly affected the architecture of the city for the next 50 years.

Art deco sculpture in Rockefeller Center

Art deco first emerged in 1925 at the Paris Exposition Internationale des Arts Décoratifs, a show intended to highlight the fine skills of French craftsmen at a time when the German Bauhaus was revolutionising the world of the decorative arts.

New York was already aware of the art deco style, however, as the Metropolitan Museum of Art had amassed a collection of the finest European work and inadvertently aided the creation of an American art deco style dubbed "moderne". With the emphasis on overall effect rather than individual craftsmanship, art moderne was tailor-made to the needs of the American market. Mass-produced terracotta and bronze friezes covered with geometric designs and floral patterns, available by mail order, soon began appearing on buildings all over the country.

This new style began to affect interiors, too. Some of New York's finest art deco entranceways and lobbies, such as the Film Center Building (see page 102), are the work of the talented architect Ely Jacques Kahn.

One of the city's earliest art deco buildings was the **New York Telephone Company** (also called the

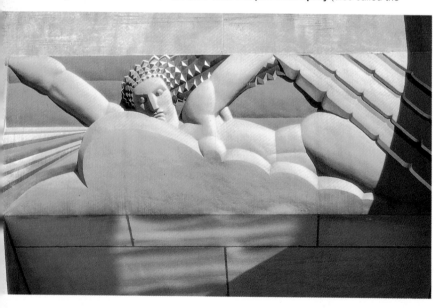

Barclay-Vesey Building, 140 West Street), described by one critic as "Mayan art deco". To get around the constraints imposed by the narrow street, designer Ralph Walker gave the building a series of pedestrian arcades decorated by a cast-concrete frieze cluttered with depictions of bunches of grapes, rabbits, elephant heads, bells and much more.

Chrysler Building The single most spectacular and lastingly impressive art deco building in New York, the Chrysler Building (see page 89) was one of the first buildings to use exposed metal. It rises in a series of cutbacks with each new level marked by a different type of decoration – a brickwork frieze of car wheels and immense winged radiator caps. Its most distinctive feature, however, is the seven-storey dome, which takes the form of a tiered arch with triangular dormer windows encased in chrome steel.

Empire State Building The Chrysler Building's status as the world's tallest building was soon eclipsed by the Empire State Building. Built purely for commercial renting, every inch of the Empire State Building was critical, and consequently the decoration was kept to an absolute minimum – allowing the structure to emerge as a fine specimen of skyscraper art deco at its most restrained and dignified.

Chanin Building Sculptor René Chambellan's façade for the Chanin Building (122 East 42nd Street), which draws the eye away from the nearby Chrysler Building, depicts swooping birds on a bronze band that winds around the building below a terracotta frieze of geometric animal forms. Inside the bronze- and marble-dominated lobby, further bas-reliefs depict the "City of Opportunity" – or New York as it was for the building's owner, Irwin Chanin, a property developer who struck it lucky.

Raymond Hood Destined to become one of the leading architects of Rockefeller Center, Hood used black brick and gold terracotta to emphasise the upright form of the **American Radiator Building** (40th Street between Fifth and Sixth avenues). He later developed this idea with vertical columns of windows and spandrels for the **Daily News Building** (see page 95).

In the former **McGraw-Hill Building** (42nd Street between Eighth and Ninth avenues), with its green and gold terracotta, Hood continued his move towards the International Style, but the building's lobby retains its impressive art deco interior.

With **Rockefeller Center** (pages 173–174), New York art deco had its greatest day. Raymond Hood had a large hand in the centre's showpiece RCA (now GE) Building. At the foot of the building, Paul Manship's golden *Prometheus* sculpture is the first of scores of art deco items decorating the entire complex. Meanwhile, Rockefeller Center's **Radio City Music Hall** takes art deco into another dimension. Its vast and extraordinarily theatrical interior is intended to be just as much a part of the evening's entertainment as the performers appearing on the stage.

The Chrysler Building, resplendent with eagle gargoyles

▶ National Academy of Design   187C1
Fifth Avenue at 89th Street (tel: 369-4880)
Open: Wed and Thu 12–5, Fri 12–6, Sat and Sun 12–5.
Admission: inexpensive. Subway: 4, 6; 86th Street
Founded in 1825 by a group of accomplished artists,
architects, sculptors and engravers – including Samuel
Morse, the artist/inventor, and the creator of Washington
Square's handsome town houses, Ithiel Town – the
National Academy of Design was established with the
intention of becoming an artist-run school and museum.
Selections from the permanent collections are shown in
the upstairs galleries, but one piece you can be certain of
seeing is the sculptured figure of Diana by Anna Hyatt
Huntington, which pivots at the foot of an elegant staircase leading up to the Academy's galleries.

▶▶ National Museum of the   104A2
American Indian
US Custom House, Bowling Green (tel: 514-3700)
Open: daily 10–5. Admission free. Subway: 4; Bowling Green
Exhibits inside the architecturally distinguished US
Custom House (see page 190) are drawn from the many
diverse native cultures of North, South and Central
America. They are presented in such as fashion as to
explain something of the beliefs and lifestyles of the peoples. While many important items have been returned to
the tribes that produced or previously owned them, the
museum retains a hugh quantity of baskets, quilts, pottery and much more, including some of the infamous
treaties that paved the way for European colonisation of
traditionally Native American lands.

164

*A focal point at the
National Academy of
Design: Anna Hyatt
Huntington's statue
of Diana*

▶ New York City Fire Museum   *IFCB2*

278 Spring Street, SoHo (tel: 691-1303)
Open: Tue–Sun 10–4. Admission: inexpensive donation
Subway: 6; Spring Street
It may not be at the top of every New York visitor's itinerary, but the New York City Fire Museum fills three floors with the buckets, hand-pumps, and horse-drawn fire-appliances that saved the city from near-total destruction on more than one occasion. The antiquated carriages are exhibited alongside an impressive collection of hose-pipe nozzles, ladders, axes, tools, fire alarms, extinguishers, uniforms and helmets.

▶ New York City Police Museum   *104A2*

25 Broadway, between Morris Street and Battery Place (tel: 301-4440)
Open: Mon–Fri 10–6, Sat–Sun 10–4. Admission free. Subway: 1; Rector Street, 4, 5; Bowling Green, J, M, Z; Broad Street
Gathered in the grand setting of the 1925 Cunard Building, where passengers of great ocean liners once bought their tickets, are guns, knives, truncheons and mugshots of public enemies that prove that policing the city's streets has rarely been an entirely peaceful affair. Among many gruesome artefacts is the machine gun used by Al Capone's gang to eliminate a rival.

▶▶ New-York Historical Society   *IFCF2*

Central Park West at 77th Street (tel: 873-3400)
Open: Wed–Sun 11–5. Admission: inexpensive.
Subway: 1; 79th Street
Predating all the city's other museums, the New-York Historical Society was founded in 1804 (dating its hyphen) and was uniquely placed to receive the bequests of wealthy New Yorkers. The society has a substantial collection of works, from early portraits of significant New Yorkers to important canvases from the country's first home-grown art movement, the Hudson River School. The society also holds a sizeable Tiffany collection and all extant watercolours in Audubon's *Birds of America* series.

THE GREAT FIRE OF 1835
The temperature in New York City on 16 and 17 December, 1835, was well below freezing, but that did not stop one of the most destructive fires in the city's history from razing 674 buildings on a 5.25 hectare site in and around the Financial District. Crowds arriving from the notorious Five Points slums looted the burned-out buildings and helped the flames engulf many more. With insurance companies enduring the same losses as many of their clients, many of the city's banks and financial institutions were unable to reopen and as a result New York endured galloping inflation for the next two years.

Top: Early equipment at the Fire Museum

In the 1930s, passengers boarding the New York–Chicago early evening service from Grand Central Terminal were, quite literally, given the red carpet treatment. Few then would have thought that just a few decades later the terminal – an architectural tour de force that was dubbed "the gateway to the nation" – would be threatened by cheap air travel and by the rising value of the land on which it stands.

166

GRAND CENTRAL STATION?

Many people, including lifelong New Yorkers, often erroneously refer to Grand Central Terminal as "Grand Central Station". In fact, as trains can only begin or end their journeys there, "terminal" is the correct word to use. The confusion was not helped by an enormously popular radio drama series which began in 1937, set in New York and titled *Grand Central Station* or by the fact that the local post office is, quite correctly, know as Grand Central Station.

Grand Central Terminal was completed in 1913 on a plot of land that then marked New York's northern edge. The land had been purchased by transport magnate Cornelius Vanderbilt (see page 37), who had gained control of all rail routes into New York. After a 10-year period of construction, the station was unveiled to wide public acclaim both as an engineering marvel and as a delight to the eye. It remains one of the world's great railway stations: an enduring symbol of the city.

In the 1960s, the Penn Central Railroad (the company in charge of Grand Central Terminal and previously responsible for the demolition of the original and much-loved Pennsylvania Station) proposed to raise a 55-storey office tower above the terminal, but these shortsighted plans were luckily thwarted by public pressure, and the building eventually became an official New York City landmark (in 1978), gaining lasting protection.

Architectural elegance The terminal's construction was a joint effort. The engineer William Wilgus and the architects Reed & Stem devised the innovative split-level design that allowed for a smooth flow of traffic – either train, subway or pedestrian – into and through the station; Whitney Warren focused on creating the terminal's graceful Beaux-Arts style. Since it was the arrival and departure point for millions of travellers (by 1939, as many people were passing through Grand Central Terminal each year as lived in the entire US), shops, hotels, restaurants and offices opened up in close proximity to the terminal, making the site a prime Midtown Manhattan plot. Many side entrances and maze-like tunnels link the terminal with its surrounding streets and adjacent office towers such as the former Pan Am Building (now the Metropolitan Life Building, see panel on page 183), just to the north.

On the terminal's southern façade you will first see Jules-Félix Coutan's 15m high figures of Mercury, Hercules and Minerva, draping themselves around an American eagle. There is also a bronze likeness of Cornelius Vanderbilt – seemingly counting potential railway passengers as they pass.

The interior Once inside, head for the terminal's second storey and look upwards. On the 46m-high vaulted ceiling,

French artist Paul Helleu used 2,500 electric lights to replicate the zodiacal constellations. The design is based on a medieval manuscript illustration, and the debate continues as to whether or not Helleu was aware that medieval illustrators commonly depicted the heavens reversed – giving God's view.

Look towards the northwest corner to spot the dark rectangle that provides an intentional reminder of the grime that had darkened the ceiling over 50 years and was removed (using a specially prepared organic soap) during the late 1990s. Another ceiling oddity is the segment that was cut out to accommodate the tip of a nuclear missile, part of a military display staged here in the 1960s.

The grandeur of the **Main Concourse** is often obliterated by the half a million commuters each day. Nonetheless, try to find a slow moment to descend the marble flight of steps onto its floor and contemplate its 23m windows, its claim to be the world's largest room (it is 114m long and 37m wide), and the once serious suggestion to develop the concourse into three separate bowling alleys.

A pearl of a restaurant The terminal's balconies and lower levels now hold a number of shops and restaurants, and a branch of the **New York Transit Museum** (tel: 878-0106; *Open* Mon–Fri 8–8, Sat 10–4. *Admission free*; see page 76). The restaurants include that of basketball superstar Michael Jordan and the **Oyster Bar**. The latter is known not only for its diverse selection of oysters and other seafood, but also for its low ceiling, covered by tan-coloured Guastavino tiles. In a vaulted area just outside the restaurant, a whisper into one corner can be distinctly heard in the other corner. However, the restaurant proper has no such magical acoustics – it's one of the noisiest eating spots in the city. Still, there are few better places in Manhattan for listening in on the lunchtime gossip of New York executives, although the suggestions that fortunes have been made on the Stock Exchange by inspired eavesdropping are apocryphal at best.

The huge scale and grand style of the Main Concourse (said to be the largest room in the world) affirm Grand Central Terminal as a monument to the halcyon days of train travel

GUIDED TOURS

For a more detailed exploration of Grand Central Terminal, join the free guided tour run by the Municipal Art Society (tel: 935-3960), which begins at 12:30 PM each Wednesday from the Information desk on the Main Concourse.

The imposing main entrance to the New York Public Library on Fifth Avenue

THE LIBRARY'S TREASURES

The New York Public Library has an extraordinary stock of rare and valuable books and prints, some of which may be on display. These include a Gutenberg bible; a 1493 folio edition of a Christopher Columbus letter describing his American discoveries; the first full folio edition of Shakespeare, from 1623; the 1640 Bay Psalm Book (the first English book published in America); a handwritten copy of George Washington's farewell address; and an early draft of Jefferson's Declaration of Independence.

▶▶▶ New York Public Library   151B2

Fifth Avenue and 42nd Street (tel: 340-0833)
Open: Mon and Wed 9–9, Tue and Thu 11–7, Fri and Sat 10–6
Hours for special exhibitions vary. Guided tours: Wed 2:30
Subway: B, D, F; 42nd Street

You cannot actually borrow a book here, the Central Branch of the New York Public Library (the 3 million or so tomes are for reference only), but you can explore one of the city's finest expressions of architecture, a Beaux-Arts temple created by the legendary firm of Carrère & Hastings and opened in 1911. Its terrace and elegant steps are decorated by a pair of sculptured lions, fountains fronting statues symbolising Truth and Beauty, and bronze flagpole bases cast at Long Island. The triple-arched portico entrance leads into the exquisitely proportioned Astor Hall – named after John Jacob Astor, founder of the nation's first library (one of the three that combined to create the present library's original holdings) – and an information desk dispensing floor plans and marking the starting point for the tours.

Immediately ahead, Gottesman Hall stages some of the library's temporary exhibitions. Turn left for the De Witt Wallace Periodical Room at the end of the corridor. Publisher De Witt Wallace spent many hours in this room scanning periodicals and abridging their contents for his fledgling venture, the *Reader's Digest*. His profits financed the room's 1983 restoration: its brass lamps and walnut chairs were joined by Richard Haas' murals of the offices of *New York* magazine and newspaper. Climb the marble stairs to the fourth floor, noting the original lamps and the drinking fountains on the way to the vaulted McGraw Rotunda, decorated in 1940 by Edward Laning's murals. This marks the entrance to the public catalogue room, complete with computer databases. Beyond the catalogue room lie the main reading rooms – the most beautiful part of the library. Across the corridor is the Edna Barnes Salomon Room, which displays the library's paintings and selections from its printed treasures.

▶▶▶ Pierpont Morgan Library 151B2

36th Street at Madison Avenue (tel: 685-0610)
Open: Tue–Thu 10:30–5, Fri 10:30–8, Sat 10:30–6, Sun 12–6.
Admission: moderate. Subway: 6; 33rd Street

Born into wealth and educated in Europe, J Pierpont Morgan had become one of New York's leading financiers by the closing decades of the 19th century. But, unlike his nouveau riche contemporaries, he trusted his own taste and judgment as he lavished a fortune on European cultural treasures, acquiring rare books, manuscripts and drawings that by 1890 had become one of the finest private collections in the country.

In 1902, Morgan commissioned the leading architect of the day, Charles F McKim, to create the Renaissance-style Pierpont Morgan Library. The Palladian porch that marks the library's original entrance on 36th Street merits a special look, though the present entrance is on the Madison Avenue side and enters a 1928 annex on the site of Morgan's son's brownstone residence.

The temporary exhibitions could hold your attention for hours, but look first around the library itself, starting at the West Room, where Morgan's study is preserved as it was on the financier's death in 1913. Once described as "the most beautiful room in America", the study is lined by Italian Renaissance paintings and dominated by Morgan's immense wooden desk.

From the study, free-standing columns of green-veined marble mark the way to the imposing rotunda and the East Room. In a nutshell, the East Room is one of the plushest reading rooms you are ever likely to see. Three tiers of bookcases, fashioned from bronze and inlaid walnut, rise to a ceiling covered by colourful murals of artists and scholars (and signs of the zodiac), while above the fireplace hangs a 16th-century Flemish tapestry.

Sumptuous though it certainly is, the East Room is never overbearing, and you could spend a long time here, poring over priceless letters and manuscripts.

THE PIERPONT MORGAN COLLECTIONS
The following are just a few items from the vast collections of the Pierpont Morgan Library: three Gutenberg bibles; a Shakespeare first folio; an autographed manuscript of Milton's *Paradise Lost*; manuscripts and early editions of Rudyard Kipling, Oscar Wilde and Gertrude Stein bearing the authors' doodles and changes; musical scores from the hands of Bach, Brahms and Beethoven; etchings and prints by Rembrandt, Rubens and Degas; and a huge selection of pre-19th century paintings and objets d'art.

169

Space for the studious: the reading room of New York Public Library. Choose your tome from the library's many kilometres of shelving and consult it here

STREET NUMBERING IN QUEENS

Anyone who has spent several days mastering the Manhattan street-numbering system will find the streets of Queens even more of a challenge. Part of the price for Queens affiliating itself to New York City in 1898 was the loss of its named streets for a numbering system imposed by the civic powers in Manhattan.

The system, it seems, is still having teething troubles. Usually streets and avenues run at right angles to each other, and an address such as 10–35 14th Street will be located on 14th Street near the junction with 10th Avenue. This is not always the case, however, and most problems occur when neighbourhoods run into each other at something other than a perfect right angle. If you get lost, the solution might be to ask a local. But then again it might not: Queens residents are often as baffled by the system as everyone else.

The interior of Bowne House, the oldest building in Queens

▶ Queens

48C3

Filling 308sq km on the western end of Long Island, Queens is easily the biggest of the City's five boroughs. Sheer size renders its layout almost incomprehensible unless thought of in the way most of its residents do: as a patchwork of separate and self-contained communities, often with little in common with each other.

While most of Queens fits the detached-house-and-two-car-garage stereotype of American suburbia, parts date back to colonial times and its population is a rich and diverse mixture echoing New York's immigration patterns. Large, yet comparatively recently arrived, communities of Chinese, Koreans, Indians and Japanese exist alongside areas long dominated by residents of Greek, Italian or Puerto Rican descent.

Even though you probably failed to realise it at the time, if your arrival point in New York was **La Guardia** or **JFK** airport, you have already had a brief taste of Queens. Both airports are sited in the borough. Planes into JFK swoop above the 52sq km of marshlands comprising the **Jamaica Bay Wildlife Refuge** (tel: 718/318-4340), a place much more interesting to migrating birdlife than to all but the most ornithologically obsessed humans.

You will need a car and a very detailed map to explore all of Queens but the main points of interest – which will also give a broad flavour of the borough's ethnic mix – are slotted into a handful of key areas, easily reached by public transport from Manhattan.

Take the subway out of Manhattan to **Flushing**, for example, and you will soon see why the route is unofficially dubbed the "Orient Express". What Flushing's Japanese supermarkets, Korean restaurants and Chinese dim sum houses do not suggest, however, are the town's 17th-century links with Quakers.

At 137–16 Main Street, a Friends' Meeting House has stood since 1694 and, on a nearby corner, the 1661 **Bowne House▶▶** (tel: 718/359-0528; *Open* Tue, Sat and Sun 2:30–4:30. *Admission: inexpensive*), one of the city's oldest houses, has further connections with The Friends. The house's owner, John Bowne, was exiled for defying a ban on Quaker meetings. However, he persuaded the Dutch West India Company – who did not want to risk losing any would-be settlers – to insist that all religious groups would be tolerated in the new colony: a step towards the religious freedoms later enshrined in the Constitution.

The house holds some of Bowne's colonial furnishings, plus those of his descendants, who lived here until the 1940s. Tours of the small modest dwelling wend their way into the kitchen, where the clandestine Quaker meetings took place. A short walk from the Bowne House, the 1774 **Kingsland Homestead** (tel: 718/939-0647; *Open* Tue, Sat and Sun 2:30–4:30. *Admission: inexpensive*) is an example of the Dutch and English architectural mix that is typical of Long Island farmhouses of the period.

Around 2km east of Flushing, **Flushing Meadows-Corona Park▶▶** (tel: 718/760-6565) began life as a swamp and rubbish dump, but by 1939 it was drawing millions to the World's Fair, which symbolised New York's emergence from the Depression. A few relics from the 1939–40 fair remain, as do many more from a second World's Fair held here in 1964–5. Among these are Philip Johnson's **New**

York State Pavilion Building – the architectural highlight of the 1960s show, but these days in a much crumbled condition – and the 43m high **Unisphere**, intended to represent the Earth and its satellites.

Another 1960s survivor, the **New York Hall of Science▶** (tel: 718/699-0005; *Open* Jul and Aug, Mon 9:30–2; Tue and Sun 9:30–5; rest of the year Mon–Wed 9:30–2, Thu–Sun 9:30–5. *Admission: moderate*), is these days crammed with hands-on computer exhibits illustrating the rudiments of science to children.

More modest-sized memorabilia from both world fairs are displayed inside the **Queens Museum of Art▶** (tel: 718/592-9700; *Open* Wed–Fri 10–5; Sat and Sun 12–5. *Admission: inexpensive*) housed in a structure that dates from the 1939–40 fair. What fascinates most here is the Panorama: a scale model of New York City that covers 1670sq m and includes every building in the city.

The park is also home to the **Queens Wildlife Center** (tel: 718/271-7761; *Open* Apr–Oct, Mon–Fri 10–5, Sat and Sun 10–5:30, rest of year daily 10–4:30. *Admission: inexpensive*), a small zoo of North American animals, as well as the **National Tennis Center** – which famously holds the annual US Open.

THE UNITED NATIONS IN QUEENS
The City Building, which houses the Queens Museum in Flushing Meadows-Corona Park, was used by the United Nations as the organisation awaited the completion of its site in Manhattan. Among the motions carried here was the one in 1947 that paved the way for the creation of the state of Israel.

A busy street in Queens

Roosevelt Avenue, in the Jackson Heights neighbourhood of Queens, is known for its bakeries and restaurants

STEINWAY
Just east of Astoria is the town of Steinway, created by William Steinway in 1872 when he moved his piano factory here from Manhattan – partly to escape the power of unions. The factory still stands at 19th Avenue and 39th Street. Steinway himself, meanwhile, moved into a stonework Italianate villa overlooking the East River at 18–33 East 41st Street. The slightly spooky villa has certainly seen better days, as has the now entirely insalubrious neighbourhood that surrounds it.

Baseball fans might note that **Shea Stadium**, home of the New York Mets, stands in the northerly section of the park. In 1965 it was the venue of a now legendary concert by the Beatles.

On the borough's northern side, facing the Bronx across the East River, **Astoria▶** is one of the world's largest Greek communities. Lining 31st Street and Ditmars Boulevard are countless Greek bakeries, cafés and restaurants, and even the graffiti on the walls is in Greek.

Not remotely Greek, though, is Astoria's **American Museum of the Moving Image▶** (36–11 35th Avenue; tel: 718/784-0077; *Open* Tue–Fri 12–5, Sat and Sun 11–6. *Admission: moderate*), which occupies part of a working studio complex. During the 1920s, Paramount shot silent movies here with legendary figures such as Rudolph Valentino, Clara Bow, Gloria Swanson and the Marx Brothers, before they relocated to Hollywood.

The museum shows cinematic classics and carries temporary exhibitions on various aspects of film history. On permanent display is a large but only mildly interesting collection of props, costumes, film-making equipment, fan magazines and vintage film posters.

Heading back towards Manhattan is heavily industrialised **Long Island City**, which is forging a reputation as an artists' enclave. In its early days, the area of Long Island City known as Hunters Point was linked by ferry to Manhattan, encouraging business development here. Some of the old warehouses and factories have been turned into artists' studios.

In Long Island City is the riverfront **Isamu Noguchi Garden Museum▶▶** (32–37 Vernon Boulevard; tel: 718/721-1932; *Open* Wed–Fri 10–5, Sat and Sun 11–6. *Admission: inexpensive donation*) devoted to the acclaimed sculptor. The son of a Japanese poet who emigrated to California, Noguchi's unconventional ideas were at first derided, but his extraordinary imagination and creativity is clear enough throughout the 12 galleries that chart his long career (Noguchi died in 1988, aged 84), and in the gardens that hold still more of his enigmatic creations.

▶▶ Rockefeller Center 151C2

47th–52nd streets between Fifth and Sixth avenues
Subway: B, D, F, 1; 47th Street – Rockefeller Center

This is the world's largest commercial and entertainment complex, through which a quarter of a million people pass each day. The project changed the face of American urban planning from the 1940s on.

The centre is named after the multimillionaire John D Rockefeller Jr, who was approached in 1928 by the Metropolitan Opera with a view to his developing a down-at-heel Midtown site, on land rented from Columbia University, as a new Opera House. Rockefeller agreed, but the Wall Street crash led to the shelving of the plans and left him with 4.5 hectares of land and a very large debt. In the country's first major pooled architectural project, Rockefeller commissioned several firms to erect 14 buildings on the site with the proviso that the structures form an aesthetically unified entity and that the complex should be a pleasing environment for working, eating, shopping and relaxing.

As a result, the art deco buildings themselves take a secondary role to the numerous cafés, restaurants, underground walkways and shopping plazas secreted in and around them, allowing a flow of light and easy movement of people. This became the blueprint for city-centre renewal initiatives throughout the country.

To reach the heart of the complex, enter from Fifth Avenue along the short Channel Gardens to the sunken **Plaza▶**, which holds an open-air restaurant and a wintertime ice rink and is presided over by Paul Manship's 1934 figure of *Prometheus*.

Rising above Prometheus' head, the 70-storey **GE Building** (better known by its original title, the RCA

ROCKEFELLER CENTER FACTS
Number employed in construction 1931–40: 75,000.
Number of telephones: 100,000.
Number of lifts: 488.
Cost of buying Columbia University's leasehold in 1985: $400 million.

GERTRUDE STEIN ON THE RCA BUILDING, 1935
"The most beautiful thing I have seen".

173

Summertime brings bright umbrellas and a holiday atmosphere to the sunken plaza amid the office buildings of Rockefeller Center

Building) is the heart of Rockefeller Center. Enter the lobby and note the murals by José Maria Sert – replacements for those of Diego Rivera, who refused to appease the anticommunist Rockefellers by removing a handsome likeness of Lenin.

The lift's top stop is the **Rainbow Room** restaurant complex, where the reward for purchasing a meal is an opulent setting around a revolving dancefloor and fantastic views over Manhattan. Return to the lobby to collect a free map from the information desk, essential as you begin weaving deeper into Rockefeller Center's impressive labyrinth.

Simple wanderings will reveal much of interest, but do not miss the **Radio City Music Hall**. The hall's 1932 gala opening was attended by the likes of Charlie Chaplin and Clark Gable, and it instantly became one of the great American entertainment palaces. More recently a favoured location for live concerts and the occasional film première, the 6,000-seat hall is still an art deco delight and can be seen on guided tours (tel: 632-4041; *Open* Mon–Fri 10–5, Sun 11–5. *Admission: moderate*). Less glamourous but still in the realms of the showbiz world, the offices and studios of **NBC Television** (tel: 664-3700; can be viewed on hour-long guided tours, daily 9–5).

▶ Roosevelt Island

187A2

Once given over to 27 hospitals that kept the incurably sick and insane (and the simply scandalous, such as Mae West) segregated from the rest of New York society, Roosevelt Island is today regarded as one of the most successful attempts at integrated mixed-income housing. Would-be residents now have to wait several years to get an apartment in the area. Besides near-total absence of crime, Roosevelt Island dwellers also enjoy automobile-free streets and a sight of the Midtown Manhattan skyline unsurpassed in most other locations in the city. For visitors, the peacefulness and the views (and the cable car that crosses to the island) are the only attractions, though the ruins of the old hospitals add a distinctly eerie note.

174

GETTING TO ROOSEVELT ISLAND

A road bridge crosses from Queens to Roosevelt Island, but to reach the island from Manhattan, use either the subway (lines B or Q) or (much the best choice) the cable-car, which makes a 3-minute jaunt over the East River from a terminal at Second Avenue and 60th Street.

The Roosevelt Island cable-car

▶▶▶ **SoHo** *113A2*

Creativity is all around you in SoHo

Named for being SOuth of HOuston Street (and bordered also by Canal, Lafayette, and Sullivan streets), SoHo is dominated by large cast-iron factory buildings put up in the mid-19th century.

The determined efforts of conservationists saved the area and its unique buildings from demolition following a decade of neglect and after 10 years of colonisation by up-and-coming artists who were attracted by spacious rooms lit by immense windows, SoHo entered a period of swift gentrification. Its loft-style apartments found favour with the city's rich and trendy – and with the art dealers who made the area internationally synonymous with contemporary art. With chic clothing shops and fashionable restaurants alongside scores of art galleries, SoHo is now transformed – but it is the dozens of remaining cast-iron buildings that shape its character.

Among the earliest examples, the **Haughwout Building** (488–492 Broadway) dates from 1857, rising in four tiers of arched windows and Corinthian columns. On Greene Street, numbers 28–30 and 72–76 show the artistry that later ironwork façades acquired, while the **Little Singer Building** (561–563 Broadway) suggests the next great architectural step: replacing cast-iron floor supports with steel – the basis of the modern skyscraper.

Art lovers not exhausted by SoHo's many galleries can also visit the **New Museum of Contemporary Art** (Broadway between Houston and Prince streets; tel: 219-1355; *Open* Wed and Sun 12–6, Thu–Sat 12–8. *Admission free*) publicising newer artists making an impact; the **Alternative Museum** (Broadway between Houston and Prince streets; tel: 966-4444; *Open* Tue–Sat 11–6. *Admission: inexpensive*) has exhibits of art often inspired by social and political issues; and the **SoHo Guggenheim** (Broadway at Prince Street; tel: 423-3500; *Open* Thu–Mon 11–6. *Admission: inexpensive*), uses a warehouse remodelled by architect Arata Isozaki for changing displays drawn from the main Guggenheim Museum (see pages 122–124) and from quality travelling exhibitions.

**RICHARD HAAS'
SOHO MURAL**
Since 1973, at the junction of SoHo's Prince and Greene streets, the neighbourhood's bringing together of contemporary art and historic cast-iron buildings has been celebrated in a witty *trompe-l'oeil* by Richard Haas, which cleverly confuses the actual features of the buildings with painted representations.

You do not have to be an art dealer or critic to find New York's thousand or more art galleries fascinating. Many galleries are in Chelsea and SoHo – very much the international nerve centre of contemporary art – though others are well established on the Upper East Side and around 57th Street. Visit the non-profit galleries, too, publicising the work considered too risky by the commercial galleries.

THE GALLERY GUIDE

The *New York Times*, the *Village Voice* and many special art publications carry art gallery listings, but the most comprehensive details are provided by *Gallery Guide*. A publication listing over 700 galleries and providing maps to help locate them, the *Gallery Guide* is published monthly and distributed free in galleries and a few selected bookshops. The thinner *New York Art World* has similar information. Many Chelsea galleries stock the free bi-monthly gallery listing, *Chelsea Art*.

Upper East Side galleries The epitome of Upper East Side elegance and sophistication, the Paris-founded **Wildenstein & Co.** (19 East 64th Street; tel: 879-0500) specialises in French impressionist works, but its holdings extend from contemporary paintings to antique objets d'art.

The diverse stocks of **Hirschl & Adler** are displayed in three separate galleries at the same address (21 East 70th Street; tel: 535-8810). The main gallery carries a broad selection of 18th- and 19th-century European pieces; Hirschl & Adler Folk gallery holds American folk art, from paintings to crafts, while **Hirschl & Adler Modern** gallery specialises in American and European names from the mid-1950s.

Focusing on modern American painters, the **Gagosian Gallery** (Madison Avenue between 76th and 77th streets; tel: 744-2313) provides a museum-like exhibition space for lesser-known works of art by well-known names, such as Jackson Pollock, Willem de Kooning, Andy Warhol and Cy Twombly.

The pocket-sized **Kahan Gallery** (922 Madison Avenue; tel: 861-3682) has a well-justified reputation for 19th- and 20th-century European works, Picasso among them. New York's oldest gallery, **Knoedler & Company,** helped develop many major private collections from the 1920s and continues to display works of note. **Margo Feiden** (699 Madison Avenue; tel: 677-5330) is lined by Al Hirschfeld's theatrical caricatures.

57th Street area galleries If you only have the opportunity to visit one 57th Street gallery, make it **Pace** (32 East 57th Street; tel: 431-3292). This deserves its place among the world's leading galleries for a stock that includes virtually every European and American name of major significance from the last 30 years.

Extremely influential in the emergence of pop art and noted for the high quality of its purchases, the **Janis Gallery** (110 West 57th Street; tel: 586-0110) has been a fixture on the New York art scene for four decades and continues to present established and new names in stimulating exhibitions.

Abstract expressionists turn up in many New York galleries but one of the better places to find works by the colour field artists is the **André Emmerich Gallery** (41 East 57th Street; tel: 752-0124).

Some intriguing historical documents from the turbulent 1930s can be seen alongside fine examples of German expressionism at **Galerie St Etienne** (24 West 57th Street; tel: 245-6734).

First established in SoHo, the **Mary Boone Gallery** (745 Fifth Avenue; tel: 752-2929) is what serious art watchers ignore at their peril. Through the 1980s Mary Boone helped launch some of the brightest new names in American art, such as David Salle and Julian Schnabel.

Around the corner on Fifth Avenue is the **Edwynn Houk Gallery** (745 Fifth Avenue; tel: 750-7070), exhibiting works by some of the world's best photographers; and the **Tibor De Nagy Gallery** (724 Fifth Avenue; tel: 262-5050) is a champion of emerging contemporary artists since the 1950s.

NON-PROFIT GALLERIES
SoHo has several non-profit galleries. **Artists' Space** (38 Greene Street, tel: 226-3970) is a launch pad for installations and video art; a SoHo branch of **DIA** (141 Wooster Street; (tel: 473-8072; see page 84) holds Walter de Maria's **New York Earth Room** with its 14 tonnes of soil; and the **Visual Arts Gallery** (137 Wooster Street; tel: 598-8221) exhibits student works.

SoHo galleries In the early 1960s, the **Leo Castelli Gallery** (2nd floor, 420 West Broadway; tel: 431-5160) brought artists such as Andy Warhol, Roy Lichtenstein, Jasper Johns and Frank Stella to wide attention. The gallery has a graphic arts annex, which can be found at 578 Broadway. Another SoHo pacesetter is the **Molly Solomon Gallery** (172 Mercer Street; tel: 941-5777).

Minimalist and conceptual art is the stock-in-trade of the highly regarded **John Weber Gallery** (142 Greene Street; tel: 629-5711), closely linked with figures such as Sol Lewitt and regularly publicising new artists.

Chelsea galleries Many galleries occupy former warehouses on the western edge of Chelsea. They include **Cheim & Read** (521 West 23rd Street; tel: 242-7727), **Feigen** (535 West 20th Street; tel: 929-0500), and **Metro Pictures** (519 West 24th Street; tel: 206-7100).

Over the past couple of decades, numerous small galleries have opened in Chelsea, providing launch pads for many new names in the art world

South Street Seaport and the cargo ship Peking

▶ South Street Seaport 104B3

Eastern foot of Fulton Street (tel: SEA-PORT)
Museum Open: Mon–Wed, Fri and Sun 10–6, Thu 10–8.
Admission: inexpensive. Subway: 2, 3, 4; Fulton Street

A large collection of shops, seafood restaurants, bars, craft centres and galleries make up the South Street Seaport district, which transformed an abandoned area beside the East River – the place where New York's 19th-century maritime trade flourished – into a history-themed pedestrian mall.

By day, however, most visitors come to Seaport itself to explore the vintage ships of the **South Street Seaport Museum** complex – which jump-started the area's gentrification some two decades ago – moored beside the South Street piers. The most interesting exhibit is the 1911 *Peking*, a four-masted cargo vessel that spent its glory days shifting nitrate from South America to the US and made several roundings of Cape Horn. Climb aboard and descend to a lower deck where a pictorial display recounts the ship's working life. Back on dry land is the **Museum Gallery**, which has a minor exhibition of maritime photos and ships-in-bottles and certificates and documents attesting to New York's historical place as one of the world's great seaports.

▶▶ Staten Island 48B1

A ride on the Staten Island Ferry (see the panel opposite) is reason enough to make the crossing from the Financial District to the hilly chunk of land wedged between New Jersey and Brooklyn, but Staten Island has much more to offer than a ferry to call its own. Settled by Dutch and French farmers in 1661 and an important British base during the Revolutionary War, the island has evolved into leafy suburbia with a tranquil mood that makes it seem a million miles from the hurly-burly of the rest of New York City. It also has some surprising collections among its museums.

The ferry docks at St George is the island's least enthralling community. Around 3km west (take bus S40

STROLL: WATER STREET
Water Street, between Wall Street and South Street Seaport, was New York's main riverside thoroughfare in the 19th century, lined by sailors' boarding houses, bars and brothels.

from the ferry terminal), Sailors' Snug Harbor is a better first stop. Founded in the 1800s as an institution for "decrepit and worn-out sailors", it is now better known as **Snug Harbor Cultural Center▶** (tel: 718/448-2500; *Open* daily dawn to dusk. *Admission free*). Restoration has kept a number of its imposing 19th-century buildings intact.

It is further south that Staten Island's real treasures are to be found (take bus S74). Visiting in 1991, the Dalai Lama himself described as "accurate" the stone cottage on Lighthouse Hill which is intended to replicate a Tibetan mountain temple and provide an apt home for the **Jacques Marchais Center of Tibetan Art▶ ▶ ▶** (tel: 718/987-3500; *Open* Apr–Nov Wed–Sun 1–5. *Admission: inexpensive*), a wondrous stock of sculptured deities, ritual objects, incense burners and many other items from the world's Buddhist cultures.

Now the largest private gathering of such material in the western world, the collection was inspired by the discovery in 1880 by the young Jacqueline Norman Klauber (who later renamed herself Jacques Marchais) of 12 Tibetan figurines that her great-grandfather had brought back

THE CONFERENCE HOUSE
Students of international summitry might consider making a trip to the Conference House (tel: 718/984-6046; *Open* mid-April–Nov, Fri and Sun 1–4). In September 1776, the stone house became the venue of the only peace talks attempted between the British forces and the American revolutionaries. The house served as a rat-poison factory before becoming a museum in 1926. The interior has period furniture and numerous items recording the revolutionary conflict, and the failed attempt to broker peace.

179

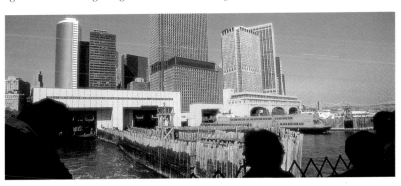

The Staten Island Ferry terminal

from a voyage to India and stored in the family attic. This experience stimulated a lifelong fascination with Buddhism and its sacraments, and she never missed an opportunity to expand the collection. Whether you are looking at a Buddhist Wheel of Life or musing over a yak butter burner, informative explanatory texts make sense of the exhibits, and illuminate their complex symbolism.

About two kilometres south is the 40-hectare **Richmondtown Historic Restoration▶ ▶** (tel: 718/351-1611; *Open* Jul and Aug, Wed–Fri 10–5, Sat and Sun 1–5, rest of the year Wed–Sun 1–5. *Admission: inexpensive*), which shows the fruits of half a century of gathering and restoring buildings dating from the 17th to the 19th centuries and equipping them with (usually) the original occupants' possessions. Local history buffs, dressed in period costume and keen to pass on their knowledge, lead tours around the old homes. These buildings range from a sparsely furnished Dutch building which doubled as local church and schoolhouse to a general store packed with 1840s consumer goods – all providing insights into earlier ways of life. Also within the complex, the Island Historical Museum presents a chronological record of Staten Island's growth, with many enjoyable exhibits from some of its early industries, from brewing to oyster harvesting.

THE STATEN ISLAND FERRY
The actual vessel is entirely ordinary, but the views from the Staten Island Ferry can be wonderful. The Statue of Liberty, Governor's Island, and the Verrazano-Narrows Bridge all appear as the skyscrapers of Lower Manhattan shrink into the distance and the green hills of Staten Island draw nearer. The ferry (pedestrians only) takes half an hour to make the 8km crossing and the journey is free.

WILD STATEN ISLAND

The hilly, bucolic interior of Staten Island holds many hectares of unspoiled land, parts of which can be explored on marked walking trails. The Greenbelt (tel: 718/667-2165) spans wetlands, woodlands, streams, rivers and parks; organised weekend activities include riding and guided nature walks. The one-time mining of clay on Staten Island's southwest shore has helped create the 100-hectare Clay Pit Ponds Preserve (tel: 718/967-1976), with pine woods and many man-made ponds that now provide wildlife habitats.

STATUE OF LIBERTY FACTS

Height: 46m
Weight: 204,120kg
Length of hand: 5m
Index finger: 2.44m
Nose: 137cm
Waist (thickness):10.7m
Best movie role: in Alfred Hitchcock's *Saboteur*.
Biggest fictional blunder: Liberty's torch is described as a sword in Franz Kafka's *America*.

If you have time to spare, visit the **Alice Austen House▶** (tel: 718/816-4506; *Open* Mar–Dec Thu–Sun 12–5. *Admission: donation*), a seafront home on Staten Island, dating from 1710 and filled by some of the 8,000 photographs taken by the untrained Alice over a 50-year period to 1934. In 1951, *Life* magazine discovered and published some of her work. Her talents were soon recognised far afield, yet she spent her poverty-stricken old age in a workhouse.

Another small and equally unexpected collection is the **Garibaldi Meucci Museum▶** (tel: 718/442-1608; Tue–Sun 1–5. *Admission free*), where Giuseppe Garibaldi – one of the founders of unified Italy – spent two years in the 1850s in the home of American-Italian Antonio Meucci. Garibaldi's place in history is assured, but fate was unkinder to Meucci, an inventor who developed a prototype telephone but failed to patent the idea. To reach both this and the Alice Austen House, take bus S51 from the ferry terminal.

▶▶ Statue of Liberty   48C2

There is no greater symbol of the nation and its promise of freedom and opportunity for all than the Statue of Liberty, which has held the flame of liberty above New York harbour since 1886. From Manhattan, a visit to the statue begins with a ferry ride from Battery Park Pier. Boats to the statue also stop at Ellis Island (see page 100).

Shut for security reasons in the aftermath of the terrorist attack in September 2001, Liberty Island (but not the monument or museum) was reopened two months later. At the statue, there are two options. If you have the time and energy, begin an assault on the 354 steps that lead up to the crown – but be warned that the staircase is narrow and that you can only climb as fast as the person in front (the ascent can take three hours). Alternatively, take the elevator to the pedestal level, from which the views are only marginally less impressive than those from the crown. There is also a museum recording the creation of the statue and the effect it had on newly arrived immigrants when seeing it for the first time. Call for the latest information (the Statue of Liberty Ferry, tel: 269-5755).

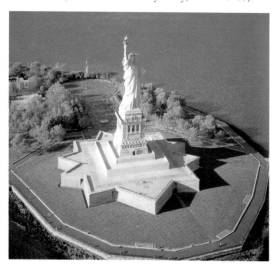

Liberty Island is in fact closer to New Jersey than to New York, but its statue is universally regarded as a fundamental part of the city

Originally intended to stand in Egypt, partly funded by a French lottery, and at first regarded in the US as a waste of money, the Statue of Liberty may be America's most famous landmark, but the story of its construction is much less straightforward than most people may realise.

Liberty in Egypt? A sculptor with a taste for monuments on the grand scale, Frenchman Frédéric Auguste Bartholdi visited Egypt and presented to the Egyptian sultan his plans for a gigantic figure of a robed female peasant holding a torch, to be sited at the entrance to the Suez canal.

The sultan rejected the scheme, but Bartholdi, on a trip to the US in 1871, found the perfect spot for his torch-carrying lady at the entrance to New York's harbour, over 6,400km from her original intended location.

French friendship The idea of a gift from France to the US to mark the nations' shared belief in democracy had been around for some time, and Bartholdi's statue idea was taken on board by France's new Third Republic, busy modelling its constitution along US lines.

As a sign of friendship, both governments agreed that the work would be shared, Bartholdi producing the statue while its pedestal was made in New York. In France, a popular lottery raised 250,000 francs towards the project, but in the US, the idea was greeted with apathy.

As *Liberty Enlightening the World* (as the statue is officially titled) took shape outside Bartholdi's Paris studio – being too large to fit inside – the pedestal had barely left the drawing board, and the American press was full of satirical cartoons and articles condemning its expense.

Raising the money After Congress rejected a bill allocating $100,000 to the work, and the mayor of New York vetoed a plan for the city to donate $50,000, newspaper publisher Joseph Pulitzer attacked the miserliness of the nation's rich, and appealed for contributions – no matter how small – from ordinary Americans.

Packed into 214 crates, the finished statue arrived in New York in June 1885. Two months later, Pulitzer announced that the goal of raising the necessary sum of $100,000 had been reached.

The statue was hoisted onto its pedestal in May, 1886 and unveiled in October. The response of the public, as Pulitzer's newspaper recorded, was "one long cheer".

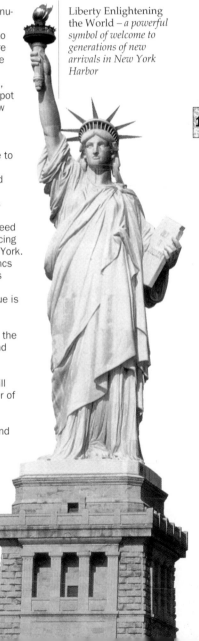

Liberty Enlightening the World – *a powerful symbol of welcome to generations of new arrivals in New York Harbor*

181

The Stock Exchange

▶ Stock Exchange 104B2

Broad Street near Wall Street (tel: 656-5167)
Open: Mon–Fri 9:15–4. Admission free
Subway: 4; Wall Street

Housed in a 1903 neo-classical building, it might be expected to form the highlight of a tour around the Financial District. Unless you have a vested interest, however, the exchange's 3440sq m dealing floor – populated by colour-jacketed brokers, reporters and pages – looks as uninteresting from behind the glass of the public viewing gallery as it does on TV. The exhibits do nothing to lessen the sense of anticlimax. Nonetheless, if you want to view the spot where the crash of 1929 plunged the nation into the Great Depression, it is best to pick up your ticket, free and time-stamped for the half-hourly tours, from the entrance soon after 9 AM.

▶ Theodore Roosevelt Birthplace 151A2

20th Street between Broadway and Park Ave (tel: 260-1616)
Open: Wed–Sun 9–5. Admission: inexpensive
Subway: 6; 23rd Street

The nation's future 26th president, Theodore Roosevelt, entered the world in 1858 in a Midtown brownstone, a building subsequently demolished but precisely reconstructed on its original site in 1923 to house a museum honouring the only president to have been a New York native. On display is an exhibition on Roosevelt's life, including hunting trophies and outdoor memorabilia.

▶ TriBeCa IFCB2

Subway: 1; Franklin Street

TriBeCa – the TRIangle BElow CAnal Street (bordered on the east by Broadway and continuing west to the Hudson River) – became the stamping ground of the artists who were priced out of their SoHo lofts (see page 175) as that district's property values soared throughout the 1970s.

Like SoHo, TriBeCa's old warehouses – formerly at the centre of New York's dairy and poultry trade – offer apartments with ample space and natural light, making perfect studios. Also like in SoHo, however, TriBeCa's artists (except for the household names) have been long priced out of the huge lofts they made desirable in the first place, as TriBeCa real estate prices exploded in a climb only slightly slowed by the WTC disaster.

Besides providing as good a picture of New York-style urban regeneration as you are likely to find, a walk through TriBeCa uncovers something of note at almost every turn. Art galleries, much less slick than their SoHo counterparts, occupy many of the former industrial buildings. A notable example is the **Clocktower** at 108 Leonard Street. Dozens of pricey restaurants nourish fashionable faces while, at 37–41 Harrison Street, a primly restored row of early-1800s Federal-style town houses makes a wholly incongruous appearance.

▶ Trump Tower 151C2

Fifth Avenue at 56th Street
Subway: E, F; Fifth Avenue

High-profile property tycoon Donald Trump was the man brave enough to put his name to this garish glass tower: with its pink marble surfaces it is a monument to

A RADICAL EXORCISM AT THE STOCK EXCHANGE
The bulletproof glass screen that shields the trading floor of the Stock Exchange from the public gallery has been in place since 1967, the year when yippie (a twist on the term "hippie") Abbie Hoffman and friends tossed 300 one-dollar bills on to the trading floor. Traders went scurrying for the cash and one of Hoffman's co-activists described the incident as "exorcising the evil spirits of the Stock Exchange".

the booming economy of the early 1980s. Step inside for some serious window-shopping in the host of designer-name boutiques.

▶ Union Square
IFCC2

Between 14th and 17th streets
Subway: 4, 5, 6, L, N, R; 14th Street, Union Square

The thoroughfares of Broadway and 14th Street meet at Union Square, where the city's theatre district was located during the late 1800s but which steadily moved further north, leaving the broad square to become a left-wing political rallying point. Such was the potency and per-ceived threat of the workers movement that police mounted machine gun placements on surrounding buildings in 1927 in anticipation of a demonstration organised to express anger at the execution of the anarchists Sacco and Vanzetti.

None of these events, or the decline that the square was subjected to during the 1970s, is apparent today in the busy but otherwise peaceful tract of land overlooked by two elegent art deco subway entrances and enlivened by a **Farmers' Market**, where fresh produce such as fruit, cheeses, bread and vegetables are sold from stalls each Wednesday, Friday and Saturday.

THE FORMER PAN AM BUILDING

Bauhaus architect Walter Gropius was among the team that designed the Pan Am Building on Park Avenue, adjoining Grand Central Terminal. The largest commercial office building ever constructed, it is also possibly the only one so closely resembling an aircraft wing. Following the demise of Pan Am, the Metropolitan Life Insurance company pur-chased the building in 1992 and set about removing its much-photographed Pan Am logo. The building itself remains as familiar a sight as ever, though still blocking the view up and down Park Avenue.

183

STROLL: DUANE PARK

By day, the streets around TriBeCa's Duane Park provide fruitful territory for a stroll. Head northwards along Hudson Street, and turn off to explore Harrison and Leonard streets.

Inside or out, nothing is understated at Trump Tower

UN GROUNDS AND GARDENS

Besides its three main buildings, the 7.3-hectare United Nations site also holds several sculptures, a small park and a rose garden. Two of the sculptures, Barbara Hepworth's bronze *Single Form* and Henry Moore's *Reclining Figure* commemorate Dag Hammarskjöld, Swedish UN Secretary General killed in a plane crash in 1961. More sculpture, each piece donated by a member state, lines the walk to and through the relaxing rose garden, where views reach across the East River to Queens and the southern tip of Roosevelt Island.

The General Assembly in session. The immense hall can accommodate delegations from up to 179 countries, and proceedings are conducted in six official languages

▶ United Nations 151C3

First Avenue between 42nd and 46th streets (tel: 963-8687)
Tours daily, every half hour 9:15–4:45. Admission: moderate
Subway: 4, 6, 7; 42nd Street – Grand Central

Given the problems blamed on its huge and infamously cumbersome bureaucracy, it might seem apt that the main building of the United Nations – the organisation of world states formed in San Francisco in 1945 and operating on this plot since 1947 – should be the entirely uninspiring Secretariat Building. This structure houses the UN's 16,000 administrative staff and rises for 39 marble-and-glass storeys above the East River.

The UN's public entrance is through the General Assembly Building. The lobby carries temporary exhibitions on international themes, and from here a stairway leads down to the souvenir shop, post office (selling United Nations postage stamps, valid only on mail that is posted here), and also to a rather gloomy cafeteria.

To see any more of the UN, other than the grounds, gardens and the Delegates Dining Room (reservations essential, see Restaurants), you need to buy a ticket for a guided tour. Departing every 15 minutes or so from the lobby, the tours last around an hour and sweep through the various UN buildings, pausing on the way at displays on the work of the UN and at artworks donated by member states. None of these matches the emotional impact of the half-melted items culled from the ruins of Hiroshima and Nagasaki, which are also on display. Assuming no meetings are in session, the tour stops by the Security Council chamber – where the calmness imposed by the empty chairs and desks belies the fact that this is the only UN body with any teeth, able to impose economic sanctions and instigate military actions – and the General Assembly room, the very size of which suggests it can never be anything more than a debating chamber.

The gridlock that ensues whenever heads of state arrive to take their places at the United Nations now seems such an established part of New York life that it is easy to forget that the organisation nearly opted for Philadelphia as its permanent home. What is more, present-day budget problems are causing the UN to reassess not only its expenditure but also its continued presence in the Big Apple.

The United Nations Charter was signed by represent-atives of 50 countries in San Francisco in April 1945, but the General Assembly held its first meeting in London in 1946, a year during which the scramble among several cities to become the organisation's permanent base grew intense. San Francisco, Boston and Philadelphia were in the running before New York's application to become the UN's home was instigated by the city's most famous (some would say most infamous) planning department chief, Robert Moses, who promised that a successful bid "would make New York the centre of the world".

Philadelphia or New York? Among those on the city's campaign committee was Nelson Rockefeller, of the Rockefeller banking dynasty, who was carving a political career for himself with the ambition of becoming presi-dent. Rockefeller persuaded UN officials to use New York as their base when sizing up the rival bids during 1946, but by December it seemed that Philadelphia would be chosen, and that city's authorities began preparing the future UN site. Meanwhile, property developer William Zeckendorf had been buying land alongside New York's East River for residential use. Rockefeller made Zeckendorf an offer he could not refuse for the land, presented the site to the UN officials and won the bid – the land being paid for with an $8.5 million grant from Rockefeller's father. The complex of buildings was com-pleted in 1963, designed by an international team of architects led by William K Harrison.

Considered by many to be New York's most boring building, the UN Secretariat towers above the East River and is home to the organisation's huge administrative machine

Mixed feelings Although not all New Yorkers could see the wisdom of diverting their taxes into easing the UN's arrival and providing incentives for its diplomats, the organisation's presence took the city's prestige through the roof and injected millions into its economy.

Overstaffing and well-publicised expenses abuses caused streamlining to be ordered in 1992, and the UN Children's Fund and UN Development Program considered leaving base for rent-free accommodation elsewhere. Meanwhile, in a move certain to gain the favour of New Yorkers (and encourage their support in a forthcoming election), mayor Giuliani announced in 1997 that UN officials would no longer be able to claim diplomatic immunity when issued with parking tickets.

Gracie Mansion, official residence of the mayor of New York, echoes the opulent feel of the Upper East Side

MUSEUM MILE
Almost all of New York's finest museums are on a stretch of Fifth Avenue that has become known as Museum Mile. From 79th Street going north, you will find the Metropolitan Museum of Art, the Guggenheim Museum, the Cooper-Hewitt National Design Museum, the Jewish Museum and the Museum of the City of New York. Just outside the officially defined mile are the Frick Collection on 70th Street, the Whitney Museum of American Art on Madison Avenue and Museo del Barrio on 104th Street.

►►► Upper East Side   151D3

Nowhere in Manhattan is the sheer pleasure of being incalculably wealthy so clearly evident as amid the mansions, high-rent apartment houses and ultra-chic shops of the Upper East Side, synonymous for a century with the kind of lifestyle only a bottomless bank account can buy.

There was a vacant space until the creation of Central Park and Manhattan's steady northwards population shift made it ripe for development. The Upper East Side's first homes were modest affairs alongside new elevated train lines that ran above Park Avenue, and the streets to its east, erected in the 1870s.

By the 1890s, the city's wealthiest people began eyeing the two-block corridor formed by Fifth and Madison avenues. The richest of the rich erected grand mansions in styles ranging from mock-Gothic to imitation Italian Renaissance along Fifth, while the merely very rich moved into the fine brownstone town houses constructed along Madison.

With a few exceptions, such as the 64-room former home of Andrew Carnegie (now the Cooper-Hewitt National Design Museum) and that of Henry Clay Frick (site of the Frick Collection), the Fifth Avenue mansions were demolished during the 1920s to make way for the luxury apartment houses that stand here now, their windows giving priceless views over Central Park and their entrances guarded by white-gloved doormen.

Through the 1950s, the Madison Avenue brownstone buildings were steadily converted to shops and offices, and now fashionably groomed locals patronise the art

Art and elegance

Giving a taste of the Upper East Side's elegance and taking in several interesting but often overlooked buildings, this walk also includes a couple of important art collections.

Begin on 65th Street at **Temple Emanu-El**, a 1929 synagogue with space for 2,500 people. Its design incorporates Romanesque and

Temple Emanu-El

Byzantine features, a mixing of East and West.

Two blocks east and to the north is the **Seventh Regiment Armory** with a drill hall for shows and sales.

Ahead, on Park Avenue, is the **Asia Society** building (page 65), west of which stands **St James Episcopal Church** (1884), with its two tiers of stained-glass windows and impressive reredos.

Facing Fifth Avenue, the former mansion home of Henry Clay Frick holds the **Frick Collection**, mostly of European Old Masters (page 110). By contrast, four blocks north and to the east, the very best of modern American art is the speciality of the **Whitney Museum** (page 191).

galleries, antique shops and designer clothing outlets of one of the nation's most exclusive – and expensive – commercial strips.

Strolling Madison Avenue dreamily window-shopping and eavesdropping on neighbourhood banter is the perfect way to acclimatise yourself to Upper East Side life.

Additional reasons to come to this area are the so-called Museum Mile (see the panel), and Gracie Mansion – the official residence of New York City's mayors since 1942 (see page 111).

"He adored New York City. He idolised it out of all proportion". These lines from the opening of Woody Allen's **Manhattan** *could easily be applied to the director himself, whose films have regularly celebrated New York and its inhabitants – and done so more convincingly than perhaps any other film-maker.*

188

REBEL WITH A CAUSE

After the much publicised wrangling with ex-wife Mia Farrow, Allen made the news again in 2000 when he opposed a developer's plans to build a high-rise apartment building on top of a bank in his own neighbourhood at Madison Avenue and 91st Street. Allen made his shortest film, just under three minutes long, to illustrate his case to the city's landmarks preservation committee, describing it as "the first film I ever made for a cause". On Mondays, Allen can sometimes be found playing jazz clarinet at Michael's Pub, inside the Lombardy Hotel, 111 East 56th Street (tel: 212/758-2272).

In 1942, the six-year-old Allen Konigsberg rode the subway from Brooklyn with his father and emerged onto 42nd Street. He would later recall that he was "in love with Manhattan from the earliest memory".

Home to New York By the mid-1950s, Konigsberg had become Woody Allen and was working as a TV gag-writer in Los Angeles when (legend has it) he proposed by phone to his Brooklyn sweetheart because he needed someone to go with to see *Casablanca* at the weekend.

Meanwhile, Lenny Bruce and Mort Sahl had reshaped stand-up comedy and paved the way for the stage-shy Allen to progress swiftly from playing tiny Greenwich Village nightspots to becoming a major figure on the national comedy circuit.

A television appearance by Allen led to his (by then ex-) wife mounting an unsuccessful $1 million lawsuit for defamation of character, but Allen's anti-wife jokes did not prevent him from remarrying, this time to an Upper East Sider through whom he claimed to have assumed "citizenship of Manhattan".

WOODY ALLEN'S

MANHATTAN

The films Allen's first film to give New York a starring role was *Annie Hall* (1977). In it Allen cast himself as a stand-up comic and writer devoted to New York. Two years later, from its George Gershwin soundtrack to its monochrome photography, *Manhattan* was as much an ode to New York as it was a tale of the "emotional alienation of the Manhattan intelligentsia". Key scenes unfolded in Central Park, the Whitney Museum of American Art and the New York Aquarium.

Perhaps Allen's best 1980s New York film, however, was *Hannah and Her Sisters* (1986), with its complex dilemmas of upper- middle-class Manhattan intellectuals. *Annie Hall* star Diane Keaton returned for the genial *Manhattan Murder Mystery* (1993) and Allen's prodigious output continued with New York-set films such as *Bullets Over Broadway* (1994), the musical *Everyone Says I Love You* (1997), *Celebrity* (1998), *Small Time Crooks* (2000), 1940s film noir tribute *The Curse of the Jade Scorpion* (2001) and *Hollywood Ending* (2002).

▶▶ The Upper West Side *151D1*

Between the modernism of Lincoln Center and the turn-of-the-century mood of the Columbia University campus, the largely residential Upper West Side has remained solidly bourgeois over the past hundred years.

Still standing in a neat cluster around 72nd Street are some of the city's first luxury apartment houses. The Dakota, the earliest of them all, is described on page 96. Another one which is well worth a second glance is the Kenilworth Apartments, at the corner of Central Park West and 75th Street. The limestone twirls decorating its façade bring fresh meaning to the term "wedding-cake architecture". Elsewhere, gracefully ageing town houses cover large sections of the area and, close to the Hudson River, several streets contain picturesque Queen Anne-style homes.

While its buildings remain, recent decades have seen marked changes in the Upper West Side's social make-up. The park-facing apartments along Central Park West have always been occupied by the well-to-do, but much of what became Lincoln Center was a slum during the 1950s, and not by accident was it chosen as the site of the 1960 film *West Side Story*.

THE NICOLAS ROERICH MUSEUM
Born in Russia in 1874, Nicolas Roerich's life was devoted to art, archaeology and philosophy. In 1929, his "Peace through Culture" banner, intended to indicate and safeguard cultural monuments and institutions during times of war, earned him a Nobel Peace Prize nomination. The Nicolas Roerich Museum (319 West 107th Street; tel: 864-7752; *Open* Tue–Sun 2–5. *Admission free*) remembers this remarkable character with a few of his books and possessions and many of his enigmatic paintings, often depicting a lone figure striving to find enlightenment amid Himalayan landscapes.

Lincoln Center's arrival was followed by an influx of academics and media folk – many of them fleeing the rising rents of Greenwich Village. They have made the Upper West Side a liberal and cultured enclave boasting bookshops, cafés and some fashionable bars. Other new arrivals are high-earning professionals with young children, taking advantage of the neighbourhood's proximity to the green vistas and playgrounds of nearby Central Park and Riverside Park.

The American Museum of Natural History is one of the Upper West Side's main draws for visitors. From it you are well placed for further exploration on foot. Aim also to investigate the curious Nicolas Roerich Museum, on the northern edge of the Upper West Side (see panel).

Central Park West from the bridge on the Lake. The Dakota and other prestigious apartment houses arrayed along here have much-prized views over the park

New York

A 1939 OPINION
Appreciation of the Custom House's Beaux-Arts style seems to be a recent phenomenon. In the 1939 WPA (Works Progress Administration) *Guide to New York* the building is described as "somewhat ponderous in its neo-classical treatment".

▶ US Custom House   104A2

Broadway at Bowling Green (tel: 514-3700)
Open: daily 10–5. Admission free
Subway: 4; Bowling Green

On the site of Fort Amsterdam, Manhattan's first permanent European settlement, the 1907 former US Custom House is an eloquent Beaux-Arts statement designed by the previously unknown Cass Gilbert.

The Custom House cost a staggering $7 million, but at the time of its construction, customs revenue was the biggest contributor to the Treasury's coffers. New York's customs – with the city established as a major seaport – were the most lucrative of all.

Heavily endowed inside and out with symbols of maritime trade, the building has at its entrance several Corinthian columns topped by the head of the Roman god of commerce and holds a frieze etched with dolphins, anchors, masts and other nautical emblems.

Raised on pedestals on the Custom House's steps, four limestone sculptures by Daniel Chester French (best known for his statue of Abraham Lincoln in Washington, DC) represent the four great trading continents: Asia contemplating her navel, Europe looking to the past, Africa an unknown quantity – and America, lively enough to leap from her seat and sprint across Bowling Green. Inside, the building is capped by an impressive rotunda and decorated by a series of 16 frescoes by Reginald Marsh, commissioned by the Works Progress Administration, a government office that created work for American artists and writers during the Depression. It shows the travels of American explorers and – much more interestingly – an ocean liner docking in New York, with Greta Garbo among the disembarking passengers.

The US Custom Service moved in 1973, and the building was closed. One section, ironically in a building packed with markers to the glories of commerce, reopened as the city's bankruptcy court. Since 1994, the US Custom House has held the National Museum of the American Indian (see page 164).

Though no longer used by US Customs, the lavishly built Custom House at Bowling Green stands as testimony to the prosperity that maritime trade once brought to New York

▶▶ Whitney Museum of American Art   187B1

Madison Avenue at 75th Street (tel: 570-3676)
Open: Tue–Wed 11–6, Thu 1–9, Fri–Sun 11–6.
Admission: moderate. Subway: G; 77th Street

In one form or another, the Whitney Museum has ignored fashion, upset critics, baffled the general public and been single-minded in its devotion to supporting emerging American artists for eight decades. It now finds itself in possession of some of the most important names – and works – of 20th-century art.

Wealthy would-be sculptor Gertrude Vanderbilt Whitney began supporting young artists in the 1910s, purchasing and displaying their output at her Greenwich Village studio. During the 1920s, she presided over the Whitney Studio Club, a celebrated art forum that displayed works by Edward Hopper, Stuart Davis and John Sloan. These and other Whitney-backed artists emerged as major creative forces in contemporary American art, though they did not do much to impress the Metropolitan Museum of Art, who rejected Whitney's offer of her personal collection in 1929. The snub encouraged Whitney to found her own museum, which moved to its present home – a severe rectangular block of granite-clad reinforced concrete designed by Marcel Breuer – in 1966.

First held in 1932 (and continuing in odd-numbered years), the Whitney Biennial continues to be a controversial, invitational exhibition of the country's latest trends – often meeting the mixed response that greeted Gertrude Whitney's earliest buys. Despite the museum's attention to emerging artists and its strong temporary exhibitions, it is the long-established names that provide the main appeal for first-time visitors. The Permanent Collection galleries are a roll-call of American greats and include such influential figures as Claes Oldenburg, Mark Rothko, Jasper Johns, Roy Lichtenstein, Andy Warhol, Willem de Kooning and Jackson Pollock. Within this area, three galleries are devoted to equally important artists with close links to the Whitney: Alexander Calder, Georgia O'Keeffe and Edward Hopper.

Most of the big names of 20th-century American art are represented at the Whitney Museum

191

THE WHITNEY BRANCH MUSEUMS
In 1973 the Whitney opened its first branch museum – staging free exhibitions on special themes – in the Financial District. By the late 1980s it had four such branches elsewhere in Manhattan (and another one in Connecticut).

Sadly, the effects of the recession have left just one branch museum remaining in the city: at the Philip Morris Building, 120 Park Avenue.

▶▶▶ Woolworth Building   *104C2*

Broadway between Barclay Street and Park Place
Subway: 2, 3; Park Place

Although once dwarfed – but certainly not outshone – by the nearby twin-towers of the World Trade Center, the Woolworth Building became the world's tallest building on its completion in 1913, when its 240m high tower, with Gothic pinnacles, canopies and gargoyles, became an instant city landmark. The Woolworth Building retained its title of "world's tallest" until it was overtaken by the Chrysler Building in 1929.

Commissioned by Frank W Woolworth as a head-quarters for his ultra-lucrative chain of 2,000 "five-and-dime stores", the building was designed by Cass Gilbert (also responsible for the US Custom House, see page 190) and officially opened in April 1913 by President Woodrow Wilson. He flicked a switch in the White House to bathe the building – nick-named "the Cathedral of Commerce" by a commentator of the time – in the glow of 80,000 light bulbs.

The exterior of the Woolworth building is certainly impressive, but the lobby – one of the richest in New York – with entrances on Broadway, Barclay Street and Park Place, is the real treat. Step inside to admire the blue, green and gold mosaics on the vaulted ceiling, wonder at the grand marble staircase, and look for the sculptured caricatures of Woolworth (depicted in the process of counting his nickels and dimes) and Gilbert (holding a model of the building), alongside other worthies.

F W WOOLWORTH
Rags-to-riches stories are seldom more spectacular than that of Frank Winfield Woolworth. He began his retail career as a humble clerk during the mid-1800s – an era when customers had to approach staff to ask about merchandise and, as likely as not, haggle over a price. In 1879, the first Woolworth "five-and-dime store" broke new ground by allowing customers to pick up and examine the stock, which was priced at either 5¢ or 10¢. By the time the Woolworth Building was commissioned, Woolworth presided over 2,000 shops and was able to uphold their no-credit credo by paying for the building in cash – a total of $13.5 million.

BATTERY PARK AREA
While much of this area was severely damaged by the 2001 World Trade Center attacks, rebuilding continues apace and a visit to the riverside Esplanade of Battery Park City to watch the sun set over the Hudson is worth every minute.

Symbol of a world-famous empire: the Woolworth Building

World Trade Center Site   104C1

The site of the World Trade Center lies between Liberty and Vesey streets on the south and north sides, and West and Church streets on the west and east. Access to the site is limited. Subway: 2, 3; Park Place

A mere 28 years old when they were destroyed in the terrorist attack of 11 September, 2001, the twin towers of architect Minoru Yamasaki's World Trade Center reached half a kilometre above Lower Manhattan. At 110 storeys, the towers became the world's tallest edifice when they were finished in 1973, a distinction they held only until Chicago's Sears Tower arrived the following year. The gigantic towers were not the most popular of skyscrapers

WHAT NOW?
At press time, hot debate over what should be built on the World Trade Center site continued. Projections ranged from a memorial park to exact replicas of the twin towers

when they were unveiled, but, as the years passed, they gained more and more fans, and the 58-second ride in the express elevator to the 107th floor – and fantastic views – was top of every tourist's must-do list.

The towers' design was unusual. They were held up by steel columns – 59 along each exterior face, and 47 at each tower's core – braced and stabilised by horizontal floor trusses of zig-zagged steel. The outer walls transferred the impact of high winds through the floors to adjacent walls and thence to the ground, and were designed specifically to withstand an impact equivalent to a Boeing 707, as the towers' great height always made aircraft collision a possibility. Nobody expected the construction to be put to the test, but when the walls were hit they did in fact absorb the impact long enough to permit thousands to escape. What caused their collapse was the infernal heat softening the steel skeleton.

During their brief lives the towers proved irresistible to a few benign pranksters. French aerialist Philippe Petit rigged (and walked) a tightrope between the tops of the towers in August 1974. He was arrested and ordered to do kids' shows in Central Park. One Owen Quinn was aquitted of recklessness charges the following year when he parachuted off the top. A less fortunate George Willig was sued by the city in 1977 for climbing a tower using crampons; his luck turned when his fine was reduced to a penny per floor, or $1.10.

Ultimately, it was the World Trade Center's symbolic status as the heart of the capitalist world – many of the tenants were international bankers and stockbrokers – as well as its height that made it a target for terrorist attack.

The WTC, impressive close up, offered great views from the 107th floor

WHEN TO GO
Wherever you go within easy reach of New York City, it's best to visit between April and September. Not only will this avoid potentially chilly temperatures, it will also enable you to enjoy the dozens of local festivals that take place throughout the summer and to visit the local museums, many of which are closed throughout the winter.

Riverside living in the tranquil surroundings of the Hudson Valley. It is hard to believe the frenetic streets of New York City are barely 50km away

Excursions

Their affluent forebears may have had summer residences the length and breadth of the state, but many New Yorkers today go weak at the knees at the thought of leaving the familiar confines of the great metropolis.

Those who take the plunge, however, are rarely less than pleasantly surprised. Within an hour's drive of Manhattan lies a countryside thick with placid villages and abundant in blissfully rural vistas.

The Hudson Valley North of the city, the Hudson River flows through the 225km-long Hudson Valley (see pages 200–205). Once the major transit route into New York from New England, the river was of great strategic importance during the Revolutionary War, and several forts were founded along its course, one of which evolved into the famous Military Academy at West Point.

Though the battle sites remain, the valley no longer echoes to the sound of musket fire: its verdant hillsides and farmlands, studded with vineyards and orchards, are the embodiment of pastoral tranquillity. These are the scenes that inspired the nation's first homegrown art movement, the Hudson River School; many examples of the artists' work can be seen in the region's museums.

Within the valley's nooks and crannies are many surprises: stately American Gothic homes, millionaires' mansions, and the homes of Washington Irving (author of *Rip Van Winkle*), and Samuel F B Morse, the inventor of Morse code. The valley stops at the urban jungle (relatively speaking) of Albany, capital of New York State.

The Catskill Mountains Halfway up the Hudson Valley, the Catskill Mountains loom to the west (see pages 196–199). The highest peak in the Catskills, Slide Mountain, reaches only slightly above 1,220m, and rather than providing scope for rock-climbers, the so-called mountains – their sides coated by pine forests and cut by tumbling streams – provide a postcard-perfect natural setting for the dozens of tiny communities enclosed in their folds.

The rounded tops of the mountains are a legacy of the last ice-age, as are the deep gorges that sometimes hold spectacular waterfalls.

Photogenic views are abundant on the lanes that wind around the hills, and the Catskills' largest village, Woodstock, has a reputation for arts, crafts and culture stretching back to the early part of the century. With streets lined by clapboard homes, and dozens of galleries and craft shops displaying and selling locally produced works, Woodstock is a lovely place to succumb to the Catskills' rural pace, and its pavement cafés are prime vantage points for people-watching.

Long Island With its south coast bordered by the Atlantic Ocean and its north coast by Long Island Sound, the appropriately named Long Island (see pages 206–211) runs for 200km east from New York City, becoming progressively less populated as it does so.

Farming and seafaring were the traditional staples of Long Island life, but New Yorkers began frequenting the south shore's fine beaches a century ago: a group of pretty seaside villages called the Hamptons became a summer retreat for the wealthy, and to this day they remain a vacation destination for affluent beach lovers.

There are more excellent beaches along the protected dune-covered sand spit of Fire Island (part of it a popular gay getaway), though many of Long Island's more intriguing stops are on the north shore, where old whaling centres and immaculately preserved farming villages nestle among mansion homes built for families such as the Roosevelts and the Vanderbilts.

Clear skies, cool temperatures and warm colours make autumn a good time for touring the Catskills

CAR HIRE AND PUBLIC TRANSPORT
In the following pages, the excursions are described on the assumption that you are travelling by car. Note, though, that you will save money by hiring a car outside New York City. All the main towns of the Hudson Valley and Long Island are well served by public transport and have offices of the major car-hire companies, so it makes sense to hire once you have arrived. A healthy alternative is to combine public transport with exploration by bicycle. Cycle-hire outlets are plentiful in most towns during the summer. To discover the best of the Catskill Mountains, however, you will certainly need a car.

Drive

Catskill Mountains

This drive goes from Kingston to Saugerties, twice crossing the ear-popping Catskill highlands and also passing some of the region's most interesting villages along the way.

The drive takes you through the colourful village of Woodstock and continues through several smaller towns, skirting forested hillsides beneath high peaks.

The breathtaking scenery is found on the drive's eastward leg, on Route 23A, as it climbs from Prattsville to Hunter – famous for its winter skiing and summer festivals. An alternative route from Prattsville would take you to East Durham, worth a detour for its two museums.

The final stretch of the drive descends sharply into the Hudson Valley towards the serene village of Saugerties. A lovely, seldom crowded place, with quaint antique shops and preserved homes, Saugerties is also within easy reach of Slabsides, the log cabin of venerated local naturalist John Burroughs.

All the important points of interest that you will pass as you travel along the route are covered in detail on pages 197–199.

▶▶ Catskill Mountains 196

Kingston and Hurley While forest-covered hills and tiny villages secreted along winding lanes are what the Catskills are really all about, the region's largest town, Kingston▶▶, should not be overlooked.

Kingston began as a Dutch trading post in 1616. By the mid-1700s it had evolved into a significant commercial base and during the Revolutionary War it became the first capital of New York state.

At 312 Fair Street is the **Senate House State Historic Site**▶ (tel: 914/338-2786; *Open* mid-Apr–Oct, Wed–Sat 10–5, Sun 1–5, also open Memorial Day, Independence Day and Labor Day. *Admission free*), which has been restored to its 1777 style to mark Kingston's two months as the seat of statehood; the senate swiftly moved south as the British approached from the north. An adjoining building displays a selection of paintings by locally born Hudson River artist John Vanderlyn as well as few by his peers.

The Senate House is one of several 17th- and 18th-century Dutch-built stone houses that occupy the Stockade District, within fortifications erected in 1658 to protect the town from Native American attack. Within easy reach are numerous old homes and the **Old Dutch Church**▶ (tel: 914/338-6759; *Open* Mon–Fri 10–4. *Admission free*). Though built in 1852, the church was founded in 1659, and its cemetery bears Dutch tombs from that time.

Kingston's second historical area is the riverfront **Rondout** district, where the indoor and outdoor exhibits of the **Hudson River Maritime Museum** (tel: 845/338-0071; *Open* May–Oct, daily 11–5. *Admission: inexpensive*) chronicle the town's heyday as a boat-building and river trade centre.

A few kilometres west of here, **Hurley**▶ had a brief spell as the state capital during 1777 and retains its share of Dutch-built stone houses. Ten of these, on Main Street, open their doors to the public every year on the second Saturday in July.

NEW PALTZ

New Paltz, south of Kingston on Route 32, was settled in 1677 by a refugee community of French Huguenots. They were expert home builders and six of their houses remain in excellent condition along the appropriately named Huguenot Street. The local historical society leads tours of the homes (tel: 845/255-1889; *Open* May–Oct, Tue–Sun 9–4. *Admission: moderate*) furnished in period style and illustrating the trials and tribulations of local 17th-century life.

On Route 42 near Shandaken

Woodstock The best-known and busiest of the Catskill villages, **Woodstock**▶▶▶ (13km west of Kingston on Highway 212) gave its name to the legendary rock festival of 1969, even though the actual gathering took place 100km away. Nonetheless, if the festival had taken place here, it would have been well in keeping with the village's long-established Bohemian character.

HUNTER AND ITS FESTIVALS
New Yorkers know Hunter (north of Woodstock on Route 214) best as a ski resort, but when the snow leaves the slopes of Hunter Mountain the area kicks into its summer season with a series of festivals remarkable for their diversity. Early July finds an Italian festival, closely followed by a German Alps festival, and the first part of a country music festival. August sees the National Polka Festival, a Celtic festival, the second part of the country music festival, and a Golden Oldies festival. Rounding out the season is the Mountain Eagle Native American Indian Festival, in early September.

In the early 1900s, an Englishman inspired by the Utopian ideals of John Ruskin and William Morris founded the **Byrdcliffe Arts Colony** (tel: 914/679-2079 or 914/339-9935) on a 12-hectare site in the hills around Woodstock (look for the signposted road off Highway 212). Artists and artisans arriving to live and work in the studios helped create a rich programme of cultural events in the village, a tradition which still continues into the present day.

West from Woodstock Continuing deeper into the Catskill hills, the roads weave and pass tiny villages such as **Phoenicia** and **Shandaken**, where white-water rafting and a rich sprinkling of gourmet-class French restaurants are the main sources of local income. Both appeal to well-heeled weekending New Yorkers, who regard this area as their own piece of heaven.

On the western side of the Catskills, **Arkville** offers a touch more diversity with the **Delaware & Ulster Rail Ride**▶ (tel: 845/586-3877; *Open* late-May–Oct, Wed–Sun 10–5. *Admission: moderate*), which operates over a 19km segment of a historic railway that makes a jaunt to Halcottsville and back several times a day and offers various other rides.

Roxbury and Prattsville North of Arkville, **Roxbury** acquired the **Jay Gould Memorial Reform Church** in 1892.

This imposing structure of limestone and oak was erected by the children of the unloved robber baron Gould, who was born here in 1836.

A more worthwhile call is to the **John Burroughs Memorial State Park▶** (tel: 315/768-7224; grounds: *Open daily dawn to dusk. Admission free*), 3km west. Here the Catskills' foremost naturalist was born in 1837 and buried in 1921. Burroughs accompanied the likes of Theodore Roosevelt, Thomas Edison and Henry Ford on camping trips into the Catskills and introduced the wonders of its nature to many more in his informative writings.

Named after local tannery-owner Zadock Pratt, **Prattsville▶▶** claims to be the first planned community in the country and backs up this assertion with some excellently maintained 1830s houses. One of them, the home of Pratt himself, stores the local history collections of the commendable **Zadock Pratt Museum▶** (tel: 518/299-3395; *Open* May–Oct, Wed–Sun 1–5. *Admission: inexpensive*).

In **East Durham** on the Catskills' northern edge, you will come across an entertaining collection with something to catch the interest of almost everyone. There are a variety of farm tools, fossils, Native American artifacts, military paraphernalia and miscellaneous household furnishings displayed in the **Durham Center Museum▶** (tel: 518/239-8461; *Open* Apr–Oct, Wed, Thu, Sat and Sun 1–4. *Admission free*). The building itself is a former schoolhouse which was built in 1825.

In complete contrast, the watery rides of the **Zoom Flume Water Park▶** (tel: 1/800 888-3586; *Open* June–Labor Day, Mon–Fri 10–6, Sat and Sun 10–7. *Admission: expensive*) close by on Shady Glen Road are the perfect way to keep cool on a hot day. Take a picnic lunch and some children with you and make the most of it.

PRATT ROCKS
Just outside Prattsville, on Route 23, are the Pratt Rocks, which carry engravings depicting Pratt and his horse. They were commissioned by Zadock Pratt during the 1860s, to enable an itinerant stone-cutter to earn the money to pay for lodgings.

Left, below and bottom: aspects of Woodstock, the classic Catskills village

Drive

Hudson Valley

Ever-changing views of the Hudson River and its beautiful tree-studded valley will guarantee lasting memories of this drive.

See map opposite.

Take two or even three days to make the most of the route, visiting some of the valley's many unique communities and historic homes – some of which have been a feature of the Hudson Valley region since its earliest European settlement.

The drive ends at Albany, New York's capital and one of the few Hudson Valley towns where modern buildings are as much in evidence as those from times long past.

The points of interest you will pass along the route are covered in detail on pages 200–205.

The Philipsburg Manor, north of Tarrytown: scenes of rural New York life during the 17th century

▶▶ Hudson Valley

Yonkers to Tarrytown Although it is unrepresentative of the pastoral scenes further to the north, industrial **Yonkers** should be your first stop out of New York City on the Sawmill River Parkway or via Metro North (taxis at every train stop will transport you locally for a few dollars).

The evocative Hudson River School landscapes gracing Yonkers' **Hudson River Museum▶** (tel: 914/963-4550; *Open* May–Sep, Wed–Sun 12–5, Fri 12–9; rest of the year Wed–Sun 12–5. *Admission: inexpensive*) will whet your appetite for what lies ahead.

Near by, a taste of Hudson Valley history is provided by the stone-built **Philipse Manor▶** (tel: 845/965-4027; *Open* Apr–Oct, Wed and Thu 11–2, Sat 12–5. *Admission free*), where Frederick Philipse III – grandson of a Dutch settler who made a fortune through shipping and slavery – led a life of ease until he was imprisoned during the Revolutionary War for supporting the British.

Further north on Route 9, just south of Tarrytown, a neo-Gothic castle, complete with battlements, towers and spires, stands beside the river, screened by woodlands. Known as **Lyndhurst▶▶▶** (tel: 914/631-4481; *Open* daily mid-Apr–mid-Oct, Tue–Sun 10–5; rest of year Sat and Sun 10–4. *Admission: moderate*), the exuberant structure is among the finest examples of American Gothic architecture and is the work of the genre's leading practitioner, Alexander Jackson Davis.

Built in 1838, Lyndhurst was purchased by the despised robber baron Jay Gould in 1880. To his credit, Gould maintained the structure well, and his descendants lived here until 1961. The building sits in 26 hectares of sumptuously landscaped grounds, and its interior is filled by a grand collection of Victoriana.

As Lyndhurst was nearing completion, author Washington Irving moved into a far less ostentatious dwelling 1.7km away at **Sunnyside▶▶** (tel: 914/631-8200; *Open* Jan–Mar, Sat and Sun 10–4; Apr–Dec, daily 10–4. *Admission: inexpensive*), where he added Dutch gables and a Romanesque tower to what was originally a 17th-century farmer's cottage. Guided tours explore the 17 rooms where the creator of *Rip Van Winkle* and *The Legend of Sleepy Hollow* spent the later years of his life.

Off Route 9 north of Tarrytown is **Philipsburg Manor▶▶** (tel: 914/631-8200; *Open* Jan–Mar, Sat and Sun 10–4; Apr–Dec, daily 10–4. *Admission: inexpensive*). This building is a reconstruction of the 17th-century mill at the heart of the Philipse family's empire. With livestock in the yard and the gristmill and granary in operation, the tours led by guides in 1750s attire are informative and fun.

Above left: Sunnyside, home of author Washington Irving, is one of several preserved buildings near Tarrytown

Excursions

Little more than a pitchfork's throw from the manor, the **Old Dutch Church**▶ (for information call Tarrytown Historical Society, tel: 914/681-8374) was built at the direction of Frederick Philipse I in 1697. Alongside those of numerous Dutch settlers the cemetery holds the tombs of Andrew Carnegie and Washington Irving. The headless hero of Irving's *Legend of Sleepy Hollow* arose from his slumbers here.

Tarrytown to West Point On the Hudson's west bank, accessible via the Tappan Zee Bridge (1-287 west) Route 9W passes close to the village of **Nyack**▶, birthplace of the great American realist artist Edward Hopper in 1882. The artist spent much of his life here, at what is now the **Hopper House Arts Center** (82 North Broadway, tel: 914/358-0774; *Open* Thu–Sun 12–5. *Admission: donation*). His finest canvases are hung in prestigious museums elsewhere, but devotees will find a few of his local landscapes here, plus a large number of souvenir prints and books.

Further north off Route 9W is the **Stony Point Battlefield State Historic Site**▶ (tel: 914/786-2521; *Open* mid-Apr–Oct, Wed–Sat 10–5, Sun 1–5, also Memorial Day, Independence Day and Labor Day. *Admission free*), the remains of a British fort attacked and captured in a midnight raid by General "Mad" Anthony Wayne in 1779. A visitors' centre describes the battle and its significance.

Beyond Stony Point, Route 9W climbs into the **Hudson Highlands**: an area of rare beauty, where the river narrows and the increasingly sheer tree-clad valley walls are studded with exposed rock.

Route 218 wends a scenic route above the river, passing through the **United States Military Academy at West Point**▶. Since 1802, West Point has sought to instil

THE NAMING OF TARRYTOWN

According to author Washington Irving, local Dutch wives were responsible for the naming of Tarrytown. It was "due to the inveterate propensity of their husbands to linger about the village tavern on market day". Less romantically inclined sources suggest the name was a corruption of the Dutch word for wheat, *Tarwe*.

The campus of the Military Academy at West Point. Visitors here can stroll in the footsteps of many famous Americans

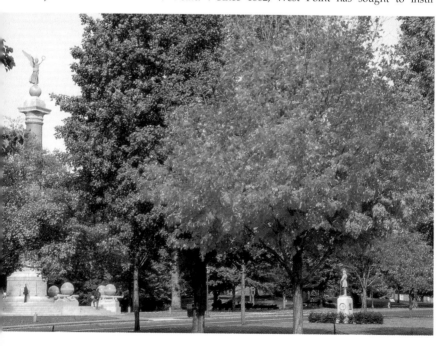

discipline, moral fibre and leadership qualities into its cadets. Numerous presidents, generals and astronauts have graduated from here; even among the drop-outs there have been some famous names, such as Edgar Allan Poe and the late Timothy Leary, the LSD guru of the 1960s.

Ports of call here include the **West Point Museum**, (tel: 914/938-2368; *Open* daily 10:30–4:15. *Admission free*) with mementos – guns, flags, medals and more – from every conflict that has ever involved the US; the remains of the Revolutionary-era **Fort Putnam**, perched 140m above the Hudson; and the **Drill Ground** (known as the "**Plain**"), where some of West Point's 4,000 cadets may sometimes be seen marching along with their geometric precision.

West Point to Poughkeepsie At **Newburgh**, the next major settlement, George Washington occupied a stone dwelling, built by Dutch settler Jonathan Hasbrouck, at 84 Liberty Street during the 16 months between the British surrender and the signing of the peace accord in Paris. Preserved as **Washington's Headquarters/Jonathan Hasbrouck House▶** (tel: 914/562-1195; *Open* mid-Apr–Oct, Wed–Sat 10–5, Sun 1–5, also Presidents' Day, Memorial Day, Independence Day, Labor Day and Columbus Day. *Admission free*), the house is one of several 18th- and 19th-century homes that make a short stroll around the town time well spent.

A better picture of the stresses of the Revolutionary period is provided by the **New Windsor Cantonment State Historic Site▶▶** (tel: 914/561-1765; *Open* mid-Apr–Oct, Wed–Sat 10–5, Sun 1–5, also Memorial Day, Independence Day and Labor Day. *Admission: inexpensive*), southwest of Newburgh near Vails Gate. Here, 10,000 of Washington's troops were accommodated in log cabins at the end of the war; only a speech by Washington himself quelled a mutiny in their ranks. During the summer months, local history enthusiasts re-create bygone scenes here, some of them firing replica Revolutionary-era weaponry.

North of Newburgh lie the foothill villages of the Catskill Mountains. In contrast, on the east bank of the Hudson is **Poughkeepsie**. A venerable institution from Poughkeepsie's past is **Vassar College▶** (for information tel: 845/437-7300), which was founded as an all-female college in 1861.

Nothing out of place: the Plain, West Point's parade ground

VASSAR COLLEGE
Strange as it may seen, profits from the production of beer helped fund Vassar College – founded in 1861 by local brewer Matthew Vassar. The intention of the rich and philanthropic Vassar was to offer women the liberal arts education that was available to men. The college did begin to admit men in 1969, although its student body remains overwhelmingly female. Besides male students, another comparatively recent addition is the Frances Lehman Loeb Art Center, built by architect Cesar Pelli, to house the college's artworks. Pelli is better known for the far grander World Financial Center in Manhattan.

THE SHAKERS

Founded in 1747, the Shakers – so named for the ecstatic trembling that followed their ritualistic dances – became one of the largest and most respected of the religious sects of the post-Revolutionary era. By the 1840s, more than 4,000 Shakers were living in twenty Shaker villages spread from Maine to Kentucky. Shaker skills and craftsmanship had enormous impact on rural America (their furniture is still highly coveted), and the sect's many inventions included the flat-headed broom, the wooden clothes peg and the circular saw. Increasing wealth led to conflict within Shaker communities, which steadily declined from 1875. Many Shakers, however, retained their beliefs until death.

204

ALBANY'S EGGSHELL

What looks like a gigantic upturned eggshell in the centre of Albany is in fact the home of ESIPA, or Empire State Institute for the Performing Arts (tel: 516/473-1061; *Open* daily 8:30–5). Inside, the eggshell has seating for 900 and a regular programme of varied musical and theatrical events.

A 3km detour south from Poughkeepsie on Route 9 leads to **Locust Grove**►► (tel: 845/454-4500; *Open* Memorial Day–late Sep, 10–3. *Admission: inexpensive*). The house was bought in 1847 by inventor Samuel Morse, who enlisted the aid of Alexander Jackson Davis to transform it into a Tuscan-style villa. A pile of Morse's telegraph equipment shares the interior of the building with a diverting cache of Victorian furnishings.

Poughkeepsie to Albany Morse may be remembered by the code that bears his name, but he could not match the achievements of Franklin D Roosevelt: destined to become the nation's longest-serving president, he was born in a clapboard house beside the Hudson in 1882, near the hamlet of Hyde Park, on Route 9 north of Poughkeepsie.

Roosevelt converted the house into a 35-room Georgian-style mansion in 1916 and used it to treat royalty and heads of state to Hudson Valley views. It is now preserved as the **Franklin D Roosevelt National Historic Site**►► (tel: 845/229-9115; *Open* daily 9–5. *Admission: moderate*), and everyone is welcome to step inside and admire the Roosevelt taste in interior design.

Within the grounds is the **Museum of the Franklin D Roosevelt Library**► (tel: 914/229-8114; *Open* May–Oct, daily 9–6, Nov–Apr, 9–5. *Admission: inexpensive*), which stores the presidential archive and has an exhibition on Roosevelt's life and achievements. A shuttle bus continues to the **Eleanor Roosevelt National Historic Site**► (tel: 914/229-9115; *Open* May–Oct, daily 9–5, rest of the year Sat and Sun 9–5. *Admission: moderate*), used by Roosevelt's wife Eleanor as a summer resort and as a permanent home during her widowhood.

The **Vanderbilt Mansion National Historic Site**►► (tel: 914/229-9115; *Open* daily 9–5. *Admission: moderate*) stands 3km further north. Frederick W Vanderbilt, grandson of millionaire Cornelius Vanderbilt, lavished $2 million of the family fortune on this three-storey Beaux-Arts mansion. Inside, the Persian rugs, Flemish tapestries and other expensive features are on display. When Vanderbilt's niece could not find a buyer for the house in 1940, she donated it to the nation.

The most imaginative home in the Hudson Valley is not a multimillion-dollar mansion but **Olana**►► (tel: 518/828-0135; *Open* Apr–Oct, Wed–Sat 10–4, Sun 12–4. *Admission: inexpensive*), on Route 9G southwest of Hudson. An inspired mix of Moorish and Middle Eastern building styles, Olana arose in the 1870s as the home of a leading Hudson River School artist, Frederick Church. Decorated with Islamic and Byzantine motifs, Olana's arched doors and windows frame gorgeous views. The interior is crammed full of eastern treasures.

On the final stretch towards Albany, make an eastward detour to Old Chatham, a base of the religious community of the Shakers from 1787. The **Shaker Museum**►► (tel: 518/794-9100; *Open* May–Oct, Wed–Mon 10–5. *Admission: inexpensive*) at Old Chatham has the most comprehensive collection of their simple and superbly crafted furnishings. There are eight buildings displaying numerous examples of Shaker achievements in carpentry, metalwork and weaving. Other exhibits detail the history of the community and its beliefs.

Marking the northern end of the Hudson Valley is **Albany▶▶**, which boomed during the 18th century as a trade and transport centre, becoming New York's state capital in 1797. A thorough restoration programme has kept many of Albany's 19th-century buildings in good order, but what dominates the town centre is the 1960s white marble modernism of **Empire State Plaza**, whose 400m-long pedestrian way is decorated by free-form sculpture. Take the lift to the observation gallery on the 42nd floor of the plaza's tallest building, the **Corning Tower▶** (tel: 518/474-2418; Observation deck: *Open* Mon–Fri 9–3:45, Sat and Sun 10–3:45), for views over the valley.

At ground level, the plaza runs out beneath the pink granite exterior of the 1898 **New York State Capitol▶▶▶** (*tours* Mon–Fri hourly 9–4, Sat and Sun 10, 11, 2, 3. *Admission free*) built at a cost of $24 million and gaining French, Italian and Romanesque features as tastes – and architects – changed during its 30 years of construction. Guided tours wind up an elegant marble staircase to the restored legislative chambers.

Across the plaza is the **New York State Museum▶▶▶** (tel: 518/474-5877; *Open* daily 9:30–5. *Admission free*), which uses exhibits and walk-through dioramas to describe the region's history, shedding light on subjects as diverse as the geology of the Adirondacks and Manhattan's architecture.

There is more on show at the **Albany Institute of History and Art▶▶** (125 Washington Avenue, tel: 516/463-4478; *Open* Wed–Sun 12–5. *Admission: inexpensive*), with Dutch settlement furniture, crockery and aristocratic portraiture, alongside a selection of Hudson River School paintings.

The state government of New York has its offices in Albany's Empire State Plaza

THE SCHUYLER MANSION
If travelling through the valley has not exhausted your appetite for period homes, the pick of Albany's stately residences is the 1762 Schuyler Mansion (32 Catherine Street; tel: 518/434-0834; *Open* mid-Apr–Oct, Wed–Sat 10–5, Sun 1–5. *Admission: inexpensive*), built for the well-connected Philip Schuyler, a successful businessman who served with distinction as an officer during the Revolutionary War.

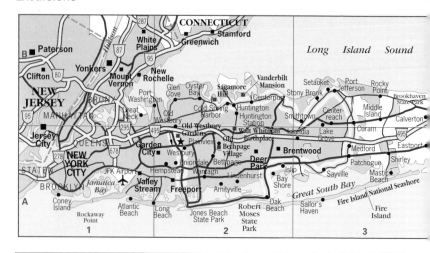

Drive

Long Island

This drive takes in some of Long Island's beaches, historic homes and atmospheric fishing ports.

From the beautifully landscaped Old Westbury Gardens, the drive continues to popular Jones Beach before passing the south-shore communities of Sayville and Patchogue. The route then passes tiny farming hamlets before reaching the picturesque villages of Setauket and Stony Brook on the north shore.

The Vanderbilt mansion can be reached down a side road off the main route, or you can continue direct to Walt Whitman's birthplace and the one-time whaling settlement of Cold Spring Harbor. The final stop is at Sagamore Hill, the stately home of Theodore Roosevelt. The points of interest you will pass along the route, as well as other highlights of a more extended visit to Long Island, are covered in detail on pages 207–211.

The beaches on Long Island's south shore are extensive enough to absorb any number of holidaying New Yorkers

►Long Island

Old Westbury and Old Bethpage Much of western Long Island is now seamless suburbia criss-crossed by freeways, but a century ago it was rural. John S Phipps, the son of Andrew Carnegie's business partner, chose a plot near Old Westbury as the site for a rambling country estate. Phipps' red-brick Westbury House was completed in 1903. Today, the 40ha grounds, known as **Old Westbury Gardens►►** (tel: 516/333-0048; *Open* May–mid-Dec, Wed–Mon 10–5. *Admission: moderate*), are the main attraction for visitors: landscaped and planted to perfection, the gardens have thousands of mature trees and an aromatic rose garden in their midst.

Long Island provides not only an escape from New York City but also, in **Old Bethpage Village►►** (tel: 516/572-8400; *Open* Mar–Oct, Mon–Fri 10–5; rest of the year reduced hours. *Admission: inexpensive*), an escape from the present day. Crushed-oystershell lanes lead into this recreation of an 1800s farming village, typical of those that

AMITYVILLE

A house on a hill in Amityville, in deepest Long Island suburbia, caused its occupants to flee in terror during the early 1970s. After the subsequent book and film, both called *The Amityville Horror*, describing (and apparently greatly exaggerating) the events, were released, locals found themselves spending a lot of their time directing sightseers to the scene of the grisly goings-on. Not surprisingly, the house has proved difficult to sell over the years and still casts a strange spell over this otherwise rather ordinary community.

THE WILLIAM FLOYD ESTATE

Close to Mastic Beach, where the road to eastern Fire Island meets the mainland, the William Floyd Estate (tel: 631/399–2030; *Open* year round, hours vary by season) is what is left of the plantation owned by General William Floyd, one of the signers of the Declaration of Independence. The simple house Floyd built in 1724 remains at the centre of the 240 hectare estate, greatly added to by successive generations of his descendants. The last of them lived here until 1975, while many of the others lie buried within the grounds in the family cemetery. The house's 25 rooms unfurl a fascinating tale of changing family fortunes.

The north shore of Long Island has great appeal for New Yorkers seeking a place in the country

dotted Long Island long before the days of freeways and suburbia. As the village's tailor, blacksmith, quilters and shopowners go about their daily tasks, it is hard not to be impressed by the thoroughness of it all.

Jones Beach and Fire Island Most New Yorkers hitting Long Island, however, are thinking not of old farming ways but about sunbathing on the south shore. On any summer weekend, **Jones Beach** is a picture of New York at play. Much the same applies to **Fire Island**, a renowned gay holiday area. The longest of the sandspits that flank the southern shore of Long Island, Fire Island is federally protected as **Fire Island National Seashore** (tel: 613/289-4810. *Admission free*). The only section of the island reachable by car is **Robert Moses State Park** (tel: 613/660-0449; *Open* daily dawn–dusk. *Admission free, fee for parking*), covering over 400 pristine hectares at the island's western extremity. Adjacent, and functioning as a visitor centre and museum documenting lighthouse keepers, shipwrecks and sea rescues, is the **Fire Island Light Station** (tel: 613/661-4876; *Open* daily 9:30–4:30, weekends only in winter. *Admission free*).

All of Fire Island is public land, although several sections are dominated by private resort communities, each with its distinctive social makeup. Day-trippers are not always welcomed with open arms at the more exclusive of them. One inviting destination for a day-trip, which can be reached by ferry from Sayville, is **Sailor's Haven▶▶** (tel: 516/589-8980). The fine beach, the nature trails weaving around the dunes, and the hardy vegetation forming the **Sunken Forest▶** should not be missed. A visitors' centre provides absorbing background material on Fire Island's subtle ecology.

The Hamptons East of Fire Island, the settlements collectively known as the Hamptons sat placidly at the centre of windmill-studded farmland until the late 19th century, when wealthy New Yorkers discovered their holiday potential and transformed them into highly desirable seaside resorts. The Hamptons are still a getaway for the rich whose huge mansions stand close to fine beaches, chic boutiques and pricey restaurants. **Southampton▶** is one of the Island's oldest towns; the **Halsey Homestead▶** (tel: 516/283-3527; *Open* mid-June–mid-Sep, Tue–Sat 11–4:30, Sun 2–4:30. *Admission free*), built in 1648, claims to be the oldest timber-framed house in the entire state. The best-looking of the Hamptons, **East Hampton▶▶**, has narrow streets bordered by neatly trimmed hedges and picket-fenced cottages. Locally born actor and dramatist John Howard Payne liked the place so much that he composed the most sentimental of songs, "Home Sweet Home", here, a fact duly acknowledged by the preservation of his house as the **Home Sweet Home Museum►** (tel: 631/324-0713; *Open* Mon–Sat 10–4, Sun 2–4. *Closed* holidays), which is mostly filled with a collection of 18th-century ceramics.

On Main Street, the 1784 **Clinton Academy►** (tel: 516/324-6850; *Open* Jul and Aug, daily 10–5, Jun and Sep, Sat and Sun 10–5. *Admission free*), once a revered seat of learning, now has exhibitions on varied facets of local life.

Cross the Robert Moses Causeway to reach the south shore

Sag Harbor Unless you want to make the 30km drive to the eastern end of Long Island (see panel), head northwest from East Hampton to **Sag Harbor► ►**. Though few people would believe it on first sight, this sleepy waterside community was once a busy port, second only to New York City in its importance. Until 1871 it boasted the world's fourth largest whaling fleet.

Recalling those glory days, a whale's jawbone frames the doorway of the former Masonic Temple that is now the town's **Whaling and Historical Museum► ►** (tel: 631/725-0770; *Open* mid-May–Sep, Mon–Sat 10–5, Sun 1–5. *Admission: inexpensive*), where piles of scrimshaw and nautical objects are stacked to the ceiling. The 1789 **Custom House►** (tel: 631/725-0250; *Open* Jul and Aug, daily 10–5. *Admission free*) is another survivor of Sag Harbor's seafaring heyday, as is the **Whaler's Church►**, built in 1841 in a curious Greek-Egyptian style. As if to mark the decline of Sag Harbor's sea trade, the church's steeple – long a landmark for seamen – was blown down by the fierce hurricane of 1938.

Shelter Island A quick ferry ride north from Sag Harbor brings you to **Shelter Island** which is not only a shortcut to Long Island's north fork (a second ferry crosses to Greenport) but also an ideal spot to relax among narrow, weaving lanes that are flanked by attractive Victorian cottages. It was previously a haunt of 18th-century pirates and Prohibition-era bootleggers.

LONG ISLAND'S EASTERN TIP
If you drive east from East Hampton to Montauk, you will kick yourself for not continuing a further 8km to Montauk Point, the last stop before the Irish coast. A lighthouse, built on the instruction of George Washington in 1797, sits at the easternmost point. The rewards for braving vertigo and dizziness to climb its 138 steps are views of Rhode Island and the Connecticut coast.

Sagamore Hill was completed in 1885 for the only US president to have been born in New York City, Theodore Roosevelt; the cost of the 22-room house was $16,975

RIVERHEAD
One reason to visit Riverhead, a town off the main routes between the Hamptons and the north shore, might be the Suffolk County Museum (tel: 631/727–2881; *Open* Tue–Sat 12:30–4:30. *Admission free*), whose exhibits range from local Native American cultures to whaling. Another reason could be the produce of the Palmer Vineyards (tel: 631/722-WINE; *Open* daily 11–6). If you are visiting in mid-August, Riverhead's Polish Street Fair and Festival should not be missed.

The north shore An exploration of Long Island's north shore is best begun at **Sagamore Hill▶ ▶ ▶** (tel: 516/922-4447; *Open* daily 9:30–4:30. *Admission: inexpensive*), a three-storey house set in 32 green hectares just east of Oyster Bay and completed in 1884 as the summer home of Theodore Roosevelt. Two floors of the main house hold roomfuls of Victorian furnishings and an extraordinary number of Roosevelt's hunting trophies. The spacious wood-panelled rooms provided the setting for Roosevelt's peace-brokering between warring Russia and Japan in 1905, for which he was awarded the Nobel Peace Prize. Further exhibits, and a short film detailing Roosevelt's life, can be viewed in the adjoining Old Orchard Home Museum, added by his son in 1938.

Continuing east on Route 25A is the **Whaling Museum** at **Cold Spring Harbor▶** (tel: 516/367-3418; *Open* Tue–Sun 11–5. *Admission: inexpensive*), which remembers the nine-ship whaling fleet based here during the mid-1880s. The exhibits include one of the few existing complete whaling vessels, and numerous smaller pieces – examples of scrimshaw, harpoons and other tools.

When the Cold Spring Harbor whaling fleet was still sailing the high seas, Walt Whitman – born in 1819, 3km away in Huntington – was busy overturning the rules of traditional verse to create *Leaves of Grass*, the work that sealed his place as a literary great. The two-storey shingled dwelling built in 1816 by Whitman's father is now the **Walt Whitman Birthplace State Historic Site▶ ▶** (tel: 631/427-5240; *Open* Memorial Day–Labor Day, daily 11–4; Sep–May, Wed–Fri 1–4, Sat and Sun 11–4. *Admission: inexpensive*), with exhibits recounting his adventure-filled life.

North of Centerport is the Spanish-style **Vanderbilt Mansion▶** (tel: 631/854-5579; *Open* Tue–Sun 12–5. *Admission: moderate*), which belonged to William K Vanderbilt II, great-grandson of Cornelius Vanderbilt. He combined his taste for opulent living with an interest in natural history, acquiring the 17,000 specimens of stuffed and mounted creatures that make a strange addition to the antiques and original furnishings on display in this shrine to luxury living. The adjacent Vanderbilt Planetarium has views of the heavens, which fail to match up to those across Long Island Sound.

Stony Brook and Setauket An almost too perfectly preserved village, **Stony Brook▶▶** was saved from neglect by wealthy philanthropist Ward Melville during the 1930s. Melville also financed the **Museums at Stony Brook▶▶▶** (tel: 631/751-0066; *Open* Wed–Sat 10–5, Sun 12–5. *Admission: inexpensive*), a complex that focuses on 19th-century Long Island life. Pride of place goes to the vintage carriages, and the paintings by William Sidney Mount, a Stony Brook resident who emerged as one of the country's most original and daring artists during the mid-1800s. First known as a portraitist, particularly noted for his painting of prominent statesmen, Mount acquired more lasting fame by capturing rural scenes on canvas, and was the first major painter to produce sympathetic images of African-Americans.

Close to Stony Brook is the similarly pretty village of **Setauket▶**, which was a hotbed of espionage during the revolutionary years of the late 1700s, and the birthplace of what is believed to have been the nation's first spy cell. One technique employed to outwit the occupying British troops was the conveying of messages using a local housewife's clothesline. The combination of clothing on the line corresponded to a prearranged code and did most damage – as far as the British were concerned – when used to alert George Washington to the approach of the French Expeditionary Force in 1780.

A TRIP TO CONNECTICUT?
Should the combination of Long Island's sea air and nautical museums give you the urge to take to the waves, you can seize the opportunity at Port Jefferson, 5km east of Setauket. From here, a ferry (taking both cars and pedestrians) makes the 30km crossing of Long Island Sound to Bridgeport in Connecticut, several times daily.

211

Framed by formal gardens, the 24-room Vanderbilt Mansion near Centerport sits at the heart of a 17-hectare estate and provides a taste of high-class living, although most visitors come for the excellent planetarium and natural history exhibits

The NYC & Company Visitor Information Center (810 Seventh Avenue between 52nd and 53rd streets, tel: 484-1222) publishes a free guide to hotels listing their addresses, phone numbers and prices, and indicating their location on a map. More opinionated descriptions of New York hotels can be found on pages 262–268.

Accommodation

From side-street fleapits with naked lightbulbs to world-class lodgings with en suite Jacuzzi and antique furnishings, the one thing all New York hotels share is inflated prices. True bargains can be extremely difficult to find; and when you do, you sometimes wish you hadn't.

Budget hotels Any hotel room priced under about $100 is unlikely to offer anything more than the basic necessities: a roof over your head and a mattress under your back, with the bathroom likely to be a shared one at the end of a corridor and equipped with erratic plumbing.

Shabby though they may be, hotels at the rock-bottom end of the market are usually safe, though some near Times Square are an exception and should be approached with caution.

Basic comforts For $100–200, you can expect a comfortable, if basic, room with colour TV (television addicts should ensure their hotel has cable channels) and a bathroom and telephone.

As you dig deeper into your budget and spend $200–250, rooms become more elegantly furnished. The TV carries more channels, a good range of complimentary soaps and shampoos should be found in the bathroom, and occasionally a complimentary newspaper will be delivered to your door each morning.

Spoiling yourself To taste the New York good life means that you can kiss goodbye to at least $250 a night. Do this, and you will be able to stretch out on a giant-sized bed in a large-sized room, with a fully equipped bathroom. Further spending will be encouraged by 24-hour room service. There should be a knowledgeable concierge available to recommend sightseeing trips, shows, galleries and restaurants, and to assist with reservations and tickets.

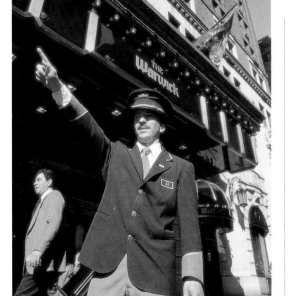

Hidden extras Although prices may seem frightening enough already, every hotel has to add on a string of taxes: New York City hotel tax (5 per cent) sales tax (8.25 per cent) and a $2 occupancy tax, per room, per night.

Therefore, what might seem an $80 bargain will actually turn out to cost $92.60, and stretching your budget to its limits for a $250 treat will land you with a bill close to $285.

Quoted rates do not include tax, and do not usually include breakfast either. Some hotels have restaurants, but going for breakfast at a nearby coffee shop or diner is always cheaper and a quintessentially New York way to start the day.

Special deals Slightly better news on the financial front is that hotel prices are often lower at weekends, when many establishments seek to tempt suburb dwellers to spend some time and money in the city by offering special cut-rate weekend deals.

Such packages can bring savings of up to 40 per cent on regular prices and are chiefly advertised in New York area newspapers. It is always worth enquiring whether a package is available. Longer-term visits will often also attract reduced rates: a few hotels give discounts for stays of two weeks or more.

Seasonal factors New York never runs short of visitors, but the peak tourist seasons match the clemency of the weather. The prime months are April, May and June. In the autumn, many hotels are filled by delegates who attend the numerous business conventions held in the city, and the months up to Christmas are spectacularly busy. So, make it a point never to turn up in New York without prearranging accommodation, at least for your first night, and do so well in advance of the date you expect to arrive.

DISCOUNTED ROOMS
In the hospitality industry, hotel rooms (like airplane seats) are considered extremely "perishable" because as soon as the night is over, the potential revenue for the room is lost. Quikbook operates like an airline broker for hotel rooms, making last-minute reservations for people in the city's best properties, often at seriously discounted rates (tel: 800/789–9887). Several websites like expedia.com and priceline.com provide a similar service.

The Upper East Side is a fittingly exclusive setting for the art deco Carlyle, a truly grand hotel

CREDIT CARDS
Most hotels accept credit cards as payment and, in fact, require your card details on arrival to cover incidentals. All major cards are widely accepted.

THE RAINES HOTEL LAW
In an effort to cut down the level of alcohol consumption among the city's down-and-outs, the Raines Hotel Law of 1896 made it illegal to sell liquor in New York on a Sunday, except in hotels to accompany meals. To circumvent this law, every seedy bar with a few spare rooms declared itself a hotel and offered inedible sandwiches to its oblivion-seeking customers. The law was soon repealed.

Reservations and payment To secure a room in advance, you will be asked to place a deposit. The simplest way of doing this is by quoting your credit card number by phone (or by fax). If you reserve a room without a deposit during a busy period and arrive after 6 PM you may find the room has been re-allocated. Always reconfirm your reservation as close to your arrival date as possible.

Payment for your full stay (or at least a large part of it) is sometimes expected on arrival by credit card, traveller's cheque, or cash (though carrying large amounts of money is not advisable in New York).

Areas of the city Manhattan is quick and simple to travel around, so you can be selective about where you stay. By far the densest concentration of hotels is in the section of Midtown Manhattan bordered by 44th and 57th streets, where some of the grandest and priciest accommodation can be found, in a knot around Grand Central Terminal and at the southern end of Central Park. The cheaper Midtown hotels (mostly around Times Square) can be unappealing, and you will get better value elsewhere.

In the southern reaches of Midtown Manhattan, where noise and traffic levels are more bearable, residential areas such as Chelsea and Gramercy Park hold several hotels full of character with attractive rates.

A handful of classy hotels with sky-high rates sit in the moneyed environs of the Upper East Side. On the other side of Central Park, the limited number of hotels on the Upper West Side are better value, especially if you like a large room, but are usually less elegant.

In Lower Manhattan, many high-rises in the Financial District are aimed at the expense-account traveller. In SoHo and TriBeCa are chic hotels that cater to the fashionable and affluent who desire a downtown aesthetic. More affordable and interesting lodgings are hotels dotted (albeit very thinly) through Chinatown and Greenwich Village.

Bed and breakfast Bed-and-breakfast accommodation is an increasingly popular alternative to staying in a hotel, but prices are not significantly lower: such is the demand for accommodation of every kind in a city where real bargains are hard to come by.

New York B&Bs fall into two categories. "Hosted" means that guests occupy a spare room or two in the apartment of a New Yorker who will provide at least a modest breakfast. Hosted B&Bs can be a source of useful insider information on the city, but there is always the risk that you might find yourself at odds with the host. With "unhosted" accommodation, guests get the run of a New York apartment whose owner is out of town.

B&B prices vary according to the neighbourhood and facilities. Many B&Bs are in outlying locations, so bear this in mind when booking. A hosted bed and breakfast is generally a cheaper option ($60–$150) than its unhosted equivalent ($80–$200). Rooms should be booked well in advance for the widest choice, although you can book the day before, if necessary. Among a growing number of bed and breakfast agencies are City Lights (PO Box 20355, Cherokee Station, New York, NY 10028; tel: 737-7049) and Urban Ventures (PO Box 426, New York, NY 10024; tel: 594-5650).

STUDENT DORMS
Further inexpensive accommodation is available (during short holiday times) in the student dorms of New York University. There is a minimum stay of three weeks and the cost per week is around $70. This kind of accommodation is extremely limited and is quickly snapped up. If you are interested, consult the New York telephone book and contact the housing office listed under the university entry.

215

Cheap and cheerful If hotels and B&Bs are beyond your budget but you still wish to see the Big Apple, the city has three YMCAs that, for slightly less than the cost of the cheapest hotel room, offer single, double and family rooms plus a range of facilities to men, women and family groups. The West Side YMCA occupies an elegant historic building at 5 West 63rd Street (tel: 787-4400).

You do not have to be a youth to stay at Hostelling International – New York's stylish and well-equipped New York hostel (891 Amsterdam Avenue; tel: 932-2300), although you do have to be a member of the International Youth Hostel Federation. Prices depend on whether you opt for a dormitory bed or a private room, but either cost substantially less than hotels and B&Bs. It is wise to make reservations in advance.

Home comforts, attractive bedrooms and excellent value for money make the Wyndham popular with New York regulars, so book well in advance

Food and drink

City that never sleeps it may be, but New York is also a city that never seems to stop eating. This gastronomic obsession is easily explained: no city on earth has such an abundance or such a variety of food available – from burgers, blintzes and catfish to dim sum and goulash – around the clock and at prices most people can afford.

Meals on the move The busier the street, the more vendors it will have. Most street vendors serve hot dogs – even the humble frankfurter in a bun has a place in New York culinary legend, and is a must-eat snack when visiting Coney Island (see page 75) – and also knishes (a doughy pastry filled with potatoes), bags of roasted chestnuts, and huge soft pretzels, crusted with salt – each for around a dollar ($1.50 in the pricey heart of Midtown Manhattan).

You are never far from the next snack in Manhattan

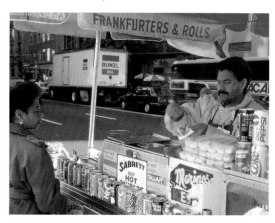

Another common sight are falafel (small deep-fried croquettes made of spiced, ground chick peas) carts and, occasionally, soup vendors. In the morning, you'll often see stands stuffed with breakfast pastries, oversized bagels and the like – breakfast-on-the-run.

In the Financial District, those working in the industry are to be seen not at chic restaurant tables, but eating their midday meal from rows of ethnic vendors lining the main thoroughfares. These pushcarts are the most convenient and quickest places to grab a bite. Here hot piles of meat or seafood and noodles are sold for only a few dollars.

The deli: a New York institution Street vendors apart, what New York has more of than any other American city is delis. The old-timers of the breed, known for their mile-high sandwiches stuffed with Eastern European meats such as pastrami, are nowadays few and far between. However, they have given their name to a variety of food sources all over the city where overstuffed sandwiches are served to eat in or take out.

More recently, Korean immigrants have given the word "deli" a whole new meaning, installing salad bars holding trays of cooked meats, seafood dishes, stir-fries, hot and cold vegetables, casseroles, salads, fruit and even sushi.

TIPPING
In any eating place that has waiter or waitress service, you are expected to leave a tip. Restaurant and coffee-shop staff depend on tips for a large part of their income, which is why the majority will eagerly attend to your needs. The precise amount that you leave should be judged according to the standard of service, but a tip of around 15 per cent of the bill is considered average. One way to estimate a tip is to double the amount of sales tax (which is 8.25 per cent) shown on your bill.

Just fill a plastic container and pay by the weight. Depending on the price (per pound) and how much you want to eat, you can have your fill for between $4 and $10. Many establishments have tables, but you may prefer to eat in the open air on the nearest bench whilst doing a spot of people-watching.

Most New York delis also serve a mind-boggling variety of sandwiches. Along with the traditional corned beef and pastrami on rye, you can also get heros (submarine sandwiches), as well as sandwiches based on food specialities of the individual deli owner's native land. In delis owned by Greeks and Middle Easterners, for instance, you may find gyros – spit-roasted beef or pork stuffed inside a pita bread envelope. Even ordinary sandwiches, such as turkey or tuna fish, are often unbelievably thick – at least an inch of meat as filling.

Bagels are served everywhere with many weird and wonderful toppings, but it is hard to beat the traditional New York way of eating them: hot out of the oven and smothered in (or with just "a schmear" of) cream cheese.

Every New Yorker has a favourite deli. Once you have found yours, start exploring the other deli specialities such as thick soups, chicken soup with the dumplings known as matzoh balls, sponge cakes and mile-high meringue pies, and blintzes – similar to crêpes – wrapped around cream cheese or fruit fillings. And don't forget to try the famous New York cheese cake.

Coffee-shop breakfasts If you are not in a rush, linger over breakfast in a coffee shop or diner. Such establishments are as prevalent as delis and street vendors and draw an equally devoted clientele. Sit at a table or at the counter and choose from a menu which is likely to include sausages, bacon, Nova (smoked salmon), pancakes, waffles, French toast, scrambled eggs, omelettes with a host of mix-and-match fillings and fried eggs. Coffee-shop breakfasts are often served with hash browns (home fries) and toast. Often your cup of coffee will be refilled for free, for as long as you like to linger there.

EATING WITH CHILDREN
New York can be a wonderful and exciting place for children to eat. There are scores of diners, theme restaurants, pizzerias and casual ethnic eateries from which to choose. Even the city's best restaurants have a reputation for being accommodating to well-behaved youngsters. If a children's menu is not offered, don't be afraid to ask for something simple; New Yorkers are not shy when it comes to ordering in restaurants.

217

A New York legend – the original Jewish deli

A coffee-shop breakfast, consisting of eggs, toast, "home fries" and coffee, will cost around $5. There are also many cafés that serve somewhat healthier alternatives like homemade muffins, oatmeal, granola with fresh fruit and fresh squeezed juices.

Lunchtime fare Lunchtime in New York usually begins at 11 and ends around 2, though it isn't hard to find something to eat throughout the afternoon. Sandwiches and salads are popular, and several establishments, such as the **Cosi Sandwich Bar** and **Mangia** food shops, have turned sandwich and salad making into an art. Here you can find savoury items such as fresh mozzarella and sundried tomatoes on a whole wheat baguette, and smoked turkey and avocado on Russian black bread; sometimes these sandwiches are so large you can barely fit them into your mouth. Cosi's many branches continually bake their own delicious bread before your eyes. The **Daily Soup** chain serves a wide variety of homemade soups as an alternative to the sandwich.

Among New York's sandwich specialities are the grilled "Reuben" (corned beef with Swiss cheese and sauerkraut on rye bread) and the "Club" (turkey with bacon, lettuce and tomato on toasted white bread). Coffee shops also serve salad plates that could feed an army and offer variations on the plain and simple hamburger such as bacon-and-cheese burgers, chili-cheese burgers and pizzaburgers as well as one made from ground chicken.

An even cheaper lunch may be found at a neighbourhood pizza joint, where slices are sold with your choice of toppings. Several pizza parlours also offer Italian hero sandwiches filled with meatballs, chicken cutlets, or eggplant and overstuffed calzones with cheese, broccoli, spinach or sausage fillings.

Many New York restaurants, whatever their culinary leaning, offer specially priced lunch menus or lunch buffets for under $8, which not only means good eating at a great price but also makes lunchtime a golden opportunity to begin your investigation of the city's innumerable ethnic cuisines. Seldom will you have the chance to sample so wide a choice of restaurant fare at such affordable prices. Some of the city's finest restaurants also offer very reasonable prix fixe deals at lunch, and during Restaurant Week in mid-June the top eateries' 3-course menus are priced to correspond to the year ($20.01, $20.02 etc) with many extending the promotion through the summer.

Italian restaurants Throughout New York City, Italian restaurants can be relied upon for excellent food at very fair prices. If you are interested in good food, then try to avoid Little Italy, where the atmosphere and the prices are designed exclusively for tourists. In its highest form, Italy's *alta cucina* carries a heavy price tag, but outside its homeland, you won't find such impressive renderings.

Little Italy's prices are also higher than they deserve to be. However, if money is no object and you are neatly dressed, head instead for the gourmet Italian restaurants recently opened on the Upper East Side.

Chinese specialities

Chinese food A short distance from Little Italy are the restaurants of Chinatown, which are unmatched for value. Because their trade is largely drawn from New York's Chinese community, the eateries can stay in profit without compromising their quality to suit western tastes.

Nobody should leave New York without dropping into a Chinatown restaurant for dim sum. Usually served until mid-afternoon on the weekends, dim sum comprises steamed dumplings and baked buns filled with meat, seafood and/or rice and noodles. Diners choose from trolleys pushed between the tables: just point at what looks good.

When you cannot eat another thing, let the waiter or waitress know and the bill will be assessed by the number and shape of empty plates on your table.

Return to Chinatown at night, when the dinner options span Cantonese, Hunan and Szechuan specialities as well as some obscure regional cuisines.

Japanese food New Yorkers first got excited by sushi and sashimi during the late 1970s when a rash of new restaurants appeared. These were intended to serve the city's fast-growing Japanese population but found themselves besieged by locals entranced by the exotic combination of raw fish and tatami mats. The city is still an excellent place for sushi and sashimi (ask any New Yorker for their suggestions), although a recent craze developed among devotees: the *okonomiyaki* restaurants, where large crêpes containing your choice of meat, seafood, vegetables or noodles are prepared on a hot slab in full view.

Affordable food to suit most tastes

MEALTIMES
To avoid crowds, or to avoid having a restaurant to yourself, be aware of the city's popular dining times. Most coffee shops open for breakfast around 6 AM and are at their busiest around 8 AM. By 10 AM, the pace has slowed as most New Yorkers are already planning their lunch. Some people eat their midday meal as early as 11:30 AM but around 1 PM is more common. By 2:30 or 3 PM coffee shops start preparing for the dinner rush, from around 5 PM to 7 PM. In restaurants, lunch hours tend to be similar to those of coffee shops but the peak restaurant dinner period is between 7 and 10:30 PM. Some of the noted after-theatre dining spots do most of their business between 11 PM and midnight.

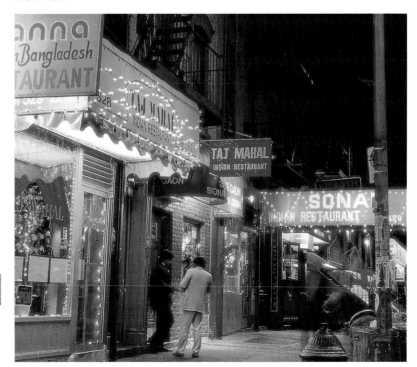

Head for 6th Street in the East Village for a dazzling array of Indian restaurants

CROSSBRED CUISINES
New York's ethnic cuisines are quick to mix with one another. To become a gastronomic explorer at the frontiers of culinary adventure (which is sometimes a long way from culinary excellence), seek out the city's Chinese pizzerias, Kosher-Italian delis and Indian-Mexican fast-food outlets, among dozens of bizarre crossbreeds.

Korean and Indian Korean is the other Asian cuisine firmly established in New York, even though few out-of-towners ever stumble on the Korean business district. Here, within a few blocks of the Empire State Building, off Fifth Avenue in the West 30s, a large number of Korean restaurants maintain around-the-clock service.

With its emphasis on barbecued beef and pork, Korean eating might be less gastronomically adventurous than Chinese or Japanese, but anyone with a liking for spicy meat should enjoy Korean *jeyuk gui*, strips of barbecued pork smothered with a very hot sauce, and the huge variety of *kimchee* (pickled condiments).

Indian food has been popular in New York for decades. The section of 6th Street between First and Second avenues in the East Village is packed with mostly mediocre Indian restaurants. Another more authentic and better quality group is to be found in Midtown Manhattan, around Lexington Avenue between 27th and 30th streets.

Spanish and Greek New Yorkers often combine dining out with a trip to the theatre, but not if they are planning to tackle one of the gargantuan helpings of paella (which might well take most of the evening to devour) served at the convivial Spanish restaurants dotted throughout the city, with several notable examples in Greenwich Village and Chelsea.

Outside the huge Greek neighbourhood in the Astoria area of Queens, Greek food is getting much easier to find. Simple Greek dishes such as spinach pie and moussaka often appear in Greek-owned coffee shops.

South American and Caribbean food You're assured of a lively evening in any of the city's increasingly well-regarded Brazilian restaurants. Churrascarias, where waiters circle the room with mammoth skewers of meat, usually offer all you can eat at great prices. Several Puerto Rican restaurants are along 116th Street in East Harlem, and they will be more than happy to serve you barbecued pig (the island's national dish).

Less daunting Puerto Rican specialities are also served, but East Harlem can be intimidating after dark. Therefore it is more sensible to restrict your food forays into the area to lunchtime.

Eastern Europe In the Yorkville district, in the 1970s and 80s streets of the Upper East Side, several Hungarian, German and Czech-Slovak restaurants are reminders of the Eastern European communities that settled here before departing for the suburbs. Look no further for rich, heavy soups, stuffed cabbage and extremely large portions of goulash.

Similarly solid but tasty fare turns up in the Ukrainian eateries of the East Village as well as in the Polish cafés that survive on the Lower East Side. In Brighton Beach's Russian restaurants, meanwhile, be ready for a Cyrillic menu or choose from a buffet table – however be prepared to dodge the vodka-sozzled dancers as you are doing so.

New York may be hard to beat for ethnic cooking but the great all-American snack still has plenty of devoted fans

221

Recipes from the regions With the foods of the world providing such competition, the regional cuisines of the nation battle hard to be noticed. Nonetheless Cajun, Tex-Mex, and southwestern cooking all have their devotees. Fried catfish, grilled swordfish, jambalaya, gumbo soup and even stuffed armadillo are among their offerings.

Being hungry in Harlem is a perfect excuse to discover soul food. Order a plateful of fried chicken or beef ribs coated in gravy, and don't skimp on the side dishes, such as black-eyed peas, corn bread and grits.

Vegetarian food Although New Yorkers are known to love steak, they are also known to start (and follow) trends. In some circles vegetarianism is chic and the food offerings to vegetarians are numerous and varied. Ethnic restaurants, particularly Southern Indian and Chinese, have much to offer. Most American restaurants offer at least one or two vegetarian entrées, and many of the fancier restaurants actually have vegetarian tasting menus available.

Steak houses One kind of establishment into which vegetarians *will* fear to tread is the New York steak house. Carnivores, however, will soon be salivating in these citadels of meat-eating, where large, thick and juicy hunks of charcoaled prime beef are served. A la carte side dishes, like hash browns or creamed spinach, are the popular accompaniments.

The crème de la crème At the top end of the dining spectrum, New York's finest restaurants not only employ some of the world's best chefs, they also engage the top waiters, managers and leading interior designers. There is a relatively new emphasis on making the diner feel as welcome and comfortable as possible.

To experience New York eating at this rarefied level requires much more than mere appetite and a big bank balance. You will also need to make a reservation (for some, a month in advance). Although the dress codes have relaxed in may places, at certain others, unless you are an extremely famous face (and sometimes even then), you may be shown the door if you are not dressed in your best for the occasion.

Expensive restaurants sometimes allow you to sample their premier offerings with fixed-price *menus dégustation*, or "tasting menus". These menus enable you to try several dishes, usually between 5 and 10, at a price below what it would cost to order them à la carte.

SMOKING IN RESTAURANTS

Any smoker who can survive without a puff for the duration of a restaurant visit would be well advised to do so. Most New Yorkers are very aware of health issues and their fear of passive smoking has helped make tobacco addicts the scourge of the city. In January 1995, smoking was made illegal in restaurants seating 35 or more people, except at separate bar areas or rooms with independent ventilation. Further restrictions on smoking are currently making their way through the city council, so it's best to ask before lighting up.

A revered New York institution: the steak house

Coffee and tea Coffee is usually freshly brewed and available in regular and decaffeinated forms. Cappuccino, caffe latte and espresso coffee, costing around $2–$3 per cup, are also extremely popular, especially on the sidewalk tables of Italian cafés. All types of coffee may be ordered "to go" from delis and street vendors, at prices graded according to the size of the cup or container. Always ask for "regular" coffee if you want milk but no sugar – to get sweetened a brew, ask for "regular with sugar".

Another Manhattan phenomenon are the coffee bars, which specialise in serving several different fine coffee blends (and usually a variety of teas and soft drinks). In addition to a variety of strengths, you can get your coffee sweetened with speciality syrups such as hazelnut or caramel. Order you drinks at the counter and wait whilst it is being prepared, then, if you are planning to have a break, take it to any seat that's free. A number of coffee-house chains are good places to linger.

Alternatively, many bookshops such as the Barnes & Noble chain, now have in-store cafés: a perfect place to sit and browse through a book or magazine while you sip your coffee.

Some New Yorkers have developed a taste for iced coffee. Both iced coffee and iced tea are great drinks for cooling you down whilst sightseeing on a hot day in the city.

Most coffee shops and delis in New York will serve hot tea if requested, but it is rarely satisfying for tea aficionados. Coffee bar tea is usually not bad, although it is seldom brewed from loose leaves. Chai lattes, spiced, sweetened tea with hot milk, are a trend and better restaurants have now begun to offer impressive selections of teas, sometimes proffered by a tea sommelier for you to sniff before you make up your mind.

For something different, try the **Wild Lily Tea Room** in Chelsea or the fairy-tale-like tea at **Mackenzie-Childs** on Madison Ave. For real extravagance, try afternoon tea at the **Four Seasons**.

Sample the wide variety of worldwide fare available in New York

TEAROOMS
There are few more welcoming sanctuaries from the mayhem of Manhattan's streets than the city's elegant tearooms (often in deluxe hotels) between 2 and 5 PM on a weekday afternoon. At this time, for a price ranging from $15 to $20, you can partake of tea – the list of blends usually spans Chinese, Indian and Russian – and nibble selectively from a silver tray laden with chicken, ham and smoked salmon sandwiches, chocolate cakes, delicate pastries and scones topped with Devonshire thick cream.

Relaxing outside the
Victory Café on the
Upper East Side

NEW YORK'S NEW BEERS

Partly as a reaction against mass-produced beers and partly because New York loves a new trend, microbrewed beers (produced in small batches, often by the bar that serves them) have become increasingly common since the mid-1990s. Hop enthusiasts can sample the likes of Brooklyn Brewery Black Chocolate Stout, Weinhard's Red, Rockefeller Red, Hudson River Porter, Gotham City Gold, Empire State Bitter and Lady Liberty Light. At the Fraunces Tavern (see page 107) they can imbibe the creamy Swig Tavern Keeper, supposedly similar to that brewed when George Washington propped up the bar.

Juice bars Sodas are fast declining in popularity among some of the more health-conscious New Yorkers, who, after a workout at the gym or a jog, refresh themselves instead with the nutritious fruit juices sold in the city's specialised juice bars. As well as fresh orange, grapefruit and carrot juice, some juice bars offer power-packed juices blended from parsley, ginger, spinach and root vegetables; expect to spend $1–4 for a glassful.

Bars and beers Bars, which are open from around midday to the early hours (legally they must stop serving at 4 AM), range from the chummy neighbourhood variety to those patronised almost exclusively by a particular social set – be it stockbrokers, art dealers or punk rockers. For more insights into the diversity of New York bars, see pages 114–115.

Most bars, especially larger ones and those with outdoor tables, have waiter or waitress service, though usually you can go to the bar and order drinks directly from the bartender – as you can if you sit at the bar. In all bars, the bartender will expect you to leave a tip when buying a round of drinks or when leaving.

Mass-market beers such as Budweiser, Miller and Rolling Rock are served in virtually every bar. Many establishments also carry a commendable selection of bottled European beers (occasionally found on tap) and Mexican beers.

Adventurous beer-drinkers should also investigate the output of the nation's many microbreweries: locally brewed Brooklyn Beer and Anchor Steam Beer, brewed in California, are commonly found.

Sports bars New Yorkers can watch the playoffs in sports bars with multiple extra-large television screens. Some favourite ones in the city include **Sporting Club** (99 Hudson Street at Franklin Street), baseball-mad **Mickey Mantle's** (42 Central Park South), **Runyons** (932 Second Avenue between 49th and 50th streets), **Scruffy Duffy's** (743 Eighth Avenue between 46th and 47th streets), **Time Out** (349 Amsterdam Avenue between 77th and 78th streets) and **The Back Page** (1472 Third Avenue between 83rd and 84th streets).

Wines and liquor Alongside beer, New York bars will also be able to serve you from a selection of wines from Europe and the United States – many of which are available by the glass. The more elegant the bar, the more extensive (and expensive) its wine stocks will be. Some good restaurants produce wine lists on regularly updated computer print-outs. Behind every bar will be a very well-stocked rack of liquor, including malt whiskies, Russian vodka and various bourbons, as well as more unusual drinks.

Cocktails Any bar describing itself as a cocktail lounge – particularly in parts of Midtown Manhattan and in the Upper East Side – is likely to be either a watering hole for the wealthy or a meeting place for the current "in-crowd". For eavesdropping on high-society gossip, cocktail lounges are unrivalled, but to spend an evening inside one you will need to be very well dressed (in black if you're downtown) and not afraid to spend $10 or more on a single drink – and on no account should you topple drunkenly from your stool.

Theme bars There are many interesting spots that are off the beaten path, and offer quirky themes along with strong cocktails. **Idlewild** (145 East Houston St), named for New York's old airport, is set up like the interior of an aircraft, complete with reclining seats and servers in groundcrew uniforms.

VINTAGE CLASSICS
Hotel bars provide exhausted sightseers with some of the best places in Manhattan. The **Plaza Hotel's Oak Bar** (Fifth Avenue and 59th Street) continues to age well with its plummy, dark-wood furnishings; it draws sophisticates, shoppers and celebrities. The **Carlyle** (35 East 76th Street) contains the charming **Bemelman's Bar** with whimsical animal murals, painted by Ludwig Bemelman, and live jazz piano music at night. At the art deco-style **Essex House** (160 Central Park South), **Journeys** bar has pure English country-style décor with rich carved wood, sporting scenes on the walls and a large fireplace. One of the most elegant, venerable spots in New York to have a glass of wine (or a cup of tea) remains the lobby bar of the **Algonquin Hotel Lounge** (59 West 44th Street), with its many literary associations.

225

Since 1913, the Grand Central Oyster Bar and Restaurant has been serving celebrities, commuters and visitors alike

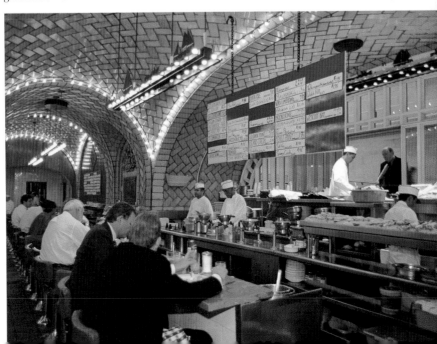

THE WINTER ANTIQUES FAIR

One way to keep warm in New York during January is to pay a visit to the Winter Antiques Fair, held at the Seventh Regiment Armory (see page 187). With all of New York's antiques dealers and antiques lovers gathered under one roof, you might not be able to afford anything, but eavesdropping on the chit-chat can be fascinating. There are plenty of fine antiques to admire, too.

Union Square now teems with shoppers choosing fresh produce at the popular Farmers' Market, which is held several times a week

Shopping

From the ultra-exclusive antiques shops of the Upper East Side to the discount clothing shops that proliferate in Lower Manhattan, New York is not only the most exciting place in the world to buy things, but also the easiest and sometimes even the cheapest. Not surprisingly, New Yorkers often like to "shop till they drop".

Antiques The New York millionaires who plundered the treasures of Europe and the Far East to furnish their mansions contributed to the city's emergence as the centre of the international antiques trade. For serious buyers, there is no better place to locate that elusive Japanese watercolour or Swiss music box. There is plenty to drool over in the upmarket antique shops of the Upper East Side. The more affordable stuff, meanwhile, can be found elsewhere.

Among the city's top-range antiques shops, **A La Vieille Russie** (Fifth Avenue at 59th Street) highlights the achievements of tsarist Russian craftsmen with Fabergé enamelware, jewel-encrusted icons, snuff boxes, clocks and assorted silverware – none of which would disgrace the finest palace.

Japanese prints, books and ornaments (18th and 19th century) are among the Far Eastern treasures that can be found at **Things Japanese** (60th Street between Park and Lexington avenues). Connoisseurs of art deco find plenty to please amid the pricey rarities at **Delorenzo** (Madison Avenue between 75th and 76th streets).

Several hours might be needed for a thorough exploration of **Asia House** (56th Street between Sixth and

Seventh avenues), packed with porcelain, lamps, vases and much more from points East.

Antiquated melodies accompany browsing at **Rita Ford Music Boxes** (65th Street between Madison and Fifth avenues), a colossal collection of music boxes and miniature handmade carousels, which the staff are easily persuaded to demonstrate.

If you lack the nerve to pose as a genuine customer in the more exclusive antique shops, you might aim instead for the friendlier environs of the **Manhattan Art & Antiques Center** (Second Avenue between 55th and 56th streets). At the **Laura Fisher Gallery**, one of the centre's 104 separate shops, you will learn more about American quilts than you thought you could know.

Another low-key spot high on potential is the **Chelsea Antiques Building** (110 West 25th Street), where 150 dealers are spread across twelve floors, and sell items ranging from 18th and 19th-century furnishings to toys, books and comics.

The mood in SoHo antiques outlets, typically set in warehouse-like shops, is much less stuffy than that of the Upper East Side shops and the prices are lower (but by no means a bargain). Among the inventory of **Back Pages** (Green Street between Prince and West Houston streets) you will find Wurlitzer jukeboxes, vintage pool tables and vending machines.

Big Apple detritus forms the eclectic stock of **Urban Archeology** (285 Lafayette Street). This is just the place to pick up a bizarre bathroom fitting or a vintage barbershop chair. Similar ephemera fills **Secondhand Rose** (275 Lafayette Street), among it neon-lit Coca-Cola signs and dilapidated peep-show machines. There are also some bizarre specialist shops: see panel.

Books New Yorkers love to read. A proliferation of **Barnes & Noble** and **Borders'** superstores cover all bases and offer pleasant environments (many with cafés) in which to browse and read. There are an equal number of independent booksellers that tailor their collections with more personality. Try **Shakespeare & Co** (716 Broadway) or **St Marks Bookshop** (31 Third Avenue). With used, review copies and remaindered books, **The Strand** (828 Broadway) is a New York institution.

Speciality book shops also abound. If your interest lies in people's lives, check out the **Biography Book Shop** (400 Bleecker Street). For mysteries and crime try **Murder Ink** (2486 Broadway) or **Partners & Crime** (44 Greenwich Avenue). If you prefer looking at pictures, venture into **A Photographer's Place** (133 Mercer Street) or flip through the pages at **Printed Matter** (77 Wooster Street). The shelves are filled with children's books at **Books of Wonder** (16 West 18th Street). The country's largest selection of gay and lesbian books is stocked at **A Different Light Bookstore** (151 West 19th Street) and the oldest at the **Oscar Wilde Memorial Bookstore** (15 Christopher Street). Serious cooks pilgrimage to **Kitchen Arts & Letters** (1435 Lexington Avenue). Comic book lovers can lose themselves at **St Marks Comics** (11 St Marks Place).

A change of identity? Anything is possible in the shops of Greenwich Village

UNUSUAL SHOPS
New York has an unusual shop at every turn. Among the curiosities you might stumble across are: New York Firefighter's Friend (Lafayette Street between Prince and Spring streets), selling firefighting paraphernalia from model fire engines to helmets and hose nozzles; Maxilla and Mandible (82nd Street at Columbus Avenue), packed with skeletons and individual bones from humans, animals and birds; and Tender Buttons (62nd Street between Third and Lexington avenues), with nothing but buttons – new and antique – tens of thousands of them.

227

BUYING RECORDS AND CDS

With 6,700sq m of floor space, the Virgin Megastore (Broadway between 45th and 46th streets) claims to be the world's largest music and entertainment shop. As you pore through rack after rack of records, CDs and cassettes, and pass through a classical section that includes space for a concert pianist, the claim is easy to believe. A second outlet can be found on Union Square. Only slightly smaller are the several branches of Tower (692 Broadway; Trump Tower, 725 Fifth Avenue; and Broadway at 66th Street).

A window-display at Armani A/X

MUSEUM SHOPS

Many museums have excellent shops. The Museum of Modern Art (pages 158–160) and the Guggenheim Museum (pages 122–124), in particular, are excellent places to find art books, unusual badges, T-shirts and other souvenirs marking their major exhibitions. A branch of the Guggenheim Museum in SoHo (575 Broadway) also has a good range of art-related merchandise, and the Cooper-Hewitt Museum (page 95) has tomes covering all aspects of the decorative arts.

For other special interests, foreign language books, religious, scholarly or used texts, consult the Manhattan *Yellow Pages*.

CDs and records CDs and tapes can be found to fit all tastes amid the eclectic and vast stocks of **Tower Records** (Broadway at 4th Street), **J&R Music World** (23 Park Row, in the Financial District) and those listed in the panel on this page.

Clothing The latest in leather, rubber and plastic street fashions can be seen being worn around the East Village, and, in general, New York is a fashion capital. Every major designer has an outlet there. Dozens of discount shops sell American casual clothing, as well as discounted designer merchandise, for a song.

Those clothes-conscious people who do not need to worry about their credit limits – or about being patronised by snooty staff – always do much of their shopping amid the designer-name shops of Midtown Manhattan and the Upper East Side. These areas are positively cluttered with the shops of world-famous names such as **Giorgio Armani** (Madison Avenue at 65th Street), **Gucci** (there are two shops on Fifth Avenue at 54th Street – numbers 685 and 689), **Hermès** (57th Street, between Madison and Fifth avenues), **Prada** (Fifth Avenue and 56th Street) and **Yves St Laurent** (Madison Avenue at 71st Street).

One pedigree designer you should visit for the setting alone, however, is **Polo/Ralph Lauren** (Madison Avenue at 72nd Street). The company occupies a French Renaissance-style Upper East Side mansion that is a show in itself. Another is **Comme des Garçons** (22nd Street and Tenth Avenue), whose trend-setting futuristic shop in Chelsea is like an attraction at an amusement park. The ultra-chic Meatpacking District department store **Jeffrey** (14th Street and Ninth Avenue) sells prohibitively priced avant-garde designer outfits.

The person of more average income and in search of quality clothing should aim instead for the scores of discount outlets, where designer clothing is piled high, unceremoniously discounted and sold for as little as half its regular price. Although their prices may be comparatively inexpensive, the shops themselves can be as classy as any. Among them are **Loehman's** (101 Seventh Avenue)

and **Daffy's** (18th Street and Fifth Avenue), selling an amazing array of discounted merchandise for men and women; **Michael's – The Consignment Shop For Women** (1041 Madison Avenue), a favourite of well-heeled Upper East Side ladies; and **Pretty Plus Plus** (1309 Madison Avenue), which stocks bargain designer wear for the larger woman.

There are some lower-priced (but not inexpensive) designer shops which specialise in chic clothes and accessories for the style-conscious traveller. One such place is **Betsey Johnson** (138 Wooster Street), which adapts New York street fashion into loud and colourful garments.

Also in SoHo is **Catherine** (468 Broome Street), a funky clothing shop known for cowboy hats in every colour of the rainbow, and **Kate Spade** (454 Broome Street), a wildly popular designer of bags and other accessories, available in a wide range of colours and styles. Style-conscious men will love **Sean** (132 Thompson Street), where proper cotton shirts come in an interesting array of colours, and **Beau Brummel** (421 West Broadway), which carries what is arguably the best selection of men's ties in the city, as well as a host of stylish suits.

Just East of SoHo is the fashionable neighbourhood of NoLiTa where independent designers peddle their wares in tiny shopfronts. Check out **Language** (238 Mulberry Street) for stylish designs, as well as beautiful objects for your home, and **Wang** (219 Mott Street) for colourful women's clothes in wearable, downtown styles. **Calypso** (280 Mott Street) sells bright island-wear, while the place for "of-the-minute" shoe styles is **Sigerson-Morrsion** (28 Prince Street).

For true bargain hunters there's Orchard Street on the Lower East Side, where shops can be found selling leather accessories, shoes and some designer duds at discount prices. (But be warned that most of Orchard Street shuts down on Saturday.)

Lower Manhattan is a good area for bargain clothing shops and stalls such as this one on West Broadway

A NOTE FOR BARGAIN HUNTERS

Photographic and electrical goods can be real bargains in New York. It is vital, however, to know exactly what you want before entering a shop and to resist the seductive patter of the salesperson. This is especially true of electrical goods, even if the sales pitch suggests otherwise.

The largest photographic discount shop is 47th Street Photo (main branch on 47th Street between Fifth and Sixth avenues; others listed in the *Yellow Pages*). It also carries a large range of videos, computers and all kinds of electrical gadgets.

Mainstream American-made clothing, particularly Levi jeans, represents exceptionally good value (especially for European visitors); prices are lowest in the scores of discount shops on and around the SoHo section of Broadway: the biggest is **Canal Jean** (between Broome and Spring streets), with a massive stock of jeans, T-shirts, jackets, sunglasses, beachwear, loud ties, all kinds of practical travelling accessories and second-hand clothing at extremely tempting prices.

Army/Navy (328 Bleecker Street, one of three Manhattan branches) is another dependable provider of items such as jeans, plaid shirts, T-shirts and reasonably priced leather jackets.

Department stores Immortalised in film, fiction and folklore, Manhattan's department stores are the stuff of legend. Generations of New Yorkers have grown up unable to imagine life without these totems to 20th-century consumerism, and while they are superficially similar, each one has a character and cachet very much its own and its own band of loyal supporters.

Among them is **Macy's** (34th Street and Sixth Avenue), famously described as the world's largest department store. The claim seems justified as you wind up its 10 floors and find half a million items for sale. There is even a section for buying pets and a branch of the Museum of Modern Art's gift shop. Large this shop certainly is but, despite revamping its image during the 1970s, Macy's is far from being the world's most exciting department store, having built its reputation by supplying middle-income family purchasers with the most middle-of-the-road tastes.

By contrast, **Bloomingdale's** (Third Avenue at 59th Street) is a wonderful shop in which to buy cosmetics, accessories, men's and women's fashions and much more. Although it is not cutting edge, Bloomies does feature a wide range of designers, in a wide range of prices.

Bloomingdale's was the first New York department store to feature now-established designers such as Yves St Laurent, Calvin Klein and Ralph Lauren, and it supports many newer ones as well. Elsewhere, there are souvenirs, the latest in electrical gadgetry, a furniture department, a well-stocked bookshop and even a fine-food level that devotes a whole section to caviar.

More opulent still is **Bergdorf Goodman** (Fifth Avenue between 57th and 58th streets). Here the ladies of the Upper East Side shop beneath crystal chandeliers for clothes, jewellery, perfumes and other luxury items. Their husbands, meanwhile, sift through the $100-a-piece tie racks in the most elegant men's shop, **Bergdorf Goodman Men**, directly across Fifth Avenue.

Spread over nine artfully designed floors, **Barneys** (660 Madison Avenue) offers all the stylish and successful

Manhattanite could wish for: cutting-edge designer names by the score, beautiful jewellery and accessories, and some classic New York attitude. Barneys is also justifiably proud of its window displays – especially at Christmas.

The antidote to all this trendiness is **Saks Fifth Avenue** (Fifth Avenue between 49th and 50th streets), which simply offers tasteful, stylish and high-quality merchandise – clothing, linens, cosmetics – in an orderly setting with efficient service.

Jewellery Dozens of jewellers occupy Manhattan's "diamond district", which fills a block of 47th Street immediately west of Fifth Avenue. This wholesale jewellery trading district is where diamonds are cut and polished, jewellery is repaired, gems are set and deals are done above the ground-level shops. More famous shops include **Tiffany & Co** (Fifth Avenue between 56th and 57th streets), with three floors of highly desirable pieces, not all of which cost the earth, and the more conservative **Cartier** (Fifth Avenue at 52nd Street), worth a call not least for the landmark building which it occupies. Another stalwart is the **World's Largest Jewelry Exchange** (55 West 47th Street), where more than a hundred retailers and repairers are under a single roof, providing ample opportunity for browsing and comparing prices.

Shoes Shoe shops abound in New York, and if you cannot find what you want (whether it's handmade Italian loafers, kitten heels, or streetwise sneakers), you are simply not trying. Aside from numerous upmarket outlets on the Upper East Side, and the extensive stocks of most department stores, many Lower Manhattan discount shops offer good deals in footwear. Manhattan also has two "shoe districts", where you will see rows of shoe shops – on West 8th Street and on 34th Street between Fifth and Sixth avenues. **Jimmy Choo** (645 Fifth Avenue) and **Manolo Blahnik** (15 West 55th Street) are the favoured shops for ultra-sexy stilettos.

Everything under one (huge) roof: Macy's

PERSONAL SHOPPING
If the prospect of roaming the city's department stores fills you with dread, consider consulting a personal shopper who will select items especially for you. All you have to do is make an appointment and pay for the goods – the personal shopper is complimentary. Telephone for details: Bergdorf Goodman (tel: 872-8757); Bloomingdale's (tel: 355-5900); Macy's (tel: 695-4400); Saks Fifth Avenue (tel: 753-4000).

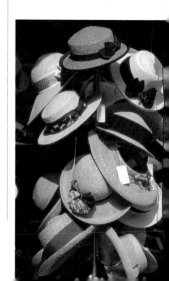

Nightlife

New York nightlife is never boring, and it's more plentiful and more diverse (and often of a higher standard) than almost anywhere else in the world. To enjoy it, all you need is energy and, in most cases, plenty of money.

Most New York-based publications carry extensive nightlife listings. The most thorough are *Time Out New York*, the *Village Voice* and the Friday and Sunday editions of *The New York Times*. For new movies and plays, the *New Yorker* is also an excellent source of opinionated reviews and information.

Theatre From the *Ziegfeld Follies* to *The Phantom of the Opera*, the theatre has been an integral part of New York nightlife for years. The section of Broadway nearest Times Square – dubbed "The Great White Way" for its multitude of lights – has long been established as the flag-carrier of commercial American theatre.

Although ticket prices can be high (as much as $100), a good reason for splurging on a night inside one of the 34

official Broadway theatres is to enjoy the sumptuous auditorium and get a taste of a little of the history and folklore that every Broadway theatre has in abundance.

Regularly hosting the city's major shows are the **Eugene O'Neill Theater** (230 West 49th Street), probably the biggest and best of the neighbourhood playhouses; the **Broadway Theater** (1681 Broadway); the **Neil Simon Theater** (250 52nd Street); the **Palace Theater** (1564 Broadway); the **Richard Rogers Theater** (226 West 46th Street); and the **Roundabout Theater Company**, which is housed in the American Airlines Theater (227 West 42nd Street). Another worth trying is the **Walter Kerr** (219 West 48th Street), as much for a renovation job that has brought back something of the 1920s grandeur of the place as for the shows themselves. **The New Victory Theater** (209 West 42nd Street; tel: 382-4000) is a wonderful renovation of a 1900 playhouse and the only theatre devoted to putting on performances geared towards youngsters.

Another venerable New York dramatic institution is the **Public Theater** (425 Lafayette Street; tel: 260-2400). Here you will discover provocative new plays and controversial adaptations of the classics in six separate theatres. Originally named for Joseph Papp, the director and producer whose credits included *A Chorus Line* and *Hair*, and who saved the building from demolition, the Public Theater hosts the New York Shakespeare Festival in Central Park for over six weeks each summer.

THEATRE TICKETS
For most Broadway and Off-Broadway productions, New York theatre goers usually order tickets by phone (Tele-Charge and Ticketmaster) or buy tickets through a ticket agent (listed in the *Yellow Pages* and local newspapers) rather than going to the theatre box office.

Another option is a "two-fer" – a coupon entitling the holder to two tickets for the price of one. These are commonly used to boost audience numbers at otherwise poorly attended shows and are handed out in ticket queues and found in hotel lobbies.

232

TKTS
Half-price day-of-performance tickets are sold from Manhattan's TKTS Discount Theatre Centre, located in Times Square (payment by cash or traveller's cheques only; there is a surcharge). There is almost always a long queue of people so be prepared to wait.

Times Square: on the mezzanine, *open* Mon–Fri 11–5:30, Sat 11–3:30.

Smaller than their Broadway counterparts, Off-Broadway theatres (seating 100–499) are a little more adventurous and among them they offer an excellent choice of musicals, comedies, revivals, classics and new works that few cities can equal. Top playwrights and leading professional actors are no strangers to Off-Broadway productions, and many of the more successful make the transition to Broadway.

A wide range of plays and shows can be seen at all of the Off-Broadway theatres. Most leading Off-Broadway theatres can be found in and around Greenwich Village, and they include the **Orpheum** (Second Avenue at 8th Street; tel: 477-2477), **Actor's Playhouse** (100 Seventh Avenue South; tel: 239-6200) and the **Cherry Lane Theater** (38 Commerce Street; tel: 989-2020). This theatre was originally built in 1817 as a silo for a local farm. It was taken over in 1924 and converted into the Cherry Lane Playhouse. A wide range of plays and shows can be seen at all of the Off-Broadway theatres.

You can go even further afield and and try your luck at an Off-Off-Broadway venue. The dozens of tiny Off-Off-Broadway theatres (seating under 100) are housed in places like converted churches or vacant schoolrooms.

It is here that daring and experimental plays are performed by unknown but often very talented actors. It is seldom necessary for you to pay more than $15 for a seat, and ticket availability is likely to be less of a problem than trying to get last-minute seats for a Broadway hit. These also stage performance art and alternative cabaret.

Among the longer-lasting are **The Kitchen** (19th Street between Tenth and Eleventh avenues; tel: 255-5793), **The Ohio Theater** (66 Wooster Street; tel: 226-9044), and **PS122** (First Avenue at 9th Street; tel: 477-5829).

THEATRE INFORMATION
Besides the listings in the *New Yorker*, *New York Times* and *Village Voice*, 24-hour recorded inform-ation on what is playing where, and on ticket availability, can be found by calling the NYC/ON STAGE hotline (tel: 768-1818).

SHAKESPEARE IN THE PARK
The Public Theater's former director, Joseph Papp, instigated the popular "Shakespeare in the Park" series: the bard's plays in Central Park's open-air Delacorte Theater (near the 81st Street entrance on the Upper West Side) between June and August. Tickets are free but limited to two per person. A very long line begins forming around noon – entertainers stroll and everyone chats and picnics: the tickets are distributed at 6 PM.

233

Bright lights in the theatre district

The golden age of neon may be long since gone, but the gaudy excitement of Times Square remains legendary

THE NEW YORK FILM FESTIVAL
Each September, specially selected new American and foreign-made films are screened at the New York Film Festival, held at Alice Tully Hall at Lincoln Center. The festival is organised by the Film Society of Lincoln Center, and tickets tend to be in short supply (tel: 875-5456).

Films New York has always had a special relationship with the cinema, playing a part in countless films over a period of more than 60 years (see pages 14–15 and 188). The city is also a great place to watch films. Not only do most high-budget Hollywood features get their first screenings here in state-of-the-art cinema complexes, but dozens of smaller film houses specialise in new independent films and rarely seen foreign films. Nostalgia buffs are in for a treat, too, with oldies – from world cinema classics to kitsch 1940s musicals – regularly showing around the city.

Multi-screen complexes show the latest releases all over the city; most art house and revival cinemas are downtown in the Village, SoHo and TriBeCa. They include the six-screen **Angelika Film Center** (Houston Street at Mercer Street; tel: 995-2000); the **Anthology Film Archives** (Second Avenue at 2nd Street; tel: 505-5181); **Cinema Village** (12th Street between Fifth and Sixth avenues; tel: 924-3363); **Film Forum** (Houston Street at Varick Street; tel: 727-8110); **The Screening Room** (Varick Street; tel: 334-2100); and the **Walter Reade Theater** (70 Lincoln Center Plaza; tel: 875-5600).

Many city museums have projection facilities and mount film series linked to a particular exhibition. The **Museum of Modern Art** and the **Metropolitan Museum of Art** also have extensive film archives of their own, and the **Museum of Television and Radio** (see page 161) is another potential source of delight for film-lovers. During the summer Bryant Park (42nd Street and Sixth Avenue) has free outdoor film screenings on Monday nights.

Classical music From free open-air recitals to concerts featuring the biggest in big names, the serious music lover will find plenty to cheer about.

Lincoln Center's Avery Fisher Hall is the home of the **New York Philharmonic**, whose season runs from mid-September to June (for information, tel: 875-5656). During July, the orchestra undertakes a free concert series in the parks of each of the city's five boroughs.

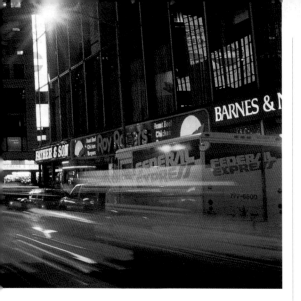

THE MOSTLY MOZART FESTIVAL
For six weeks each July and August, New Yorkers shake off their summer slumbers with the enormously popular Mostly Mozart Festival, held at Lincoln Center's Avery Fisher Hall. Featuring many star performers and conductors, the festival is also the only chance many people get to afford front row seats: for the festival, all seats are charged at a single (low) price.

The **New York Chamber Symphony** (tel: 996-1100) is based at the 92nd Y (92nd Street at Lexington Avenue). The oak-walled **Kaufmann Theater** (also 92nd Street Y) is strong on both acoustics and atmosphere and is a popular venue with visiting soloists and other chamber groups.

At Lincoln Center, **Alice Tully Hall** (tel: 875-5050) is another good place for chamber music, and all around the city numerous other venues regularly give all forms of classical music an airing. Historic **Carnegie Hall** (Seventh Avenue and 57th Street; tel: 247-7800) offers chamber music and solo recitals; the compact **Merkin Concert Hall** (67th Street between Broadway and Amsterdam Avenue; tel: 362-8719) showcases more unusual fare, such as ethnic music and choral groups; a broad-ranging programme is offered at the **Town Hall** (43rd Street between Sixth Avenue and Broadway; tel: 997-1003).

Music fans of meagre means should scan the newspapers' listing sections for free and moderately priced concerts, held at the Financial District's **St Paul's Chapel**, the Upper West Side's **Riverside Church** and at the city's schools of music – the major one being the **Juilliard School of Music** at Lincoln Center.

Ballet and dance Based at Lincoln Center's **Metropolitan Opera House**, the **American Ballet Theatre** (tel: 362-6000) gets rave reviews for its interpretations of classical and contemporary pieces. The season runs from April to June. **New York City Ballet** is based at Lincoln Center's **New York State Theater** (tel: 870-5570). Their performances run from November to February and from April to June, with the *Nutcracker* on during the Christmas season. Tickets vary widely in price and sell out in advance. Sometimes you can pick up tickets at the box office on the day of the performance, or (sold at face value or less) outside the theatre just before curtain time.

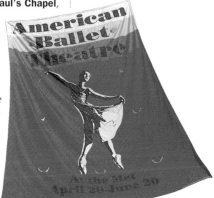

Many of the world's finest dancers perform at the Met

THE FIRST MET

Generation after generation of New York's longstanding wealthy would demonstrate their social aloofness by occupying all of the few boxes available during the opera season at the Academy of Music (on Irving Place), leaving the *nouveau riche* of the mid- to late-19th century to face the social indignity of sitting below them. In retaliation, millionaires William Henry Vanderbilt and Jay Astor financed the first Metropolitan Opera House. The huge building that arose, opening in 1883, was criticised for its ugliness, but did provide the grand boxes from which the city's self-made millionaires could symbolically flaunt their affluence.

In summer, top international guest companies, such as the Bolshoi or the Paris Opera, often come for a two-week run. Bear in mind that the cheaper seats are very high and far from the stage, not really a great bargain in the theatre.

Another important but much more intimate dance venue, **City Center** (55th Street between Sixth and Seventh avenues; tel: 581-1212), hosts a trio of innovative companies: the **Alvin Ailey American Dance Theater**; the **Dance Theater of Harlem**; and the **Merce Cunningham Dance Company**. A further small but interesting venue is the **Bessie Schonberg Theater** (219 West 19th Street between Seventh and Eighth avenues; tel: 924-0077), where the **Dance Theater Workshop** pioneers experimental dance. Bigger and more mainstream than the DTW, but smaller than the City Center, the **Joyce Theater** (175 Eighth Avenue; tel: 691-9740) has the Feld Ballet in residence amongst others. The promising talent of many future dance stars can be seen in the workshop performances of the prestigious **School of American Ballet** (tel: 875-5456) at Lincoln Center's **Juilliard School of Music**.

Such is the excellent quality of its productions that dance-loving Manhattanites regularly cross the East River to attend shows at the **Brooklyn Academy of Music** (tel: 718/636-4100). The US's first centre for the performing arts, the Academy was founded in 1861 and moved to its current site in 1908. Artists from Enrico Caruso to Laurie Anderson have graced its boards. Established as a major centre of modern dance, the Academy hosts the Next Wave festival each autumn.

Opera During its late-September to mid-April season at Lincoln Center's vast **Metropolitan Opera House**, the **Metropolitan Opera** company's performances

The Metropolitan Opera House

(tel: 362-6000) are as much social as musical occasions, especially Monday evenings. The company is criticised as unimaginative but seldom turns in anything other than exceptionally polished performances. Tickets are highly priced and can be hard to get without booking a long time in advance. Standing room tickets are available.

Also based at Lincoln Center is the increasingly innovative **New York City Opera** (tel: 870-5600), usually performing at the **New York State Theater**.

Among a sprinkling of smaller opera companies, with lower prices and cosier settings, is the **Amato Opera Company** (319 Bowery; tel: 228-8200). From June to August, **New York Grand Opera** mounts free shows at Central Park's Summer Stage (www.summerstage.org).

Comedy clubs New York's comedy clubs have given a break to the careers of Eddie Murphy, David Letterman, Robin Williams and innumerable others over the years. Don't expect Las Vegas-style gags and routines – New York comedy clubs can be boisterous places and the crowds may be cruel if they dislike a particular comic.

Most clubs have two shows nightly. It is wise to make a reservation for performances on Fridays and Saturdays.

THE POETS' SLAM
Listening to unknown poets reciting their latest verse may sound like an unexciting way to pass an evening, but at the Nuyorican Poets' Café (234 East 3rd Street between avenues B and C; tel: 505-8183), the Friday night "Poets' Slam" finds a bunch of rowdy poets locked in combat, each one hoping to impress the audience – and a panel of invited judges – with their work. A winner is chosen at the end of this lively and bizarre – but very New York – event. Nuyorican also hosts some other interesting events like wild Latin jazz nights and experimental film screenings.

237

Music is a way of life for many New Yorkers. The city offers plenty of scope for talented performers

Expect to pay more (if you can get tickets) for a "name"; "open mike" nights (when amateurs take a turn, usually on Mondays) are almost always free, but you will still be expected to buy a drink.

The most extensive comedy club listings are carried by the *Village Voice*. With a range of well-chosen up-and-coming talent, and the occasional big name, the most reliable clubs are **Caroline's on Broadway** (Broadway between 49th and 50th streets; tel: 757-4100); the **Comic Strip Inc** (Second Avenue between 81st and 82nd streets; tel: 861-9386); **Dangerfield's** (First Avenue between 61st and 62nd streets; tel: 593-1650); and **Stand Up NY** (78th Street and Broadway; tel: 595-0850).

Nightclubs New York nightclubs are always in a state of flux. The last 20 years have seen the rise and fall of the jet-set Studio 54; the arty Mudd Club, which helped rejuvenate SoHo; and a batch of punky East Village clubs that reshaped many New Yorkers' notions of what a night out could be.

Bright lights on the club scene

The city's nightclub scene in general is thriving. The action has tended to move further downtown, away from the traditional Midtown area, but there are still scores of places of different kinds where you can dress up (or dress down), pose, preen or just dance well into the small hours.

For non-regulars, the biggest potential hazard at any club is the doorman, who will decide whether you are a suitable person (judged by your clothes and general manner) to be admitted. The arrogance of doormen is legendary, but being turned away is no problem – simply try somewhere else.

No nightclub worth its salt gets into gear before 1 or 2 in the morning (most are open until 4 AM and some until noon the next day). Arrive before midnight and you will probably have the place to yourself. One advantage of arriving early, however, may be a reduced admission charge. Drinks in nightclubs are more expensive than in bars, and sometimes extortionately so.

Many clubs have different entertainment, and therefore an entirely different crowd, on particular nights of the week: always phone ahead to check. The best places for information on the club scene are *Time Out New York* and *Paper Magazine*.

New York nightclubs open, close and change address with incredible rapidity; the following suggestions are intended as a representative cross-section.

One of the longer-established upmarket clubs, the polo-stick-and-croquet-mallet-decorated **Au Bar** (58th Street between Madison Avenue and Park Avenue; tel: 308-9455) attracts a designer-dressed and rather staid crowd, dancing primly to fairly bland disco music. Likewise, **Webster Hall** (11th Street between Third and Fourth avenues; tel: 353-1600) is unadventurous, but appreciated by its regular crowd of suburbanites.

Lively and youthful, and packed to the gills on busy nights, **Tunnel** (220 Twelfth Avenue; tel: 695-4682) is an entertainingly varied club with different rooms featuring different sounds, from hip-hop to acid jazz; the audience can be similarly eclectic. **Twilo**, across the street, boasts the strongest sound system in town. The dizzyingly designed **Centro-Fly** (45 West 21st Street; tel: 627-7770) is known for its DJs and atmosphere. **Fun** (130 Madison Street; tel: 964-0303), located underneath the Manhattan Bridge, is a bi-level emporium of entertainment, from the video projections on the wall to the futuristic lounge. Latin American rhythms – and mambo lessons – can be found at **SOBs** (Varick Street at Houston Street; tel: 243-4940).

Opening in the mid-1980s, the subdued ambience of **Nell's** (14th Street between Seventh and Eighth avenues; tel: 675-1567) was intended as an antidote to flashing lights and pulsating music; this Victorian-style living room has faded from fashion but is still worth a visit.

GAY AND LESBIAN NIGHTCLUBS

New York has many gay and lesbian nightspots, and many Lower Manhattan nightclubs are intended predominantly or exclusively for gay men or lesbians on certain nights of the week. The latest details can be found by reading the *Village Voice*, *New York Press*, *Time Out New York* and the many smaller gay- and lesbian-aimed publications found in speciality bookshops such as *Different Light Books*, 151 West 19th Street.

239

Radio City Music Hall is a popular rock venue

However, a new trend is rapidly evolving: the "lounge", a quiet place where the more sedate nocturnal New Yorker can just lounge and chat.

Rock music Rock music's big names always include New York on their international touring schedules. If they are not filling the 55,000-capacity Shea Stadium in Queens, they are most likely to be found in venues such as the **Beacon Theater** (Broadway at 75th Street; for ticket information tel: 496-7070), **Madison Square Garden** (Seventh Avenue between 31st and 33rd streets; tel: 465-6741), or **Radio City Music Hall** (Sixth Avenue at 50th Street; tel: 247-4777) which stages musicals, dance and rock music shows.

Up-and-coming bands from the US and Europe who have outgrown the small club scene but are not yet ready for the large concert halls turn up most nights of the week in mid-sized venues such as **Irving Plaza** (17 Irving Place; tel: 777-6800), the **Roxy** (515 West 18th Street; tel: 645-5156 or 627-0404), and **Roseland** (52nd Street between Eighth Avenue and Broadway; tel: 247-0200), the legendary ballroom of the Big Band era.

ROCK MUSIC TICKETS
Tickets for major rock shows (usually $35–$75) and for most shows at medium-sized venues ($10–$30) can be booked by phone and paid for by credit card through Ticketmaster (tel: 307-7171).

Other venues worth checking out are **The Bottom Line** (4th Street near Fifth Avenue; tel: 228-7800), featuring new signings to major labels and also booking some ageing 1960s cult names, and **Wetlands** (Hudson Street, three blocks south of Canal Street; tel: 966-4225), with 1960s psychedelic décor, organic food and books and pamphlets on ecological issues – as well as a full roster of rock, reggae and funk bands.

Another dependable spot for local talent and sometimes more, is **Brownies** (169 Avenue A, between Tenth and Eleventh streets; tel: 420-8392).

New York's own rock music scene is highly incestuous – some bands might be huge in a particular neighbourhood but unknown outside it. Plenty of exotically named hopefuls can be heard every night for free, or a few dollars, in dozens of tiny clubs secreted throughout the East Village and SoHo. For details, read the ads in the *Village Voice* or look for the handwritten notices pinned up in local cafés and bars.

Talking Heads and Blondie were just two of the big names that emerged from the New York punk scene of the mid-1970s, which centred on the still-surviving **CBGB** (Bowery at Bleecker Street; tel: 982-4052). Unknown bands play here every night of the week, while performance art and readings are also billed at the **CB's 313 Gallery** next door (tel: 388-2529).

Experimentally minded musicians explore rock's avant-garde fringe at the **Knitting Factory** (74 Leonard Street; tel: 219-3055).

A popular jazz venue, Birdland is named after a club that was a 1940s legend

Jazz and blues Since the 1940s, New York has been well endowed with smoky jazz clubs, usually occupying basements in Greenwich Village. Their floorboards will have been trodden by many of jazz's most illustrious figures.

Most jazz clubs have two or three nightly shows. Cover charges range from around $8 to $20 or more and, depending on the venue and, sometimes, the band playing, you may have to pay per set, rather than for the whole evening. Sometimes there will also be a two-drink minimum charge (around $6).

The long-established and excellent **Village Vanguard** (Seventh Avenue at 11th Street; tel: 255-4037) epitomises the dark-and-smoky Greenwich Village basement jazz club. Several top names play here regularly. Major jazz stars are also frequent visitors to the atmospheric **Blue Note** (3rd Street at MacDougal Street; tel: 475-8592), where cover charges can sometimes be very steep.

Among the city's newer jazz venues is the **Iridium Jazz Club** (1650 Broadway at 51st Street; tel: 582-2121), highly rated for its excellent roster of live acts and its quirky architecture. An older venue in a fresh setting is **Birdland** (315 West 44th Street; tel: 581-3080) which aims to re-create the style of a 1940s supper club. It offers three nightly jazz sets as well as a Sunday jazz brunch session.

A lower-key Greenwich Village venue is **55 Bar** (55 Christopher Street; tel: 929-9803), where quality piano and bass duos and more thrive in an intimate atmosphere.

Elsewhere around town, the pricey **Michael's Pub** (118 West 57th Street; tel: 758-2272) specialises in New Orleans-style jazz. On Monday nights, Woody Allen usually adds his clarinet to the exuberant musical melée. An appreciative audience helps make **Smalls** (183 West Tenth Street; tel: 929-7565) a likely place to catch emerging talents, and the **Knickerbocker Bar and Grill** (9th Street and University Place; tel: 228-8490) offers some line-ups that include established jazz stars. Blues and R&B, meanwhile, seldom come rawer or raunchier than the nightly acts at **Terra Blues** (149 Bleeker Street; tel: 777-7776). For more mainstream acts check out **B.B. King Blues Club and Grill** (243 West 42nd Street; tel: 997-4144).

Folk Greenwich Village was the epicentre of the early 1960s folk revival. Judy Collins, Bob Dylan and other legends started here. The days of hootenannys are long gone, but legendary folk venues such as the **Bitter End** (147 Bleeker Street; tel: 673-7030) remain, alongside newer ones such as the welcoming **Centerfold Coffeehouse** (Church of Sts Paul and Andrew, 263 West 86th Street; tel: 866-4454).

Country music Listening to country music seems somewhat incongruous in ultra-urban New York, but **Full Moon Saloon** (Eighth Avenue at 46th Street) features a mixture of new wave and traditional country sounds. **O'Lunney's** (44th Street near Fifth Avenue; tel: 840-6688) and the **Rodeo Bar** (Third Avenue at 27th Street; tel: 683-6500) are smaller, more intimate, venues.

Greenwich Village jazz: a costlier night out than 50 years ago, but the atmosphere remains the same

FOR CHILDREN IN THE OUTER BOROUGHS

Brooklyn's Children's Museum (145 Brooklyn Avenue) is an architecturally innovative affair, with exhibits to encourage understanding of the basics of science and nature. Older children might prefer a romp through the vintage subway cars displayed at the New York Transit Museum (see page 76).

A ride on the Staten Island Ferry is enjoyable in its own right. Once ashore, the Richmondtown Historic Restoration (see page 179) has traditionally attired guides bringing local history to life in a colourful and informative way. Elsewhere, the Bronx Zoo (see pages 70–71) has a children's section; in Queens, the New York Hall of Science (page 171) has a mass of entertaining hands-on exhibits.

Alice and friends in Central Park

New York for children

A number of Manhattan museums have sections intended for children but only the **Children's Museum of Manhattan** (in the Tisch Building, 83rd Street between Broadway and Amsterdam Avenue) is purpose-designed: a wonderful play-as-you-learn facility using computerised interactive exhibits and displays. The Children's Museum's four floors of informative fun include the Brainatarium, exploring the functions of the human brain, and the Time-Warner Center for Media, where children can film, edit and star in their own videos. The Urban Tree House explores the environmental conflicts between city life and the natural world.

Still with an educational role, the **American Museum of Natural History** (see pages 63–64), with its dinosaur skeletons, giant model whale and scores of stuffed creatures, is usually popular. At the **Sony Wonder Technology Lab** (550 Madison Avenue), there are regular programmes for children which explore animation and other media-related subjects with interactive computers and special workshops.

For city views, the **Empire State Building** is the star, and its nerve-shattering **New York Skyride** provides thrills. A boat trip (page 67) can be combined with a clamber around the historic ships of the **South Street Seaport** (page 178).

In Central Park, the main **Central Park Wildlife Center** is behind the Arsenal at 64th Street and Fifth Avenue (tel: 408-0271). Sea lion feeding times are at 11:30 AM, 2 PM and 4 PM. Storytelling takes place on Saturdays at the Hans Christian Andersen statue by Conservatory Water (tel: 794-6564 for details). On the northern edge of Central

Park are the exhibits of the **Charles A Dana Discovery Center** (110th Street and Fifth Avenue), which explore environmental themes. Special events include beginners' birdwatching and walks.

For a treat, go to the delightful **Enchanted Forest** (85 Mercer Street), where expensive stuffed animals inhabit a make-believe medieval forest, or **FAO Schwarz** (Fifth Avenue between 58th and 59th streets), packed with the kind of toys children dream about – including top-of-the-range items.

Above: Getting to grips with the game in Central Park

Above left: The Bronx Zoo, described on pages 70–71

Left: Rollerblading in Central Park

244

Throughout the summer, the Brooklyn Arts Council (for details, tel: 718/625-0080) hosts free musical events at several locations, including Brighton Beach. The Bronx's Hall of Fame for Great Americans (pages 71–72) is always free, as is the Bronx Zoo (pages 70–71) from Tuesday to Thursday, although a voluntary donation is expected. In Queens, the New York Hall of Science (page 171) is free Thursday and Friday afternoons during Sep–Jun. Staten Island's Garibaldi Meucci Museum (page 180) has free admission, and there is no charge for the July concert series at Snug Harbor (tel: 718/448-2500).

Window-shopping, Manhattan-style: a live window display at Macy's department store

New York for free

Even paupers can have fun in the Big Apple. Many of New York's finest things – architecture, pulsating streetlife, distinctive neighbourhoods, fantastic department stores – can be seen without spending any money. Study the suggestions below for more ways to enjoy New York for free.

Free in Manhattan Several of the city's major museums described in the A-Z section of this book offer free admission on selected weekday evenings: the **Cooper-Hewitt Museum** (*Open* Tue 5–9 PM); the **Guggenheim Museum** (*Open* Fri 6–8 PM. *Admission donation*); the **Museum of Modern Art** (*Open* Thu 4:30–8:15 PM. *Admission donation*); and the **Whitney Museum of American Art** (*Open* Thu 6–8 PM. *Admission donation*). Among the smaller institutions with temporary shows, the **National Academy of Design** allows free entry to its exhibitions on Friday evenings (5–6 PM), as does the **International Center of Photography** (*Open* Fri 5–8 PM. *Admission donation*).

Museums and galleries to which admission is free are the **American Numismatic Society** (page 65); the **American Bible Society** (page 61); the **Forbes Magazine Galleries** (pages 107); the **Hispanic Society of America** (page 126); the **Museum of American Folk Art** (page 155; a suggested donation of $3); the **Museum of American Illustration** (see page 62); the **Nicolas Roerich Museum** (page 189); and the **New York City Police Museum** (page 165).

Visiting **Federal Hall** (page 102) and the **General Grant Memorial** (page 110) costs nothing, and both **Lincoln Center** (page 134) and the **Stock Exchange** (page 182) offer free guided tours. When tickets are available, you can listen for free to delegates' speeches at the **UN General Assembly** (page 184).

Free musical and theatrical entertainment can be found in the summer in **Central Park** (tel: 360-2777), in **Prospect Park** (tel: 718-8999), at **Rockefeller Center** (tel: 664-4602), on the plazas of **Lincoln Center** (tel: 875-5350) and at **South Street Seaport** (tel: SEA-PORT).

Travel Facts

Arriving and departing

Entry formalities British citizens require a full 10-year passport to visit the US but, like the citizens of most European countries, do not need a visa if their intended stay in the US is less than 90 days and they have a return ticket. It is necessary, however, to fill out the green visa-waiver form issued on the plane.

Before landing, passengers will also be given US customs and immigration forms to complete. These forms require fairly simple information about the duration of your stay and the address where you will be spending your first night and should present no difficulties if you are visiting the US on holiday or on a business trip. Should you be planning to live and/or work in the US, however, you need to obtain permission to do this – and the relevant paperwork – from a US embassy before arranging your flight.

If your trip is long (more than three weeks, for example) you are likely to be asked to show evidence of sufficient funds to support yourself during your stay. A wallet full of credit cards and a thick wad of traveller's cheques will soon put the minds of suspicious immigration officials (who might think you are planning to work illegally in the US) at ease.

If you are travelling with one of the major airlines, it is possible that an

Use only licensed cabs from the official airport taxi ranks

246

immigration check (a computer check of the passengers' names against those of known miscreants) will be carried out when you check in at the airport. A sticker will then be attached to your passport to speed your passage through immigration control when you land. Otherwise, anticipate a wait of at least an hour to be processed by immigration. Once you reach the desk, hand the officer your passport and the immigration form that you filled in on the plane, and have your return ticket ready for inspection.

Assuming there are no problems, your passport will be stamped with the date and part of the immigration form will be fixed to your passport showing the date by which you must leave the country (usually several months ahead); this is removed only when you leave the US.

By air: International flights into New York land either at John F Kennedy Airport (tel: 718/244-4444; in Queens, about 24km east of Manhattan) or Newark (tel: 973/961-6000; in New Jersey, about 24km west of Manhattan). Both these airports also receive domestic flights, as does the city's third airport, La Guardia (tel: 718/533-3400; also in Queens, 13km east of Manhattan).

Wherever you land, travel into Manhattan is fairly straightforward if somewhat time-consuming: once clear of immigration and customs, depending on traffic, travel between the airport and the city can take from 30 minutes upwards. Each airport has a Ground Transportation desk where you can check routes, timings and fares into the city.

Besides the public transport services detailed below, taxis operate from each of the three airports and should be taken from the clearly signposted official taxi ranks, outside the terminals. If you are approached in person, the taxi driver is likely to be unlicensed, and therefore uninsured. Never ride in independent taxis; stick to yellow taxis, and look for the medallion – the official flat bronze-coloured disk affixed to the roof.

Taxi fares from the airports into Manhattan are high: expect to spend around $35–45 (road and bridge tolls

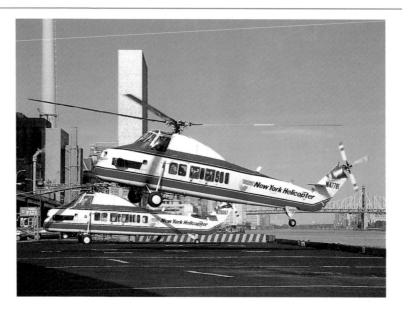

Helicopters provide a speedy but costly way to sightsee or reach the airport. Most travellers prefer to use the bus

are extra) from Newark, $20–30 from La Guardia. From JFK there is a flat fare of $30 plus tips and tolls.

"Share and Save" group rates are available between 8 AM and midnight at Newark and La Guardia; make arrangements with the airport's uniformed taxi dispatcher. Remember that traffic can be particularly dense around each airport and can add further to taxi charges.

From **JFK** free shuttle buses run to the nearest subway station, Howard Beach, leaving a 60-minute ride into Manhattan. Other buses link the airport to other subway lines, intended for New Yorkers who want to get home without changing lines. (Before using the subway, see **Public transport** on pages 256–257.)

Olympia Trails Airport Express (tel: 964-6233) has separate buses leaving every 20–30 minutes between 6 AM and midnight to either Grand Central Terminal and the Port Authority. The $11 ticket is sold at the Ground Transportation desk and by the driver.

Nervous tourists arriving at JFK for the first time and carrying luggage should ignore the subway and instead use the New York Airport Service

(tel: 718/706-9658), which departs for stops in Manhattan every 15–30 minutes between 6 AM and midnight. One-way tickets can be bought, for much less than half the cost of a taxi, from attendants at airport terminals.

A slightly more expensive but quicker option is to use a shared minibus like Gray Line Air Shuttle (tel: 800/451-0455). Purchase a one-way ($14) or round-trip ($28) ticket from an agent at the Ground Transportation desk near the baggage claim. The vans run from 7 AM to 11:30 PM and stop at Manhattan hotels between 23rd and 63rd streets.

From **Newark** Olympia Trails Airport Express (tel: 908/354-3330) operates as from JFK, as does Gray Line Air Shuttle (tel: 800/451-0455), operating shared vans from Newark airport to hotels in Manhattan.

From **La Guardia** local buses run to the rest of Queens, but the best way to reach Manhattan is with Gray Line Air Shuttle van (tel: 800/451-0455). The vans have the same schedule as those serving JFK, but serve Manhattan hotels between 23rd and 125th streets. Olympia Trails (see above) also operate from La Guardia. You could also try Service Express Bus (718/706-9658), which departs for six Manhattan stops every 20 minutes between 6 AM and midnight.

For general information on travel to and from New York's airports, call 1-800/AIR-RIDE.

By sea: New York's great days as a seaport may be long gone but the QE2 keeps the tradition and the sheer luxury alive. After the crossing, you will glide into New York beneath the Statue of Liberty and put ashore at Midtown Manhattan's gleaming Passenger Ship Terminal on Twelfth Avenue between 50th and 52nd streets.

By bus: Long-distance buses into New York complete their journeys

at the country's largest and busiest bus station, Port Authority Bus Terminal (tel: 564-8484), which stretches between 40th and 42nd streets on Eighth Avenue.

By rail: Most local commuter trains pull into Grand Central Terminal, at 42nd Street between Lexington and Park Avenue: for more information and history regarding the Terminal, see pages 166–167. Amtrak's long-distance trains pull into New York's other station, Penn Station, at 31st Street and Eighth Avenue. For information tel: 800/872-7245.

Car hire

With traffic lights on almost every corner and a lack of affordable parking, as well as being infamous for its gridlock, Manhattan – and New York City generally – is a dire place in which to drive. For excursions outside the city, however, a hire-car is a near-essential accessory.

The majority of international car-hire companies have desks at New York's airports (and offices in the city), where you can collect a pre-booked car or hire one on the spot. You will save money, but not necessarily any time, if you travel out of

Life on the move in New York City

the city by public transport and then hire a car in a smaller town. Hiring a car at an airport branch is usually less expensive than at the same agency's Manhattan branch.

The address of the nearest major car-hire outlet can be found by calling the following freephone numbers: Avis (tel: 800/230-4898); Budget (tel: 800/527-0700); Hertz (tel: 800/654-3131); National (tel: 800/227-7368). Many more hire firms are listed in the *Yellow Pages*, though the international companies are often safest.

New York has outlawed the sale of Collision Damage Waiver (CDW), an optional form of insurance that can add considerably to costs. In New York you pay only for the first $100 of damage to a rental car. Check also whether or not the vehicle has to be returned with a full tank of petrol.

Any non-US citizen under 25 and/ or without a credit card may find problems hiring a car in New York.

In the unlikely event of your hire car breaking down, simply phone the car hire firm you hired from. Should you break down far from a phone, stay with your vehicle and wait for a Highway Patrol to come by.

If any other passing motorist stops to offer help, there is every chance that the approach will be genuine – but treat the offer with caution. Usually, the best help is for the person to make a call on your behalf.

Climate

New York City attracts visitors all the year round. Those who avoid the hot, sticky months of July and August and the snowfalls and sub-zero temperatures, which are common between December and February, get the best deal in terms of climate. The city generally emerges from its winter freeze by mid-March. By April, the numerous outdoor events that make New York so appealing are beginning to get into full swing, making springtime a good period to be around. After the ferocious summer heat, when air-conditioning machines are run at full-pelt and New Yorkers tend to become irritable, autumn finds the humidity disappearing although temperatures remain

appealingly mild, usually well into October. Outside New York City, where summers are much more pleasant, the best time to travel is April to September.

Crime

Careful advance planning, staying alert on the street and in the subway will all help to reduce what is already a statistically very slender chance of your being robbed or attacked. Once an infamous city, New York's crime rates have fallen dramatically.

However, as in any large city, caution is still advised: Don't leave money and valuables in your hotel room and enquire whether the hotel has a safe. Keep an eye on your wallet or purse; don't go into dark or deserted areas, epecially at night; and after midnight take a taxi instead of the subway. With less traffic, the ride will be much faster and cheaper than during the day.

Lost or stolen traveller's cheques are relatively easy to replace (read the instructions when you buy the cheques and make a note of the relevant details). Replacing a stolen passport, however, can be much harder and begins with a visit or telephone call to your country's nearest consular office (see details on pages 252–253).

Customs regulations

Duty-free allowances for non-US citizens entering the country include one US quart (just under a litre) of alcoholic spirits or wine (no one under 21 may bring alcohol into the US), 200 cigarettes or 50 cigars, and up to $100-worth of gifts. Among things you may not bring into the US are meat, fruit, plants, chocolate liqueurs and lottery tickets.

Be warned that bottles of pills and other forms of medication are likely to excite the interest of US customs officers. Unless you have a doctor's certificate, even drugs which are available over the counter in the UK may be confiscated if they are prescription-only in the US.

The import of wildlife souvenirs sourced from rare or endangered species may be either illegal or require a special permit. Before purchase you should check your home country's customs regulations.

Travellers with disabilities

In New York, as in the US generally, facilities for travellers with disabilities are impressive. By law, public buildings have to be at least partially wheelchair-accessible and all must provide toilets for people with disabilities (the design of which sometimes differs from those found in Europe). Almost all New York buses have rear-door lifts for wheelchair-users and most are also able to "kneel" to make access easier from the kerb. The subway is an entirely different story, however, with access almost impossible for wheelchair users.

Elevated subway in Williamsburg

US trains and airlines are obliged to provide services for people with disabilities if requested, and Amtrak (the US train service) has earned a reputation for doing this well. Though buses are less comfortable than the trains, Greyhound are more frequent and allow a companion to travel free provided you have a doctor's certificate stating that this is necessary.

Some major car-hire companies can arrange vehicles with hand controls provided they receive advance notice.

For more information, contact the Mayor's Office for People with Disabilities, tel: 788-2830.

Domestic travel

If you are combining your trip to New York with travel further afield in the US, you will find that the country's domestic transport services are (considering the distances involved) usually cheaper than their European counterparts. Foreign visitors are often entitled to discounted passes which can reduce costs further.

By air: Not only the fastest way to get between cities, air travel in the US can also be a bargain. Seemingly no end of cut-price domestic air fares are advertised by US travel agents and airlines as they seek to fill seats on flights outside peak periods. Look in any newspaper or travel agent's window for the latest bargains.

Many international airlines will offer connecting flights (with their own domestic service or with that of their US partners) at little, if any, extra cost above the transatlantic fare. It is usually a simple matter to arrive and depart from different airports within the US, provided travel is with the same airline. In the wake of the 11 September bombing, the FAA has introduced additional security checks on internal flights, so arrive at the airport in plenty of time for your flight. You will not be able to take on board anything that could be used as a weapon (including items such as golf clubs or insect repellent). If you are in any doubt, pack it in your checked-in luggage or leave it behind.

By bus: Long-distance bus services in the US are run by Greyhound and,

250

by a few dollars, are the country's cheapest form of long-distance travel. All departures from New York are from the Port Authority Bus Terminal (see page 248). Although Greyhound buses are comparatively comfortable – with air conditioning, reclining seats, toilets on board and stops every few hours for refreshments and leg-stretching – journeys can be very long (five hours from New York to Boston, for example) and monotonous. The buses nearly always take the fast but tedious Interstate Highways rather than more scenic country or coastal roads. Costs over several very long journeys can be reduced with an Ameripass ticket, which offers unlimited Greyhound travel over a fixed period – from 4 to 30 days. Ameripass tickets can be bought outside the US. Details can be obtained from your local travel agent.

By car: If you are travelling beyond New York or embarking on any of the excursions described on pages 194–211, the cheapest and most convenient way to do so is by car. In the US, petrol costs a fraction of its European price and car-hire rates (outside New York City) are very reasonable. For further details, see Car hire (page 248). Driving in the US is legal with a valid licence of most European countries or with an International Driver's Licence. See Driving tips (page 252).

By train: Before the advent of cheap domestic air travel, rail was the swiftest and most stylish way to travel around the US and New York's Grand Central Terminal was truly the gateway to the continent. These days, the trains – equipped with sleeping berths, dining cars and comfortable carriages – are as plush as ever, but prices are often no lower than the cheapest air fare on the same route. For non-US citizens touring the country (or part of it) by train, a variety of regional and country-wide rail passes can save money over regular fares provided they are used to their fullest extent. Visitors from Europe should note that the US rail network is far from comprehensive and, in many instances, services between major cities are not particularly frequent.

CONVERSION CHARTS

FROM	TO	MULTIPLY BY
Inches	Centimetres	2.54
Centimetres	Inches	0.3937
Feet	Metres	0.3048
Metres	Feet	3.2810
Yards	Metres	0.9144
Metres	Yards	1.0936
Miles	Kilometres	1.6090
Kilometres	Miles	0.6214
Acres	Hectares	0.4047
Hectares	Acres	2.4710
US Gallons	Litres	3.7854
Litres	US Gallons	0.2642
Ounces	Grams	28.35
Grams	Ounces	0.0353
Pounds	Grams	453.6
Grams	Pounds	0.0022
Pounds	Kilograms	0.4536
Kilograms	Pounds	2.205
US Tons	Tonnes	0.9072
Tonnes	US Tons	1.1023

MEN'S SUITS

UK	36	38	40	42	44	46	48
Rest of Europe	46	48	50	52	54	56	58
US	36	38	40	42	44	46	48

DRESS SIZES

UK	8	10	12	14	16	18
France	36	38	40	42	44	46
Italy	38	40	42	44	46	48
Rest of Europe	34	36	38	40	42	44
US	6	8	10	12	14	16

MEN'S SHIRTS

UK	14	14.5	15	15.5	16	16.5	17
Rest of Europe	36	37	38	39/40	41	42	43
US	14	14.5	15	15.5	16	16.5	17

MEN'S SHOES

UK	7	7.5	8.5	9.5	10.5	11
Rest of Europe	41	42	43	44	45	46
US	8	8.5	9.5	10.5	11.5	12

WOMEN'S SHOES

UK	4.5	5	5.5	6	6.5	7
Rest of Europe	38	38	39	39	40	41
US	6	6.5	7	7.5	8	8.5

*Driving in NewYork is best left to
the experts*

All train departures from New York
are from Grand Central Terminal or
Penn Station.

Driving tips
Driving in New York City is not
recommended (not least because
New Yorkers drive like maniacs and
parking can be very expensive), nor
is it necessary. Venture beyond the
city to the Catskill Mountains, the
remoter parts of the Hudson Valley,
Long Island or New Jersey – or further afield – and wheels of your own
become essential (for these excursions
see pages 194–211).

On US roads, signposted distances
are always given in miles (although
elsewhere distances may be
expressed in terms of the time it
takes to drive somewhere). Traffic
travels on the right-hand side, and
overtaking is permitted on both the
inside and outside lanes of Interstate
Highways.

A speed limit of usually 55mph
(88kph) or 65mph (104kph) is in
force on Interstates (in some places
there may also be a minimum limit).
In built-up areas lower speed limits
are indicated. It is illegal to drink and
drive, and hefty fines and prison
sentences are frequently imposed.
New York City is now confiscating
drunk drivers' cars – permanently.

Parking infringements also attract
stiff fines (or worse: your car could
be towed away), so read the signs
carefully. Equally, never park within
3m of a fire hydrant.

Except for some minor routes, the
roads are of a high standard with
petrol (or "gas") stations easy to find
in all but the most secluded or inhos-
pitable regions. Virtually all cars use
unleaded petrol, sold by the US
gallon (3.8 litres). Tolls are charged
for some Manhattan bridges and tunnels, and for some stretches of road
in the Outer Boroughs.

If you are a member of a motoring
organisation at home, it is
worthwhile checking if it has links
with US counterparts: several
provide a range of free services to
members of suitably affiliated
motoring organisations.

Electricity
The US electrical supply is 110 volts
(60 cycles) and appliances use two-
pin plugs. European appliances are
designed for 220 volts (50 cycles) and
can only be used with an adapter,
which can be bought before leaving
or in the US.

Many electrical goods such as CD
players, computers and videos are
sold in New York at prices much
lower than in Europe and the rest of
the US. If you are tempted, be sure to
check (preferably with the manufacturer rather than the eager-to-please
sales assistant) whether or not the
item is compatible with European
electricity supplies.

Embassies and consulates
Most countries have their US embassy
in Washington DC. The following are
consular offices in New York:
Australia, 150 East 42nd Street (tel:
351-6500); Canada, 1251 Sixth Avenue
(tel: 596-1600); Denmark, 1 Dag
Hammarskjöld Plaza (tel: 223-4545);
France, 934 Fifth Avenue (tel: 606-
3688); Germany, 460 Park Avenue (tel:
308-8700); Ireland, 800 Second Avenue
(tel: 319-2555); Italy, 690 Park Avenue
(tel: 737-9100); Netherlands, 1
Rockefeller Plaza (tel: 246-1429); New
Zealand, 780 Third Avenue (tel: 832-
4038); Norway, 825 Third Avenue (tel:
421-7333); Portugal, 630 Fifth Avenue

(tel: 246-4580); Sweden, Dag Hammarskjöld Plaza (tel: 583-2500); United Kingdom, 845 Third Avenue (tel: 745-0200).

Emergency telephone numbers

For **ambulance**, **police** or **fire**, dial 911 (no money required) and ask for the relevant service.

Other emergency numbers include **Safe Horizon** (tel: 577-7777) and **Rape and Sexual Assault Hotline** (tel: 227-3000).

Health and health insurance

It is essential, though not compulsory, to have insurance when you travel anywhere in the US. Besides the obvious benefits of compensation for stolen articles and disrupted travel, taking out travel insurance will guard against an astronomical bill if you are unfortunate enough to need medical treatment while in the US.

Comprehensive insurance cover for a stay in New York should include medical insurance of, at the very least, $1 million. If you book a package tour to New York, incidentally, you are likely to find that the optional insurance cover offered will be the

City street-life takes many forms in the Big Apple

more expensive and/or the less comprehensive than that available from a specialist company. For a reduced rate, some insurance companies will offer cover for the US which includes only medical bills.

If you need to see a doctor or dentist whilst in New York, find one by looking under "Physicians and Surgeons" or "Dentists" in the *Yellow Pages*, or phone one of the doctor and dentist referral services listed under "Hospitals". New York hospitals with 24-hour casualty departments include St Luke's Roosevelt (59th Street at Ninth Avenue) and St Vincent's (Seventh Avenue and 11th Street).

Language

New Yorkers not only talk fast, they also talk American English, a language only superficially resembling British English. Besides the well-known variations such as "elevator" instead of lift, "sidewalk" instead of pavement, and "being through" instead of having finished, Americans also commonly use "sir" and "madam" (usually abbreviated to "Ma'm") as a polite way of addressing strangers, and will say "excuse me" rather than "pardon" if they mishear or do not understand what somebody has said.

253

Lost property

Lost at JFK Airport, tel: 718/244-4225.
Lost at La Guardia tel: 718/533-3988.
Lost at Newark tel: 961/961-6633.
Lost in a taxi, tel: 302-8294. Lost on a
bus or the subway, tel: 712-4500.

Media

New York has literally hundreds of
TV and radio channels, as well as
newspapers and magazines. Free
publications aimed at visitors can be
found littering every hotel lobby.
However, they should not be all dis-
regarded as they include *City Guide*
and *Quick Guide*. Also free and useful
are *Village Voice* and *NY Press*. For a
full run-down on the city's media,
see pages 132–133.

Money matters

Before arriving in the US, convert
your spending money to US dollar
traveller's cheques, which can be used
as cash (simply sign and hand over
the cheque, then wait for your
change) in New York and all over the
country in hotels, restaurants and the
larger shops. Most hotel cashiers will
happily exchange guests' US dollar
traveller's cheques for cash.

Trying to change foreign currency –
or foreign-currency traveller's
cheques – in the US is much more of

*Street advertising is an art form New
York could call its own*

an ordeal, although New York (rare
among US cities) does boast several
banks with foreign-exchange desks,
and a small number of exchange
bureaux. Money can also be changed
on arrival at JFK and Newark airports.

Companies that offer currency
exchange include Chase Manhattan
(tel: 935-9935) and Thomas Cook (tel:
800/287-7362). Both have many
branches throughout the city and
phoning the numbers above will elicit
the address of the nearest one to you.

US dollar traveller's cheques can be
changed for cash in a bank, but you
will have to show ID and may be
charged a commission fee. Ask first.
New York City banking hours are
generally Mon–Fri 9–5 or 6. Some
branches may open on Saturday.

Credit cards are a common form
of payment and all the major cards
are widely accepted. Europeans who
know their credit card pin number
can also get cash through American
cash-dispensing machines (known as
ATMs) which display the appropriate
credit-card symbol.

The currency that you will handle
most frequently is the identically
sized and coloured notes: $20, $10, $5

and $1; and the variously sized coins: 25¢ (a "quarter"), 10¢ (a "dime"), 5¢ (a "nickel") and 1¢ (a "penny").

National holidays
Banks and all public offices will be closed on all the following holidays, though shops may be open on some of them: New Year's Day (1 Jan), Martin Luther King's Birthday (third Mon in Jan), Presidents' Day (third Mon in Feb), Memorial Day (third Mon in May), Independence Day (4 Jul), Labor Day (first Mon in Sep), Columbus Day (second Mon in Oct), Veterans' Day (11 Nov), Thanksgiving Day (fourth Thu in Nov), Christmas Day (25 Dec). In some cases, the actual dates vary if the holiday falls on a weekend.

Opening hours
New York shop opening hours vary greatly. Many big shops will open on weekdays and Saturdays from 9 to 8, but smaller or more specialist shops may open as late as 11 or noon and close at 9 or 10. On Sundays, opening times are from 11 or 12 till 6 or 7.

Museum opening times also vary. Many are open from 10 or 11 to 6 on weekdays and Saturdays (though several are closed on Mondays). Some also open on Sundays, and several keep late hours on selected days.

Bank opening hours are Mon–Fri 9–3:30. Many keep longer hours and may open on Saturday.

Pharmacies
Pharmacies are plentiful in New York, however, visitors from Europe will find many familiar medicines under unfamiliar names. Some drugs that are available over the counter in Europe are available in the US only with a prescription.

If you need to take medication regularly, the safest course is to bring a supply with you (but see the relevant section of Customs regulations on page 250). Should you be intending to buy prescription drugs while in New York, bring a note from your own doctor. (To find a doctor in New York, see the information on Health on page 253.)

Times Square – the heart of the city that never sleeps

Places of worship
New York's places of worship are many and varied. Some of the principal ones are described in the A-Z section of this book, and on pages 120–121. Your hotel reception will be able to advise of those in your neighbourhood, and the telephone book carries a comprehensive list. Several companies offer Sunday gospel trips to Harlem.

Police
"New York's Finest", the city's police, are helpful and efficient. Besides patrolling in cars, officers are regularly seen on the street and are well represented in crowd situations.

If you are unfortunate enough to be the victim of theft, you may want to call at a police station to have your insurance claim authorised. Every New York neighbourhood has a police station. To find the one nearest you, dial 374-5000. If you need the police in an emergency, dial 911.

255

Policemen will be happy to help

Post offices

New York's main post office, at Eighth Avenue between 31st and 33rd streets, stays open around the clock, every day of the week. Elsewhere in the city, larger post offices are open on Monday to Friday from 8 to 6 and on Saturdays from 8 to 1. The many smaller post offices keep shorter hours. Post-boxes are blue.

As well as from a post office, stamps can be bought (at inflated prices) through vending machines found in some shops and in many hotel lobbies.

Public transport

Spending most of your time in Manhattan will leave you much less reliant on public transport than you might expect. Not only are distances small, but much of Manhattan is best seen on foot. If you are exhausted, in a rush, planning to visit the Outer Boroughs or simply commuting between uptown and downtown, you will need to make use of the city's buses, subway or taxis.

City buses Substantially slower than subway trains, New York buses at least allow passengers to view the city as they travel through it. Many people find them less intimidating than the underground transit system. The bus network is comprehensive (free maps are available from the tourist information office listed on page 260) and the majority of routes run north–south and east–west (crosstown) with free transfers between another bus or subway journey.

Bus stops are close to street corners – marked by an MTA sign and route number – and most have a route map and frequency schedule for the buses that use that stop. The route is displayed on the front of each bus. Most buses stop every two or three blocks; those marked "limited" (which can only be found at rush-hour) make fewer stops, usually only at major junctions.

As with the subway, there is a flat fare (currently $1.50) for all journeys. This can be paid with a MetroCard or in coins (exact change only; no dollar bills) or a subway token (see below) on boarding.

When using your MetroCard, whether on the bus or the subway, you will be entitled to a free transfer to another bus or subway journey. This is automatically encoded on the card and valid for two hours. If you use coins or a token, ask the driver as you get on the bus for a transfer slip.

Especially during rush-hours, New York buses can become solidly packed; crosstown buses make only slightly better headway than pedestrians. If you are wedged in a crowded bus and think your stop may be coming up soon, start making your way towards the exit doors (which are in the middle of the bus – though you can also get off at the front door) in plenty of time; otherwise there is every chance you will not reach the doors before they shut and the bus moves on.

The subway The much-maligned New York subway system is a swift, inexpensive and largely efficient way to get about the city. The system has benefited greatly from a multi-million dollar clean-up that saw the replacement of graffiti-covered carriages with cleaner and (usually) more comfortable models.

A tangle of lines denoted by numbers and letters, the subway system map (available free from subway station token booths and from the tourist information office listed on page 260) initially seems hopelessly confusing. In fact, the system is relatively easy to use provided you remember that "Uptown" trains go north (towards the Upper West and East sides and Harlem) and "Downtown" trains travel south (towards Lower Manhattan). Any train labelled "Brooklyn Bound" is indeed bound for Brooklyn but will stop in Lower Manhattan on the way.

What can be more confusing is the choice between "Express" and "Local" trains. While local trains stop at all stations on a particular line, express trains stop only at selected stations (see pages 54–55 for further details on distinguishing between the two). Board an express train by mistake and you can sometimes find yourself some distance from where you want to be, and possibly in a dangerous neighbourhood. If this happens then take the next train back.

Know which line and direction you want to travel in before entering the station and follow the relevant signs to the platform. If you do not know, enquire at the ticket booth or ask a uniformed transit police officer. On the platform, approaching trains are usually announced over loudspeakers (though such announcements can often be inaudible). Each train has the relevant letter or number and its destination shown along its side, in a colour corresponding to the subway map.

During the day, trains arrive every 10–15 minutes (more during rush-hours). Between midnight and 5 AM the usual wait is around 20 minutes. To enter the subway system, you need to use a MetroCard or drop a subway token (currently $1.50) into a slot and pass through a turnstile. Tokens can be bought from the booths found at every station (most all booths are open 24 hours) and also from a few major museums. MetroCards (tel: 800/METROCARD) are plastic smartcards encoded at the ticket booth for $3–80 worth of fares, or in fixed-fee versions: the $4 Fun Pass lasting a day and the $17 Unlimited Ride card lasting seven days. The subway does have its share of pickpockets – but if you stay alert, you should have no problems.

Taxis These are expensive, and liable to be stuck in traffic for long periods of time. Sometimes, however, cabs are the most time-efficient way to get where you are going, especially at night. When you want one, simply hail the next empty one to pass by. You know a cab is empty if the sign on its roof is lighted.

Always wear the seat-belts provided, and get a receipt from the driver before you get out. If you leave something in the taxi, the receipt could help in getting it back. Use only the official "medallion" cabs. These are yellow with "NYC Taxi" stencilled on the side and a light and medallion on the roof. Any other vehicle touting for passengers will be unlicensed (known colloquially as a "gypsy cab") and should be ignored. Official taxi charges currently begin at $2 and gain 30¢ for each fifth of a mile (322m) travelled and 20¢ for

257

Take care on the subway

each minute stopped in traffic. There is a 50¢ surcharge between 8 PM and 6 AM; a 15–20 per cent tip is the norm.

Student and youth travel

Coming from Europe, students in full-time education and anyone under 26 may qualify for discounted transatlantic flights offered by travel agents that specialise in youth and student travel. Students carrying International Student Identity Cards (ISICs) will be entitled to reduced admission to many New York museums and other attractions. While not exclusively for young and student travellers, the city's YMCAs and youth hostels (see page 215) offer inexpensive accommodation and a chance to socialise with other young visitors from around the world.

On the down side, travellers under 21 should remember that US law forbids them to buy alcohol; they may also be denied admission to some New York nightclubs. Under-25s may also encounter problems hiring a car in some parts of the US.

Telephones

Americans are inclined to pick up the telephone for routine enquiries more frequently than their counterparts in Europe. Many companies and businesses have freephone numbers (prefixed 800, 877 or 888) allowing the public to phone them free of charge (first dial "1").

Public telephones are easy to find: in the street, hotel lobbies, train and bus stations, bars and restaurants and most public buildings.

The telephone has slots for quarters, dimes and nickels, which should be inserted before dialling. By European standards, phone calls are cheap. A local call costs 25¢ for the first three minutes. The definition of "local", however, often only covers an area of a few square kilometres; calls further afield – from Manhattan to Staten Island, for example – can be costly.

Almost without exception, hotel room telephones have much higher charges than public telephones. Sometimes hotels even charge for dialling freephone numbers. Emergency calls (dial 911), calls to the operator (dial 0) or the international

operator (dial 800/874-4000), or calls for directory assistance (411) are free.

Throughout this book, freephone numbers are given where available. The predominant area code (212) for Manhattan is omitted on the asumption that your call is from another 212 number. Some newer Manhattan numbers use 917 or 646 – when calling these numbers from a 212 number (or vice versa), a "1" plus the full area code must be dialled. Area codes in the Outer Boroughs are 347 and 718.

Time

New York uses Eastern Standard Time, 5 hours behind the UK, 6 hours behind the rest of western Europe, and 13–15 hours behind Australia. These differences will vary by an hour for a few weeks in March/April and October/November, when US Daylight Saving Time begins and ends.

Tipping

In the US, tipping is a long-established fact of life and many people in jobs that involve serving the general public rely on tips to make up a large proportion of their relatively low wages.

How much you tip is entirely up to you, but the general rule in a coffee shop or restaurant is to leave the person who served you 15 per cent of the total bill. (An easy way to calculate the approximate amount is to double the sales tax figure – which is 8.25 per cent – shown at the bottom of the bill.) The money should be left on the table, or in a box beside the cashier. Do not leave a tip at any food outlet where you serve yourself or where the food is sold to be taken away.

After a taxi ride, it is customary to tip the driver around 15–20 per cent of the fare. The amount need not be exact, however, and most people (if the amount works out within reason) allow the driver to keep the change as they pay for the fare.

Tipping hotel porters is also the done thing, especially if they are red in the face and short of breath after carrying your suitcases up several flights of stairs. Again, the amount you tip is entirely discretionary, but reckon on about $1 per bag. If a porter simply helps move your luggage from the lobby into a taxi outside the hotel, a total of $1–$2 should usually be sufficient. In some hotels, envelopes bearing the maid's name are left in the rooms. These are intended to hold tips for the maid, though you need not feel obliged to leave anything, particularly if your stay is only lasting a few nights.

Toilets
Every public building is obliged to provide public toilets (look for the signs saying "Rest Rooms" or "Bathrooms"). Although intended for people with reason to be in the building, such toilets can be used by anyone who does not look overly scruffy. They are almost always in immaculate condition, as are those in hotel lobbies, restaurants and most bars.

Tourist information
The New York Convention and Visitors' Bureau (NYCVB), 810 Seventh Avenue (Mon–Fri 8:30–6, Sat and Sun 9–5; tel: 800/NYC-VISIT), can answer queries, provide free bus and subway maps, and leaflets detailing restaurants, hotels and attractions.

The New York Division of Tourism (1 Commerce Plaza, Albany, New York, NY 12245, tel: 518/474-4116 or 800 225-2697) offers help and information on a state-wide basis – useful if you are planning excursions.

259

From a restaurant meal to a shoe-shine… don't forget that tipping is expected in the US

Tours on foot

There are many guided tours on offer in New York. The **Museum of the City of New York** (tel: 534-1672) and **New York City Cultural Walking Tours** (tel: 979-2388) visit the city's architecture, landmarks and historic sites. Other guided tour companies include **Adventures on a Shoestring** (tel: 265-2663) and **Urban Explorations** (tel: 718/721-5254).

The **Big Apple Greeters** (tel: 669-8159), who are volunteers, will match your particular interest in the city with a local who can tell you all about it on a 2 to 4-hour jaunt. The service is free and tips are not accepted. The Greeters extend their service to those with disabilities. More walking tours are suggested in the panel on page 56.

Web sites

Many New York museums, tourist attractions, newspapers, hotels and restaurants have websites. Details

Americana for sale in a flea market in Little Italy

of them and much more can be found from general sites such as NYCVB (www.nycvisit.com), Citysearch (www.newyork.citysearch.com) and the New York City government site (www.ci.nyc.ny.us).

Women travellers

As in any other city, females on their own – be they residents or visitors – may attract unwelcome attention. This is likely to be more annoying than threatening, and can usually be dealt with simply by ignoring it.

A woman travelling alone is by no means uncommon in New York, but common sense dictates that she should avoid cheap hotels in seedy areas, which are unsafe at night. Otherwise, women travellers face many of the same problems as their male counterparts (see page 249). If you are in trouble and need help, see the Emergency numbers on page 253.

Billboard on Midtown Westside

Hotels and Restaurants

Hotels and Restaurants

The following recommended hotels have been divided into three price categories:
Inexpensive (£): under $125
Moderate (££): $125–$250
Expensive (£££): over $250
Prices do not include taxes (see page 213). Note also that telephone numbers prefixed 800 are free outside the 212 code area when dialed within the United States (dial "1" first); local numbers follow the freephone number, the code for Manhattan being 212 (see also page 258).

HOTELS

CHINATOWN

Holiday Inn Downtown (££)
138 Lafayette Street, at corner of Howard Street tel: 800/HOLIDAY; 966-8898
The only hotel in Chinatown, with very small rooms offering two telephones, in-room films and individual climate control. Eat Chinese seafood in the Pacifica restaurant, or head for the many cheaper alternatives in the busy streets around the neighbourhood.

FINANCIAL DISTRICT AND TRIBECA

Regent Wall Street (£££)
55 Wall Street tel: 845-8600
Perhaps the hotel with more history than any other in the city. The 144-room Regent's land-mark 1842 building, the work of Isaiah Rogers, started out as the New York Merchants Exchange. It then did time as the New York Customs House in the late 19th century, until McKim, Mead and White renovated it in 1907 for use as an Italian Renaissance-style bank. The Greek revival exterior, complete with its massive columns, has not changed, while the interior has retained a great deal of its grandeur, thanks partly to its magnificent scale. Bedrooms are huge – at 150–300 square metres – and rich with velvets and silk damasks, while managing a modern effect. All have the usual luxury amenities, plus private fax/printer/copy machines, cordless phones and voicemail, plus big marble bathrooms with oversized tubs and separate showers. Those with Wall Street business will find the location convenient, but it's also a 15-minute walk to downtown, and a 10-minute subway ride to midtown.

Ritz-Carlton New York, Battery Park (£££)
2 West Street tel: 800/241-333/344-0800
Opened in January 2002, the 298-room Ritz-Carlton is full of oil paintings and reproduction antiques, as is typical of this business travellers' hotel company. It is the only upmarket Manhattan hotel with views of the Statue of Liberty from the bedroom windows, and it also boasts a generous 1200 square metre fitness centre and spa. Part of the complex is luxury condominiums, lending a slightly residential feel to the property, enhanced by the riverside parks of adjacent Battery Park City.

Tribeca Grand (£££)
2 Avenue of the Americas tel: 519-6600
Taking up a whole city block, this is the first major hotel to open in the area. It is configured as an atrium which looks down on the chic Church Lounge, which is a catch-all bar, lounge and café. There is even a cinema in the hotel available for private screenings. Rooms are modern and very comfortable with tall windows that look out over lower Manhattan.

GREENWICH VILLAGE

Washington Square Hotel (£)
103 Waverly Place
tel: 800/222-0418; 777-9515
There is no better placed or better priced Greenwich Village base; this hotel is just opposite a corner of Washington Square Park. The rooms tend to be somewhat small but are clean and pleasantly furnished, and the staff are extremely helpful. In a previous life as the Hotel Earle, this was the first New York home of Bob Dylan and was also where John Phillips of the Mamas and the Papas penned the 1960s hit song "California Dreamin" for his homesick wife Michelle.

LITTLE ITALY AND SOHO

60 Thompson (£££)
60 Thompson Street tel: 431-0400
Considering that SoHo is one of the smallest of New York's neighbourhoods it is amazing the number of upmarket hotels that have opened here. 60 Thompson is a luxury, boutique hotel that is attracting notice from travelling trendsetters. In addition to mini-bars filled with goodies from the supreme gourmet store Dean & Deluca and a chic restaurant, personal laptops, mobile phones and DVD players are on the list of amenities.

Mercer Hotel (£££)
99 Prince Street tel: 888/918-6060, 966-6060
Small and sleek, this downtown hotel caters to an affluent insiders crowd. The rooms are luxurious in an urban way and the services and amenities match the overall cool feel of the place. If your interests lie predominantly in downtown Manhattan, there is no better perch. The Mercer Kitchen in the basement is home to superstar chef Jean-Georges Vongerichten and it is most definitely worth the wait to get in.

Off-SoHo Suites (£££)
11 Rivington Street
tel: 800/OFF-SOHO; 979-9808
These mini-apartment-style suites are very good value if you want to be within walking distance of SoHo, Little Italy and the Lower East Side. Rates are very reasonable, but the suites are tiny, and the area, just the wrong side of the Bowery, may not be to everyone's taste. For inexpensive accommodation, however, this is certainly well worth considering. Each suite is supplied with cable TV and VCR, and there is also a laundry and fitness room on the premises. Make use of the hotel's 24-hour discount cab service.

SoHo Grand (£££)
310 West Broadway
tel: 800/965-3000; 965-3000
Many considered the arrival of the first
full-scale hotel in SoHo the beginning of the
end of the neighbourhood's charm. However,
the understatedly elegant design of this
trendy hostel attracts a crowd that is in perfect
keeping with its environment. The rooms are
comfortable and the lounge and bar in the
second-floor lobby are particularly popular on
weekend nights.

MIDTOWN MANHATTAN

Algonquin (££)
44th Street, between Fifth and Sixth avenues
tel: 800/548-0345; 840-6800
It took a Japanese company to restore this
literary landmark (home of the Round Table,
presided over by Dorothy Parker and friends
from 1919) to its former glories. Above the
sumptuous lobby and famed bar areas,
however, the Algonquin's rooms are only
adequate, and there are plenty of better-value
alternatives in the area.

Ameritania (£)
Broadway at 54th Street
tel: 800/922-0330; 247-5000
An inexpensive hotel next to the Ed Sullivan
Theater and six blocks from Central Park.
Everything is designed in a modern style, from
overstuffed leather armchairs in the lobby to
the sleek lounge. The low prices are a major
attraction – book early.

Beekman Tower (£££)
3 Mitchell Place at First Avenue and
49th Street tel: 800/ME-SUITE; 355-7300
The 1928 Gothic-style Beekman Tower holds
an all-suite hotel with sensible prices,
especially good for long-term stays – which
explains its popularity with officials from the
nearby United Nations. All the suites have
kitchenettes with microwave ovens and
coffee-makers, and there is a fully equipped
fitness centre.

Best Western Manhattan (£)
32nd Street, between Fifth Avenue
and Broadway tel: 800/567-7720; 790-2705
Best Western is now part of the Apple Core
chain of reasonably priced hotels, and it
offers unelaborate but functional rooms in
the heart of the compact Korean business
district almost in the shadow of the Empire
State Building.

Box Tree (£££)
49th Street at Second Avenue tel: 758-8320
The perfect choice for an indulgent weekend,
the Box Tree fills two adjoining brownstones in
the Turtle Bay area of Midtown. *Trompe-l'oeil*
decorations are on the walls, and a
Gaudiesque main staircase leads upstairs from
the restaurant to a series of tiny, private dining
rooms, most of which have Versailles-like
themes. The 13 bedrooms are decorated in
different styles – for example Chinese,
Egyptian and Japanese – and the bathrooms
are tiny but delightfully stylish.

Drake Swissôtel (£££)
Park Avenue at 56th Street
tel: 800/DRAKENY; 421-0900
The lobby's wood and brass fittings (and the
bowls of complimentary Swiss chocolates) set
a comfortable, low-key mood that continues
into the comfortable, airy rooms.

Dylan (£££)
52 East 41st Street, between Park and
Madison avenues tel: 338-0500
This boutique hotel is housed in the gorgeous
1903 building that was once home to the
Chemist's Club. The rooms are small but boast
high ceilings and formal bathrooms lined with
marble and are filled with plush furnishings.
Chef Didier Virot, a protégé of Jean-Georges
Vongerichten, has opened an upmarket
restaurant within the hotel.

Edison (££)
47th Street at Eighth Avenue
tel: 800/637-7070; 840-5000
A partial refurbishment of this art deco-era hotel
has made some of the rooms bright, airy and
welcoming, while others remain rather shabby.
The good rooms come at a fair price, although
the hotel's size (1,000 rooms) and its theatre-
district site make it very much a tourist hotel.

Elysée (££)
54th Street, between Madison and Park
avenues tel: 753-1066
Refurbishment has sadly obliterated the highly
individual "Lucy goes to Hollywood" older
rooms, but some of the original furnishings
have been kept and have been incorporated
into the brand-new, Regency-inspired rooms.
Most of the doubles are small – opt for a suite
if you want space. VCRs are standard features,
as are safes and marble baths.

Essex House (£££)
Central Park South, between Sixth and Seventh
avenues tel: 800/654-5687; 247-0300
From the etched brass and black marble
features of the art deco lobby to the amply
proportioned and tastefully furnished rooms,
the Essex House is stylish and enjoys an
enviable position facing Central Park. The
best views are from the luxurious suites. The
hotel is also the home of the Alain Ducasse's
New York eatery.

Four Seasons (£££)
57th Street, between Park and Madison
avenues tel: 800/332-3442; 758-5700
The Four Seasons is not only the tallest hotel
in New York – designed by the celebrated
IM Pei, it rises 52 storeys – but also the most
opulent. On average, each room cost a million
dollars to deck out in stylish contemporary art
deco form and acquire amenities such as
enormous bathtubs that fill within 60 seconds.

Gorham New York (££)
55th Street, between Sixth and Seventh
avenues tel: 245-1800
An excellent location to enjoy the best features
of Midtown Manhattan. The staff are noted for
courtesy and friendliness, and the more costly
of the very comfortable rooms feature
whirlpools, kitchenettes with microwave ovens,
and the latest in temperature-controlled baths.

 263

Hotels and Restaurants

Helmsley Middletowne (££)
48th Street, between Lexington and Third avenues tel: 800/221-4982; 755-3000
Owned by the controversial hotelier Leona Helmsley, the Middletowne occupies a 17-storey former residential apartment house conviently near the United Nations. The property has a mellow ambience, and the pleasant rooms have kitchenettes. Some rooms open on to terraces or have fireplaces.

Herald Square (£)
*31st Street near Fifth Avenue
tel: 800/727-1888; 279-4017*
Occupying the 1893 *Life* magazine building, the rooms here are small and spartan but with clean, tiled bathrooms. Most rooms have TV and phones, and prices are cheap.

Hilton Times Square (££)
234 West 42nd Street, between Seventh and Eighth avenues tel: 642-2500
Located on 42nd Street near top Broadway theatres, this hotel is built above a huge retail and entertainment complex (the lobby is on the 21st floor) which includes a 25-theatre multiplex and Madame Tussaud's wax museum. The Hilton can provide a perfect base for families and other travellers who appreciate the neon-lit hustle and bustle of Times Square. Although the rooms are rather standard in design, most have interesting city views.

Holiday Inn on 57th Street (££)
*440 West 57th Street
tel: 800/231-0405; 581-8100*
Unexciting but dependable branch of a nationwide chain of hotels, this is near the Midtown sights but with a lacklustre location.

Howard Johnson's 34th Street (£)
34th Street, between Seventh and Eighth avenues tel: 800/633-1911; 947-5050
Small, functional rooms are adequate for a night's rest if you don't mind the slightly sleazy location, opposite Penn Station. Each room is has cable TV and a private bathroom; the low prices are the main attraction.

Hudson (££)
356 West 58th Street, between Eighth and Ninth avenues tel: 554-6000
Hudson owner, Ian Schrager, started the trend toward hotel chic more than a decade ago when he opened the Royalton. He's done it again with the Philippe Starck designed Hudson, which actually puts out velvet ropes in the evening to control the scantily-clad hordes who want to romp all night in the white-hot Hudson bar. Prices here can vary tremendously and all of the 1,000 rooms, though very chic with see-through shower walls destined to make even the steeliest blush, are very small.

Iroquois (££)
*44th Street, between Fifth and Sixth avenues
tel: 800/332-7220; 840-3080*
A much-needed refurbishment has made a definite improvement to this always dependable but once very shabby hotel. The more expensive rooms are equipped with kitchenettes; almost all are tastefully decorated in relaxing pastel shades. The excellent restaurant adds to the draw.

Library Hotel (£££)
*299 Madison Avenue at 41st Street
tel: 983-4500*
This elegant new Midtowner takes its theme very seriously; each of the ten floors of the hotel is dedicated to one of the ten major categories of the Dewey Decimal System (used to organise library collections) with rooms numbered according to the System, and are decorated in a style corresponding to a topic within that category. Though the idea is rather quirky, the Library is not meant to attract those expecting a fun-park: it is a boutique hotel with plush guestrooms and full-service amenities.

Mansfield (££)
*44th Street, between Fifth and Sixth avenues
tel: 800/255-5767; 944-6050*
A place with few pretensions, the Mansfield offers very affordable accommodation in a prime Midtown location (the more famous Algonquin Hotel is just across the street). The turn-of-the-century building was designed by noted New York architect Stanford White.

Michelangelo (£££)
*51st Street at Seventh Avenue
tel: 800/237-0990; 765-1900*
Genuine 18th- and 19th-century European art and a wealth of marble and crystal help the Michelangelo to rank among New York's most luxurious hotels. The large rooms come in art deco, Empire or country French styles with seemingly every possible amenity, including TV in the bathroom. There is even a free unpacking service if you have too much luggage to tackle alone. The atmosphere here is a bit hushed, but this de luxe, self-styled palazzo is one of the fanciest places to stay around Broadway.

Morgans (£££)
Madison Avenue, between 37th and 38th streets tel: 686-0300
The brainchild of the former owners of the famous Studio 54, Morgans has a minimalist design and a colour scheme based on black, grey and white. The bathrooms feature unique stainless steel basins and fittings, and every room has a video player as standard. The clientele is predominantly young and fashionable – and not short of a dollar or two.

Muse (£££)
130 West 46th Street, between Sixth and Seventh avenues tel: 485-2400
So named because of its proximity to the Broadway theatre it is billed as "a place to stay inspired". Though the lobby is pleasant enough it is rather standard in design, but the guest rooms are larger than average with separate sitting areas and decently sized bathrooms. The restaurant, District, continues the theatre theme with deconstructed elements, such as a curtain of iron that separates the dining areas.

Pickwick Arms (£)
51st Street, between Second and Third avenues tel: 800/PIC-KWIK; 355-0300
A comfortable lobby, a cocktail lounge and a roof garden go some way towards compensating for the small rooms. This is a well-priced option for the area, just a few minutes' walk from the heart of Midtown Manhattan.

Plaza (£££)
Fifth Avenue at Central Park South
tel: 800/759-3000; 759-3000
New York's leading hotel since opening in 1907, the Plaza's past guests include Teddy Roosevelt, F Scott and Zelda Fitzgerald, the Beatles and Solomon Guggenheim, who lived in one of the suites and decorated its walls with the art that later became the core of the Guggenheim Museum's collection. Property tycoon Donald Trump snapped up the Plaza for $400 million in 1988 and put his then wife Ivana in control of a $100-million face-lift. Still the epitome of class, the Plaza has every possible facility. Some tiny viewless rooms have been made into suites; the pricier accommodation has unbelievable panoramas of Fifth Avenue or Central Park.

Portland Square Hotel (£)
47th Street, between Sixth and Seventh avenues tel: 800/382-0600
An unknown James Cagney was just one among many struggling actors who used this long-established budget-priced hotel in the heart of the Broadway theatre district. The rooms have a few more frills than the Portland's sister hotel, Herald Square: there are places to sit in the lobby, lockers and a drinks- and ice-machine.

Quality Hotel (££)
40th Street, between Fifth and Madison avenues tel: 800/228-5151; 447-1500
Unfancy but crisply decorated rooms offer all the usual amenities in a good location at a very fair price.

Remington (£)
46th Street, between Broadway and Sixth Avenue tel: 221-2600
Clean, no-frills accommodation in the theatre district. The cheapest rooms lack private bathrooms, but all are fair value for their low price. Located very close to Times Square.

Roger Smith (££)
Lexington Avenue at 47th Street tel: 800/445-0277; 755-1400
Just north of Grand Central Terminal, the Roger Smith offers attractively furnished rooms and the intimate, personal atmosphere most Midtown hotels can only strive for.

Roosevelt (££)
Madison Avenue at 45th Street tel: 800/223-1870; 661-9600
Once a pre-eminent New York hotel catering to the thousands who poured into the city at nearby Grand Central Terminal, the Roosevelt has matured into a slightly staid but dependable hotel. Renovations are now complete and the beautiful, vast, neo-classical lobby has been spruced up. Many of the rooms have been upgraded too; with the very reasonable room rate, this is one of Midtown's better deals.

Royalton (£££)
44th Street, between Fifth and Sixth avenues tel: 800/635-9013; 869-4400
Another ultra-trendy hotel from the team that created Morgans, the Royalton is designed with a cool artistry throughout and finds favour with the "in-crowd". Rooms are small but attractive.

Salisbury (££)
57th Street, between Sixth and Seventh avenues tel: 800/223-0680; 246-1300
This is a small, welcoming and professionally run hotel. Its location across the road from the Russian Tea Room makes it convenient for shopping. The décor is frumpy, but the rooms are spotless and comfortable, with some offering microwaves and fridges. If you want even more space, opt for an apartment-sized suite.

San Carlos Hotel (££)
50th Street, between Lexington and Third avenues tel: 800/722-2012; 755-1800
Little sets it apart from other Midtown Manhattan hotels, but the San Carlos offers good quality rooms with ample cupboard space and adequately equipped kitchenettes.

Sherry Netherland (£££)
Fifth Avenue at 59th Street tel: 355-2800
One of the grand French château-style buildings put up along Fifth Avenue across from Central Park during the 1920s, the Sherry Netherland offers soaring park views and impeccable service. Rooms are spacious, with video recorders and microwaves, and plenty of personal touches. The sky-high rates are worth it if you have a huge range of hard-to-satisfy demands. Room service is by the acclaimed restaurant, Harry Cipriani, located at ground level.

Sofitel New York (£££)
45 West 44th Street, between Fifth and Sixth avenues tel: 354-8844
The first New York property of this European chain, the Sofitel is a large and comfortable hotel perfect for the upmarket business traveller and anyone who wants to be in the heart of Midtown. The lobby and guest rooms are adorned with plenty of dark wood and the rooms are spacious and soothingly designed in a neutral palette. There is an expansive and exclusive brasserie, named after a French ex-patriot actress of the 1920s, which also features a piano bar.

Vanderbilt-YMCA (£)
47th Street, between Second and Third avenues tel: 755-9600
Make an early booking to stay at the most popular and best-located of New York's YMCAs. Open to both men and women, the renovated, but small, single and double rooms are available at very low prices plus extra facilities such as a brand-new restaurant, luggage lockers, a swimming pool, a gym and a launderette.

W New York (£££)
Lexington Avenue at 49th Street tel: 877/946-8357, 755-1200
The flagship of a chain of urban spa hotels, this smart property in the former Doral location is abuzz with trend-setters. The design is chic, the atmosphere comfortable, and the amenities – like an elegant day spa and fitness centre – indulgent. Drew Nieporent's Heartbeat restaurant serves creatively healthy fare prepared by chef Michel Nischan.

Waldorf-Astoria (£££)
Park Avenue, between 49th and 50th streets
tel: 800/WALDORF; 355-3000
After the Plaza, the Waldorf-Astoria is New York's most famous hotel. It was the birthplace of the charity ball and the prime rendezvous for New York high society from the 1930s – although it has taken $150 million to restore its grandeur. A sense of opulence strikes as soon as you enter the art deco lobby, and all the rooms are stylishly appointed with marble bathrooms. Only in the top-price suites and the Tower rooms, however, will you encounter a level of luxury to match the hotel's rich history.

Warwick (£££)
65 West 54th Street
tel: 800/223-4099; 247-2700
Built by William Randolph Hearst in 1927, the Warwick is popular with business travellers. It has over 400 rooms (all with TV and telephone), plus a restaurant and fitness facilities, and is convenient for all the main Midtown sights.

Wellington (££)
Seventh Avenue at 55th Street
tel: 800/652-1212; 247-3900
Except perhaps for the lobby, there is nothing fancy about the sizeable Wellington, where the rooms are clean and simple and reasonably priced for their prized central location.

MURRAY HILL, GRAMERCY, FLATIRON AND CHELSEA

Carlton Arms (£)
25th Street at Third Avenue tel: 679-0680
Each wacky, threadbare room has been designed and decorated by a different (unknown) artist, and what the Carlton Arms lacks in cleanliness and creature comforts, it makes up for through its sheer eccentricity. Book well in advance for a room with a bathroom. Many struggling artists make this their New York home, so expect bizarre fellow guests and exceptionally low prices.

Chelsea Hotel (££)
23rd Street, between Seventh and Eighth avenues tel: 243-3700
Arthur Miller reputedly relocated here from the Plaza Hotel because he was fed up with having to put on a tie to go down to the front desk to collect his post. The Chelsea still attracts refugees from more formal establishments, with its laid-back but solicitous service and the atmosphere of a run-down but arty apartment building. For more on writers and artists who have stayed here see the feature on page 85.

Chelsea Inn (£)
46 West 17th Street, between Fifth and Sixth avenues tel: 645-8989
Good value rooms with kitchenettes in a 19th-century town house; the least expensive have bathrooms shared with one other room.

Chelsea Savoy (£)
202 West 23rd Street tel: 929-9353
A no-frills option in the heart of the increasingly trendy Chelsea neighbourhood, this moderately priced hotel offers no amenities but puts you near art galleries and nightclubs.

266

Comfort Inn Murray Hill (££)
35th Street, between Fifth and Sixth avenues
tel: 800/228-5150; 947-0200
This branch of the nationwide chain predictably has higher rates than its far-flung counterparts but nonetheless represents good value for New York City, with tidy, comfortable rooms.

Gramercy Park (££)
21st Street and Lexington Avenue
tel: 800/221-4083; 475-4320
Facing Gramercy Park this gracefully ageing hotel may have slow lifts and few recent furnishings, but it does have lots of character, offers discounts at weekends and for long stays, and is usefully placed on the borders of Midtown and lower Manhattan.

Martha Washington (£)
30th Street, between Park and Madison avenues tel: 689-1900
Spartan accommodation in a semi-residential area. The rooms are gloomy and range from small to comparatively spacious; should you feel the need for a private bathroom and TV, you can expect to pay extra for them. Bookable by the night or at very tempting weekly rates; additional discounts for longer stays (there is a one month maximum).

Roger Williams (££)
31st Street, between Madison and Park avenues tel: 800/637-9773; 448-7000
Located in a quiet semi-residential area of Midtown, this is a friendly, modestly priced hotel. Every room has a kitchenette and cable TV, and there is a good choice of suites for families. The furnishings may have seen better days, but the hotel is good value.

Wolcott (£)
31st Street at Fifth Avenue tel: 268-2900
For a remarkably low rate, the Wolcott offers smallish but well-furnished, comfortable rooms complete with private bathrooms and cable TV. The mirror-lined, baroque-style lobby is a surprise bonus in this impressive budget hotel.

UPPER EAST SIDE

Barbizon (££)
63rd Street at Lexington Avenue
tel: 800/753-0360; 838-5700
By the standards of the high-priced Upper East Side, the Barbizon is good value for its smallish but cosy rooms and the dozen terraced suites (some with good views) that occupy the red-brick building's Gothic tower. Until 1981, the Barbizon was a women's residential hotel, and famous former guests include Grace Kelly, Candice Bergen and Liza Minnelli.

Carlyle (£££)
76th Street at Madison Avenue
tel: 800/227-5737; 744-1600
For years, the understated elegance of the Carlyle has provided a home for high-ranking dignitaries and those so wealthy that they have no need to flaunt their affluence. Crystal chandeliers hang above the public spaces, and the rooms are decorated with antiques, tapestries and fresh flowers. Sink into the marble bathtub and you will find a phone at your elbow.

Lowell (£££)
*63rd Street, between Park and Madison
avenues tel: 838-1400*
A small, luxurious hotel, the Lowell occupies an
art deco building in the Upper East Side.
Chinese porcelain, 18th- and 19th-century prints
and wood-burning fireplaces decorate the
rooms; service is personal and attentive. There
is a fitness room for all guests, but if you prefer
private workouts, go for the Gym Suite.

Mark (£££)
*77th Street at Madison Avenue
tel: 800/843-6275; 744-4300*
In-room whirlpools, video players (select films
from a well-stocked library), and courteous
staff help attract a fashionable, jet-setting
clientele. When the rich and famous don't
want to be noticed, this is where they stay.

Pierre (£££)
*Fifth Avenue at 61st Street
tel: 800/332-3442; 940-8101*
There is nothing surreal about the mural-lined
corridors or the enormous, well-furnished rooms
of the Pierre, even though this was Salvador
Dali's favourite New York hotel. Packed with
antiques and lined with lush carpets, the
hotel's somewhat tired but nevertheless
aristocratic ambience is heightened by the
afternoon tea served beneath the rotunda.

Plaza Athénée (£££)
*64th Street, between Park and Madison
avenues tel: 734-9100*
With Louis XIV-style furniture filling every corner
and marble and crystal fittings wherever you
look, the Plaza Athénée is intended to evoke
the grandeur of a European royal palace.
Even though some find it pretentious, plenty
of wealthy guests bask happily in the
pre-revolutionary Versailles atmosphere, and
standards of service are high.

Regency (£££)
*Park Avenue, between 60th and 61st streets
tel: 800/23-LOEWS; 759-4100*
The lobby may be stuffed with French antiques,
but the Regency, while extremely stylish, is a
lot less snooty than many of its Upper East
Side rivals. Be they financial wheeler dealers or
rock stars on the rise, the clientele appreciate
the tastefully furnished, airy rooms and the
efficient, attentive staff.

Stanhope (£££)
*Fifth Avenue at 81st Street
tel: 800/828-1123; 288-5800*
With high-quality reproduction Louis XIV
furniture filling the lobby and antique porcelain
sitting beside state-of-the-art electronic
gadgets in every guest room, the Stanhope is
an interesting blend of old and new but has a
rather hushed and hallowed atmosphere.

Surrey (£££)
*76th Street at Madison Avenue
tel: 800/ME-SUITE; 288-3700*
A small, quiet and welcoming hotel, where
all the rooms include kitchenettes – though it
is hard to imagine the guests opting for
self-service snacks when room service
operates around the clock and the acclaimed
Café Boulud is located on the premises.

Wales (££)
*Madison Avenue at 92nd Street
tel: 800/428-5252; 876-6000*
One of New York's longest-serving hotels, the
Wales has been in business since 1900, and
the attractive rates reflect its location on the
northern edge of the neighbourhood – though
public transport links to Midtown and lower
Manhattan are swift. The price of the nicely,
but not opulently, furnished rooms includes
afternoon tea and a light breakfast.

UPPER WEST SIDE

Beacon (££)
*Broadway at 75th Street
tel: 800/572-4969; 787-1100*
A bustling, professionally run, small hotel, ten
blocks north of Lincoln Center and within easy
reach of most Upper West Side attractions.
The large rooms all come with cable TV and
kitchenette, and Zabar's, one of the city's best
gourmet delis, is just up the street.

Excelsior (£)
*81st Street, between Central Park West and
Columbus Avenue tel: 800/368-4575;
362-9200*
Standard but entirely acceptable rooms with
spotless, old-fashioned bathrooms make this a
good bet, in a residential area of the Upper
West Side. Central Park, the American
Museum of Natural History and Columbus
Avenue bars and eateries are near by.

Hostelling International New York (£)
*Amsterdam Avenue at 103rd Street
tel: 932-2300*
The largest youth hostel in the US occupies an
architectural landmark – dating from 1883, the
building was designed by the man responsible
for the base of the Statue of Liberty. Very clean
and welcoming, with small dormitory rooms
and a host of additional services.

Malibu Studio (£)
*Broadway, between 102nd and 103rd streets
tel: 800/647-2227; 222-2954*
Bordering a district that can be intimidating at
night, though close to Columbia University and
the Cathedral Church of St John the Divine, the
Malibu offers student-residence-style rooms at
very low rates. They are unelaborate but homy,
and a few extra dollars bring a colour TV,
kitchen facilities and private bathroom.

Mayflower on the Park (££)
*Central Park West at 61st Street
tel: 800/223-4164; 265-0060*
On the border with Midtown Manhattan, and
with some rooms overlooking Central Park, the
Mayflower offers tidily appointed rooms a
stone's throw from Lincoln Center.

Milburn (£)
*76th Street, near Broadway
tel: 800/833-9622; 362-1006*
One of the Upper West Side's best budget
choices, the Milburn offers not only a quiet,
graceful lobby and rooms with kitchenettes,
but also prompt, friendly service. The spacious
suites make ideal family accommodation; there
is a self-service laundry on the premises.

267

Hotels and Restaurants

Olcott (£)
72nd Street, between Central Park West and Columbus Avenue tel: 877-4200
Worn furnishings and occasional offhand service may be offputting, but many theatrical and musical performers stay here for the inexpensive weekly rates. Shorter stays are subject to availability. However, early booking is essential and credit cards are not accepted.

On the Ave (££)
2177 Broadway at 77th Street tel: 362-1100
Despite many hotels in the neighbourhood the Upper West Side remains a mostly residential area. On the Ave is the first hotel – apart from notables like the Trump International – that actually looks and feels like a full service hotel. It is in a great location for exploring Central Park and all of the uptown museums, and is excellent for giving guests a taste of real New York life. This is also a safe bet for families. Rooms are comfortable, if basic.

Radisson Empire (££)
Broadway at 63rd Street tel: 800/221-6509; 265-7400
A luxury chain hotel, refurbished to the tune of $30 million, it offers small, well-furnished rooms all with CD players and tape decks as well as colour TVs and video players. The grand, high-ceilinged lobby displays a beautiful collection of model stage sets – appropriate for a hotel a few steps from Lincoln Center.

Riverside Tower (£)
Riverside Drive at 80th Street tel: 800/724-3136; 877-5200
Located in a dull residential section of the Upper West Side, its spartan and somewhat dreary rooms do have phones and TVs. However, as there are no other facilities, use the Riverside as a cheap place to sleep and for the superb views over the Hudson.

Trump International (£££)
1 Central Park West at 60th Street tel: 299-1000
With the opulent taste of Donald Trump dictating the design, this hotel, perched on the southwest corner of Central Park, was bound to be as swank as they come. The rooms are not large, but are very nicely conceived with top-of-the-range bedding, marble bathrooms and small kitchens – you can enlist one of the chefs from the top-notch Jean George to come upstairs and cook you dinner if you don't feel like leaving the room.

West Side YMCA (£)
63rd Street, near Central Park West tel: 787-4400
Book well ahead to stay in these simple but usefully situated and reasonably priced rooms. These are available as singles or doubles in a large, echoey building close to the Lincoln Center. The price includes the use of a well-equipped gym and a large swimming pool, safe-deposit boxes, a coin-operated laundry and 24-hour security.

RESTAURANTS

The restaurants listed below are divided into three categories (prices are based on the average price of a main course):

Inexpensive (£): up to $12
Moderate (££): $12–$22
Expensive (£££): over $22

CHINATOWN

Golden Unicorn (££)
18 East Broadway tel: 941-0911
A favourite for large family banquets or big parties. Large selection, from savoury appetisers through dim sum to duck, fresh fish and tofu.

Grand Sichuan (£)
125 Canal Street tel: 625-9212
Unlike most of the Szechwan food you'll find around town, the fiery authentic cooking at this Chinatown restaurant is remarkable, as is the fact that they take (and honour) reservations and have a menu translated into English. However cash only is accepted.

Joe's Shanghai (£)
9 Pell Street, between Bowery and Mott streets tel: 233-8888
One of the best Chinese restaurants in the city, known for its rich and satisfying Shanghai cooking – soup, dumplings, braised pork shoulder, lion's head, handmade Shanghai noodles and more. Worth the long wait. Cash only.

Mandarin Court (£)
61 Mott Street, near Canal Street tel: 608-3838
Wonderfully chaotic dim sum parlour, which is busiest on Sundays when the communal tables are packed.

New York Noodle Town (£)
28 Bowery Street tel: 349-0923
Providing plenty of what its name suggests in many more varieties than you ever imagined possible. Duck with flowering chives is a must.

Nha Trang (£)
87 Baxter Street, between Bayard and Canal streets tel: 233-5948
Excellent, inexpensive Vietnamese. BBQ pork chops, crispy squid and other regional specialities never disappoint.

Oriental Garden (££)
14 Elizabeth Street tel: 619-0085
The seafood at this Cantonese restaurant is as fresh as you can find – it flops its way from the tanks in the window to the kitchen. The drunken shrimp are actually cooked live at your table.

Shanghai Cuisine (£–££)
89–91 Bayard Street tel: 732-8988
Small and unpretentious venue for enjoying the Chinese cuisine of the moment: Shanghai.

Sweet 'n' Tart Café (£)
76 Mott Street at Canal Street tel: 334-8088
The menu is arranged according to rules of traditional Chinese medicine. Expertly prepared, fast and super-inexpensive.

Thailand Restaurant (£)
106 Bayard Street tel: 349-3132
Inexpensive Thai favourites, and some lesser-known dishes, fill a lengthy, delicious menu.
Triple 8 Palace (££–£££)
88 East Broadway tel: 941-8886
On the top floor of a building beneath the Manhattan Bridge, this is wildly popular with locals who show up mostly for the lunchtime Hong Kong-style dim sum.
Vegetarian's Paradise (£)
68 Mott Street tel: 406-6988
A vegetarian cubby hole does wondrous things re-creating regular Chinese dishes but using nothing that ever walked, crawled or swam.
Viet-Nam (£)
11 Doyers Street tel: 693-0725
An unpretentious setting for some of the best and probably most authentic Vietnamese cuisine in New York.
Wong Kee (£)
113 Mott Street tel: 966-1160
Fine selection of Cantonese dishes at irresistible prices; deservedly crowded.

EAST VILLAGE AND LOWER EAST SIDE

Acme Bar and Grill (££)
9 Great Jones Street tel: 420-1934
Cajun cooking and lots of it – gumbo, jambalaya and deep fried oysters.
Angelica Kitchen (£)
12th Street, between First and Second avenues tel: 228-2909
Tasty and very inexpensive natural foods.
Benny's Burritos (£)
Avenue A at 6th Street tel: 254-2054
Burritos with a host of inventive fillings are dispensed here to a lively East Village crowd.
Caffè della Pace (£)
7th Street, between First and Second avenues tel: 529-8024
This low-key spot is worth seeking out for its stylishly presented Italian food at very reasonable prices.
Christine's (£)
Lexington Avenue at 40th Street tel: 953-1920
Christine's serves omelettes, salads and sandwiches, but knowing regulars choose the Polish dishes – tripe, home-made pirogi or blintzes – and leave room for babka dessert.
Dojo (£)
24 St Mark's tel: 674-9821
An intriguingly combined Japanese and health-food restaurant, with a predominantly youthful and trendy clientele.
Emerald Planet (£)
2 Great Jones Street tel: 353-9727
Exotic variations on the Mexican burrito with a range of creative fillings and garnishing such as jasmine rice and mango salsa.
First (££)
87 First Avenue, between 5th and 6th streets tel: 674-3823
This clubby bistro serves an intriguing menu of whimsically updated American favourites until 4 AM. Everything is cooked on the premises.

Great Jones Café (££)
54 Great Jones Street tel: 674-9304
This is where you will find the cutting-edge East Village faces selecting their late-afternoon breakfasts from the daily specials – cajun-southern fare – chalked on a blackboard.
Il Bagatto (££)
192 East 2nd Street, between Avenues A and B tel: 228-0977
Surprisingly authentic home-made pastas and entrées at bargain prices in a lively setting. Always busy; always good.
Indochine (££)
Lafayette Street, between Astor Place and 4th Street tel: 505-5111
Dine amid palm fronds on a tremendous mix of Vietnamese, Thai and Cambodian fare; open for dinner only.
Katz's Delicatessen (£)
East Houston Street, near Orchard Street tel: 254-2246
Legendary for providing pastrami and corned beef sandwiches for over a century, Katz's has found more fame in the 1989 film *When Harry Met Sally*.
Miracle Grill (£)
112 First Avenue, between 6th and 7th streets tel: 254-2353
Among the first in the wave of ambitious, inexpensive restaurants in the area, the Southwestern food at this restaurant still satisfies. Lovely garden, great brunch.
Mitali (££)
6th Street, between First and Second avenues tel: 533-2508
The quality Indian cuisine draws adventurous diners from all over New York. It's best for Indian Rou.
No. 9 (££)
109 East 9th Street, between Third and Fourth avenues tel: 529-5333
A gorgeously streamlined "downtown" space that has wonderful food to match. Tuck into the marvels on offer such as Chilean sea bass seared in orange marmalade, or lush herb-crusted venison loin.
Pommes Frites (£)
123 Second Avenue, between 7th and 8th streets tel: 674-1234
The aroma of Belgian-style French fries crisping in peanut oil and the wide array of home-made mayonnaises attracts queues to this new East Village takeaway, but it does have limited seating at the back.
Pop (£–££)
127 Fourth Avenue, between 12th and 13th streets tel: 767-1800
Stylish and sleek with extremely flattering lighting, quite an in-crowd are known to gather here. Pop's food is American with an added Asian accent: think sesame-crusted sea bass with udon noodles.
Radio Perfecto (£)
190 Avenue B tel: 477-3366
Come for the roast chicken (available with a variety of sauces) and the comfortable environment. A collection of antique radios adorn the walls.

269

Second Avenue Kosher Deli (££)
Second Avenue at 10th Street
tel: 677-0606
This family-run Jewish deli is one of the last remaining places where you can sample kasha, kugel, knishes and knaidels in authentic forms. The side room features memorabilia from the Lower East Side's Yiddish Theater.

Two Boots (£)
Avenue A at 2nd Street tel: 505-2276
Two Boots incorporates an enterprising mixture of Italian and Cajun-style cookery: shrimp pizza is just one example.

Veselka (£)
Second Avenue at 9th Street
tel: 228-9682
Earthy, filling Ukrainian and Polish fare is served around the clock and in large quantities to a surprisingly diverse East Village crowd. For something light, stick to the blintzes.

Yaffa Café (£)
97 St Mark's Place tel: 674-9302
This is a hangout for East Village characters, and a great place to sample local atmosphere. Graze happily on croissants or burgers inside or out in the garden.

FINANCIAL DISTRICT AND TRIBECA

Bridge Café (££)
Water Street at Dover Street tel: 227-3344
If you have just crossed the Brooklyn Bridge on foot, why not reward yourself with a delicious lunch in this cosy red-brick dining room sited just beneath the bridge itself? Along with the usual lunch and dinner favourites, there is an appetising selection of well-prepared seafood dishes.

Bouley Bakery (£££)
120 West Broadway at Duane Street
tel: 964-2525
Under one of the city's best chefs, this tiny, elegant bakery/restaurant offers exquisite, deceivingly simple French food with an unmatched selection of breads. It is well worth the wait.

Capsouto Frères (£££)
451 Washington Street at Watts Street
tel: 966-4900
You practically feel the breezes from the nearby Hudson River in this airy brick-walled dining room. This is an unusual French bistro, serving food with flair, that is great for brunch on Saturday and Sunday.

Chanterelle (£££)
2 Harrison Street at Hudson Street
tel: 966-6960
For 20 years, David and Karen Waltuck have set the standard for New French cuisine and hospitality at this elegant, placid space. A great wine list and state-of-the-art cheese cart complete the perfect evening.

City Hall (£££)
131 Duane Street tel: 227-7777
The latest venue for Cub Room chef Henry Meer features large portions of updated classics like she-crab soup and prime rib.

The Harrison (££)
355 Greenwich Street at Harrison Street
tel: 274-9310
Lovely home-style dishes are served in a white-walled bistro with brown leather banquesttes. This is the second of a duo whose simple, welcoming formula has already proven popular.

Le Zinc (£–££)
139 Duane Street, between Church and West Broadway tel: 513-0001
Chanterelle's owners (see above) have now bestowed a casual bistro upon the same neighbourhood. House-made charcuterie, crisp duck wings and Hungarian stuffed cabbage are served in the warm, mirrored space.

Montrachet (£££)
239 West Broadway, between Walker and White streets tel: 219-2777
One of the first great restaurants in TriBeCa, this cosy bistro features terrific French food, great service and a reasonably priced wine list of hard-to-find selections.

Nobu (£££)
105 Hudson Street at Franklin Street
tel: 219-0500
Sister to London's hotspot and LA's film-star hangout, this Japanese-inspired restaurant has won awards both for design and for food. Nobu Next Door operates on a first come, first served basis. Superb.

Odeon (£££)
West Broadway at Thomas Street tel: 233-0507
A favourite for its contemporary American food and its art deco and neon-decorated setting.

TriBeCa Grill (£££)
Greenwich Street at Franklin Street
tel: 941-3900
Co-owned by actor Robert de Niro and set in what is now a film company building, the TriBeCa Grill draws a star-spotting crowd, but its real attraction is the gourmet-pleasing food, especially the carefully crafted fish dishes.

GREENWICH VILLAGE

Anglers and Writers (£)
Hudson Street at St Luke's Place
tel: 675-0810
Plays up the neighbourhood literary links and serves snacks, tea and coffee amid antiques and rows of frequently thumbed books.

Babbo (£££)
110 Waverly Place tel: 777-0303
The food is robust and flavourful, the atmosphere welcoming, the service friendly and attentive. Try the five-course pasta tasting menu, but reservations can be difficult to get.

Benny's Burritos (£)
113 Greenwich Avenue tel: 727-3560
Like the branch in the East Village, its burritos are stuffed with as much cheese, beans, meat or vegetables as they will hold.

Blue Ribbon Bakery (££)
33 Downing Street tel: 337-0404
A 100-year-old oven inspired this bistro-cum-bakery, owned by the Bromberg Brothers of Blue Ribbon fame. The menu offers small and large plates of classic French fare.

Caffè Rafaella (£)
134 Seventh Avenue, between Charles and 10th streets tel: 929-7247
Sandwiches, salads and desserts tempt in this living-room setting, where people-watching is as good as it gets.

Caffè Reggio (£)
119 MacDougal Street tel: 475-9557
Claimed to be the country's oldest coffee shop, it has a dark, atmospheric interior and a selection of pleasing coffees and cakes.

Clementine (£££)
1 Fifth Avenue at 8th Street tel: 253-0003
Contemporary American food distinguishes this bar-restaurant from being just another scene. The cocktails are exceptional.

Corner Bistro (£)
331 West 4th Street tel: 242-9502
Late-night, busy, no-frills stop for bistro burgers (served on paper plates) and chilled beer.

Cowgirl Hall of Fame (£)
519 Hudson Street tel: 633-1133
Photos of famous cowgirls grin down at you from the walls and country music plays on the jukebox as plaid-shirted staff dispense substantial helpings of Tex-Mex fare – and potent margaritas.

Cucina Stagionale (£)
275 Bleecker Street tel: 924-2707
Simple, inexpensive and very pleasing Italian food; be prepared to queue and make sure you bring your own alcohol.

Florent (££)
69 Gansevoort Street tel: 989-5779
Bistro specialising in, but not limited to, delectable meat dishes. Being open around the clock with breakfast available from midnight finds an intriguing assortment of club-going New Yorkers arriving through the small hours.

Gotham Bar and Grill (£££)
12th Street, between University Place and Fifth Avenue tel: 620-4020
From the perfect architecture to the perfectly presented food, the Gotham Bar and Grill is an impeccably stylish New York classic.

Home (££)
20 Cornelia Street, between Bleecker and West 4th streets tel: 243-9579
The reasonably priced food is surprisingly elegant and delicious. Accompaniments such as home-made relishes and sausages.

Il Cantinori (£££)
32 East 10th Street, between Broadway and University Place tel: 673-6044
Upmarket Italian with fine pasta and Tuscan specialities. Although the service can be variable, the overall experience is lovely, if slightly overpriced.

Japonica (££)
100 University Place tel: 243-7752
Spartan setting for substantial helpings of sushi and other Japanese fare.

John's Pizzeria (£)
278 Bleecker Street tel: 243-1680
Long popular – not least with Woody Allen – it serves perfect oven-baked pizzas in more than 50 varieties. The various outposts around town are also reliable, but no slices available.

Le Gigot (££)
18 Cornelia Street, between Bleecker and West 4th streets tel: 627-3737
Tiny French bistro with excellent food and reasonable prices. Le Gigot also offers an inexpensive wine list and friendly service.

Marquet Patisserie (£)
15 East 12th Street, between Fifth Avenue and University Place tel: 229-9313
Charming French bakery and café with fresh salads, soups, pastries and café au lait served in bowls. Breakfast and lunch only.

Minetta Tavern (££)
Minetta Lane and MacDougal Street tel: 475-3850
A historic Greenwich Village saloon decorated with 1930s artworks and memorabilia; very satisfying Italian lunches and dinners.

Moustache (£)
90 Bedford Street, between Barrow and Grove streets tel: 229-2220
There's always a wait for one of the 10 tables at this Middle Eastern restaurant, with freshly baked pittas straight from the oven.

Pearl Oyster Bar (££)
18 Cornelia Street tel: 691-8211
This tiny counter of a seafood restaurant has recently expanded. The buckets of steamers, lobster rolls and other New England seafood preparations remain superb.

Petite Abeille (£–££)
466 Hudson Street tel: 741-6479
This tiny restaurant (now a mini chain of three) started the recent Belgian craze. Salads, entrées, sandwiches and omelettes from the minuscule short-order kitchen are top notch.

Sammy's Noodle Shop (£)
453 Sixth Avenue at 11th Street tel: 924-6688
Bustling Chinese restaurant where everything is made from scratch, including the noodles, baked buns and barbecued duck.

Strip House (££–£££)
13 East 12th Street, between Fifth Avenue and University Place tel: 328-0000
The lusty red bordello setting and vintage striptease photos will enhance your appetite for what this place is really about: New York strip steak. All the steakhouse classics are to be found here.

Sushi Samba 7 (££–£££)
87 Seventh Avenue South at Barrow Street tel: 691-7885
The largest – and newest – downtown sushi emporium also features seviche, smashing cocktails and a gorgeous roof deck. It's easy to rack up a big tab, but worth it.

Taka (££)
61 Grove Street, between Bleecker Street and 7th Avenue tel: 242-3699
Unusual because the sushi chef is a woman, this Japanese restaurant is extremely popular.

Tanti Baci Caffè (£)
163 West 10th Street, between Seventh Avenue and Waverly Place tel: 647-9651
Inexpensive Italian trattoria with the feel of a grotto. Combine your favourite pasta and sauce or choose from one of the daily specials.

Tea and Sympathy (£)
108 Greenwich Avenue tel: 989-9735
As well as the traditional high tea, they also serve shepherd's pie, fish cakes and stodgy "school dinner" desserts.

Tortilla Flats (£)
Washington Street at 12th Street tel: 243-1053
Tex-Mex eatery where the emphasis is on rowdy good times as much as on consuming fiery food and alcohol in very large amounts. Bingo night can be hilarious.

LITTLE ITALY

Ballato's (££)
55 East Houston Street tel: 274-8881
While there might be better Neapolitan food at other restaurants, few can match this one for Little Italy atmosphere.

Caffè Roma (£)
385 Broome Street tel: 226-8413
In business since the 1890s, Caffè Roma offers excellent coffee and superb freshly baked pastries and cakes to indulge in.

Ferrara (£)
195 Grand Street tel: 226-6150
Lacks the atmosphere of Caffè Roma, but a nice place to sip a cappuccino and nibble a selection from a tempting array of baked goods.

Taormina (££)
147 Mulberry Street tel: 219-1007
A touch pricier and classier than its neighbours, Taormina serves Neapolitan dishes in a sedate setting.

MIDTOWN MANHATTAN

East and West Midtown
Alfredo of Rome (££–£££)
4 West 49th Street, near Fifth Avenue tel: 397-0100
Fettucine Alfredo was invented in 1914 at the Roman original of this poised new Rockefeller Center resident, and it leads the menu here. Don't miss the *frito misto*.

Aquavit (£££)
13 West 54th Street, between Fifth and Sixth avenues tel: 307-7311
It's not easy to make Swedish food alluring, but this elegant restaurant raises herring and smoked fish to new gastronomic heights.

Atlas (££–£££)
40 Central Park South, between Fifth and Sixth avenues tel: 759-9191
Critically exalted British chef Paul Liebrandt creates some of the most original dishes in town in this lovely and intensely popular place. Preparations like fresh water eel, watermelon, crystallized violets and red wine glaze may sound dreadful, but they're simply revelatory.

Avra (£££)
141 East 48th Street, between Lexington and Third avenues tel: 759-8550
If it's achingly fresh grilled fish you crave, you won't do better than Avra: ridiculously delicious grilled octopus and roasted royal dorado lead the school. Entrée fish is priced by the pound, which can really add up.

Ben Benson's (£££)
123 West 52nd Street, between Sixth and Seventh avenues tel: 581-8888
The most masculine steakhouse in town, with a hunting lodge motif, is also quite female-friendly. All the great classics are on hand, in perfectly delicious renditions, brought to you by a well-choreographed staff.

Carnegie Delicatessen (£–££)
854 Seventh Avenue at 55th Street tel: 757-2245
Mile-high sandwiches and oversized portions – the food's still good at this perpetually busy deli. Be prepared to share tables.

Delegates' Dining Room (££)
United Nations, First Avenue at 46th Street tel: 963-7626
Armed with a reservation and proper attire, the general public can rub shoulders with United Nations officials and delegates on any weekday lunchtime. Top value is the buffet.

JUdson Grill (£££)
152 West 52nd Street, between Sixth and Seventh avenues tel: 582-5252
You will feel like you're in the vast dining room of an ocean liner. Bill Telepan's New American fare is nothing short of sensational.

Kaplan's Deli (£–££)
59th Street, between Park and Madison avenues tel: 755-5959
An unexciting but reliable standby, it has sandwiches, soups and the usual deli fare in an otherwise pricey area.

Kuruma Zushi (£££)
7 East 47th Street tel: 317-2802
This small, second-floor eatery only serves sushi. If you are feeling rich, sit at the sushi bar and order the omikase (chef's tasting). Beware, dinner can cost upward of $200 per person – but it's well worth every penny.

Le Bernardin (£££)
155 West 51st Street, between Sixth and Seventh avenues tel: 489-1515
Acknowledged in many quarters as the best restaurant in America, this Midtown mecca elevates fish and seafood to the *hautest* level of cuisine. The impeccable, doting service and an exceptional wine list complete the package.

The Leopard (£££)
253 East 50th Street, between Second and Third avenues tel: 759-3735
A peculiar and delightful restaurant, set in a beautiful little townhouse. Best on the prix fixe menu are the obligatory fresh pea soup and marvellous boned quail with minced duck/wild rice stuffing.

Lespinasse (£££)
St Regis Hotel, 2 East 55th Street, between Fifth and Madison avenues tel: 339-6719
Christian Delouvier produces inspired French cooking in a very formal setting: superb.

Lutèce (£££)
50th Street, between Second and Third avenues tel: 752-2225
The classic French menu has been streamlined and updated. The service can have an attitude, but some of the modern French innovations are worth it.

Maloney & Porcelli (£££)
37 East 50th Street, between Madison and Park avenues tel: 750-2233
Bring a large appetite to this whimsical American eatery.

Manhattan Ocean Club (£££)
57 West 58th Street, between Fifth and Sixth avenues tel: 371-7777
A no-nonsense, even austere space that lets you concentrate on your aquatic fare. Best are baked oysters in a morel mushroom cream and tuna loin with braised whole shallots and sliced applewood-smoked bacon.

Marichu (££)
342 East 46th Street, between First and Second avenues tel: 370-1866
Around the corner from the UN, this charming restaurant offers authentic Basque cooking.

Molyvos (££–£££)
871 Seventh Avenue tel: 582-7500
Up-market Greek food is served in this large, friendly restaurant. The meze are superb, and pricey entrées do not disappoint.

Oceana (£££)
55 East 54th Street, between Madison and Park avenues tel: 759-5941
A dining room like a cruise ship with totally inspired cooking. Elegant seafood preparations and warm service.

One CPS at the Plaza (£££)
1 Central Park South at Fifth Avenue tel: 583-1111
Set in the stirring Edwardian Room of the Plaza, this new incarnation features fresh shellfish "bouquet", rack of lamb with shepherd's pie and German chocolate "horse and buggy" cake, in honour of its equine neighbours visible just outside the gigantic windows.

Osteria del Circo (£££)
120 West 55th Street, between Sixth and Seventh avenues tel: 265-3636
This up-market Italian trattoria mixes contemporary with traditional Tuscan fare.

Peacock Alley (£££)
At the Waldorf-Astoria, 301 Park Avenue, between 49th and 50th streets tel: 872-4895
Laurent Gras ranks among the best chefs in New York. He's devised a "create-your-own-tasting-menu" that utterly enthralls. And you won't find a more bacchanalian Sunday brunch buffet. Pricey, but worth every penny.

Rothmann's Steakhouse (££–£££)
3 East 54th Street at Fifth Avenue tel: 319-5500
Some argue that this newcomer is the best steakhouse in Manhattan. It certainly has pedigree: chef Robert Dickert is steak pioneer Peter Luger's great nephew, and the original Rothmann's in Long Island is nearly 100 years old. Absolutely superb Porterhouse.

Russian Tea Room (£££)
150 West 57th Street, near Seventh Avenue, next to Carnegie Hall tel: 974-2111
Sumptuous fare in an even more sumptuous setting make for an unforgettable and extravagant evening. House-infused vodkas are a must, as are the caviar, blini and chicken Kiev.

Smith & Wollensky (£££)
797 Third Avenue at 49th Street tel: 753-1530
It appears to be about 1958 in this timeless, roomy restaurant, in every sense (except prices, of course). Dry-aged steaks flaunt their sheer beefiness, and all the trimmings are on offer.

Sparks Steak House (£££)
210 East 46th Street tel: 687-4855
This quintessential New York steak house features prime aged beef and "all the fixins" with magnums of fine Bordeaux to match.

Town (££)
15 West 56th Street, between Fifth and Sixth avenues tel: 582-4445
A "downstairs" space with a four-storey ceiling, Town showcases the masterful fare of Gregory Zakarian, who gives a spins to every classic he touches, such as escargot risotto, fluke carpaccio and ribeye steak with short ribs.

Utsav Festive India (££)
1185 Avenue of the Americas, enter on West 47th Street, between Sixth and Seventh avenues tel: 575-2525
With a distinctly different Indian menu and a dash of sheer originality at every turn, chef Walter D'Rozario is also unafraid of heat. His searing shards of skirt steak are unforgettable, and he's come up with the only great Indian desserts in existence.

Vong (£££)
200 East 54th Street tel: 486-9592
Brainchild of one of the city's most talented chefs, Jean-Georges Vongerichten. Reserve in advance to sample the French–Thai food.

Zarela (££)
Second Avenue, between 50th and 51st streets tel: 644-6740
Zarela Martinez raises Mexican cuisine to lofty heights with exotic yet subtle creations.

MURRAY HILL, GRAMERCY, FLATIRON AND CHELSEA

11 Madison Park (£££)
11 Madison Avenue tel: 889-0905
Union Square Café and Gramercy Tavern owner Danny Meyer owns this bustling American eatery (along with Tabla next door; see below). Elegant, almost retro art deco décor and Kerry Heffernan's contemporary American cuisine.

Alva (££)
36 East 22nd Street, between Broadway and Park Avenue tel: 228-4399
American bistro at its best; roast chicken, lamb, fish, mashed potatoes – all served in a neighbourhood atmosphere.

Bendix Diner (£)
219 Eighth Avenue at 21st Street tel: 366-0560
The menu has a little of everything – American, Thai, Italian, you name it – and it's all good and inexpensive. A hot brunch spot.

Bolo (£££)
23 East 22nd Street, between Broadway and Park Avenue South tel: 228-2200
Creative Spanish food, deftly flavoured and skilfully prepared.

Hotels and Restaurants

Bottino (££)
246 Tenth Avenue tel: 206-6766
Most restaurants that are this trendy and this jam-packed with beautiful people don't usually take the food very seriously. But this Chelsea gallery-area hotspot features reasonably priced Italian fare of exceptional quality.

Bright Food Shop (£)
216 Eighth Avenue, between 21st and 22nd streets tel: 243-4433
Unusual Asian–Southwestern food in a 1930s coffee-shop. Odd-sounding menu selections turn out to be delicious.

Chat 'n' Chew (£)
10 East 16th Street, between Fifth Avenue and Union Square West tel: 243-1616
Huge helpings of American classics in a comfortable setting. Sandwiches, entrées and desserts are the best.

Chelsea Bistro & Bar (££–£££)
358 West 23rd Street, between Eighth and Ninth avenues tel: 727-2026
A neighbourhood French bistro that attracts gourmets from around the city. Foie gras ravioli and other equally innovative dishes are not to be missed: it's gorgeous and cosy.

Chicama (££–£££)
35 East 18th Street, between Broadway and Park Avenue tel: 505-2233
Having led the Nuevo Latino revolution in New York, Douglas Rodriguez has now reinvented seviche – fish "cooked" in a citric acid marinade – by adding all sorts of unexpected ingredients. It is luscious fare not to be missed.

The City Bakery (£)
3 West 18th Street, near Fifth Avunue tel: 366-1414
The relocated and considerably expanded restaurant serves beautiful sandwiches, salads, soups, cookies and a dazzling buffet. Superb tarts and, during the winter, hot chocolate.

Coffee Shop (££)
16th Street and Union Square West tel: 243-7969
Despite its name, this is actually a lively and fashionable spot for consuming American-Brazilian food and generally being seen by the right faces. Serves a great jazz brunch.

Ess-a-Bagel (£)
359 First Avenue at 21st Street tel: 260-2252
Probably the city's best bagels. Smoked salmon, cream cheese and other accompaniments are worth queuing up for. Its also best for takeaway.

Hangawi (££)
12 East 32nd Street, between Fifth and Madison avenues tel: 213-0077
If you don't know what "vegetarian mountain Korean food" is, order the Emperor's Menu. Some 12 courses later you will understand the allure of this unusual and enticing restaurant.

Follonico (££)
6 West 24th Street, between Fifth and Sixth avenues tel: 691-6359
Among the most authentic-feeling trattorias in town. A wood-fired oven gives the Tuscan fare a welcome rustic flavour.

Gramercy Tavern (£££)
42 East 20th Street, between Broadway and Park Avenue South tel: 477-0777
The Tavern redefines four-star dining with prix fixe, multicourse menus of inspired modern French–American cooking. There is a lighter menu available in the bar.

I Trulli (£££)
122 East 27th Street tel: 481-7372
An authentic trattoria with a beautiful garden in season, offering home-made pasta and other sophisticated Italian fare. Enoteca next door has a selective menu and a huge wine list.

Kang Suh (££)
1250 Broadway at 32nd Street tel: 564-6845
Skip the sushi bar and head straight upstairs for the Korean menu. Oyster and scallion pancakes, tableside barbecue and *kim chee* are served into the small hours.

Keens Steakhouse (££–£££)
36th Street, between Fifth and Sixth avenues tel: 947-3636
Keens has been providing no-fuss meat-and-potatoes fare since 1885; mutton chop with mint is what they do best, although there are some hearty seafood options.

Les Halles (££)
411 Park Avenue South, between 28th and 29th streets tel: 679-4111
Perhaps the most authentic French bistro in town, with a glistening butcher's shop at the front and faux tobacco stained walls. Great frites and flavourful meats of every kind. Gets crowded and loud.

Lola (££)
22nd Street, between Fifth and Sixth avenues tel: 675-6700
American food bearing a West Indian influence, and some genuine Caribbean and South American dishes, prepared to an exceptional standard. A "Gospel brunch" is served on Sundays. Outstanding fried chicken.

Merchants, NY (££)
112 Seventh Avenue at 17th Street tel: 366-7267
Pub-like atmosphere with good bar food and outdoor seating.

Mesa Grill (££)
102 Fifth Avenue, between 15th and 16th streets tel: 807-7400
Considered the city's best Southwestern. Hefty portions and friendly service make this a favourite among well-dressed city-dwellers. Funky, award-winning design.

Negril (££)
362 West 23rd Street, between Eighth and Ninth avenues tel: 807-6411
Traditional and innovative Jamaican food served in a bustling, noisy setting. Be warned, there is a wait for a table at the weekends.

Olives NY (£££)
201 Park Avenue South at 17th Street tel: 353-8345
One of the most important new restaurants in town. Chef Todd English has brought his luscious Boston act south, with an impressive degree of panache and is known for combining large numbers of succulent ingredients.

Park Bistro (££)
Park Avenue, between 28th and 29th streets
tel: 689-1360
Among the better of New York's many French bistro-style restaurants, this is deservedly popular for providing lovely food in a lovely setting.

Patria (£££)
250 Park Avenue South at 20th Street
tel: 777-6211
Inspired, boldly flavoured and stunningly presented Nuevo Latino cooking keeps this trendy restaurant packed. Lunch is a bargain – dinner is prix fixe.

Periyali (£££)
35 West 20th Street, between Fifth and Sixth avenues tel: 463-7890
Simple Greek food with a few creative touches served in a friendly Mediterranean setting.

Pipa (£–££)
38 East 19th Street, between Broadway and Park Avenue South tel: 677-2233
Across the hall from Douglas Rodriguez's Chicama is his lively tapas restaurant, and it's no less ambitious and delightful. Almond-stuffed serrano-ham-wrapped dates and sangria to start, then mini paella and baby eels in garlic and oil. A real party.

Pongal (£)
110 Lexington Avenue tel: 696-9458
Authentic southern Indian cooking (as well as vegetarian and kosher) is the bill of fare at this popular restaurant. Try one of the thalis to sample a variety of dishes.

Scopa (££–£££)
27 East 28th Street, between Madison and Park Avenue South tel: 686-8787
Vincent Scotto's rustic Italian cooking is often breathtaking: some of the tastiest pizza in town, gorgeous pastas, steaks and desserts.

Tabla (£££)
11 Madison Avenue tel: 889-0667
Chef Floyd Cardoz's cooking shows heavy Indian influences. The food is fragrant with spices and elegantly presented. A more casual bread bar on the first level is less expensive.

Tamarind (££)
41–43 East 22nd Street, between Broadway and Park Avenue South tel: 674-7400
The most enthralling new Indian restaurant to arrive in town in years. Resplendently appointed space with three very busy tandoori ovens. Unusual offerings include tandoori scallops and venison chops in a spicy coating.

Union Pacific (£££)
111 East 22nd Street tel: 995-8500
Chef Rocco Dispirito's prix fixe menu offers some of the most daring and delicious culinary creations in town. An interesting wine list.

Union Square Café (£££)
16th Street and Union Square West
tel: 243-4020
State-of-the-art contemporary American cookery and the very cordial staff have made this restaurant a particular favourite.

Zen Palate (££)
34 Union Square East tel: 614-9291
Vegetarian food with an Asian accent presented in delicately arranged portions.

SOHO

Aquagrill (£££)
210 Spring Street at Sixth Avenue
tel: 274-0505
Fresh fish and seafood in a trendy SoHo setting. Creative entrées balance simple preparations. Try the signature snail snaps and roasted cod and great desserts.

Balthazar (£££)
80 Spring Street at Crosby Street
tel: 965-1414
The closest you'll come to a Parisian brasserie. A white hot, ultra-loud scene where power-brokers enjoy chilled seafood platters, roasted chicken, braised short ribs, and other brasserie fare. Reservations necessary.

Ceci Cela (£)
55 Spring Street at Lafayette Street
tel: 274-9179
This tiny French bakery with six tables at the back has the best croissants and classic French pastries this side of the Atlantic.

Honmura An (£££)
170 Mercer Street, between Houston and Prince streets tel: 334-5253
Handmade soba is the highlight of this serene outpost of a Tokyo favourite.

Lombardi's (£)
32 Spring Street, between Mott and Mulberry streets tel: 941-7994
The 1905 coal-fired oven gives the pizza at this parlour an unusually flavourful crust. Many consider it the best on the island.

Omen (££)
Thompson Street, between Spring and Prince streets tel: 925-8923
This relaxed Japanese restaurant's house speciality is indeed Omen – a spicy soup dish with vegetables and noodles.

Palacinka (£)
28 Grand Street tel: 625-0362
The pancake's the thing at this pan-European crêperie which produces unusual variations on a familiar theme.

Quilty's (£££)
177 Prince Street, between Thompson and Sullivan streets tel: 254-1260
Named after a character in Nabokov's *Lolita*, this elegant bistro serves creative modern fare.

Raoul's (£££)
Prince Street, between Sullivan and Thompson streets tel: 966-3518
A winning New York version of a French restaurant: a tempting array of main courses and desserts and an impressive wine list.

Rialto (££)
265 Elizabeth Street, between Houston and Prince streets tel: 334-7900
Reasonably priced, upmarket American menu with charming garden and hip atmosphere.

Soho Steak (££)
90 Thompson Street, between Prince and Spring streets tel: 226-0602
Don't be put off by the wait or the sardine-like seating in this tiny bistro. The menu – which features more than just steak – is expertly prepared and exceptionally well priced.

275

THEATER DISTRICT

Becco (££)
355 West 46th Street, between Eighth and Ninth avenues tel: 397-7597
All-you-can-eat antipasti and home-made pasta arrive as soon as you sit down. If you have room for an entrée, you won't be disappointed.

Brasserie de Boeuf (££)
258 West 44th Street, between Broadway and Eighth avenues tel: 869-4440
David Ruggerio's whimsical, but totally masterful cooking has moved him all around town. He's currently enthralling the Theater District with reasonably priced French and steakhouse classics. Look for the giant cow above the door.

China Fun (£–££)
1653 Broadway at 51st Street tel: 333-2622
One of the city's most enterprising and exacting Chinese restauranteurs and chefs, Dorothea Wu's China Fun offers dim sum from noon to midnight, and a great deal more – 170 offerings in all – from a spotless display kitchen.

Churrascaria Plataforma (££)
316 West 49th Street, between Eighth and Ninth avenues tel: 245-0505
An authentic Brazilian barbecue, where one price gets you a lavish salad bar and a parade of marinated and grilled meats.

District (££)
130 West 46th Street, between Broadway and Sixth avenues tel: 485-2999
Sam DeMarco, one of the most irrepressible and playful chefs in town, offers some extraordinary dishes at this Times Square refuge. Think butter-poached lobster meat bathed in fennel-scented cream foam with citrus supremes.

Firebird (£££)
365 West 46th Street, between Eighth and Ninth avenues tel: 586-0244
Pre-revolutionary, aristocratic Russian cooking in an ornate setting. Blini, caviar, kasha and other delicacies haven't been so good since the rise and fall of Communism.

Jezebel (££)
Ninth Avenue at 45th Street tel: 582-1045
Soulfood favourites, such as fried chicken, catfish and grits, feature in a setting themed as a Deep South bordello.

Joe Allen (££)
46th Street, between Eighth and Ninth avenues tel: 581-6464
Burgers, bowls of chili and other simple American food served in large portions amid Broadway show posters.

Landmark Tavern (££)
Eleventh Avenue at 46th Street tel: 757-8595
Hearty lunches and dinners – fish-and-chips, and shepherd's pie alongside the ubiquitous burgers and sandwiches – are served in wood-panelled rooms dating from 1868.

Little Saigon (£)
374 West 46th Street tel: 956-0639
A useful pre- or post-theatre stop for very well-priced Vietnamese dishes.

Sardi's (££)
44th Street, between Broadway and Eighth avenues tel: 221-8440
A noted theatrical hangout and lair of the gossip-columnists, Sardi's is well past its prime, but the caricatures of Broadway stars still line its walls and the service is still as off-hand as ever. Choose from an Italian menu.

Stage Deli (££)
Seventh Avenue at 54th Street tel: 245-7850
Long time rival of the Carnegie Deli, the Stage Deli provides much the same staple New York deli fare in equally generous portions, though the staff can often be less than gracious.

Virgil's Real BBQ (£–££)
152 West 44th Street, between Broadway and Sixth avenues tel: 921-9494
Casual American barbecue joint with tender, tasty ribs, chicken, shrimp, corn bread and other favourites in giant portions.

UPPER EAST SIDE

Al Baraka (£–££)
1613 Second Avenue, between 83rd and 84th streets tel: 396-9787
An utterly transporting experience awaits you at the back of this storefront, thanks to the tireless efforts of owner/designer Sam Ben Safi. Moroccan food is often ranked by connoisseurs with French and Chinese as the best on earth: Al Baraka shows you why.

Arizona 206 (££–£££)
206 East 60th Street tel: 838-0440
The vibrant cooking at this busy and loud restaurant emphasises the bright bold flavours of southwest America.

Aureole (£££)
34 East 61st Street, between Madison and Park avenues tel: 319-1660
The exquisite upmarket American food and startling presentations make this one of the city's best restaurants.

Brother Jimmy's BBQ (£)
1644 Third Avenue tel:426-2020
Substantial sandwiches, soups, barbecued ribs and other accompaniments to beer drinking and watching sports TV.

Brunelli (£–££)
1409 York Avenue at 75th Street tel: 744-8899
A handsome, dashing space, Brunelli serves up perfect Roman fare with a few American twists. Don't miss the spiedino or the unbelievable veal chops.

Café Boulud (£££)
20 East 76th Street tel: 772-2600
The ever-changing menu at this casual cousin to Daniel Boulud's more formal four-star restaurant is overseen by top chef Andrew Carmellini, and it is just as good.

The Dining Room (££–£££)
154 East 79th Street, between Lexington and Third avenues tel: 327-2500
Mark Spangenthal's celebrated downtown fare moves uptown with dishes such as pan-fried artichokes, delicious foie gras with spiced peaches and luscious roasted ribeye steak.

EAT (£)
Madison Avenue, between 80th and 81st streets tel: 772-0022
Continental Jewish snacks and sinful desserts.

Felidia (£££)
243 East 58th Street tel: 758-1479
A perennial favourite for regional Italian cooking with an emphasis on game and specialities of Friuli. Lidia Bastianich stands guard, ensuring an impeccable experience.

Fred's at Barneys (££–£££)
10 East 61st Street at Madison Avenue tel: 833-2200
A favourite of the "ladies who lunch" (and shop) and Upper East Side socialites.

India Grill (££)
240 East 81st Street tel: 988-4646
Well-priced menu of Indian fare, and often offering daily specials.

J G Melon (£)
Third Avenue at 74th Street tel: 744-0585
Its American diner menu is a cut above the average, served at low cost in the homy environment of a wood-panelled bar.

Jo Jo (£££)
160 East 64th Street, near Lexington Avenue tel: 223-5656
Jo Jo's serves superb French bistro fare with a modern twist. Choose between the loud and packed main dining area and the more serene rear room.

Le Perigord (£££)
405 East 52nd Street, between First and York avenues tel: 755-6244
Few have mastered the art of bonhomie as well as proprietor Georges Briguet, and it is unlikely that you will soon forget Jacques Qualin's turbot with a comté breadcrumb crust in champagne sauce. A luscious, highly dignified place.

Lenox (£££)
1278 3rd Avenue, between 73rd and 74th streets tel: 772-0404
The smooth service and sophisticated cooking at this neighbourhood favourite make it a perfect place to rest after a day of shopping.

Maya (££–£££)
1191 First Avenue, between 64th and 65th streets tel: 585-1818
Jammed night after night with people who know that chef Richard Sandoval is turning out some of the best Mexican food on the Eastern seaboard. Roasted corn soup is as good as it gets, and the shrimp/manchego stuffed chile relleno could entice you to return the following night.

Park Avenue Café (£££)
100 East 63rd Street at Park Avenue tel: 644-1900
You can't help but laugh at the witty and whimsical interpretations of modern American cooking. Everything tastes even better than it looks. A favourite for weekend brunch.

Payard Bistro (££)
1032 Lexington Avenue tel: 717-5252
There is a terrific bistro behind the popular patisserie.

Pig Heaven (££)
Second Avenue, between 80th and 81st streets tel: 744-4333
With renovated décor and an improved Chinese menu, this place is quite a local favourite.

Revel (££–£££)
24 East 81st Street, between Fifth and Madison avenues tel: 249-5720
Quite near the Metropolitan Museum, this "modern Italian" elegant space is utterly captivating. Don't miss the parmesan "ice cream" with balsamic "fudge sauce", perfect crab cakes and duck two ways.

Rosa Mexicano (££–£££)
1063 First Avenue at 58th Street tel: 753-7407
The Mexican food at this venerable restaurant is painstakingly authentic. Tableside guacamole with fresh corn tortillas and braised lamb shank with three-pepper sauce are not to be missed. There is a casual bar area in the front with a more formal restaurant towards the back.

7th Regiment Mess (£)
643 Park Avenue, between 66th and 67th streets tel: 744-4107
American home-cooking is served here in an old wood-panelled restaurant inside the Seventh Regiment Armory. This place is great for children; booking is advisable.

UPPER WEST SIDE

Alouette (££)
2588 Broadway tel: 222-6808
This is the type of French bistro that you'd expect to find in Greenwich Village, not the Upper West Side. The cooking is sophisticated and delicious.

Avenue (££)
520 Columbus Avenue tel: 579-3194
Breakfast, lunch and dinner are all terrific at this neighbourhoody French bistro. Children are especially welcome.

Baci (££)
412 Amsterdam Avenue tel: 496-1550
Cramped and often crowded, but has some of the best Italian food in the area.

Barney Greengrass (£–££)
Amsterdam Avenue, between 86th and 87th streets tel: 724-4707
The epitome of a New York Jewish deli-diner and owned by the Greengrass family since 1908. House specialities include sturgeon and salmon; breakfast and lunch only.

Blue Nile (££)
77th Street at Columbus Avenue tel: 580-3481
One of New York's few Ethiopian restaurants. The food is scooped up and devoured with spongy chunks of injera bread.

Café des Artistes (£££)
67th Street at Central Park West tel: 877-3500
The 1930s Howard Chandler Christy murals create quite a lusty atmosphere for wonderful French classics. Reserve for dinner and Sunday brunch.

Hotels and Restaurants

Café La Fortuna (£)
71st Street, between Central Park West and Columbus Avenue tel: 724-5846
Sip coffee and sample an excellent pastry to feel at home in this neighbourhood favourite.

Café Lalo (£)
83rd Street at Amsterdam Avenue tel: 496-6031
This café attracts would-be writers, artists and media folk who drink cappuccino and gorge themselves on a selection of irresistible cakes.

Café Luxembourg (£££)
70th Street, between Amsterdam and Columbus avenues tel: 873-7411
This is an art deco bistro aiming for a 1930s Parisian ambience. The top-rated food draws fashionable faces from all New York.

Calle Ocho (££)
446 Columbus Avenue tel: 873-5025
The menu at this striking restaurant features classic and contemporary dishes inspired by the cuisines of Latin America. The flavours are vibrant and bold.

EJ's Luncheonette (£)
Amsterdam Avenue, between 80th and 81st streets tel: 873-3444
Retro diner complete with chrome fittings and historic Coke advertisements. The sandwiches (try the grilled Cajun chicken breast) are huge.

Gabriela's (£)
685 Amsterdam Avenue at 93rd Street tel: 961-0574
Inexpensive Mexican eatery that's always packed. The posole is particularly good, but for the price, you can't go wrong with anything that you select.

Good Enough To Eat (££)
Amsterdam Avenue, between 83rd and 84th streets tel: 496-0163
Grand selection of American staples, from ham and eggs to strawberry waffles, for breakfast, lunch or dinner in cosy surroundings.

Indian Café (££)
Broadway at 108th Street tel: 749-9200
Competitively priced Indian food includes inventive vegetarian selections, such as chick-peas with spinach and tomato, and sautéed lentils with garlic and ginger. Alternatively, feast on a selection of appetisers.

John's Pizzeria (£)
48 West 65th Street, between Columbus Avenue and Central Park West tel: 721-7001
A cousin of the original Greenwich Village John's, it has pizzas that are every bit as good and the atmosphere is a little more pleasant.

Josie's (£–££)
300 Amsterdam Avenue at 74th Street tel: 769-1212
The health-food-inspired menu has a number of vegetarian options and fresh salads.

La Caridad 78 (£)
Broadway at 78th Street tel: 874-2780
Inventive Chinese-Cuban dishes are served without fuss in informal surroundings.

Marika (££–£££)
208 West 70th Street, between Amsterdam and West End avenues tel: 875-8600
Perhaps the most significant restaurant to open on the Upper West Side in a decade. Truly stunning décor, with chef Joel Somerstein's succulent fare, like deeply flavoured roasted lobster and lamb three ways – stuffed, braised and roasted. Simply not to be missed if you're in the Lincoln Center area.

Ollie's (£)
Broadway at 84th Street tel: 362-3712
Chinese fare prepared in full view of diners. The noodle soups are flavourful and cheap.

Picholine (£££)
35 West 64th Street, between Broadway and Central Park West tel: 724-8585
Expertly prepared modern French food in a country setting with its own cheese cave.

Rain (£)
100 West 82nd Street, between Amsterdam and Columbus avenues tel: 501-0776
The Thai-inspired menu fills this bustling eatery with a young crowd. There is a long wait, however, at weekends.

Sarabeth's West (££)
Amsterdam Avenue, between 80th and 81st streets tel: 496-6280
A refined place for smoked salmon sandwiches and fluffy omelettes. Has a scintillating selection of home-made cakes.

Savann (££)
414 Amsterdam Avenue, between 79th and 80th streets tel: 580-0202
An imaginative, but often crowded, American bistro with a French accent.

Shark Bar (£)
74th Street, between Columbus Avenue and Broadway tel: 874-8500
Tallahassee grilled shrimp, Louisiana fried crab cakes, or pan-blackened catfish – the tastiest fare from all over the south.

Shun Lee (£££)
43 West 65th Street, between Columbus Avenue and Central Park West tel: 595-8895
Upmarket Chinese served by tuxedoed waiters. The chef is talented, but the bill can be high.

Spazzia (££)
366 Columbus Avenue tel: 799-0150
Fresh and flavourful Mediterranean cooking is a welcome addition to a neighbourhood overrun by mediocre food.

Symposium (£)
113th Street at Amsterdam Avenue tel: 865-1011
Authentic, inexpensive Greek fare popular with students from nearby Columbia University. In summer, you can dine in the garden.

Tavern on the Green (£££)
67th Street at Central Park West tel: 873-3200
More famous as a New York landmark, the tavern serves erratic – but usually excellent – meals beneath Venetian crystal chandeliers.

Vince and Eddie's (£££)
70 West 68th Street, between Columbus Avenue and Central Park West tel: 721-0068
A cosy, American bistro that's a favourite of quiet celebrities and Lincoln Center regulars.

HARLEM

Copeland's (££)
*145th Street, between Broadway and
Amsterdam Avenue tel: 234-2357*
This is where the high-flyers of Harlem don
their finery and dine on a creative mix of
soul-food and nouvelle cuisine.

Sylvia's (££)
*Lenox Avenue, between 126th and 127th
streets tel: 996-0660*
A landmark soul-food restaurant, serving huge
helpings of Southern favourites, like spicy
barbecued ribs and fried chicken.

BROOKLYN

Cucina (£££)
*256 Fifth Avenue, between Carroll Street and
Garfield Place tel: 718/230-0711*
Even island-bound Manhattanites will
travel to this Park Slope trattoria for the
friendly atmosphere, flavourful pastas and
large entrées.

Junior's (£)
*386 Flatbush Avenue Extension at DeKalb
Avenue tel: 718/852-5257*
A Brooklyn institution known for its large
breakfasts, corned beef and pastrami
sandwiches and award-winning cheesecakes.
As a point of reference, Junior's is near to the
Brooklyn Academy of Music.

Lemongrass Grill (£)
*61A Seventh Avenue, between Berkeley and
Lincoln places tel: 718/399-7100*
The Grill serves inexpensive Thai food that's
flavourful, fresh and fast. There is also a pretty
garden on view.

Mrs Stahl's Delicious Knishes (£)
*1001 Brighton Beach Avenue
tel: 718/648-0210*
Delivers exactly what its name suggests:
expertly made knishes available with a host of
fillings. Buy several.

New Prospect Café (£)
*393 Flatbush Avenue
tel: 718/ 638-2148*
Lively locals' eating spot, situated near the
Brooklyn Museum.

Noodle Pudding (££)
*38 Henry Street, Brooklyn Heights
tel: 718/625-3737*
Although the name conjures images of lokshen
kugel, it is actually a loose translation of the
owner's last name, which he shares with a
Neapolitan dessert. The food is Italian, not
Jewish, and if you are to eat one meal in
Brooklyn Heights, this is where it should be.
The chef excels at fish, usually generously
portioned and lightly grilled.

Odessa (££)
*1113 Brighton Beach Avenue
tel: 718/253-1470*
The best way to enjoy Odessa's is to come
with a group. One price buys a bottle of vodka
and all you can eat from the Russian–Georgian
buffet table. Be warned that you should be
ready to dance.

Patsy Grimaldi's (£)
*19 Old Fulton Street, between Front and Water
streets tel: 718/858-4300*
Pizza *aficionados* consider Patsy's among the
city's best. Red-chequered tablecloths and
plenty of Sinatra provide the atmosphere to
enjoy thin-crust pies with myriad toppings.

Peter Luger Steak House (£££)
*178 Broadway at Driggs Avenue
tel: 718/387-7400*
Considered by many to be the best steak
house in the country, what it lacks in its turn-of-
the-century German beer hall ambience it
makes up for in dry-aged porterhouse, buttery
home fries and creamed spinach. Cash only.

Teresa's (£)
*80 Montague Street, Brooklyn Heights
tel: 718/797-3996*
Very filling, very well-priced Polish food.

THE BRONX

Dominick's (££)
2335 Arthur Avenue tel: 718/733-2807
Strong on atmosphere, with southern Italian
food. The menu is recited by the waiters.

Mario's (££)
2342 Arthur Avenue tel: 718/584-1188
Often as busy as Dominick's, but with slightly
better food, much of it Neapolitan.

QUEENS

Elias Corner (££)
*24–02 31st Street at 24th Avenue, Satoria
tel: 718/932-1510*
Grilled fish and other traditional Greek fare.

Happy Dumpling (£)
*135–29 40th Road, Flushing
tel: 718/445-2163*
Chinese fare, and rarely bettered for stuffed
dumplings or noodles.

Jackson Diner (£)
*74th Street, between Roosevelt and 37th
avenues tel: 718/672-1232*
Probably the best priced of a glut of Indian
restaurants in this section of the borough.

KB Garden (£)
*136–28 39th Avenue, Flushing
tel: 718/961-9088*
Come for the raucous weekend dim sum or for
the lengthy à la carte menu.

Penang Malaysian Cuisine (££)
*38–04 Prince Street at Roosevelt Avenue,
Flushing tel: 718/321-2078*
An exotic menu of Malaysian specialities
ranging from Indian curry to coconut shrimp.

Ping's (££)
83–02 Queen's Boulevard tel: 718/396-1238
Ping prepares classic Chinese dishes fit
(and priced) for a king – braised abalone,
giant lobster on noodles, shark's fin and
other delicacies.

Yao Han (£)
*135–21 40th Road, Flushing
tel: 718/359-2828*
Chinese and Vietnamese food make another
great find for noodle-lovers.

Index

A

Index

Index

285

New York Subway

East River

Main St-Flushing 7

Willets Point-Shea Stadium

111 St

103 St Corona Plaza

Junction Boulevard

90 St-Elmhurst Av

82 St-Jackson Hts

74 St-Broadway

La Guardia
International Airport

46 St   Norther Boulevard   65 St   Elmhurst Av   Grand Av-Newtown   Woodhaven Boulevard-Queens Ctr   **Jamaica Center** E

ay St   **Jamaica-179 St** F

Roosevelt Av-Jackson Hts   **71-Continental Avs** G,R

69 St

61 St Woodside

33 St   40 St   46 St   52 St

ins Plaza

QUEENS

Metropolitan Av-Middle Village M

Fresh Pond Rd

Forest Av

Seneca Av

ham Av   Montrose Av   Jefferson St   Myrtle Av   Halsey St   **Jamaica Center** J,Z

Grand St   Morgan Av   DeKalb Av   Wilson Av   Van Siclen Av

Wyckoff Av   Bushwick Av   Alabama Av

Knickerbocker Av

Lorimer St   Flushing Av   **Myrtle Av** M   Central Av   Chauncey St   Broadway-Eastern Parkway

Av   Kosciuszko St   Gates Av   **Euclid Av** C

Myrtle-   Broadway-East New York   Liberty Av   **Lefferts Boulevard** A

ghby Avs   **Far Rockaway-Mott Av** A

Rockaway Av   **Rockaway Park-Beach 166 St** A

ord-
and Avs   Ralph Av

Av

Franklin Av S   Nostrand Av   Utica Av   Atlantic Av

Clinton-Washington Avs

New Lots Av 3

Kingston-Throop Avs

rette Av   Park Place   Van Siclen Av

Sutter Av   Pennsylvania Av

Nostrand Av   Kingston Av   Sutter Av-Rutland Rd   Rockaway Av   Livonia Av

Franklin Av   President St   **Utica Av** 4   Saratoga Av   Junius St   New Lots Av

Eastern Parkway
Brooklyn Museum   Botanic Gardens   Sterling St   East 105 St

b Av   Winthrop St

Alantic Av   7 Av   Church Av

evins St   Bergen St   Grand   Beverly Rd

Pacific St   Army   Newkirk Av

Bay Parkway M   Plaza

Bay Ridge-95 St R   **Prospect Park** S   **Canarsie-Rockaway Parkway** L

oney Island-Stillwell Av **N,W**   **Coney Island-Stillwell Av** Q   **Flatbush Av-Brooklyn College** 2,5

Acknowledgements

Picture credits

The Automobile Association would like to thank the following photographers, libraries and associations for their assistance in the preparation of this book:

J ALLAN CASH 127a Market. **ALLSPORT UK LTD** 90a American Football (S Dunn). **AMERICAN CRAFT MUSEUM** 62 Museum interior (Dan Cornish). **BETTMANN ARCHIVE** 22b Damon Runyon (UPI/BETTMAN NEWSPAPERS), 42b *The Brains* (THE BETTMAN ARCHIVE), 43a William O'Dwyer (THE BETTMAN ARCHIVE), 44b East River (THE BETTMANN ARCHIVE), 119a P Orbvsky & A Ginsberg, 119b A Poole in our time (THE BETTMAN ARCHIVES). **BRIDGEMAN ART LIBRARY LTD** 29a Irish immigrants disembark at the Battery in New York, 1855 (Museum of the City of New York, 1855/Bridgeman Art Library, London), 32a New York after Independence, seen from East River by George Torino (18th C) (Private Collection/Bridgeman Art Library, London), 36a Cartoon depicting Andrew Carnegie, 1903 (Private Collection/Bridgeman Art Library, London), 97b *Campbell's Soup* by Warhol, Andy (1930–87) (Wolverhampton Art Gallery, Staffs/Bridgeman Art Library, London). **CORBIS/ROBERT HOLMES** 117A, **CORBIS/GAIL MOONEY** 121a, 228, **CORBIS/ BILL ROSS** 233, **CORBIS/CHARLES O'REAR** 234/5. **D CORRANCE** 92 The Cloisters, 110 Frick Museum, 123 Guggenheim Museum, 177 Soho Martin Lawrence Gallery, 179 Staten Island Ferry, 241 Greenwich Village Jazz. **HULTON GETTY** 16a, 16b **HULTON DEUTSCH COLLECTION LTD** 73b Malcolm X © 1999. **KELLY/MOONEY PHOTOGRAPHY** 18, 117b, 118b, 166, 167, 236. **KOBAL** 15a King Kong. **MAGNUM PHOTOS LTD** 97a Eyes Warhol (Philipe Halsam), 188a Woody Allen (Ernst Haas). **MARY EVANS PICTURE LIBRARY** 22a Manhattan Transfer, 23b Henry James, (Mary Evans/ J Morgan) 30a Dutch Land on Staten Island, 33 Declaration of Independence, 34–5 Immigration, 41a,b Wall St Crash, 105a Immigrants at Ellis Island. **METROPOLITAN MUSEUM OF ART** 143a Egyptian Funerary Customs – Coffins (Rogers Fund 1915 (15.2.2), 145a,b Islamic Eastern Mediterranean Glass (Rogers Bequest of Edward C Moore 1891 (91.1.1530), 147a Henri Matisse painting (Robert Lehman Coll. 1975 (1975.1.194), 147b Jacopo Bellini painting (Gift of Irma N Straus 1959 (59.187). **MUSEUM OF MODERN ART NEW YORK** 129 Jackson Pollock painting, 158b *The Starry Night* Van Gogh. **MUSEUM OF TV & RADIO** 161 Int Lonsdale Room. **PICTURES COLOUR LIBRARY** 24–5 East 47th Street. **REX FEATURES LTD** 17a, 17b, 132. **ROBERT HARDING** 168, 238. **RONALD GRANT ARCHIVES** 15b *Saturday Night Fever*, 188b *Manhattan* Woody Allen. **SPECTRUM COLOUR LIBRARY** 26b Chinese New Year, 27 Flute Player, 154a St Patrick's Day, 154b Pipe Band, 240 Birdland Jazz Club. **THE MANSELL COLLECTION** 30/1 New Amsterdam, 31 Landing of Hendrick Hudson, 32b P Stuyvesant, 34b Entering a New World, 36b Andrew Carnegie, 37 Pierpont Morgan, 38b Brooklyn Bridge, 38–9 New York 1851, 45b SS *Queen Mary*. **TONY STONE IMAGES** 221. **TOPHAM PICTURE POINT** 46, 47. **UNITED NATIONS** 184 Int, UN Building. **ZEFA PICTURE LIBRARY (UK) LTD** 11 Tompkins Sq Park, 14 Times Sq, 39 Harlem, 40 Wall St 73a Boy & Water, 138 Delancey St, 155 Folk Art Mus, 173 Rockefeller Plaza, 176 Soho Gallery, 185a U N Building, 189 Central Park, 203 West Point Parade, 205 Albany, 237 Musician & bike.

All remaining pictures are from the Association's own picture library (AA PHOTO LIBRARY) with contributions from:

P BAKER 127c. **D CORRANCE** 4, 6–7, 13, 20b, 25, 67a, 72, 78, 79, 87, 89, 96, 101, 106, 118a, 126, 128–9, 135, 137, 146, 148, 159, 160a, 162a, 171c, 175, 181b, 182, 185b, 192, 214, 215, 218b, 229, 232, 242, 246, 257, 259b. **R ELLIOTT** 3, 5a, 7, 10a, b, 12–13, 19, 20a, 21, 24, 28, 43b, 44a, 45a, 50, 51, 52, 53, 56, 60, 61a, 63, 64, 66a, 68, 70, 74, 81a, b, 86, 88a,b, 90b, 94, 99, 100, 112, 113, 114a, 115, 116, 124a,b, 125, 131, 139a, b, 140, 141a,b, 142, 143b, 144, 150, 151, 153, 156, 157, 158a, 160b, 163, 164, 165a,b, 169, 171a,b, 172, 174b, 178, 180, 183a,b, 187, 190, 191, 193a,b, 194, 195, 196, 197, 198, 199a,b, 200, 201, 202, 206–7, 208, 209, 210, 211, 216, 220, 223a, 226, 227, 238b, 239, 244, 247a, 250, 253, 254, 256a, 258. **J HENDERSON** 127b. **P KENWARD** 2, 5b, 5c, 6c, 9, 12, 18a, 23a, 26a, 54a, 57, 66b, 71a, b, 75a, b, 76, 84a, b, 91, 93, 102, 103, 104, 109, 120a, 132a, 134, 136a, b, 152, 162b, 170, 174a, 181a, 186, 213, 218, 219, 224, 231a, b, 235, 243a, b, c, 245a, b, 247b, 259a, 261b. **S MCBRIDE** bottom left and right front cover, 8, 54a, 55, 58, 59, 67b, 69, 80, 98, 121b, 149, 212, 217, 225, 248, 252, 255, 260a,b, back cover. **D POLLACK** 65, 85a, b, 108, 109, 111, 120b, 261. **E ROONEY** spine, 9b, 29b, 49b, 83, 222. **C SAWYER** top front cover, 105b.

Contributors

Original copy editor: Donna Dailey
Revision verifiers: Mick Sinclair, Jane Miller,
Tom Steele, Emmanuelle Morgen and Kate Sekules

288